Integrated Teaching Methods:

Theory, Classroom Applications, and Field-Based Connections

Integrated Teaching Methods:

Theory, Classroom Applications, and Field-Based Connections

Bruce M. Frazee
Trinity University
San Antonio, Texas

Rose A. Rudnitski
State University of New York
College at New Paltz

Delmar Publishers
An International Thomson Publishing Company

Albany • Bonn • Boston • Cincinnati • Detroit • London • Madrid • Melbourne
Mexico City • New York • Pacific Grove • Paris • San Francisco • Singapore • Tokyo
Toronto • Washington

NOTICE TO THE READER

Cover design courtesy of Cronin & Prusko

Delmar Staff

Acquisitions Editor: Erin J. O'Connor
Senior Project Editor: Andrea Edwards Myers
Project Editor: Colleen A. Corrice
Production Coordinator: Sandra Woods
Art and Design Coordinator: Doug Hyldelund/Timothy J. Conners

COPYRIGHT © 1995
By Delmar Publishers
a division of International Thomson Publishing Inc.
The ITP logo is a trademark under license

Printed in the United States of America

For more information contact:

Delmar Publishers   International Thomson Editores   International Thomson Publishing Europe
3 Columbia Circle   Campos Eliseos 385, Piso 7   Berkshire House 168-173
Box 15015   Col Polanco   High Holborn
Albany, New York 12203-5015   11560 Mexico D F Mexico   London WC1V7AA
                                                                            England

International Thomson Publishing GmbH Thomas Nelson Australia   International Thomson Publishing Asia
Königswinterer Strasse 418   102 Dodds Street   221 Henderson Road
53227 Bonn   South Melbourne, 3205   #05-10 Henderson Building
Germany   Victoria, Australia   Singapore 0315

Nelson Canada   International Thomson Publishing - Japan
1120 Birchmount Road   Hirakawacho Kyowa Building, 3F
Scarborough, Ontario   2-2-1 Hirakawacho
Canada M1K5G4   Chiyoda-ku, Tokyo 102
                                      Japan

1 2 3 4 5 6 7 8 9 10 XXX 01 00 99 98 97 96 95 94

Library of Congress Cataloging-in-Publication Data

Frazee, Bruce.
   Integrated teaching methods : theory, classroom applications, and
field-based connections   /   Bruce M. Frazee, Rose A. Rudnitski, — 1st ed.
      p.   cm.
   Includes bibliographical references and index.
   ISBN 0-8273-5959-4
   1. Teaching   2. Teacher participation in curriculum palnning-
-United States.   3. Action research in education—United States.
4. Student teaching—United States.   I. Rudnitski, Rose A.
II. Title.
LB1025.3.F735   1995
371.1'02—dc20

LB
1025.3
.F735
1995

94-10250
CIP

08-04426

Contents

Preface

The deepest understanding one can have in any field is an understanding of pedagogy.

—Aristotle

Introduction

The year 1994 marks the centennial of the publication of Francis W. Parker's *Talks on Pedagogics,* a series of lectures on his theory of the integration of curriculum and instruction. We believe that though there has been much "shuffling around" of ideas in the century since Parker's book, too often educators have ignored the ideas of the past only to reinvent them with new names. For this reason, we chose Parker's term, *pedagogics,* as the appellation for the main idea of this book: the integration of curriculum and instruction as pedagogy, based on the best and latest research on how students and teachers learn, and how schools work best.

Though they are based on recent research, many of the ideas in this book are firmly rooted in the past. We symbolically demonstrate our respect for those roots in our adoption and adaption of the term first used in the field by Francis W. Parker.

Rationale

Teacher education needs to prepare individuals to internalize knowledge, experiences, and behaviors that are necessary to begin and sustain their careers throughout recent and future educational reform. Future teachers must know pedagogy and be provided with the knowledge, skills, and field experiences necessary to practice teaching. Educational reform in teacher education that combines theory and practice in a school setting is necessary in order to connect theory to practice.

Recent research indicates that teacher education programs might be more effective if they were more connected to the field (The Holmes Group, 1986; Goodlad, Soder, & Sirotnik, 1990). Many colleges and universities have adapted programs to include involving students in field experiences while they are enrolled in graduate or undergraduate education courses. This text is designed for use by interns (student teachers or preservice students) and their mentors (cooperating or supervising teachers) in those field-based programs.

In the past two decades, the teaching profession has undergone many changes. The role of teachers has progressed from one of implementer of curricula developed by experts to actual developer of the curriculum. Teaching is moving toward professionalization as teachers are placed in decision-making positions on building planning teams and as they are asked to develop integrated and subject area curricula. These collaborative problem-solving activities require a strong knowledge base as well as experience and skill in working in cooperative group settings. This book provides the basis for developing the knowledge and skills needed by future teachers, professionals who will be practicing a vibrant profession in challenging contexts.

Lasting improvement in teacher education depends on partnership with schools and teacher preparation institutions sharing in educational reform. New partnerships with schools will focus on university professors and teachers working together in the school setting to prepare better teachers. Interns (students) working with mentors (master teachers) in professional development schools is a successful model that current research and professional organizations view as an important priority for teacher preparation institutions. Students at universities must be assigned to a school to make sense of theory in the real-life environment. The opportunity to practice pedagogical strategies, theories, and practical activities in a school setting is a fundamental premise of this textbook.

This comprehensive text connects and synthesizes the various subjects taught in the schools to common pedagogical practices. The text organizes core theories of teaching skills that relate to classroom teaching practices in a collaborative school environment.

Philosophy

This book represents a particular point of view. We believe good teachers develop from their own experiences in conjunction with their knowledge of educational history, philosophy, theory, research, and practice. This development requires deep reflection on one's educational experiences and on what one observes in classrooms as well as what one does in one's own teaching. It also requires study in a variety of fields and application of what is learned to real classroom situations.

This book is designed to aid students in their reflection and study as they attend classes at the university and work in classrooms and schools. It is designed to connect those two contexts by relating ideas and activities. Throughout the course of the book, students will be working on independent projects and participating in activities to share with their mentor teachers and with each other. They will also work on their own professional portfolios, which are intended to be used in much the same manner as artists' portfolios. The portfolio will represent the intern's best work in the field through a curriculum unit, research, direct observation of a child, and a philosophy of education.

Goals

The primary goal of this textbook is to assist university students in developing a personal educational belief system and values. To prepare future teachers, it is important that they systematically develop and articulate reasons for choosing specific pedagogical beliefs and behaviors in their instruction and classrooms.

The second goal is to help students write an organized plan that implements this belief system in a specific classroom context. This plan, called a curriculum unit, is meant to demonstrate expertise in an authentic writing task in teaching.

Audience

This book is useful for a wide variety of undergraduate and graduate courses in teacher preparation that integrate theory and field-based practice. It is especially appropriate for prestudent teaching methods courses, practica, and seminars. It is also useful as a resource for interns or student teachers and is particularly helpful to first–year teachers. Mentor teachers, who supervise education students, will find this text to be a valuable reference for initiating and maintaining a collaborative field-based learning community. The book's format covers fundamental pedagogical content and skills that integrate the variety of school subjects and grade levels to enhance empowered teachers and students to self-efficacy in the school culture.

Purpose

The purpose of this book is threefold: first, to identify the knowledge, pedagogical skills, and research relevant to successful teaching and learning; second, to provide a guide to link theory and practice in a school-based environment; and third, to encourage reflection in order to develop a personal educational belief system. Teachers and university students who complete this text in conjunction with a field-based experience are expected to choose and articulate their beliefs regarding the theory, pedagogy, and practice of teaching and learning.

Assumptions

This textbook is founded on the following assumptions.

1. There is a need for a pedagogical framework that is built on a strong research base.
2. Pedagogy is best learned when practiced in schools.
3. There are specific and basic pedagogic principles that cross disciplines and are used by good teachers at the appropriate time.
4. University professors, teachers, school administrators, and university students need to be partners in developing future teachers.
5. Students learn best when encouraged to make connections to broad themes through interdisciplinary strategies.
6. Reflective teaching is essential to successful learning.
7. Mentors, interns, professors, and students need to articulate beliefs and actions.
8. Teaching is a collaborative endeavor that involves the whole school culture and community.
9. Active teaching and learning increases student performance and learning is more than information transmission.
10. Teachers *do* make a difference in helping all children to learn.

Organization

The book chapters are organized to facilitate the coordination of a university course to a field-based experience. The format of the text is sequential in the development of key pedagogical concepts as teachers and students engage in theory, practice, and activities that encourage and guide them to learn and experience in a coherent and reflective manner. The book progresses from a more theoretical perspective (Section I) to a practical one. The later chapters (Section II) include more case studies and suggestions for the field. Each chapter incorporates the following format and sequence:

1. **Theory.** Classic and current research is reviewed at the beginning of each chapter.
2. **Classroom Application.** A brief summary of what the research means in terms of real classrooms. This section provides guidelines and suggestions for developing meaningful practice.
3. **Field-Based Connections.** A variety of experiences and activities is suggested for intern students to enhance the experience of theory and application of pedagogy in a field-based environment. Throughout the book, interns will be working on reflective journals and projects to place in their professional portfolios. Major projects include an integrated unit and a child study.
4. **Summary and Discussion Questions.** Closure is provided to wrap up all the key elements of the chapter. Provocative questions at the end of the chapter inspire reflection and direction for connections between the theory, practice, and field experiences.
5. **Case Studies.** A real-life situation is presented to inspire discussion and reflection. These classroom analyses were written by veteran teachers, first-year teachers, interns, and preservice students. Case study questions initiate sharing and articulation of experiences and beliefs between practitioners in the field and students in university classes.

6. **References and Suggested Readings.** This section includes works cited and literature for further research and study. We strongly encourage self-directed reading and independent research for students and teachers.

Chapter-by-Chapter Overview

This book is divided into two sections, Section I and Section II.

Section I of the book provides essential background to create and build a philosophical and knowledge base for getting ready to teach. We believe that understanding the implicit and explicit functions of a school and their effect on students is a necessary prerequisite for effective teaching. The reflective practitioner combines knowledge, experience, and practical skills to the teaching and learning process and is better prepared to develop a personal educational belief system. There are six chapters in the first section of the book, which provide the theoretical foundation for the more practical second section.

Chapter 1 reviews pedagogical history and defines pedagogy as a means to study and connect teaching methods and practices. We believe that evolving pedagogical practice and study introduces and initiates reflective thought as a primary means for making decisions from a knowledge base.

Chapter 2 offers an in-depth analysis of factors affecting students in terms of teaching and learning. We believe that all students can learn, particularly when time is taken to study, understand, and develop a compassion for the variables affecting the development of students.

Chapter 3 develops a broader perspective of the whole schooling process by analyzing culture and climate. The collaboration of teachers, parents, and community in the school setting has an enormous impact on school effectiveness. We believe that understanding the responsibilities of individual and group roles is necessary in building positive working relationships.

Chapter 4 develops a reference for formative assessment. We believe that early identification and acknowledgement of goals and specific learner outcomes is essential in the beginning of any educational experience. This chapter describes and discusses various ways to build a repertoire for evaluating the various tasks teachers perform.

Chapter 5 examines the leadership role of the teacher in various perspectives of the curriculum. We believe that teachers with proper training and support must be empowered to design and develop curriculum that meets the wide variety of student needs in the classroom.

Chapter 6 identifies ways of integrating the content of major school subjects with skill instruction. We believe that integrated thematic units are a viable and necessary means for developing connections between content, skills, and real-life experiences.

This section establishes a philosophical and knowledge base upon which teachers can build an educational vision. Teachers need to reflect on their beliefs and practice as they make pedagogical decisions about curriculum and instructional delivery systems.

Section II provides practical pedagogical strategies and guidelines to implement and fine tune the craft of teaching. In order to fully comprehend delivery systems teachers and students must have time to observe, discuss, collaborate, reflect, and share their delivery system experiences. We believe that studying and practicing integrative instructional strategies leads to knowledgeable teachers who are capable of choosing, creating, and articulating sound pedagogical practices. These chapters provide a transition to the field.

Chapter 7 describes the necessity of developing a classroom management system. We believe the first task to successful delivery of instruction is to communicate and establish classroom expectations.

Chapter 8 describes the various strategies for implementing curriculum. Basic teaching practices and styles are compared and analyzed to offer methods to meet individual and group needs. We believe that the teacher and student should be active partners in the instructional process.

Chapter 9 covers the relationship between thinking and questioning while implementing instructional strategies. We believe that thinking and questioning are important elements of classroom communication and are crucial components of effective teaching practices.

Chapter 10 examines the realm of summative assessment. We believe that authentic assessment with student involvement is an integral part of any successful evaluation model.

Chapter 11 explores the increasing and ever changing role of technology in the classroom. We believe that an understanding of technology for implementing delivery systems is necessary in preparing teachers for the twenty-first century.

Chapter 12 cycles the book back to the initial focus on reflective teaching pedagogy. We believe that pedagogical reflection continually builds and refines professional growth and commitment for responsible, caring teachers.

Teaching is a complex activity that requires making pedagogical judgments to improve and reform education. There are no guarantees that any pedagogy will be successful in every situation. Therefore, knowledge and reflection must be fostered to develop the critical judgment skills necessary for successful teaching and learning. Teachers who reflect on their experiences can develop lifelong decision-making skills that will lead to thoughtful judgments about personal educational belief systems.

References

Goodlad, J. I., Soder, R., & Sirotnik, K. A. (1990). *Places where teachers are taught*. San Francisco: Jossey-Bass Publishers.

Holmes Group, The. (1986). *Tomorrow's teachers*. East Lansing, MI: The Holmes Group, Inc.

Parker, F.W. (1894). *Talks on pedagogics: An outline of the theory of concentration*. New York: E. L. Kellogg.

Acknowledgments

We want to thank our families for their support and understanding for the time away from them while we prepared the book. Thanks to our spouses, Cecilia Frazee and Donald Rudnitski, whose thoughtful comments on early drafts are especially appreciated. Thanks also to our children, Bruce (Beaver) and Felicia Frazee, and Joseph and Stephen Rudnitski.

We recognize our mentor teachers and students who encouraged us while we taught what we believed in our university classes and our field-based courses. Special thanks to the students and teachers who contributed case studies and the mentor teachers who helped us fine-tune our ideas and make them applicable to real life in the classroom. We appreciate principals Maureen Fitzgerald-Gray and Alicia Thomas for allowing us to work with them as partners in professional development schools.

We have learned much from the schools, teachers, and students.

We wish to acknowledge former interns, now teachers, Debbie Alaniz for her contributions and preparation of the text and Cyndi Hartman for her contributions and thoughtful comments, and Janet Lewis-Teal for her support.

Thanks to Erin O'Connor, associate editor, for her guidance, the reviewers for their suggestions, and the staff at Delmar Publishers for their editorial and production assistance. The authors and staff at Delmar Publishers wish to express their appreciation to the reviewers of this manuscript whose thoughtful and constructive suggestions resulted in a much improved text.

This book was written equally by both authors, whose names appear in alphabetical order.

Reviewers

George M. Christ
University of Dallas
Irving, TX

Martha S. Gage
Ottawa University
Ottawa, KS

Mary Hughes
Iona College
New Rochelle, NY

Margaret A. Laughlin
University of Wisconsin–Green Bay
Green Bay, WI

Norma Jean Strickland
Rust College
Holly Springs, MS

About the Authors

Bruce M. Frazee is an associate professor of education at Trinity University in San Antonio, Texas. He received his undergraduate degree from Edinboro State College, his master degree from the University of Akron, and his Ed.D. from Memphis State University. He was an elementary school teacher in Ohio for five years. At Trinity, Dr. Frazee serves as a clinical faculty member in partnership with Hawthorne and Cambridge Elementary Schools. There he works with mentors, interns, and practicum students for Trinity's on-site teacher education program.

Dr. Frazee is a consultant for numerous school districts across the country. He is active in supporting teachers who initiate curriculum change through the Core Knowledge Foundation in Charlottsville, Virginia. He is currently conducting a study with five schools across the country to assess the student and teacher impact of the Core Knowledge curriculum.

Dr. Frazee authored a popular social studies series about *Families and Their Needs,* and *Communities and Their Needs* (1989). This curriculum is a basic learning system for first and second grades, published by Silver Burdett and Ginn. Recently, he co-authored a map reading book entitled, *Helping Your Child with Maps and Globes* (1994), published by

GoodYear Books. In addition, he has published over twenty journal articles and several book chapters.

Rose Rudnitski is an assistant professor of education and director of the Master of Science in Teaching Program and coordinator of the graduate programs in reading at the State University of New York at New Paltz, New York. A member of several national and international professional organizations in education, she is chair of the Conceptual Foundations Division of the National Association for Gifted Children and a member of the Committee on Teaching about Genocide and Intolerance of the National Council of Teachers of English.

Professor Rudnitski earned the doctorate in Curriculum and Teaching from Teachers College, Columbia University, where she continues to serve as a visiting assistant professor of education. She is a member of the editorial review board of *The Gifted Child Quarterly* and Roeper Review. Her research interests include the history of the curriculum, interdisciplinary curriculum, global conceptions of gifted education, comprehension and semiotics in reading and writing across the disciplines, and the development of social consciousness through curriculum and teaching.

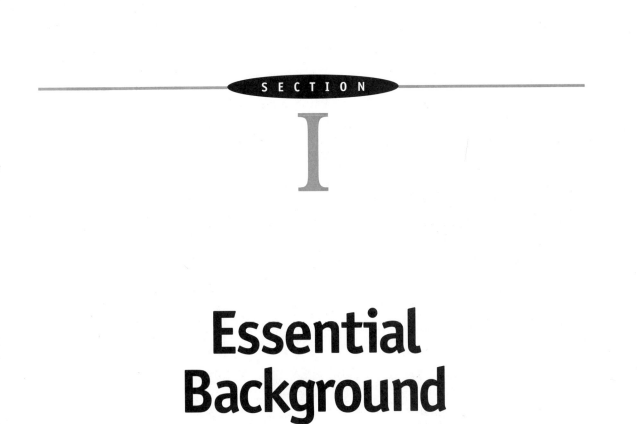

SECTION

I

Essential
Background

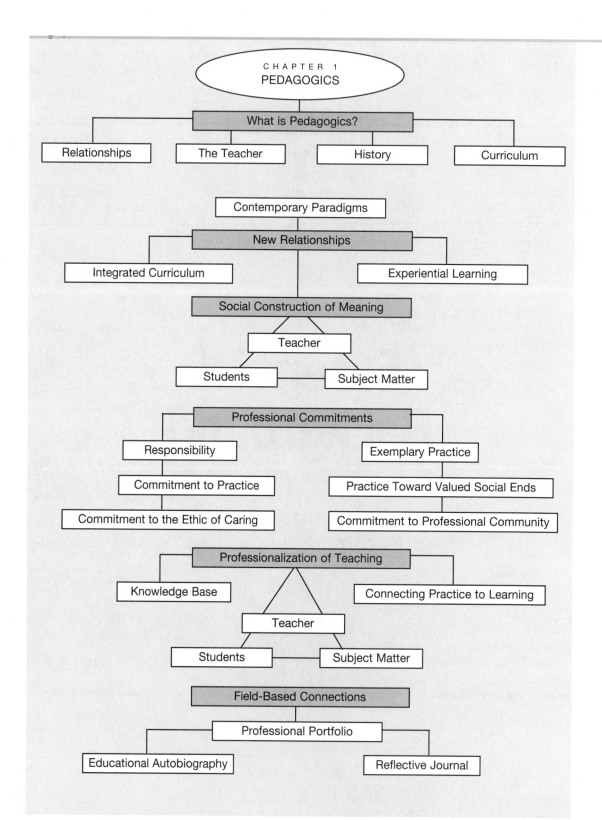

"Being aware of oneself as the instrument of one's teaching and aware of the story that makes one's life sensible allows for greater change and growth as well as greater intentionality in teaching choices."

—*William Ayers, 1988*

Pedagogics

Introduction

The Importance of Relationships

We define *pedagogics* as the study of pedagogy that integrates the many traditional discipline-based methods courses to highlight the relationships among them. However, relationships can be both explicit and implicit. The explicit relationships between the disciplines may be found through over-arching universal principles or skills that cross disciplinary lines. The implicit relationships involved in pedagogy are, perhaps, more difficult to define. They encompass the relationships between the teacher and the subject matter and the students and school community as well as between the teacher and him/herself.

▶ THEORY

The quotation at the beginning of this chapter was chosen because it epitomizes the *essential* aspect of our definition of pedagogics that makes it different from traditional conceptions of the study of pedagogy, and different from its original meaning as well. The teacher makes decisions based not only on knowledge of the subject and the teaching of it (what Shulman calls pedagogical content knowledge), but is also based on knowledge and awareness of self, society, and students. Teachers may reach an expert level of competence in using pedagogical content knowledge in decision-making, yet lack a deep awareness of how they feel about such fundamental issues as diversity, teacher autonomy, curriculum priorities, and how teachers should be taught to teach. Though that teacher's decisions are affected by those feelings, his/her lack of awareness could lead to decisions that may perpetuate existing inequities and faulty practices. This may ultimately shortchange the students, society, and the teaching profession. The practitioner of pedagogics is as aware of these sometimes hidden issues and effects as they are of the needs and interests of their students. In pedagogics, it is through the integration of reflection and critical thinking that the teacher acquires a truly professional level of skill and awareness, which translates to informed action in practice.

The Importance of the Teacher

With the increase in interdisciplinary teaching at all levels of schooling, and the increase in multi-disciplinary problem-solving teams in research and industry, it is necessary for teachers to develop and model the skills of relationship-finding and building in order to foster their development in their students: the citizens and workers of the future. We believe that pedagogy should not be simply integrated across subject-area lines, but should also include a personal dimension: the integration of the human beings involved, with a primary emphasis on the teacher as the mediator between the document we call "The Curriculum" and the learner.

John Dewey (1933) perceives the importance of the teacher in connecting the curriculum to the student, and views the teacher as an agent.

> Books, especially textbooks, are the chief representatives of the past, while teachers are the organs through which pupils are brought into effective connection with the material. Teachers are the agents through which knowledge and skills are communicated and rules of conduct enforced. (p. 18)

Teachers connect students to materials, activities, and knowledge; as agents of the curriculum they choose the answers to the basic curriculum questions:

- What is taught;
- To whom;
- Through what method;
- Using what resources;
- In what order; and
- For what amount of time.

This holds even if the answers to those questions are specified in the textbook or document.

Teachers also connect students to the norms and values of the larger society through what Dewey calls "rules of conduct." The teacher determines what behaviors are appropriate in the hundreds of experiences planned for the students each year, in addition to answering the questions:

- How should the students feel/believe about the subject;
- Which students are best suited for certain activities;
- In what way will the students be grouped;
- How will I react when a student behaves in an unacceptable manner; and
- What makes some things unacceptable in school, etc.

In choosing answers to these and myriad other questions, teachers rely on their own life experiences and beliefs as much as they rely on their knowledge of content and pedagogy. This makes teaching a purposeful, value-laden activity that requires personal integrity as well as technical competence. Thus the teacher is an agent mediating between the student and the curriculum, and between society, the curriculum, and the student.

History—Building on the Past

The term pedagogics was first used by Colonel Francis W. Parker (1894) to describe his theory for developing natural methods of teaching that used real experiences and involved the students in active rather than passive learning, practices which were quite revolutionary for his time. These methods emanated from his experience as Superintendent of Schools of Quincy, Massachusetts from 1875 to 1883, where he became widely known for his "Quincy System" of teaching. Parker's methods were based on his theory of "concentration," the integration of subject matter into a core of central subjects that were taught through unified methods. The relationships between the subjects were emphasized in Parker's pedagogics in order to make the curriculum more relevant than the traditional discipline-based curriculum with its isolated subjects. This also resulted in the alleviation of some of the overcrowding in the curriculum, especially at the elementary level, which had increased substantially since the inception of the common school (Tanner & Tanner, 1980).

Parker thought that pedagogy should be based on the two modes of learning: attention and expression. Attention was based in observation, hearing language, and reading, basically taking in information through processes that were primarily mental. The study of language, in his method, was integrated with the study of the content, the beginnings of what is now called the whole language method.

The modes of expression in Parker's pedagogics were primarily physical: gesture, voice, music, speech making, modeling, painting, drawing, and writing; these involved action and the use of the information and mental processes of attention. In practice, this would correspond to an emphasis on the application level of Bloom's Taxonomy (1956), the dominant model of cognition currently used in curriculum development. Thus,

in Parker's method, reading and writing were integrated with the study of geography or natural science in much the same way as they are in integrated units in a whole language classroom today. Many involved in the whole language movement in education trace their roots to the progressive education movement and philosophers like Francis W. Parker and John Dewey (Goodman, 1989). Our conception of pedagogics is founded in some of the same principles shared by those two movements: an equal focus on the whole picture as well as the parts, and an emphasis on relationships between ideas and people. In the classroom, these principles have translated into such practices as curriculum integration, experiential learning, cooperative learning, and group problem-solving.

Conclusion to Theory

There are teaching practices that cross disciplines. Some of them, teaching through mental models, teaching for transfer, and curriculum integration, were outlined in this chapter. In pedagogics, the teaching of skills is wholistic, while in content, the focus is conceptual. The curriculum is centerd on basic understandings and principles, and several topics are explored in depth, instead of the broad coverage of many.

In the subject areas, some best practices have been delineated, but the over-arching principles of a conceptual focus and wholistic skills instruction in a social context are common to all. Perhaps the most revolutionary idea in teaching today is the social construction of meaning for both the students and the teacher. Pedagogics, in all subject areas, reflects this revolution.

▶ **CLASSROOM**
▶ **APPLICATIONS**

Contemporary Paradigms

Curriculum Integration

We chose the name pedagogics for our theory of integrative teaching methods because we felt a need to acknowledge our debt to those who laid the foundation for our ideas. There is currently a resurgence in an emphasis on curriculum integration that stems from that initiated by Parker, Dewey, and others at the turn of this century. Though this progressive line of educational philosophy and practice has existed throughout this century, its roots were formed at that time (Kliebard, 1986). In 1902, in *The Child and the Curriculum,* Dewey wrote:

> Again, the child's life is an integral, a total, one. He passes quickly from one topic to another, as from one spot to another, but is not conscious of transition or break... The things that occupy him are held together by the unity of the personal social interests which his life carries along... He goes to school, and various studies divide and fractionalize the world for him. Geography selects, it abstracts and analyzes one set of facts, and from one particular point of view. Arithmetic is another division, grammar another department, and so on indefinitely. (pp. 5-6)

Almost a century ago, Dewey perceived the fragmentation and lack of cohesion of the traditional curriculum. We have inherited many aspects of traditional curriculum that have become entrenched over time. Scheduling by subject, textbook writing by subject, teaching methods courses by subject in teacher education, and even teacher certification by subject are all norms that have all contributed to the perpetuation of the traditional fragmented curriculum.

In light of new research on cognition and the workings of the brain, educators are again changing the curriculum to make it more relevant and understandable to the learner (Caine & Caine, 1991; Perkins, 1991). The changes being made include the integration of subject matter when appropriate, and when it illuminates what is being taught. These changes encompass more than simply modifying what each teacher does in the classroom. They have prompted the restructuring of institutional arrangements, which were formerly held as immutable. Teachers now work together in cooperative groups to plan and develop curriculum. Team teaching is a common practice in interdisciplinary units, and schedule changes that increase flexibility and freedom of choice are being implemented in order to make more curriculum integration and group work possible (Jacobs, 1989). This is an exciting time to be a teacher, if one is unafraid to take risks and accept the challenge of paving a new path.

Experiential Learning

With curriculum integration comes the integration of the teaching of skills along with the content that is being taught. The "what" and the "how" are inextricably intermeshed, changing the focus of lesson plans and perhaps even eliminating the need for objectives, which reflect an out-dated behavioristic point of view (Caine & Caine, 1991). There is less time in the pedagogic classroom for "teacher telling" and direct instruction, modes of pedagogy for a time when the memorization of facts was considered to be a major goal of learning (Baroody & Ginsburg, 1990).

Instead, opportunities are set up for individuals and groups to construct meaning through activities and experiences in and out of the classroom. Though there are many definitions and degrees of belief and practice in this theory, much of experiential learning comes under the rubric of "constructivism." Constructivist learning experiences are founded in the belief that all knowledge is constructed, built up by each student through interaction and active participation in the learning process (Noddings, 1990; von Glasersfeld, 1990).

Experiential learning activities utilize both long- and short-term projects for groups and individuals. They include apprenticeship programs through which students may observe and learn from working experts in a variety of fields. Students may also experience real-life situations in computer and classroom simulations and experiments. It is through experiential educational activities such as those just cited that a diversity of students learn to develop working explanations of the world (Gardner, 1991).

Relationships and the Social Construction of Meaning

The translations of the work of Vygotsky (1962; 1978) and the influence of scholars from fields such as psychology (Gardner, 1983), anthropology (Bateson, 1972), and neuropsychology (Samples, 1992), among others, have caused a transformation in the way we view learning. No longer is learning viewed as something which occurs solely in the individual. It is something that we do together as we socially construct meaning from shared experiences.

The classroom is a shared experience in which everyone influences each other in ways that are both obvious and hidden. The obvious ways are those in which competition and cooperation are evident in the activities fostered by the teacher and the school environment. The hidden ways are the ways that the teacher's values and biases are evident in the choices made in teaching and in the curriculum. These biases may manifest themselves in such ways as a teacher's never having the time for science in the curriculum, allowing males to monopolize classroom discussions (AAUW, 1992), or even in lower expectations for culturally different students. Again, the truly professional teacher is aware of both the overt and the hidden aspects of the curriculum and teaching. Pedagogics and the methods outlined in this book will help you, as a teacher, to address those aspects of your craft.

Curriculum and the Learner: Teacher as Connector

Connecting What the Teacher Learns to What the Teacher Does

Teaching has traditionally been viewed as a complex, lonely activity fraught with the responsibility inherent in the thousands of decisions a teacher makes every day (McPherson, 1972; Lieberman & Miller, 1984). A profession plagued by a reputation for low standards in its educational programs, lack of preparation, and low status and pay, teaching and teacher education have been the focus of reform efforts in the United States for well over one hundred years (Lortie, 1975; Goodlad, 1984).

How can such an admittedly important profession suffer from such a lack of respect and efficacy? There have been many suggestions proffered in answer to this question: with everything from teaching's history as women's work, to its transience as an occupation, to naive conceptions of what teaching entails being implicated as reasons (Apple, 1987; The Holmes Group, 1986). Though these factors may have contributed to the present state of teaching, it is up to you as a present or future teacher, no matter what your preparation has been so far, to take the responsibility for changing those conceptions. The first step is to take responsibility for not only your preparation and your teaching, but for the profession as a whole.

Taking Responsibility for the Teaching Profession

In taking responsibility for your profession, you must be aware of the depth of the commitment you have made in choosing teaching as a career. As a teacher, you accept the responsibility of stewardship through which society virtually entrusts you with its next generation. You accept responsibility for your students: a moral commitment to usher them from one stage to another, with little regard for extrinsic reward for yourself.

You also accept what Sergiovanni (1992) has called professional virtue. Professional virtue has four dimensions which, if embraced

by all who practice the art, would eradicate the plagues just cited and help to elevate teaching to status as a true profession. These dimensions are:

1. A commitment to practice in an exemplary way;
2. A commitment to practice toward valued social ends;
3. A commitment to one's own practice and to the practice itself; and
4. A commitment to the ethic of caring. (p. 43)

To the dimensions of professional virtue, we would add a commitment to the professional community: to collegiality and sharing. Taken separately, each of these dimensions has many facets of its own. Though each will be dealt with in greater depth in later chapters, they are outlined briefly here.

Practice in an Exemplary Way

Exemplary practice, to the professional teacher, means reading professional literature and keeping abreast of developments in theory before they reach practice. Many teachers have little sense of the theories involved in their actions each day, and exhibit even less understanding of the historical antecedents of current practices. This is one of the sources of criticism of education for being ahistorical and for our perpetually reinventing the wheel (Cuban, 1984; Jackson, 1992).

As a practitioner, you must set high standards for yourself and your colleagues. This means not only keeping up with current literature, but sharing ideas and trying them in your classroom. In doing this, you would enlist the support and help of colleagues, community, and students; you would set an environment for risk-taking in your classroom, and act as a role model for those around you, most notably your students. For exemplary practice is characterized by risk-taking as much as it is by a sound basis in theory.

Another facet of exemplary practice is that of reflection on one's practice and the feelings and reasons behind one's actions (Schon, 1983). Teachers who reflect on their practice are more deliberate and purposeful in their teaching, and tend to have a more thoughtful climate in their classrooms (Onosko, 1992). They model the habits of and dispositions toward the higher order thinking which characterizes reflection, and foster those attitudes and dispositions in their students and the classroom environment (Dewey, 1933). It is through reflection that the teachers connect what they are and know to each situation in the classroom. It is also through reflection that the teacher is aware of him/herself and the students. It is also through reflection that the teacher grows.

Reflection alone, however, is not enough. It must be accompanied by informed action. In order to have reflection inform the actions of the teacher in practice, Smyth (1989) suggests four stages, translated into questions, which might prove helpful in providing a framework for translating reflection into action.

1. Describe...what do I do?
2. Inform...what does this mean?
3. Confront...how did I come to be like this?
4. Reconstruct...how might I do things differently? (p. 13)

The purpose of reflection in exemplary practice is to change action and align it with the needs of the students, the curriculum, and society, prioritized in accordance with one's beliefs and values as an informed professional.

Practice Toward Valued Social Ends

In committing to practice toward valued social ends, a teacher accepts a sense of stewardship or agency (Sergiovanni, 1992; Greene, 1989). Maxine Greene (1989) regards the sense of agency as concomitant with reflective practice:

> It is difficult to imagine students discovering what they think and what they do not yet know if there is no space of conversation, no space of engagement in diversity. A sense of agency is required of the teacher if such things are to happen; and it is hard to conceive of a teacher who is a reflective practitioner but who lacks a sense of agency. (p. 23)

A sense of agency, according to Greene (as it did with Dewey), connects the teacher, the students, and the school to the surrounding world. The worthwhile questions in study are inspired by the problems and conditions extant in the world and society. They are the questions that are real and which will result in informed action on the part of the students and teacher as citizens of the community. According to Dewey (1899), these are the questions which will cause these students, the future citizens, to help society to progress and develop in meaningful, positive ways.

A Commitment to One's Practice and to the Practice Itself

A major feature of the commitment of the professional teacher who practices pedagogics is the commitment to the practice itself. This includes, in our view, a commitment to the professionalization of teaching and to raising the conception of teaching as a profession. It is a commitment to teaching as a vocation, a calling for which the rewards are intrinsic and from which the teacher derives personal meaning, even while helping students to construct meaning of their own.

A commitment to the practice itself also entails the commitment to sharing and a responsibility for one's peers. It means helping a colleague who is having trouble. It means taking the time to come to consensus as a school community and to define shared values and norms of professional behavior and beliefs. Beliefs are complicated and diverse, and consensus may never be reached, but it is the discussion of beliefs and the awareness of their effects on teaching situations that are important.

A commitment to the practice itself also means defining success, not in terms of what is happening in one's classroom, but in terms of what is happening in one's school and the larger educational community in society (Sergiovanni, 1992). As members of a profession, we share as much responsibility for our students and their achievements as we do for our practice. Therefore, it is important that, as a professional, you accept responsibility for your chosen profession.

A Commitment to the Ethic of Caring

The fourth professional virtue encompasses all of the others, for one cannot make a commitment to the others without caring. In this sense, the caring is not just what one feels for the students; it is a level of accountability that can only come with a total commitment to the profession as a human endeavor. Noddings (1986) writes that an ethic of caring,

> "takes fidelity to persons as primary and directs us to analyze and evaluate all rec-

ommendations in light of our answers to questions concerning the maintenance of community, the growth of individuals, and the enhancement of subjective aspects of our relationship." (p. 510)

It is through our caring that we make the effort to discuss our beliefs and to analyze all aspects of our relationships in the school community.

The word education is derived from the Latin word, *educare,* which means to draw out or bring forth that which is within the person. In order to do this, we must not only know our students, we must also know ourselves and our colleagues. We are in a continuous state of growth, and if we forget that, we will not be able to fully assist our students in their own growth. In order to educate, it is not enough to know, however. We must also care enough to form and maintain a relationship with our students. This relationship has a specific purpose and should not be confused with a deeply personal relationship. Teachers, in Noddings' view (1986), model caring through "meticulous preparation, lively presentation, critical thinking, appreciative listening, constructive evaluation, general curiosity" (p. 503).

A Commitment to the Professional Community

We believe that a commitment to the professional community is important enough to delineate as a professional virtue unto itself. This commitment is enacted through collegiality and sharing, and reflects the contemporary paradigm of the social construction of meaning and group problem-solving cited in the section on pedagogics. Pedagogics does not just reflect this emphasis on society and relationships, it draws upon them as building blocks in teaching practice and the educational process. Relationships, to the professional practitioner of pedagogics, may be likened to negative shapes in art (Figure 1–1). To those who are unaware, they are the spaces between things, but to those who are aware, they are a part of the work: a piece of the picture. It is this awareness that distinguishes good teaching as moral action rather than as competent behavior.

Part of the commitment to the professional community is a commitment to induct new members into the profession. Professional virtue carries with it the responsibility to see that those who have chosen the profession are welcomed and supported in their early years by caring mentors—those who spend time reflecting on practice with novice teachers. It is not only our professional duty to communicate high standards and inclusive norms to student teachers and interns, it is also our duty to model caring and professional practice.

Cooperating teachers and mentor teachers make the commitment to maintain a profes-

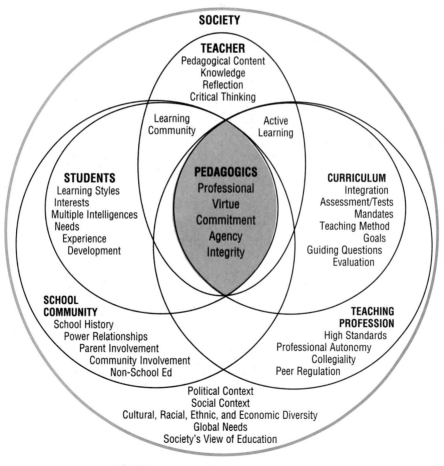

FIGURE 1–1   Society's View of Education

sional community and promote its development whenever they accept a student teacher or intern. Maintaining a professional community takes effort and may be likened to maintaining a high level of communication in a long-term relationship, or to maintaining a personal reputation for integrity and high standards. It means ascertaining the context and adjusting to changes in it. It means a commitment to communicating and listening, and maintaining a realistic view of oneself and one's colleagues. This commitment is not "above and beyond the call of duty;" it is an intrinsic part of professional duty to those who practice pedagogics.

The Professionalization of Teaching

The integration of values and pedagogy elevates teaching to a moral activity, based as much on relationships as on knowledge and skills. The awareness and appreciation of the moral aspects of teaching are as basic and essential to the development of a professional practice of teaching as the technical aspects (Sergiovanni, 1992). It is through pedagogics that we hope to integrate the moral, technical, personal, and relational to develop truly professional teachers. These teachers will contribute to elevating teaching to the professional status it deserves.

Though the discussion of the professionalization of teaching has primarily centered on the development of a knowledge base, raising standards of entry, restructuring, and the improvement of teacher education programs (The Holmes Group, 1986; Elmore, 1992), we believe that the primary responsibility for professionalizing teaching rests with teachers. The determination that a career is a profession should come from within its own ranks, not from without. That determination is made by the commitment to professional practice, to the professional community, and to a commitment to professional virtue and personal integrity on the part of those in the profession. Those who make those commitments realize that naive and disparaging conceptions of teaching are based in bias or on the actions of the few who have not committed to the development of those qualities in themselves as individuals.

It is up to teachers to monitor their profession and to ensure that all who teach make the necessary commitments on a personal and professional level. Just as the teacher is the central connecting force in pedagogics, so is the teacher the force connecting teaching as a technical skill with teaching as a profession.

The Knowledge Base for Teaching

As with every field of knowledge, the knowledge base for teaching is in constant flux, reflecting new knowledge in education and related fields as well as reflecting new methods of inquiry in educational research. The field has come a long way since the process-product research of the 1970s defined discrete behaviors exhibited by teachers and catalogued them as "effective teaching." (This early research is exemplified by such studies as Rist, 1973; Rosenthal & Jacobson, 1968; Berliner, 1977; Good & Grouws, 1977.) Yet, that body of research provided the foundation for the continuously developing knowledge base for teaching.

We now know a great deal about teacher expectations and how they affect student achievement; about "time on task" and the most effective sequence of teaching behaviors for presenting a lesson. Teachers can build upon this knowledge with the added perspectives of context and self, and their impact on classrooms to either enhance or hinder education. Art Costa (1984) observes, "Teaching, like all other forms of human interface with environmental phenomena, is a dynamic interaction between both exterior and interior forces—the exterior world of the classroom and the interior meaning of the teacher" (p. 202). The most recent information in the knowledge base for teaching reflects both interior and exterior knowledge. Pedagogics builds upon the old and the new to help you, as a teacher, chart your own course of action.

The new knowledge base includes our knowledge of how learners learn, and makes use of what we know about learning to change what we do in teaching. In later chapters, we will explore, in depth, the diverse forms of knowledge and knowing and the social nature of knowledge. Of all the recent developments in the field of cognition, none has had as profound an effect on pedagogy as the social nature of learning (Leinhardt, 1992). It has caused a significant shift in our conception of curriculum and teaching, to the point of changing our thinking of teaching from that of presenting information to one of guiding students in the use of cognitive strategies which they will eventually use on their own.

Our wholistic view of pedagogy enlarges the professional knowledge base to give equal value to personal integrity, critical reflection, technical skills, situational problem-solving, and multiple modes of learning and expression for the students and the teacher. Pedagogics is each of these features working in relation to the others and in the context of human relationships, making it more than the simple sum of all of them. We will elaborate on these points in Chapter 3 on the teacher.

Pedagogics in Action

Connecting Patterns of Teaching with Patterns of Learning

There are some over-aching principles of good teaching which cross subject-area lines as well as those which are subject-specific. In pedagogics, we integrate the large concepts with the specific skills to become teaching professionals with a commitment to professional virtue. Some of the methods which foster deep understanding, according to Perkins (1991), are teaching with mental models, coaching understanding performances, teaching for transfer, and connecting the curriculum (curriculum integration).

Teaching with *mental models* means first approximating the mental models of what is to be taught to those which exist in the students' minds. In the past, this was called determining prior knowledge, but that phrase may also imply the use of pre-tests. Pre-tests, though sometimes appropriate, are not viewed as the sole source of knowledge of the students' existing models. Brainstorming on the topic, discussion, picturing and imagery, creating metaphors, role playing, graphic representations and symbols, and other means can also provide the information.

In the context of a subject area, a practice for using a mental model comes from the teaching of reading: K-W-L (Ogle, 1986). In this model, the teacher and the children first ask themselves what they already know about the subject. Then they ask what they would like to know, or predict what they might find out about the subject through reading, observing, experiencing, etc. The last step is to determine how they will show what they have learned. For example, if the students are reading a short passage, they might simply discuss and answer questions; but if they are embarking on a long educational project, then they might publish a paper on the subject or work on a performance or exhibition to demonstrate their expertise in that area.

This is where *coaching understanding performances* comes in. As students delve into a topic in depth (another characteristic of good subject matter teaching that crosses subjects), they learn the behaviors that experts in that area display as they acquire knowledge of the subject (Brophy, 1992). Their learning experiences are actual representations, simulations or real experiences in which the students are able to use some of the skills that an expert in that area would use. They are provided with opportunities to approximate expertise, and are guided and coached in these experiences, either by the teacher or by a mentor or expert in the field, depending on resources and their availability.

Again, in the field of reading, this approximation of expertise would be demonstrated in the teacher's use of the writing workshop to encourage the students to employ the writing process in their own writing. In the writing workshop, students approximate expertise by behaving like authors. They, in fact, are authors, sharing their work, editing, learning new techniques in mini-lessons, and conferencing with the teacher; the teacher models the desired behaviors and attitudes, and coaches the students, supporting and encouraging them to develop more complex mental models as they hone their own writing skills. Since students write in all subject areas, the writing workshop activities can be used for all writing that the students are doing in school.

In *teaching for transfer,* the teacher encourages the students to employ techniques from the writing workshop to any other writing that they may be doing. The teacher coaches the children to see connections between the writing they do in school and writing they do out of school. Teachers also model what they are coaching the students to do, and give students examples of reports, etc., that were edited, re-written, and improved on. This is where it is crucial that the teacher be a model and demonstrate the desired behaviors honestly and with integrity. There is more to teaching for transfer than the simple transfer of skills. The students must be encouraged to transfer the dispositions, values, and knowledge as well as skills to other contexts (Brophy, 1992). The teacher must be willing to care enough to commit to being an author and transferring the skills and ideas being taught in the classroom to personal life.

Integrating the *content of the curriculum* around a limited set of powerful concepts and ideas, basic understandings and principles, is another key factor in connecting patterns of teaching with patterns of learning. In researching the effects of integrated curricula, Jacobs (1989) found that the students transferred skills and knowledge to other areas of their lives more readily than when they experienced discipline-based curricula. Perceiving relationships is a skill, and the students, with practice, got better at seeing the connections between what they were learning in school and what they did outside of school. It is also notable that the students related and got along better *during* and *after* integrated units than they did *before* experiencing them.

The Role of the Teacher in Pedagogics

The role of the teacher in the classroom in which pedagogics is practiced is one of a guide or coach. The teacher helps the students to scaffold and build schemata, and does not spend the majority of the time presenting information. The empty vessel metaphor does not apply to the pedagogic classroom.

Though the teacher is a guide for the learning in the classroom, this does not imply that the teacher is not the expert on education in the situation. It is the teacher who is ultimately responsible for the learning that takes place in the classroom environment, and therefore must take great care to create an environment which is a learning community. In this community, risk-taking is encouraged: The students, and sometimes the teacher, make mistakes in their attempts to approximate expertise. It is an environment where social interaction and dialogue promote deeper insight and understanding. It is a climate of inquiry, fostered by the guidance and questioning of the teacher. The teacher in the pedagogic classroom uses questioning to structure the inquiry and discovery of the students to help them to elaborate their knowledge and skills well beyond those held in their textbooks.

The Role of the Student in Pedagogics

The student plays an active role in the pedagogic classroom. Here, the student performs tasks that call for problem solving or critical thinking. The students are actively engaged in authentic tasks in which they employ higher order thinking skills and processes as they construct meaning in the context of the curriculum. *Application* is the primary level of instruction in the pedagogic classroom. This is especially true at the elementary level, where the students are at Piaget's Concrete Operational stage of cogni-

tive development and need to be performing hands-on activities rather than sitting and listening to the teacher talk.

Gardner (1983) has helped us to reconceptualize intelligence and broaden our definitions to encompass the many modes of attention and expression delineated by Parker in 1894, and to view them as viable bases for the development of appropriate teaching practices. The students in the pedagogic classroom are aware of these strengths or "frames" of mind and experiment with modes of learning, thinking, and expression as a means of finding their own talents and abilities through active participation in their own and each other's learning.

Relationships Between Teaching Practices and Various Subjects

There is a move in almost every discipline in the curriculum toward wholistic skills instruction (Brophy, 1992). The practitioner of pedagogics teaches skills in context in all subjects, and does not isolate skills or pieces of skills for drill and practice alone. In reading, this translates into practices such as teaching for meaning from whole texts rather than the decoding of phonemes within words. Students are engaged in reading whole texts for a number of purposes and they employ all levels of language: oral, written, and the reading of texts both silently and aloud in their search for meaning. They share their ideas about books and often read literature which ties in with a theme on which they are focusing for study.

In the pedagogic classroom, reading is inextricably intertwined with writing, and each enhances the development of skills in the other. Writing is viewed as a medium of communication and expression, with skills taught within those broader contexts. Writing is shared among the students and the teacher, and each helps the other through the process of revision through the final copy. In the pedagogic classroom, students respond to their reading in writing and respond to each other's writing both orally and in writing. With the focus on communication and response, writing and reading have real purposes in pedagogics, even as we are attempting to give equal status to non-verbal means of learning, communication, and expression whenever we can.

In the pedagogics classroom, the focus for social studies is on integration of social science concepts with other subject areas while students engage in critical thinking and problem solving. They collect, analyze, and interpret information culled from as many primary sources as possible in their study of history, the heart of the social studies. In the current paradigm, history and geography provide the framework for the social studies curriculum (NCSS, 1990).

At the core is a curriculum of inclusion on many levels, with less emphasis on the old concept of "expanding environments" or going from the near community to places farther away as students go through the grades. Students study global diversity as they engage in activities which help them to explore issues of cultural diversity and civic decision-making locally. They are involved in community activities and perform community service projects as part of their curriculum, as well as participate in experiences such as the Circle of Friends to help them to understand what being different is like (Forest & Pierpoint, 1992) even as they help someone who differs from them.

The mathematics curriculum is focused on problem-solving, with students exploring, reasoning, and estimating to solve a variety of non-traditional problems. The memorization of math facts is secondary in the pedagogics classroom to the development of skills through use and application to problems. Operations are performed with calculators, and students and teachers spend more time engaged in discourse on the meaning of concepts underlying the work (NCTM, 1989). Here, too, the teacher is a guiding force rather than a forceful authority, while the student is an active participant in the process.

In science, there is no longer an emphasis on the layers of many different disciplines making the cake at the secondary level. Each year, students study each scientific discipline from a descriptive to an abstract level over the course of their secondary education, integrating all of the sciences every year rather than taking a different course each year. There is no longer an emphasis on earth science in ninth grade, biology in tenth grade, chemistry in eleventh grade, and physics in twelfth grade. All sciences are studied every year. Throughout their schooling, students learn habits of mind, understandings, and attitudes that are "necessary for all citizens in a scientifically literate society," through hands-on activities in situations that are as authentic as possible (AAAS, 1990).

The textbook and the teacher in the pedagogics classroom connect the students to what they have learned and what they are doing. The teacher presents a model of inquiry for the students and acts as a mentor, helping the students to build their scientific reasoning through scaffolding, questioning, and guidance. The students formulate hypotheses and test them, using empirical methods, then select alternatives when necessary (Brophy, 1992). The focus is no longer on the "what" in the pedagogic classroom, but on the "how" and especially the "why."

FIELD-BASED CONNECTIONS

Guidelines for Interns

The Reflective Journal

This activity is suggested for both the intern/student teacher and the mentor/cooperating teacher. Each of you should keep a reflective journal of your classroom experience together. The journal does not have to focus on your relationship, but, as a starter, might follow your own personalized variation on the four guiding questions suggested in this chapter. Here are ours:

1. What did I do?
2. Why did I do it? What are the beliefs and values inherent in my actions? What do they mean?
3. How did I come to believe/feel/think this way?
4. How do I want to change my practice to more closely reflect what I believe to be true and right? Do I want to change what I believe to reflect my practice instead?

You may be reluctant to keep a journal. It is difficult to find the time to write, especially at the end of the day when one is tired. It is important that you understand that you are developing the disposition to reflect in yourself as much as you would like to develop it in your students. It takes discipline and practice to be a reflective professional. It takes discipline to keep a journal. Try it. It might be difficult and tedious at first, but once you get used to it, you will find that you look forward to the few minutes you have to think back on your practice and look into yourself for the reasons for your actions. Getting to know yourself better will be a pleasurable experience.

Another reason in support of keeping the journal is your role as a model for the students. No matter what grade level or subject you teach, you probably will, at some point, ask your students to keep a journal. Typical journal frameworks are the reading response journal, the writing journal, the reflective journal, the science journal (recording both observations and reflections), and even the math journal as an adjunct to a math portfolio. It is imperative that you model the disposition to keep a journal and reflect on your actions as much as you model the behavior for your students.

You might try writing in your journal when the students are writing in theirs, rather than doing other things at your desk. In fact, it is very important that you model the behaviors you expect of your students. You could write in your journal for a few minutes during your preparation time at school rather than waiting until evening or the end of the school day.

Your journal can also be a place to gestate ideas. The artist has the sketchbook; the inventor, the notebook. Even Beethoven kept a notebook of his ideas for themes. His notebook is our evidence that he made seventeen tries before he finally came up with the final four-note theme for his Fifth Symphony. Though you might use this as an example of drafting and revision in writing, we use it here as an example of perseverance. The purpose of your journal is not to draft and revise writing; it is actually much deeper: You are looking at yourself from without through recalling your actions, and you are revising yourself from within through reflection. It is the single most important activity we will suggest in this book.

Lessons in the Field

Take a lesson from the teacher's manual of any textbook or the basal reader, if your mentor uses them, and try to alter it to fit a pedagogic paradigm. You are not out to change the world in this activity, so don't try to do too much alteration.

Try translating the objective of the lesson to an overall question. Then structure the lesson so that you guide the students to ask the questions that are listed for the teacher to "parrot" in the teacher's manual.

Your main goal in this activity is to make the students active investigators who are responsible for their learning rather than for sitting still and listening to the teacher talk and ask questions. Shift the onus of inquiry to the students.

Another goal of this activity is for you to exercise your powers of creativity. If you are now mentally protesting that you are not creative, don't bother. We don't believe you. The more you practice using your creativity, the better you will get at it. This is why we are asking you to practice it in terms of planning lessons. We want you to get a lot of practice at being creative in this context.

The Educational Autobiography

You teach who you are. It's important, therefore, for you to know how you came to be who you are as an educator. Over the course of this semester, you will be working on compiling an educational autobiography as a preamble to creating your personal philosophy of education.

We suggest that you start thinking about assembling a professional portfolio for use when you are entering the profession after you graduate. It should contain your philosophy of education, which should cite theory and research and not just seem like it came "out of the blue." It could also contain a curriculum unit you developed, a child study, and/or a paper that you have written that reflects your scholarly abilities and interests, and perhaps your educational autobiography. The educational autobiography is a first step to discovering who you are as a learner and as a teacher, both of which are two sides of the same coin. A sample educational autobioigraphy is included at the end of this chapter.

Try to recall your elementary or secondary school years. Was there a teacher who had a particularly profound effect on you? Was she/he (90% of elementary teachers are female) exceptionally sensitive and understanding? Was she/he tough and uncompromising? Did this teacher let you know that she/he expected the best from you? How did you know this? How would you like to be like this teacher? How would you be different? Was there anyone else in your educational experience who was significant in your education and life? Explain.

▶ CHAPTER CLOSURE

Summary

This chapter was an introduction to the concept of pedagogics. Pedagogics encompasses many facets of teaching and classroom relationships as well as the relationships between teachers and the profession of teaching with the school community and the larger society. Traditionally, there have been some aspects of these relationships that teachers have not been aware of, yet which have affected decision-making in the classroom. In pedagogics, we take these aspects out of hiding and address them as we become aware of them, reflect upon them, and take deliberative action.

The teacher who practices pedagogics accepts a commitment to a professional virtue which has many facets. As professionals, make a commitment to the profession and people as well as to principles and ideals. We also make a commitment to ourselves—to our own growth and development as caring, responsible human beings as we help our students to grow.

Pedagogics is teaching based on our knowledge of teaching and of learners, both as individuals and as part of a learning community. We construct a community in our classrooms, with the help of our students while we all construct meaning from our shared experiences there. Just as students build new knowledge on prior knowledge, we as teachers build our practice on who we are. In the pedagogics classroom, we value group interaction as much as individual projects, and we value multiple modes of learning and expression as much as we value the traditional verbal/mathematical means of communication prevalent in classrooms today.

Chapter Discussion Questions

1. The concept of pedagogics is not a new one. Was there anything in your own educational experience that reflected a pedagogic point of view? Do you remember a teacher taking the time to adapt lessons for different learning styles or individual needs? Do you remember a teacher who went beyond the textbook in order to make learning more relevant and fun?

2. How do you think you might put such concepts as reflective teaching or a commitment to professional virtue into action in your practice as a teacher?

3. Look at the curricula or textbooks for your grade level in the classroom in which you are placed, and make a list of the subjects expected to be covered at that level. Do not forget subjects taught by special teachers: music, art, health, and physical education. Compare your list to the subjects you studied in elementary school. Discuss why or why not there are differences.

4. Is there anyone in your class, or do you know anyone, who went to a progressive school? Perhaps they attended a private school or a Montessori school. Compare their educational experience with yours. Discuss the advantages and disadvantages of both.

CASE STUDY

The case study example can be used for analysis in small or large groups. Questions follow the case study as suggestions for discussion

CASE STUDY 1–1: Lisa

Lisa is a very unusual sixth grader in a suburban elementary school. She has unique mannerisms which most people find irritating. She screams when angry or upset. When she is excited, the volume and pitch of her voice rise, and she lengthens the pronunciation of vowels. "Oooohhh," she shrieks when another girl calls her a derogatory name.

In class, Lisa is quite bright, even brilliant at some things. She is highly verbal and it is obvious that she processes information and can learn at a very fast pace. In terms of depth, however, she seems to fall short. Though mature beyond her years in intellectual pursuits, her insight into human nature and interactions is lagging. Emotionally, she is quite excitable and is prone to tantrums when upset, making her difficult to control in some classroom situations.

To add to this unevenness, Lisa is very uncoordinated physically. Whenever she's upset or excited and is shrieking vowels, she almost seems to be conducting an orchestra, accompanying the sounds with her hands flailing next to her face. When she walks, Lisa's heels barely touch the ground, and she seems to be walking on her toes and balancing with her outstretched hands. This distinctive gait is widely imitated by the other students as they joke about Lisa and make fun of her.

Lisa is quite unpopular and has no friends. In fact, few students interact with Lisa unless they have to for a class activity. They avoid her as much as possible. At this age, her unpopularity is becoming a source of sadness and discomfort for Lisa. She has joined the school chorus, though she doesn't sing very well, and belongs to the Girl Scouts. She often makes overt efforts at friendship, but to no avail. She is simply ignored, or worse, used by the other children.

Lisa is the only child in an upper middle-class home. Her father is a research scientist with the local chemical laboratory and her mother is a teacher in another school district. They are proud of their daughter's abilities and high grades on her report cards. They seem unaffected by reports from Lisa's teachers of her unpopularity and problems with social adjustment. They say that the other children are jealous of their daughter's intelligence and insinuate that perhaps the teachers are, too.

The teachers are actually no pillars of virtue and mimic and deride Lisa mercilessly behind her back, especially in the faculty lounge. The music teacher is quite upset by this behavior, but lacks the courage to tell her colleagues. She either becomes silent and ignores their ridicule of Lisa or leaves the room when it starts.

She is currently casting the school musical, which she directs. It is a cooperative endeavor and a major yearly event at the school. The school chorus is the cast, while the teachers make the costumes and the set and give many hours of their free time to make the musical a memorable event for the children. The faculty actually enjoys working on the musicals. They are proud of the quality of the productions and the students' accomplishments in them. The music teacher has built a reputation for excellence and integrity through the musicals over the years, and her colleagues respect her for her talent and abilities.

This year, the musical is a comic version of "Cinderella," a play written to be performed by adults for children. This has not deterred the music teacher who has written a score to transform the play into a musical, complete with production numbers and special effects. Today, she walks into the faculty lounge and announces to the sixth-grade teachers, who are there eating lunch, that she has cast the production. She has cast Lisa in a major role as one of the comic step-sisters. The teachers are aghast. "Are you crazy? She'll ruin the show!"

Case Study Discussion Questions

1. What are Lisa's strengths as a student? What are her weaknesses? How might you use her strengths to help her to work on her weaknesses in classroom situations?

2. What dimension of professional virtue is most lacking in the faculty of this school? What professional virtue is dominant? How is the music teacher attempting to strengthen the faculty in their area of weakness? How can she succeed? What if she fails?

3. What can be done to help Lisa's parents see a more realistic view of their daughter's social needs? How can they help her to gain more acceptance from her peers? Should they help her? Does she need the acceptance of her peers?

4. How can the teachers help Lisa to strengthen her social position with her peers? Do you think that the music teacher made the right choice? What do you think motivated her?

▶ SAMPLE EDUCATIONAL AUTOBIOGRAPHY

I attended public schools until ninth grade when I transferred to Cathedral Preparatory Seminary in New York City. It is a Catholic high school for boys considering the priesthood. I knew at that time that I wanted to enter a service profession, but wasn't sure which. I had never considered the priesthood, so I decided to explore this option in high school.

By the time I graduated I had decided not to become a priest, but to pursue a career in social work. I continued my education at Nazareth College of Rochester where I focused my studies on youth services, and received a B.S. in social work. While in college and after graduation I worked with various populations of young people. The first group I had experience with was mentally retarded teenagers, followed by juvenile delinquents. Next I worked with developmentally disabled children, and then emotionally disturbed youngsters. The last group I worked with was emotionally disturbed pre-schoolers. With each new population, I gravitated toward children with more potential for growth. I learned that I am not good at maintenance. I need to see progress in those I work with. Even though the pre-schoolers had the most potential out of all the groups I worked with, it wasn't enough. Out of confusion and frustration I left social work, took training and became a radio disc jockey.

After two years, I decided to quit radio in order to take a journey around the country. It was something I always wanted to do, and it was something I had to do. I had reached a low point in my life, and I needed enlightenment.

The desire to take this trip was born when I was a little leaguer who cheered Reggie Jackson on and idolized Tom Seaver. I always wanted to tour the country visiting every major league ballpark. When I finally took my journey, I did manage to visit five ballparks and the Field of Dreams in Iowa. However, as an adult, I had many other reasons for going.

Two books that fueled my desire to venture out were John Steinbeck's *Travels With Charley* and William Least Heat Moon's *Blue Highways*. Like these two authors, I wanted to experience America. I wanted to visit small towns, talk to the people, learn their history, and see how they live. Also, I wanted to view the natural wonders of our land as well as the big cities.

On my trip I did all of these things and more. I visited such natural monuments as the Badlands, Devil's Tower, the Rocky Mountains, and the Grand Canyon. I fulfilled another childhood dream of driving my car through that giant redwood tree in California. I also viewed man-made wonders such as the Sears Tower, Mount Rushmore, Hoover Dam, Los Angeles, Las Vegas, and Epcot Center.

This experience profoundly changed my life. Through it I was able to deal with and resolve many personal issues as well as learn some new things about myself. I also acquired a tremendous amount of information in a number of areas: the environment, Native-American history, modern architecture, the military, the oil industry, Mexican-American history, farming, natural history, the space industry, etc. This experience awakened in me an incredible thirst for knowledge, and all I wanted to do when I returned was to share what I had learned.

My decision to become a teacher was solidified when, soon after returning, I got a job supervising fourth and fifth graders in an after-school program. These were "normal" kids whose parents both worked, and they had nowhere to go in the afternoons. Immediately my eyes were opened to the tremendous amount of potential these children had. It was then that I realized that this was the population I wished to serve.

At the time I had no money, so I decided to work for a few years in order to save up enough to go back to school. I got a job managing a video store and quickly I moved up to district manager. After three years I had accumulated the funds necessary to return to school. In March of 1993, I resigned that job and entered my application to the graduate school at the State University of New York at New Paltz. I was accepted into the Master of Science in Teaching program, and hope to complete my studies by December of 1994.

After taking only four classes, I have already learned a great deal about the history of education in America and the direction it is taking today. This has caused me to struggle with my beliefs in order to form my own philosophy of education. I began by looking at my childhood experience.

I grew up in middle-class suburbia sixty miles north of Manhattan, and until high school I went to large public schools. My educational experience was uneventful. My strongest memory of kindergarten is when I learned the difference between the girls' and boys' bathrooms by going into the girls'. In first grade I remember asking myself "I won-

der what would happen if I stuck my finger in this pencil sharpener?" Luckily I needed no stitches. I also remember crying one day because I didn't know which reading group I was supposed to be in. Instead of offering consolation, my teacher yelled at me, saying that only babies cried.

In second grade I had a great teacher because she gave us candy if we memorized our times tables. In third grade, multiplication was a source of trauma for me. The teacher held a competition in which the members of two opposing teams raced to the board to complete multiplication problems. The excitement was high, the race close. When it was my turn I ran to the board, and with everyone screaming, I blanked. As I struggled to remember the answer, the other team surged ahead and won. I cried as the other kids on my team taunted me and the bully of the class made fun of me.

The only thing I remember about fourth grade was this really cool fox I made out of paper-mache. Also, the music teacher sent me to his closet to retrieve a jacket. When I handed him his overcoat, he told me in front of the whole class that he meant a record jacket. So he humiliated me in order to teach us what a record jacket was. Thanks to him I will never forget that vital piece of information.

In fifth grade my friend John had all of his baseball cards taken away and I received five stitches in my lower lip after colliding with another kid in a kickball game. Sixth grade was great because I had the coolest male teacher in the school. I don't remember anything he taught us, but he was cool.

I remember school as being tedious and boring. I usually received high grades, but was seldom challenged. Most of the time I remember being frustrated at having to wait for the teacher to finish helping the other kids before we could move on. I also could never understand why we had to do page after page of long division and multi-digit multiplication. Most of all, I hated sitting around waiting for the teacher to deal with discipline problems.

Learning history was particularly annoying to me. I could never understand why we had to memorize all those dates. Whenever I asked what it all had to do with real life, the answer was that learning history was important.

All through my elementary education I was given the role of passive receptor. The teachers simply imparted information on me either through lectures or strict use of the textbooks. Homework consisted of answering questions at the end of a history chapter or completing a math worksheet. I did get to do some writing (which I enjoyed), but I don't recall doing very much reading. Besides the fox in fourth grade, a quilt we made in second grade, and a few field trips, the active experiences I had consisted mostly of memorization drills. I could not relate to the subject matter. It had no meaning in my life. I lost interest in school and thought of it as a waste of time.

Exploring the differences between the way I was taught and the more progressive methods I am learning about now has caused me to look back at my schooling with anger. In exploring that anger, I have come up with some conclusions that have become a compelling force in my desire to teach.

Through my studies of the social foundations of education, I have learned that traditionally schools have been used to preserve the status-quo. The educational system is a tool utilized by the rich and powerful to subjugate the weak masses in order to retain their wealth and power. By looking at my own experience, I can see that the methods used create

controllable, passive citizens. Horace Mann believed that schools could be used to maintain social order by "socializing children from the political system" (Spring, 1991, p. 10). Spring paraphrases Johann Fichte's assertion that schools "would prepare the individual to serve the government and country by teaching obedience to the rules of the school and developing a sense of loyalty to the school" (1991, p. 11). Under this much control, not only will the masses not oppose the leadership, they are willing to provide cheap labor and, as Fichte said, fight wars for it (Spring, 1991).

It is unjust for one group to assert power over another. By doing so, our leaders are making a mockery of our democratic society by violating the most important principle upon which it was founded—freedom. The goal of our educational system should be freedom for all who pass through it. Freedom results from autonomy and, as Maxine Greene says, "autonomy, many believe, is a prime characteristic of the educated person" (Shapiro & Purpel, 1993, p. 337). She goes on to point out that autonomy characterizes the highest level of development according to both Piaget and Kohlberg. The traditional emphasis in teaching has not been on autonomy, but rather on passive obedience. Greene says there must be "a concern for the critical and the imaginative, for the opening of new ways of 'looking at things,' " but that this approach "is wholly at odds with the technicist and behaviorist emphases we still find in American schools" (Greene in Shapiro & Purpel, 1993, p. 337). However, the necessary changes are taking place and I feel compelled to help bring about those changes.

I am becoming a teacher for three main reasons. First, this is the best way for me to fulfill my long held desire to serve youth. Second, as a result of my trip, I wish to share my new-found thirst for knowledge. Finally, because of my belief in freedom as the goal of education, I feel compelled to help bring about the reforms necessary to insure that each student has an equal opportunity to achieve this goal.

Thomas A. Rubeo
Pre-service Teacher
New Paltz, New York

References for Sample Educational Autobiography

Least Heat Moon, W. (1982). *Blue highways: A journey into America.* New York: Fawcett Crest.

Shapiro, S. H. and Purpel, D. E. (1993). *Critical social issues in American education toward the 21st century.* New York: Longman.

Spring, J. (1991). *American education: An introductin to social and politial aspects.* New York: Longman.

Steinbeck, J. (1962). *Travels with charley: In search of America.* New York: The Viking Press.

▶ REFERENCES

American Association of University Women (AAUW), with The Wellesley College Center for Research on Women. (1992). *How schools shortchange girls: A study of major findings on girls and education.* Boston: AAUW Educational Foundation and National Education Association.

Apple, M. W. (1987). *Teachers and texts: A political economy of class and gender relations in education.* Boston: Routledge and Kegan Paul.

Ayers, W. (1988). *Giving headaches: On teaching and the reform of teacher education.* Paper presented at the Midwest Region Holmes Group Conference, Chicago.

Baroody, A. J. & Ginsburg, H. P. (1990). Children's learning: A cognitive view. In *Constructivist views on the teaching and learning of mathematics.* Reston, VA: National Council of Teachers of Mathematics.

Bateson, G. (1972). *Steps to an ecology of mind: Collected essays in anthropology, psychiatry, evolution, and epistemology.* San Francisco: Chandler Publishing Co.

Berliner, D. C. (1977). Tempus educare. In P. L. Peterson and H. J. Walberg (Eds.), *Research on teaching.* Berkeley, CA: McCutchan.

Bloom, B. et al. (1956). *Taxonomy of educational objectives: Vol. I, The cognitive domain.* Chicago: University of Chicago Press.

Brophy, J. (1992). Probing the subtleties of subject-matter teaching. *Educational Leadership, 47*(7), 4–9.

Caine, R. N. & Caine, G. (1991). *Making connections: Teaching and the human brain.* Alexandria, VA: ASCD.

Costa, A. L. (1984). A reaction to Hunter's knowing, teaching, and supervising. In P. L. Hosford (Ed.), *Using what we know about teaching.* Alexandria, VA: ASCD.

Cuban, L. (1984). *How teachers taught: Constancy and change in American classrooms: 1890–1980.* New York: Longman.

Cubberley, E. P. (1920). *The history of education.* Boston: Houghton Mifflin.

Dewey, J. (1899). *The school and society.* Chicago: University of Chicago Press, Combined Edition, 1956.

Dewey, J. (1902). *The child and the curriculum.* Chicago: University of Chicago Press, Combined Edition, 1956.

Dewey, J. (1933). *How we think.* Boston: D. C. Heath.

Elmore, R. F. (1992). Why restructuring alone won't inprove teaching. *Education Week, 49*(7).

Forest, M. & Pierpoint, J. C. (1992). Putting all kids on the MAP. *Educational Leadership, 50*(2), 26–32.

Gardner, H. (1983). *Frames of mind: The theory of multiple intelligences.* New York: Basic Books.

Gardner, H. (1991). *The unschooled mind: How children think and how schools should teach.* New York: Basic Books.

Good, T. L. & Grouws, D. A. (1977). Teaching effects: A process-product study in fourth grade mathematics classrooms. *Journal of Teacher Education, 28* (May/June), 49-54.

Goodlad, J. I. (1984). *A place called school.* New York: McGraw-Hill.

Goodman, Y. (1989). Roots of the whole language movement. *The Elementary School Journal,* April/May.

Greene, M. (1989). Reflection in teacher education. *Current Issues in Education, IV*(2).

Holmes Group, The. (1986). *Tomorrow's teachers.* East Lansing, MI: The Holmes Group, Inc.

Jackson, P. W. (Ed.). (1992). *The handbook of research on curriculum.* New York: Macmillan.

Jacobs, H. H. (Ed.). (1989). *Interdisciplinary curriculum: Design and development.* Alexandria, VA: ASCD.

Kliebard, H. M., (1986). *The struggle for the American curriculum: 1893–1958.* Boston: Routledge & Kegan Paul.

Lieberman, A. & Miller, L. (1984). *Teachers, their world and their work.* Alexandria, VA: ASCD.

Leinhardt, G. (1992). What research on learning tells us abo⸺ ꞏhing. *Educational Leadership, 49*(7).

Lortie, D. (1975). *Schoolteacher: A sociological study.* Chicago: University of Chicago Press.

McPherson, G. H. (1972). *Small town teacher.* Cambridge, MA: Harvard University Press.

National Council for the Social Studies (NCSS). (1990). *Charting a course: Social studies for the 21st century.* Washington, DC: NCSS.

National Council of Teachers of Mathematics (NCTM). (1989). *Curriculum and evaluation standards for school mathematics.* Reston, VA: NCTM.

Noddings, N. (1986). Fidelity in teaching, teacher education, and research for teaching. *Harvard Educational Review, 56,* 496-510.

Noddings, N. (1990). Constructivism in mathematics education. In *Constructivist views on the teaching and learning of mathematics.* Reston, VA: National Council of Teachers of Mathematics.

Ogle, D. M. (1986). K-W-L: A teaching model that develops active reading of expository text. *The Reading Teacher, 39*(6), 564–570.

Onosko, J. J. (1992). Exploring the thinking of thoughtful teachers. *Educational Leadership, 49*(7).

Parker, F. W. (1894). *Talks on pedagogics: An outline of the theory of concentration.* New York: E. L. Kellogg.

Perkins, D. N. (1991). Educating for insight. *Educational Leadership, 49*(2).

Rist, R. (1973). *The urban school: A factory for failure.* Cambridge, MA: MIT Press.

Rosenthal, R. & Jacobson, L. (1968). *Pygmalion in the classroom.* New York: Holt, Rinehart and Winston.

Samples, B. (1992). *The metaphoric mind: A celebration of creative consciousness,* 2nd ed. Rolling Hills Estates, CA: Jalmar Press.

Sergiovanni, T. J. (1992). Why we need substitutes for leadership. *Educational Leadership, 49*(5).

Schon, D. (1983). *The reflective practitioner: How professionals think in action.* New York: Basic Books.

Smyth, J. (1989). *Developing and sustaining critical reflection in teacher education. Current issues in education. IX, Fall.* Normal, IL: Illinois State University for the John Dewey Society for the Study of Education and Culture.

Tanner, D. & Tanner, L. (1980). *Curriculum development: Theory into practice* (2nd ed.). New York: Macmillan.

von Glasersfeld, E. (1990). An exposition of constructivism: Why some like it radical. In *Constructivist views on the teaching and learning of mathematics.* Reston, VA: National Council of Teachers of Mathematics.

Vygotsky, L. S. (1962). *Thought and language.* Cambridge, MA: MIT Press.

Vygotsky, L. S. (1978). *Mind in society: The development of higher psychological processes.* Cambridge, MA: Harvard University Press.

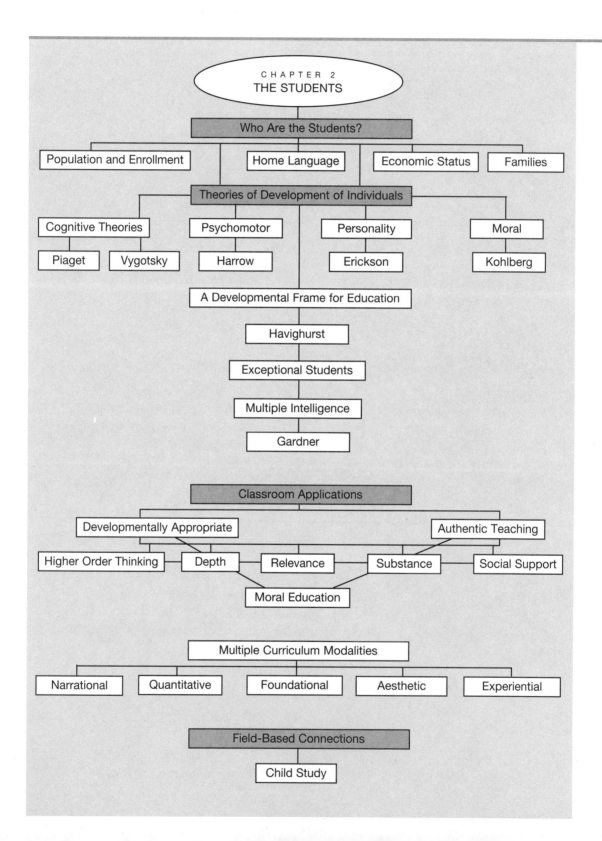

The Students

Introduction

One of the most important elements of your knowledge base as a teacher is your knowledge of your students: their nature, their needs, and the best strategies for you to use in creating a classroom and school environment that nurtures their growth. This chapter attempts to answer some questions you may have regarding who your students will be:

- the general theories of how students develop;
- what the forces are that have helped to shape them into the people that they are when you meet them in the school setting;
- how the students may differ; how students learn; and
- what motivates them to learn.

We have devoted an entire chapter to the students because they are at the core of the elements that one considers in developing curriculum and planning learning in the school setting (Figure 2–1).

Who Are the Students?

The following sections are designed not only to provide a picture of students in the United States around the turn of this century into the next, but also to delineate social aspects of the students that correlate with their educational achievement. These factors are race/ethnicity and home language, economic status, and family life. When these factors are suited to the way schools have been traditionally structured, a student is more likely to achieve at high levels. When these factors do not fit the traditional profile, the student is more likely to be at-risk for failure in school. Oaks, Worthy, and Ramaley (1993) described at-risk students in these words:

> Students at risk of dropping out frequently come from families of relatively low socioeconomic status. Quite often, students at risk are members of a minority group. In addition to lacking the basic necessities, such as clothing and food that so many people take for granted, minority

at-risk students may also have to contend with a large number of intangible obstacles. They may be unable to "fit in." Language barriers, incompatibility with fellow students and teachers, racism and discrimination, and the inability to reach teacher- and school-established expectations are problems that community, state, and federal assistance programs cannot easily overcome. (p. 91)

We will see that this description may fit more of the students who will be in school in the coming century than it ever has before. With the changing nature of work in our infor-

---

FIGURE 2–1 Factors Influencing Educational Decisions

Society
Social, Cultural,
Political, Economic

Knowledge
Epistemological,
Philosophical,
Pedagogical

Teacher
Philosophical Beliefs
and Assumptions,
Professional Knowledge,
Knowledge of Subject Matter,
Pedagogy

Student
Cognitive, Affective,
Developmental,
Environmental

---

mation-age society it is becoming increasingly important to keep these students in school, as well as those who have traditionally done well in school, and provide them with an appropriate educational environment. This is one in which they can succeed and learn the skills, knowledge, and attitudes that they need to be successful citizens.

Population and Enrollment Projections

The overall school population in America is expected to increase by about 30 million between 1990 and 2010 (Gerald & Hussar, 1991). The number of students in kindergarten through grade eight is anticipated to increase by about 1 percent per year until the year 2002, when some projections estimate that it will drop slightly (Legters & Slavin, 1992). Others project increases in student enrollments at all levels of schooling, including the college level, by the year 2002 (Evangelauf, 1992).

The students of the late twentieth and early twenty-first centuries will be the most diverse group ever to attend public and private schools in America. With high levels of immigration and large disparities in birth rates between white and non-white citizens, the entire population is becoming more ethnically and culturally diverse. This diversity is becoming even more pronounced in the school population (Hass & Parkay, 1993). In a demographic study of students and the factors that contribute to their success and failure in schools, Natriello, McDill, and Pallas (1990) estimate that the total population of school-age children (under eighteen years of age) in the United States will rise from 63.6 million in 1988 to 66.4 million in 2020.

One result of the rise in immigration and steadily declining birth rates among the white population is that the proportion of white school age children in the total population is estimated to decrease from about 70 percent to 50 percent by 2020. The proportion of Hispanic children is expected to increase from about 10 percent to about 25 percent. The proportion of African American students is expected to increase as well, but at a slower rate, and to actually decrease between the years 2000 and 2010. The proportions of Asian and Pacific Islander students in American schools is estimated to increase from 1.1 million to 1.4 million in the two decades between 1990 and 2010 (U.S. Department of Education, 1991) (Figure 2–2).

Language Spoken in the Home

Children who demonstrate limited English proficiency (LEP) are often those for whom English is not their first language or those who have limited exposure to conventional English. Usually, another language or dialect is spoken at home by these children, when they are with their families and friends. This creates obvious incongruities between the home and school environment; even if the child does well in school it may cause conflict for the child, who could be caught between two worlds. (For interesting reading in this area, we recommend *Hunger of Memory*, by Richard Rodriguez, published in 1982 by David R. Godine, Boston, MA.)

It is difficult to determine the number of LEP students in the United States. Though the United States Department of Education uses eleven indicators of limited English proficiency in identifying LEP students, many local school districts use a variation of an instrument called the Home Language Survey. A basic assumption of these surveys is that speaking a second language in the home is the strongest indicator of limited English proficiency, though this is not necessarily true. The United States Office of Education estimates the number of LEP students in the United States to be about 1.5 million children. If one were to use the speaking of a language other than English at home as the sole indicator, then the number of children speaking a primary language other than English is anticipated to double by the year 2020, increasing from 2.2 million students to 5.5 million, or from 4 percent to 8 percent of the total student population (Legters & Slavin, 1992).

Economic Status

The number of children living at the poverty level rose from 17.9 percent to 19 percent of all children in the 1980s. The highest proportion of children living in poverty are under six years old and are non-white minorities, who represent 31 percent of all young children and 59 percent of all children under six living in poverty (U. S. Department of Education, 1991). This situation is expected to grow worse as we approach the twenty-first century. The number of children living in poverty is expected to increase by 33 percent, with schools educating 4 million more economically disadvantaged children in 2020 than in 1989 (Natriello et al., 1990).

Family Life

The structure of the American family has changed in the last few decades, with many more children living in single parent households than ever before in our history. This is a cause for concern particularly because there is

FIGURE 2–2 Projections of the Population, Birth to Age 24, by Race/Ethnicity and Age: 1990 to 2010

Race/ethnicity and age	Population, in millions				Percentage change			
	1990	1995	2000	2010	1985 to 1990	1990 to 1995	1995 to 2000	2000 to 2010
Total, all ages	249.7	259.6	268.0	283.2	4.6	4.0	3.2	5.7
All races	90.1	90.8	92.0	92.5	-1.6	0.8	1.3	0.6
Under 5	19.2	18.6	17.6	18.0	4.0	-3.0	-5.3	2.0
5 to 13	32.2	34.4	34.4	31.9	8.5	7.0	-0.2	-7.3
14 to 17	13.0	14.1	15.4	15.0	-12.1	8.7	9.2	-2.6
18 to 24	25.8	23.7	24.6	27.7	-10.2	-8.1	3.8	12.4
White, non-Hispanic	64.1	63.1	62.5	59.9	-4.1	-1.6	-1.0	-4.1
Under 5	13.2	12.5	11.5	11.2	2.4	-5.4	-8.2	-2.7
5 to 13	22.7	23.8	23.2	20.3	6.1	4.6	-2.2	-12.6
14 to 17	9.3	10.0	10.6	9.9	-15.3	7.5	6.4	-6.9
18 to 24	18.9	16.9	17.2	18.6	-12.4	-10.7	1.8	8.0
Hispanic	9.5	10.5	11.5	13.3	10.0	10.4	9.5	16.0
Under 5	2.3	2.4	2.5	2.9	14.2	5.7	3.5	14.3
5 to 13	3.5	4.0	4.4	4.8	15.8	16.6	8.3	9.0
14 to 17	1.4	1.5	1.8	2.1	5.5	11.5	21.0	13.5
18 to 24	2.4	2.5	2.8	3.6	1.6	5.2	10.2	30.1
Black*	14.1	14.6	15.2	16.1	1.9	3.7	4.1	6.1
Under 5	3.2	3.2	3.1	3.3	5.2	-1.6	-2.7	7.2
5 to 13	5.1	5.7	5.8	5.6	14.6	12.1	1.1	-2.2
14 to 17	1.9	2.2	2.5	2.5	-9.5	11.0	17.9	0.0
18 to 24	3.8	3.5	3.8	4.6	-8.2	-6.7	6.5	21.9
Other*	3.0	3.3	3.5	4.0	7.6	8.6	7.7	13.7
Under 5	0.6	0.7	0.7	0.8	1.7	10.1	7.8	14.5
5 to 13	1.1	1.2	1.3	1.4	13.2	4.4	7.7	15.6
14 to 17	0.5	0.5	0.5	0.6	7.0	18.0	-3.5	20.0
18 to 24	0.8	0.9	1.0	1.1	5.4	8.0	14.6	7.5

* Includes small numbers of Hispanics.

Note: Details may not add to totals because of rounding. Percentages are computed on unrounded data.
Source: U.S. Department of Commerce. Bureau of the Census. Current Population Reports. Senes P-25. *Projections of the Hispanic Population: 1983 to 2080.*
From: U.S. Department of Education (USDE), Office of Educational Research and Improvement (1991). Youth Indicators. Washington, DC: USDE.

Courtesy of U.S. Department of Commerce, Bureau of the Census.

a strong correlation between financial difficulties and single-parent female-headed households (Moles, 1987), and because there is a much higher proportion of single-parent families among minority populations. Ascher (1987) reported that the proportion of female-headed families is 74 percent among blacks, 55 percent among Hispanics, and 49 percent among whites (Ascher, 1987).

Hetherington et al. (1981) reported that there were no differences in intelligence or ability between children from one- or two-parent families, but that there was a significant disparity in grades between these two groups. They attributed the difference in grades to teacher perceptions of the students, students' having less time for homework, and to students' behavior. They found that children of single-parent families are more likely to:

- be truant, absent, or tardy;
- have inefficient study and work habits; and
- drop out of school.

In contrast, in a large-scale study of high school students, the National Association of Elementary School Principals (1980) found that though the fact that a child is growing up in a single-parent household might *not* be a problem when there is adequate income, when income factors exacerbate risk factors, the single-parent structure is a definite factor.

The demands of educating an increasingly diverse and economically challenged student population in the near future are considerations for any new teacher entering the profession. Students of the late twentieth and early twenty-first centuries will need to be more highly educated than any of their age peers of past generations (Colorado Commission on Higher Education, 1992). Deep understanding

of the students, assessment of students' prior knowledge and needs, and solid principles of curriculum development are part of the essential knowledge base a teacher must have to meet the educational needs of our society and its children.

▶ THEORY

Individual Development of Students

Theories of Development

In the last section, we focused on social aspects of the lives of students in describing them. In the following sections, we will focus on psychological aspects of the development of individual students, revealed through several widely accepted theories of development. Though theories of development may be characterized by domain: cognitive/intellectual, psychomotor, and affective/personality/moral, the domains are interactive and synergistic. Together, and along with the previously mentioned social factors, they help shape us as individuals, and affect each individual student's ability and motivation to learn (and teach). Since cognition and oral and written language development are closely intertwined (Piaget, 1955; Vygotsky, 1962), a major theory of cognitive development is presented here using stages of language development as benchmarks.

Piaget's Theory of Cognitive Development

Piaget viewed cognitive development as being related to maturation, and separate from environmental factors. Though environmental factors correlate with educational achievement, they do not necessarily correlate with intelligence and cognitive capacities (Hetherington et al., 1981). Piaget also viewed the stages of cognitive development as sequential, with a child only moving from one stage to the next after "completing" the previous stage. Under this theory, each child moves from one stage to another at his/her own pace, but the path for each must be the same. These differences in developmental pace were termed "de callage" by Piaget.

Kohlberg (1975), a believer in a moral theory of development, assigned the following attributes to the stage concept in human development:

1. Stages are consistent, structured wholes. A person at a particular stage of development consistently acts as one would at that stage.

2. Stage sequences are invariant and immutable. A person may never go backwards through stages or skip a stage.

3. Stages are hierarchical. Thinking at a particular stage encompasses all the thinking at previous stages. (pp. 670–71)

Sensorimotor Stage. The sensorimotor stage is the earliest stage of human cognitive development, according to Piaget (1950). It lasts from birth to approximately two years of age, and is the time when a child gains control over perception and motor responses in relation to objects, but not people. The child at this stage does not see others as separate entities, and engages in what Piaget calls egocentric speech (1955). Though egocentric speech may be heard by others, it is primarily directed at the child, herself, and at fulfilling her own needs.

Preoperational Stage. At the preoperational, or representational stage, from the ages of around two to seven years, the child begins to direct speech toward others. Language becomes more socially oriented; Piaget called this socialized speech. The child is able to see herself as separate from others, and to use words to interact with others beyond just the meeting of her own needs. The child at this stage is also able to understand and use a word as a symbol to represent an object or a concept. It is during this stage that most children enter kindergarten, and it quickly becomes apparent that those who have a larger vocabulary are generally the children with the most knowledge of concepts, and the highest capability to learn.

Though Piaget believed that intelligence was predetermined and inherited, it is now also believed that environmental factors may make a difference in vocabulary knowledge. The relationship between vocabulary knowledge and intelligence is a strong one (Marzano & Hutchins, 1988). Anderson and Freebody (1981) cited the relationship between vocabulary knowledge and intelligence as one of the most important findings in the history of intelligence theorizing and testing.

One of the major cognitive concepts that the child acquires during the preoperational stage, according to Piaget (1950), is decentration, the ability to perceive parts of an object as they relate to the whole. This is a very important milestone in the child's ability to learn to read, something else that is a major factor in the child's educational life at this stage. Most children learn to read in first grade, and even though a child may be taught to read by a method that does not emphasize learning word parts before the whole, *phonemic awareness* and the ability to segment phonemes (the sound units of words) is the most essential skill in learning to read a language (Clay, 1993; Gillet & Temple, 1992).

Two other cognitive concepts that children acquire in the preoperational stage are the concepts of *conservation* and *reversibility* (Piaget, 1950). When a child has acquired the concept of conservation, she can perceive that the mass of an object does not change when the shape of the object is changed. The ability to see that relationships between people and objects may be reversed—for instance that the child has a mother, and also that the child is a daughter—is the concept of reversibility. Both of these concepts relate to language and reading development, and are vital to the child's ability to recognize words out of their usual contexts. For example, before attaining these concepts, a young child may recognize the name of her favorite fast food restaurant when she sees it on the building, but not when it's on a word card.

Concrete Operational Stage. This is the stage that ranges from seven to around twelve years of age (Piaget, 1950), most of the years a child is in elementary school. It is during the concrete operational stage that a child learns to solve problems and deduce information. Language skills developed during this period include the ability to ascertain relationships such as sequence, cause-effect, main idea, and word and conceptual categories. In terms of language development, it is at this stage that the child is able to deduce the meaning of words from context and environmental clues. A child may not know the word, hamburger, but may deduce its meaning from knowledge of its letters or some phonemes, and the fact that it is on the sign at the favorite fast food restaurant. Piaget asserts that, at this stage, concepts are learned primarily through the manipulation of objects and interaction with people in the environment.

Formal Operational Stage. At this, the last stage of cognitive development, twelve years to adult, according to Piaget, the child learns to think abstractly, to hypothesize and theorize, and test ideas through inquiry and experimentation. Language may be used to denote abstract, distant concepts and events. Language becomes a tool to transcend the limitations of space and time.

Vygotsky's Theory

Piaget believed that language development depended on cognitive development; Vygotsky, a Russian contemporary of Piaget, believed the opposite and asserted that cognitive growth was a product of language use. Vygotsky believed that language was a social construction, and that words have meaning because the members of a society agree on their meaning. We, for instance, agree to call the outdoor expanse above our heads the sky. We could call it something else—the bowl or the ocean—but the consensus is to call it the sky. These *negotiated* meanings are learned through social interaction, according to Vygotsky (1962; 1978); the more a child interacts with others through language, the farther and faster the child will develop cognitively.

The idea that a child may be taught to move through developmental stages by social interaction was the main way in which Vygotsky diverged from Piaget. Piaget believed that one should not try to teach a child something until the child had reached that stage of development and could understand the concept on her own. Vygotsky believed that if the teacher could find the child's "zone of proximal development," the difference between what a child could do alone and what she could do in collaboration with others, then the teacher or other students could help a child do what she could not do on her own. The expectation, in Vygotsky's theory, is that the child can eventually do alone what she has done with others (Smith, 1988). The seeds of cooperative learning and the whole language movement, practices that have revolutionized teaching, may be found in the theories of Vygotsky. Leinhardt (1992) has asserted that, "Of all the 'new' ideas, the social nature of learning is probably the most radical" (p. 23).

Psychomotor Development

Educators work with an array of taxonomies and stage theories in their efforts to know and promote the growth of the developing humans with whom they work. You will probably use a taxonomy of learning in your curriculum development. The most commonly used taxonomy is that conceived by Benjamin Bloom and his associates in the book, *Taxonomy of Educational Objectives, Handbook I: The Cognitive Domain,* generally called Bloom's Taxonomy. The following taxonomy deals with physical growth and the development of control over physical aspects that every child must learn.

Harrow (1972) delineated the categories of physical development important to full mat-

uration. These processes are synergistic with cognitive, affective, and social factors that affect a child's development (Figure 2–3).

One can see how these skills might affect the mastery of many common school activities: from holding a pencil or writing at the computer, to playing the violin or acting in a school play, to conducting a dissection in a biology class.

Personality Development

In a now classic work, *Identity, Youth and Crisis,* psychologist Erik Erikson (1968) outlined a theory of personality development. Using the characteristics of a healthy personality as guides, he delineated a sequence and pace of personality development, which he validated through many cross-cultural psychological and anthropological studies. Like the stages of Piaget, Erikson's developmental stages are immutable and biologically driven. He asserted that a healthy personalty could only develop if it followed the schema described here.

Trust. The sense of trust is developed in the infant in the first year and a half of life, according to Erikson. It is reinforced daily as the mother comforts the child, provides sustenance, love, and attention. It is also developed as the infant gains control over his own body and activities, such as being able to grasp and shake a rattle. Infants deprived of love, hope, and the opportunity to bond with a caring adult develop unhealthy personalities, and may become mentally ill or even psychopathic.

Autonomy. Once the child has developed a strong sense of trust, he is ready to venture forth and test his independence between the

---

FIGURE 2–3 Psychomotor Development

1.0 Reflex Movements

2.0 Basic-Fundamental Movements
    2.1 Locomotor movements
    2.2 Nonlocomotor movements
    2.3 Manipulative movements

3.0 Perceptual Abilities
    3.1 Kinesthetic discrimination
    3.2 Visual discrimination
    3.3 Auditory discrimination
    3.4 Tactile discrimination
    3.5 Coordinated perceptual abilities

4.0 Physical Abilities
    4.1 Endurance
    4.2 Strength
    4.3 Flexibility
    4.4 Agility

5.0 Skilled Movements
    5.1 Simple adaptive skill
    5.2 Compound adaptive skill
    5.3 Complex adaptive skill

6.0 Nondiscursive Communication
    6.1 Expressive movement
    6.2 Interpretive movement

Reprinted, with permission from A. J. Harrow, *A Taxonomy of the Psychomotor Domain.* (New York: David McKay Longman, 1972.)

---

ages of twelve to eighteen months. The child is discovering that he is an independent human being, with a will and emotions of his own. Many parents call this the time of the "terrible twos." Erikson believed that the physiological basis for this stage was the development of the child's muscular system. At this stage, the child is able to coordinate several actions, like walking and talking or throwing things: actions which he repeats over and over.

Parents with children at this stage must deal with conflicts between their desire to keep the child safe and the child's desire to explore and experiment. This is the stage where discipline is first introduced to the child. It is important that the parent be firm, yet affirming and positive with the child when disciplining at this stage.

Initiative. The child develops the sense of initiative and purpose around the ages of three to six, according to Erikson. This is a time of imagination, when the child tries on many adult roles, pretending to be a fireman, nurse, or racing car driver. This is also a time of immense curiosity.

A child at this stage is also developing a sense of right and wrong, and a conscience to go along with it. The conscience helps the child to control his behavior as well as to limit experiments and projects. This is the preschool stage, and it is important that the teacher encourage the child to explore and discover, as well as share and participate as much as possible. Encouragement is key, and though initiative is developed at this stage, it needs to be encouraged throughout the child's life.

Summary: Erikson's First Three Stages. These three stages are prerequisites for the following stages. They are the building blocks that form the foundation for the rest of the personality to develop. If they are weak, it is difficult for the personality to form in a healthy way.

Industry. Erikson's period of industry almost coincides with Piaget's concrete operational (seven to twelve) stage. It starts at around six years of age, and ends at early adolescence.

This is the stage at which the child develops a sense of mastery of many tasks. In addition to a sense of accomplishment, the child develops the ability to function in a social environment; in short, to play games and to follow the rules.

If a child is unable to develop a sense of industry or accomplishment during this time, he may develop feelings of being a failure and inadequacy. The key to helping children to develop this sense is to provide them with activities that are challenging, but not too difficult to master. A teacher must also provide a safe, secure environment in the classroom, making it a place where each child is free to take the risks involved in developing expertise, without risking shame or ridicule from peers or adults.

Identity. This period begins with the start of adolescence, which is brought about biologically by physiological changes and rapid growth, in Erikson's view. During this time, the student is questioning all that he formerly accepted, in an effort to determine his own sense of self. In many societies, this is a time for a major rite of passage, usually one in which the child's strength and character are tested, after which the adolescent is accepted into the adult age-set. In modern Western societies, such rites do not formally exist. Our society is too diverse for all of our children to experience the same rites and rituals, so adolescence can become a time of great turmoil and individual inner conflict.

In the past, educators had difficulty maintaining a positive, encouraging atmosphere in schools; one in which adolescents could develop a strong sense of identity while maintaining a strong sense of trust, autonomy, initiative, and industry. The middle school, with its team structure, interdisciplinary curriculum, and cooperative group arrangements is one way that educators have adapted structures to meet the developmental and educational needs of students (George et al., 1992).

Intimacy. This stage is one that Erikson places at late adolescence; it is characterized by a need to like yourself and form intimate relationships with a person of the opposite sex and with friends. The person who does not develop a sense of intimacy at this stage, but shies away from deep interpersonal relationships, or maintains formal relationships at very stereotypical levels never forms truly intimate relationships, Erikson believes. This stage is reinforced culturally by our expectation that young adults form these relationships and eventually marry.

Summary: Erikson's Last Two Stages. The last two stages of Erikson's theory are adult stages of personality development, and though educators should looks for signs of readiness to encounter these stages, it would be very rare for a school-age child to move through them. The last two stages of personality development, according to Erikson, are: generativity (development of the parental sense), and the development of a sense of integrity.

In developing the parental sense, a person develops an interest in having and caring for children. The person is ready to take care of and nurture his own children, or to take responsibility for the children of others.

The sense of integrity is developed when a person develops a sense of acceptance of one's own life, and the sense that one's life is one's own responsibility. The individual with integrity has a true sense of who he is and his place in the overall scheme of things. Erikson believed that it was essential that children be exposed to adults who had developed a sense of integrity. It is crucial that teachers reach this stage.

A Theory of Moral Development

Lawrence Kohlberg is credited with developing a universal theory of moral development that has gained wide acceptance in education. Gilligan (1984) was the chief critic of Kohlberg's work. She maintained that men and women think differently, and that while men base the ethic of justice on principles, women base it on an ethic of caring. Though we believe this to be true, research has found no gender differences in moral development when rated by Kohlberg's scale; but rather gender differences in the bases for moral reasoning. Though his theory has been criticized for these reasons, Kohlberg's theory is presented here to serve as a guideline for your study of the students you will teach. The stages of moral development are intertwined with cognitive and emotional maturity. They do not stand alone, and should be viewed as part of a whole developing person when using them as guides.

Preconventional Level. At the preconventional level, moral judgment resides outside of the individual. Cultural labels of right and wrong are unquestioned, and serve as guides for action only in terms of physical reward or punishment of the individual. This level encompasses two stages: Stage One, the obedience-punishment stage, where there is deference to superior power and authority; and Stage Two, the naive egoistic stage, when the individual chooses behavior that is naively egalitarian, sometimes pleasing himself, and sometimes pleasing others.

Conventional Level. This is the level at which the individual conforms to social norms to meet the expectations of others. This level also encompasses two stages: Stage Three, the interpersonal concordance—good-boy, nice-girl stage—in which one seeks the approval of others; and Stage Four, the authority and social-order orientation, in which there is an orientation to following rules and doing one's "duty."

Postconventional Level. This level marks the "true" morality. Moral values and principles are employed with regard to, but not as a result of authority or conformity to group norms and values. These may be seen as valid, but the person makes his own decisions. This level also contains two stages: Stage Five, the contractual/legalistic orientation, in which there is an awareness of the relationship between personal values and those of others; and Stage Six, the conscience or principle orientation, in which a person chooses the universal principles to which he will adhere as personal values. These values will guide all of the individual's actions. Examples of individuals who have reached Stage Six, according to Kohlberg (1970), would be Gandhi or Albert Schweitzer.

Summary: Kohlberg' Theory. Though the above is a stage theory, Kohlberg reported that, in studies of junior high school students who were engaged in instruction in moral education, some students in lower stages did move up at least one stage on his scale. This research indicated that when purposeful moral education is implemented in an atmosphere infused with a sense of justice and fairness, progress through the stages may be fostered (Blatt & Kohlberg, 1975).

A Stage Theory for Education

Havighurst's Developmental Tasks. Havighurst (1972) contended that there were certain developmental tasks that each individual must master in order to develop into a happy, productive member of society (Figure 2–4). He defined a developmental task as

> . . . a task which arises at or about a certain period in the life of the individual, successful achievement of which leads to success with later tasks, while failure leads to unhappiness in the individual, disapproval by the society, and difficulty with later tasks. (p. 2)

The significance of Havighurst's (1953) developmental tasks for educators is that they may serve as guidelines in developing curriculum and planning instruction for students at these levels. He provided some guiding questions as criteria for evaluating school programs in terms of the developmental tasks. They have been condensed here.

- Is the school aware of where each child stands in terms of accomplishing the developmental tasks, and is it assisting each child according to his/her needs?
- Does the entire school community take part in discussions about the development of its students, and is there a clearly articulated policy in which they are all involved?

FIGURE 2–4   Havighurst's Developmental Tasks

I.   TASKS OF INFANCY AND EARLY CHILDHOOD
1. Learning to walk
2. Learning to eat solid food
3. Learning to talk
4. Learning to control one's body functions
5. Learning gender differences
6. Achieving physiological stability
7. Forming concepts of social and physical reality, and developing the language to represent them
8. Learning to relate to others
9. Learning to distinguish between right and wrong, and to develop a sense of conscience

II. TASKS OF MIDDLE CHILDHOOD
1. Learning the physical skills to play games
2. Building wholesome attitudes toward oneself as a growing human being
3. Learning to get along with peers
4. Learning an appropriate gender role
5. Developing skills in reading, writing, and computation
6. Developing concepts necessary for everyday living
7. Developing conscience, morality, and a sense of values
8. Achieving personal independence
9. Developing attitudes towards social groups and institutions

III. TASKS OF ADOLESCENCE
1. Achieving new and more mature relations with age-mates of both sexes
2. Achieving a masculine or feminine social role
3. Accepting one's physique and using one's body effectively
4. Achieving emotional independence from parents and other adults
5. Selecting and preparing for an occupation
6. Preparing for marriage and family life
7. Developing intellectual skills and concepts necessary for civic participation
8. Desiring and achieving socially responsible behavior
9. Acquiring a system of values and ethics as a guide to behavior

---

Adapted from R. J. Havighurst, *Developmental Tasks and Education,* 3rd Edition (New York: David McKay Longman, 1972.)

• Does the school see the strengths and weaknesses in the other community institutions in providing for the attainment of the developmental tasks by its children?

• Are the teachers and other adult members of the school community effective role models for the children in their own attainment of the developmental tasks?

• Does the school promote reflective thinking in terms of the developmental tasks? (Adapted from Havighurst, 1953)

There are many valuable suggestions for educators in these questions. The idea of the articulation of services was a very avant garde one for the time that Havighurst was writing. It is a major goal of many schools today, especially in urban areas, where the students have access to, and need for, many social services. His questions are also a model for school committees which currently make educational decisions for special education students who need more help in performing the developmental tasks.

Exceptional Students

The previous sections on human development provide guidelines for education of children who fall within the range of characteristics and abilities we call "normal." Normal, in this case, means an average range within a set of norms, which vary according to the tasks required for students to perform. For example, the norms for a standardized test in language arts differ from the norms for a test of artistic ability. In this section, we provide a brief discussion of exceptionalities beyond the norm. We must say here that a curriculum that calls upon students to perform engaging, interest-ing tasks rather than to sit and absorb knowledge in the traditional manner can be adapted to the needs of individual students, including exceptional students. Chapters 5 and 6 provide a process for developing a curriculum that can be suited to the different needs, interests, and abilities of all students in classrooms where exceptional students are included.

Inclusion. Since the enactment of Public Law 94-142, Education for All Handicapped Children Act in 1975, states and local school districts have wrestled with definitions of exceptionality and the meaning of the phrase, "least restrictive environment," a key phrase describing the optimal context for educating exceptional children. Though that law was designed to provide due process for handicapped students, it spurred federal legislation in 1978, and policies for delineating services for gifted and talented students in almost every state of the union (Passow & Rudnitski, 1993). This reveals an issue in the education of exceptional students: that of definition. Though the federal government has never included gifted and talented students in its definition of exceptionality, the Council for Exceptional Children (CEC), a national professional organization dedicated to the appropriate education and welfare of handicapped and gifted and talented children and youth, includes the gifted in its definition and advocacy efforts for exceptional students.

Public Law (P.L.) 94-142 introduced several unprecedented federal mandates into local education, including:

• the requirement that every state develop a statewide plan for educating its handicapped children and youth, and that it be revised every year;

- mandating that every state develop nondiscriminatory and bias-free screening, testing, and identification procedures for locating all handicapped children and youth in the state;

- the mandate that each state provide a free, appropriate education to all handicapped students from age five to age twenty-one;

- the mandate that handicapped children and youth be educated in the least restrictive environment possible, based on the assessed needs of the student, and that the student, whenever possible, be placed with non-handicapped peers;

- directing each state to ensure the rights of due process and confidentiality to all handicapped students;

- requiring that each identified child be provided with an individualized educational plan (IEP), which includes goals based on the assessed needs of the individual handicapped student.

This law revolutionized the education of handicapped students in the United States. In this decade, the interpretation of P.L. 94-142 has evolved to include the concept of "inclusion," a direct descendent of "mainstreaming." On a continuum ranging from separate full-time classes in a separate school building, to a separate classroom in a regular school, to a resource room arrangement, to mainstreaming, to inclusion; inclusion is the model in which the exceptional student is in the regular classroom for the most time and for the most activities.

The rationale for inclusion encompasses many social reasons. As adults, these students will be living together in the same society. Conventional wisdom tells us that the more they are segregated from each other in school,

the more they will be separated in society when they grow up. Conversely, the more they are exposed to each other and placed together in school, the more they will be able to work together and get along as adults. Research has also shown that programs provided for exceptional students of all abilities and backgrounds are not always equal to the mainstream educational experience (Passow, 1989; Anderson & Pellicer, 1990; Kozol, 1991; U.S.D.E., 1993). If separate programs cannot provide the quality of contexts, teaching, and experiences equal to those in regular classrooms, then all students should be provided with a better quality education if they were in the regular environment. Though it is not our purpose to argue the advantages and disadvantages of inclusion, it has gained increasing popularity as policy in school districts and states across the United States. You will most likely have exceptional students included in your classroom. If you focus on professionally and objectively assessing and meeting the needs of all your students through your curriculum, and if you seek help and guidance when you need it, you will be a successful teacher of *all* students.

Physically Challenged Students. More students with physical and health challenges are included in regular classrooms today. The nature of the physical challenges involves orthopedic disbilities such as the absence of limbs, cerebral palsy, and paralysis. Health challenges emanate from diseases such as heart conditions, tuberculosis, and diabetes or from other health conditions that result in communication problems and an impaired ability to concentrate and learn (U.S.O.E., 1977). The educational implications of this exceptionality, as with all the others, are tied to the nature of the impairment of educational ability. Essentially, physical and health problems negatively affect the student's ability to learn by affecting school attendance with doctor's visits and hospital stays. The ability to engage in physical activities is also affected. These students are also at risk for developing dependent behaviors and for having lower self concepts than their peers (Salend, 1990).

Visually Impaired. Students with visual impairments are those whose ability to see affects their educational performance, even after correction through glasses and contact lenses. This includes students whose ability to see is limited, but who are not totally blind. These students need to have books on tape and descriptions of visual material provided for them in class. They probably learn best through abstract concepts and through the aural narrational and expressive, the kinesthetic, and the foundational curriculum modalities described later in this chapter. If partial visual impairment remains undetected in young children, it can adversely affect cognitive and social development (Hoot & Parmar, 1992).

Hearing Impaired. A hearing impaired student has trouble processing linguistic information aurally, with or without amplification (U.S.O.E., 1977). Even if it is not permanent, a slight hearing impairment, normally due to frequent ear infections early in life, can affect a student's verbal language and reading abilities in school. A hearing impaired student in the classroom needs to have information presented visually and through hands-on modalities.

Learning Disabilities. Learning disabilities are usually neurological in origin and affect the processes of understanding or using language. Students with learning disabilities may demonstrate a diminished ability to listen, think, speak, read, write, spell or do mathematical computations. This definition does not include students who have learning difficulties due to visual, motor or hearing impairments, and those whose difficulties are the result of mental retardation, emotional disturbance or environmental, cultural or economic disadvantage (U.S.O.E., 1977). Students with learning disabilities may have difficulty learning in some or all of the content areas, with uneven success and development. Like all students, they differ from each other and are unique individuals. Their needs are best met by professional teachers who help them to compensate for their disabilities and to avoid the "learned helplessness," that is so common among students of this group. Students with learning disabilities tend to feel that they have little control over their academic success and that no matter how hard they try, they will not succeed (Salend, 1990). Their best teachers help them to learn optimism through providing them with appropriate experiences that challenge, but do not frustrate them (Seligman, 1991).

Mental Retardation. Mildly to moderately mentally retarded individuals are included in regular classrooms. These students have difficulty paying attention to tasks and activities for extended periods of time, may take longer to learn material, and may have less cognitive capacity and memory than the norm. They may also have difficulty thinking abstractly or grasping abstract concepts (Heflin & Bullock, 1992; Salend, 1990). Hands-on learning experiences that engage them in a variety of modalities work well with these students.

Emotional and Behavioral Disorders. Students with emotional and behavioral disorders that adversely affect their ability to learn in school are generally identified for special education under this category. Some of the characteristics of emotionally disturbed students are:

- inability to learn that cannot be explained by intellectual, sensory or health factors;

- inability to start or maintain satisfactory interpersonal relationships with peers and teachers;

- inappropriate behavior or emotions under normal circumstances;

- a general, deep, pervasive unhappiness or depression;

- a tendency to develop physical symptoms or fears associated with personal, school, and social problems. (U.S.O.E., 1977)

The student should exhibit these behaviors consistently over a long period of time before being classified as emotionally disturbed (E.D.). The teacher can support these students with help at setting and achieving personal social and behavioral goals, and through modifying curriculum activities and projects as needed for each individual student.

Gifted and Talented. It has been argued that the most neglected exceptional students are the gifted and talented   (Passow, 1980; Tannebaum, 1983). A recent federal report (U.S.D.E., 1993) described the state of education for these students in regular classrooms:

> The vast majority of talented students spend most of the school day in a regular classroom where little is done to adapt curriculum to their special learning needs.

> Exciting pedagogy and teaching strategies have been developed and refined in some special programs for gifted and talented. Programs for gifted and talented students have served as laboratories of innovation in educational practice. However, few of these approaches have made their way into the regular classrooms. (p. 19)

If this is the case, gifted children and youth, especially those with no mandated IEPs, (the policy in most states) need to have more adaptations made for them in the regular classroom.

All teachers have gifted children in their classes. Some may be identified for programs, but many are not. Who are these students? The United States Department of Education (1993) defines gifted students in this way:

> [They are] children and youth with outstanding talent or [those who] show the potential for performing at remarkably high levels of accomplishment when compared with others of their age, experience or environment. These children and youth exhibit high performance capability in intellectual, creative, and/or artistic areas, possess an unusual leadership capacity or excel in specific academic fields. They require services or activities not ordinarily provided by schools. Outstanding talents are present in children and youth from all cultural groups, across all economic strata, and in all areas of human endeavor. (p. 26)

Though gifted students were, in the past, identified primarily through IQ tests, methods of identification congruent with today's performance-based curriculum and standards are utilized in formal identification for gifted programs. Even if you do not have a program in your school, methods of observation and qualitative assessment presented in Chapter 4 may be used to identify students for educational adaptation as gifted students in your classroom. Remember that any student with a very strong interest in a topic or subject and who performs at levels beyond those of his/her peers may be potentially gifted. With careful observation and assessment, you can meet the needs of that student by addressing his/her strengths and interests through the curriculum.

How Students Learn

We have briefly discussed Piaget's theory of cognitive development, which serves as a kind of map in thinking about children's learning. There are other theories of cognitive development, most notably that of Jerome Bruner (1960), who proposed that the child approaches subject matter in much the same way as a developed scholar, but at a different level. We have come to view learning as a highly individual process that may be influenced by interaction with others. We know that much of the understanding that we derive from learning experiences is based on our own prior knowledge and experience (Pearson et al., 1979; Smith & Neale, 1991). We also know that individuals organize new knowledge in their brains according to their own filing systems or schemata (Rumelhart, 1980). Much of how we see the world depends on the culture in which we live, in interaction with our individual cognitive make-up or style, which depends on our own strengths, or what Howard Gardner (1983) calls "Frames of Mind." Though there are many theories on learning styles (Dunn & Dunn, 1978; Gregorc, 1982; Jung, 1971; Witkin & Goodenough, 1981), and the curriculum modalities to cater to them (Barbe & Swassing,

1979; Butler, 1984; McCarthy, 1980; Samples, 1992), we have chosen the theories of Gardner to highlight in this book because we feel that they are the most widely used in classrooms across the United States.

Multiple Intelligences

Gardner's theory of multiple intelligences (1983) has done much in the past decade to help further our understanding of our students and their individual differences. He delimited seven areas in which humans may have strengths of mind; and though we all have each strength to some degree, we are each stronger in some than in others.

Verbal/Linguistic Intelligence. Linguistic intelligence is related to words and language. It includes written expression, oral expression, and verbal memory. It is the dominant means of delivering instruction and expressing understanding in our schools, and therefore dominates schooling. Two of the three Rs are reading and writing, skills which demand linguistic intelligence. People with this intelligence are poets, lawyers, and academics.

Logical/Mathematical Intelligence. This strength of mind is related to numbers and number systems as well as the ability to think and deduce and induce information. People with this intelligence are good at abstract reasoning, especially with numbers, and can recognize patterns and categories. These are the scientists and mathematicians.

Visual/Spatial Intelligence. This intelligence hinges on the sense of sight in the ability to visualize objects and create mental pictures and images. People with this intelligence solve spatial problems very well, and are good chess players, surveyors, and navigators as well as artists and sculptors. They may even be, as was George Washington, great military strategists.

Bodily/Kinesthetic Intelligence. This intelligence is related to physical movement, and the ability to use and control all parts of one's body to learn and express oneself. People who are strong in this area may be dancers, basketball players or actors. (For a view of a student with high bodily/kinesthetic intelligence in the classroom, see Chapter 6.) They may also be mechanics, mimes, and surgeons.

Musical/Rhythmic Intelligence. This intelligence is related to auditory function and the ability to recognize and remember tonal patterns and sounds. The person with this intelligence exhibits the ability to remember and create musical themes as well as to play them. This person may be a composer, performer or arranger of music.

Interpersonal Intelligence. This intelligence is a factor in social and interpersonal relationships. People with this intelligence are leaders, those who can understand the needs of others and who will help them to achieve their goals. They are the best teachers, politicians, and religious leaders.

Intrapersonal Intelligence. This intelligence is related to metacognition, the ability to think about one's thinking; and reflective thinking, the ability to think about one's feelings. This involves the knowledge of one's own range of emotions as well as the ability to use them as a means of understanding the world.

Conclusion to Theory

It is important to remember that the intelligences are in everyone to some degree, and that schools really teach to just two, the linguistic and the mathematical. It follows, then, that if we broaden our methods and curriculum modalities to include the others we may reach students who are strong in intelligences, but are not currently recognized in the school curriculum. Curriculum modalities are discussed in the next section.

► CLASSROOM ► APPLICATIONS

Developmentally Appropriate Practice

Theories of development have sometimes been used to create restrictive, regimented curricula. That is not their purpose: They can be useful to the pedagogic teacher in the *development* and *testing* of curricula, but should not be used to *lower expectations and standards* for any child. Theories of development should only affect curriculum planning as guides, and as part of an array of factors that influence curriculum.

Elkind (1989) suggests that developmentally appropriate curriculum and instruction view the learner as having developing mental abilities. This means, if some children are at a lower stage of development than others, the teacher will not view the children as "behind," but as children who are exhibiting a slower rate of growth. He makes the distinction between psychometric teaching and authentic teaching. The psychometrically oriented teacher often asks questions of the students. These questions have a "right" answer that the teacher is seeking. The authentic teacher often asks questions for which the answer is not known. The seeking for an answer or solution becomes the task for both the teacher and the students in developmentally appropriate teaching. He states,

> To put the difference more succinctly, the developmental approach seeks to create students who want to know, whereas the psychometric approach seeks to produce students who know what we want. (p. 115)

Teachers should develop and field test or pilot their own curricula and materials. Elkind (1989) believes that teachers are the best people to determine what works and what doesn't for their children. He also believes that this changes with each new class every year, so that the this development and testing is an ongoing activity of teachers throughout their careers. These, of course, are some of our goals as teachers who practice pedagogics.

Authentic Teaching

Authentic teaching, as defined by Elkind (1989), is a major goal of the pedagogic teacher. We will now explore the concept in more detail. Though this chapter is about the students, the presence of a section on authentic teaching is an indication of how closely tied teaching and learning are to the learner.

Newman and Wehlage (1993) proposed five standards to determine if instruction is authentic. They provide a good framework for assessing the authenticity of the lessons you design for your students. They are:

1. Higher order thinking
2. Depth of knowledge
3. Connectedness to the world
4. Substantive conversation
5. Social support for student achievement

Higher Order Thinking. Higher order thinking can be defined in many ways. In Chapter 5, we introduce Bloom's Taxonomy (1956), probably the most common framework for assessing levels of thinking in classroom instruction. Remember: Higher order thinking is characterized by the using of content knowledge to solve a problem or perform a task or complete a project, and not the memorization or recall of the content. When higher order thinking is emphasized in a lesson, the students are manipulating information and ideas. At the elementary level, if the instruction is developmentally appropriate, at the concrete operational stage, the students are manipulating information and ideas as well as objects. At the secondary level, they may be manipulating just the ideas, and not necessarily concrete objects.

Depth of Knowledge. This criterion is related to the importance of the information that the students know: to society, to the students, and to the disciplines. One way to insure that you are meeting this criterion is to write a strong rationale for each topic or concept to which you choose to devote classroom time. The importance of a clear rationale cannot be understated. As Gardner asserted, "The first question the teacher should ask is, 'Why am I doing this? Do I believe it's important? Can I convey that to kids?' Not just because it's the next lesson or comes from the textbook" (Brandt, 1993).

Connectedness to the World. Newman and Wehlage (1993) presented the following criteria by which to measure instruction for connectedness to the world. They are presented here in light of our pedagogic philosophy.

- Students experiencing authentic instruction address real-world public problems. These problems tend to be interdisciplinary in nature, and knowledge from a number of fields is needed to help solve them. Many schools have community service requirements for their students in order to help them to develop a sense of civic responsibility. We think that such requirements, though worthy, are not enough, and that working toward the solution of real public problems should be tied to the regular classroom curriculum as much as possible.

- Students experiencing authentic instruction use personal experiences as a context for applying knowledge. Such skills as conflict resolution and peer mediation are meaningless unless they are applied in a meaningful context. The children's own conflicts and disputes are the best place for them to practice these skills. Moral dilemmas, or stories to spark discussions on morals and ethics (presented in the next section), should also emanate from the children's own experiences as much as possible.

Substantive Conversation. These criteria also apply to the discussions of moral issues. They also contain the same message as Elkind's (1989) discussion of questioning in the section on developmentally appropriate practice. The level of questioning and facilitation on the part of the teacher is the key to substantive conversation. Newman and Wehlage (1993) give the following criteria:

1. There is considerable interaction about the ideas of a topic (the talk is about disciplined subject matter and includes indicators of higher order thinking such as making distinctions, applying ideas, forming generalizations, raising questions; and not just reporting experiences, facts, definitions or procedures).

2. Sharing of ideas is evident in exchanges that are not completely scripted or controlled (as in a teacher-led recitation). Sharing is best illustrated when participants explain themselves or ask questions in complete sentences and when they respond directly to comments of previous speakers.

3. The dialogue builds coherently on participants' ideas to promote improved collective understanding of a theme or topic. (p. 10)

Social Support for Student Achievement. The teacher has high expectations for all students, and those with less skill or expertise are treated with just as much respect as the most proficient students. There is an explicit value held in the classroom for excellence, and all students are encouraged by everyone in the classroom community to do their best. Negative comments regarding the performance of others or oneself are minimal in this classroom, and when mistakes are made,

they are viewed as problems to be solved and not as failures.

Moral Education

Much moral education happens as a result of classroom activities and problems that the students solve together as a group. Teachers should be aware of opportunities to discuss moral issues as a response to classroom events at the elementary and middle school levels. At the high school level, these discussions are often sparked by current and historical events and figures. These discussions are opportunities for the students to practice the skills of higher levels of development than they may currently have attained. Thinking that is more sophisticated and mature than their own is very appealing to children. A lapse to less sophisticated levels should be regarded as temporary (Krogh & Lamme, 1985).

Krogh and Lamme (1985) provided the following guidelines when developing educational activities and curricula to foster the moral development of children:

1. Keep the activities concrete, even if, while discussing a story, the children must be drawing pictures to go along with it.

2. The discussion group should be small enough to give each child a chance to join the discussion many times. Parent volunteers, school librarians, special teachers, and other interns are possible choices as group leaders to help maintain small group size.

3. Try to form groups that are diverse. The more points of view, the better.

4. The length of the discussion should be geared for the developmental levels of the students. For primary students, this could be fifteen to twenty minutes; for elementary students, it could be twenty-five to thirty-five minutes; for middle school students, thirty-five to fourty-five minutes; and for high school students, forty-five minutes and longer. Of course, the moral dilemmas are more complex for older students.

Stories in children's and adolescent literature may also be used as the basis for moral discussions and role plays, as can movies, computer games, and videos. The point is to take the opportunity to have discussion on developmentally appropriate moral issues as much as possible in your classroom. It will foster the moral development of your students.

Multiple Curriculum Modalities

If we were to use Gardner's multiple intelligences concept as guides in curriculum development, many more varieties of acceptable activities and projects would be the result. Gardner (1991) and Kornhaber and Gardner (1993) criticized the lack of variety in acceptable curricular choices in schools, citing the dominance of linguistic and mathematical intelligences in our classrooms. They argue that outside of school there are many ways to develop and demonstrate expertise in every domain; and that people with different profiles or combinations of intelligences may become successful in many different ways, while in school, the ways are limited.

One way to change the curriculum to better reflect the varieties of the students' ways of knowing is to use a variety of what Gardner

(1991) calls "entry points" to deep understanding. He delineates five entry points: Narrational; Quantitative/Logical; Foundational; Aesthetic; and Experiential.

Narrational Entry Points. This is the entry point that relies on the universal appeal of a story as communication and meaning. In utilizing narrational entry points, a teacher developing a unit in American history might use the stories of famous people, or the journals of participants in great historical events. One might also make use of autobiography and biography and any of the other subjects. The important point is to use the *story-like aspects* of the content to bring it to life for the students who are more inclined toward this entry point.

Quantitative/Logical Entry Points. A teacher making use of the quantitative/logical entry points to subject matter would choose to focus, with some of the students, on the *rational aspects* of the content and skills. For example, in biology, the study of evolution would be conducted through the "lens" of genetics if this entry point were emphasized.

Foundational Entry Points. Foundational entry points emphasize the *philosophical concepts* and issues within each domain. In the study of evolution, a teacher and students emphasizing this entry point would perhaps regard the issues involved in the conflicting views of evolutionists and creationists, or the ethical issues of cloning human beings.

Aesthetic Entry Points. Aesthetic entry points rely on the artworks and literature related to the content and skills of the curriculum as well as other aspects of the curriculum that may be perceived through the *senses*. In the study of evolution, students could be asked to discern the different features of plants or animals, and to devise a system of classification for them. For a child who is strong in bodily/kinesthetic and spatial intelligences, the teacher might provide an opportunity to classify animals or insects by their methods of locomotion, and to perhaps choreograph a dance or performance piece using those movements.

Experiential Entry Points. This is the entry point that relies on *hands-on* experience. The key here is that the students physically experience the subject matter. This would mean, in the study of evolution for example, that the students might breed fruit flies and record variations and mutation across a number of generations (Kornhaber & Gardner, 1993).

Though Gardner admits that the concept of entry points or modalities is not a new one, his framework provides teachers with a basis for developing and testing curriculum with their own students. In this way, the students may be engaged in a variety of ways and in a variety of domains (Kornhaber & Gardner, 1993). He states, "We need to give kids a chance in school to enter the room by different windows, so to speak—but to be able to see the relationships among the different types of windows" (Brandt, 1993).

Kornhaber and Gardner (1993) recommend these practices to teachers:

- Model the use of a variety of entry points in your own learning, and demonstrate it explicitly to your students.
- Connect your efforts in the classroom to the rest of the world.

- Externalize your thinking through think-alouds and cognitive coaching. Bring metacognition out into the open.

- Try to arrange, as much as possible, for your students to engage in apprenticeships outside of school in areas in which they have expressed a strong interest.

▶ FIELD-BASED CONNECTIONS

Guidelines for Interns

Child Study

Conduct a child study of an individual in your class. Be sure to obtain written permission from the child and the parent. Choose a child you would like to observe and follow over a period of time (at least two weeks). Observe the child in a number of different settings (at least ten) to collect your data, and record your observations in a variety of ways (anecdotal recollections of routine incidents and anecdotal recollections of critical incidents; and timeline observations, where you record the student's behavior every minute for fifteen minutes). Write up each observation following this format: Rationale for choosing this time to observe, description of incident, and reflection on the student's behavior. Use the sample case study provided at the end of this chapter as a guide. Interview the child and record the interview.

Write a vignette of your child, starting with a physical description, a personality profile, and a description of the child's background, if you have access to that information. Is the child's behavior consistent or inconsistent? How does the child use language? Use the theories of development provided in this chapter as frameworks to discuss the child's physical, emotional, cognitive, and moral development. After observing the child in a number of learning situations, what do you think are his/her strengths of mind?

Conduct an Experiment

Choose two children you think have similar, non-traditional strength of mind profiles. It would be good if they were both spatially oriented, for instance. Take a series of "traditional" lessons that you or your mentor teacher have prepared for the class, and do them with one of the children, as usual. Adapt them for the other spatially oriented child, perhaps by using aesthetic entry points instead. Record their responses. Reflect on what happens.

▶ CHAPTER CLOSURE

Summary

There are a number of ways in which students may differ, be it race or culture, development, or strength of mind. This chapter presented a broad overview of the most prevalent theories of human cognitive, personality, psychomotor, and moral development. It also presented a picture of how students may vary in ways by which they understand the world. What a child knows is what its mind perceives in interaction with the world, and not as a passive viewer or receiver of information. These are important considerations for the teacher when planning teaching and learning in the classroom, and in assessing student understanding and performance.

Chapter Discussion Questions

1. The ideas of Piaget, Erikson, Kohlberg, and Havighurst overlap to some extent. Discuss the four stage theories, paying particular attention to connections between them.

2. How might being at-risk as a result of social factors affect the cognitive development of a child? Physical development? Moral development? The accomplishment of the developmental tasks?

3. What might a school day look like, if the entry points to deep understanding of Gardner were utilized throughout your school?

4. Looking at the seven intelligences of Gardner, what do you think your strengths of mind are? Why? Discuss this with a friend in the room to provide and receive another point of view.

5. The concepts of decentration, conservation, and reversibility are major milestones for the preoperational child to attain. With the large number of immigrants coming to the United States— many of them with children in the preoperational stage—it is important that you think about ways in which you can provide developmentally appropriate instruction for them in your classroom, even if you do not speak their language. What might you do with a preoperational first or second grader who speaks a language other than English or Spanish to help the child develop deep understanding of the concept of the seasons, for instance?

▶ SAMPLE CHILD STUDY ▶ FOR FIELD-BASED CONNECTIONS

General Information
Peter Williams (Pseudonym)

The subject student was born in March of 1982. His parents are divorced. He lives with his mother, stepfather, and two stepsisters. He was retained in the first grade. Some information in his background data indicates that he is Mexican-American. Other forms say that he is Anglo. Peter is an avid baseball player. His

mother thinks that he has the potential to play professionally.

He began attending his present school in the second grade after transferring from a school in Phoenix. He was retained in the first grade, but his age is appropriate for a third grader, so I cannot ascertain exactly why he was held back. That is, his standardized Iowa test scores (2/91) indicate that he is well above the national average in his verbal, quantitative, and nonverbal abilities, and his age indicates that he is not older than his classmates. It is probable that he was retained for reasons other than any related to academic performance.

Peter received several unsatisfactory grades in conduct during the second grade. He has a history of not completing his homework, which persists in his present situation. His third grade teacher this year has talked with his mother on the telephone concerning his homework. The mother's involvement has resulted in improved performance in this area.

Peter's mother seems concerned. Her involvement is probably a key factor in ensuring Peter's academic success. She informed Peter's teacher that Peter's father dropped out and never graduated from high school. She is worried that Peter might follow in his father's footsteps.

To date, Peter's grades are all in the A-B range.

Observation During P.E., October 30, 9:00–9:25 AM

The purpose of this observation is to watch the subject student in a recreational setting. The game being played in P.E. is "Frisbee Mania." Students are broken up into teams and then instructed to go to specific areas of the gym. The P.E. instructor places a bowling pin in the center of the room. The four groups of children surround the pin, one group on each side of the square room. They are in a line within their group so that when the teacher calls out the number three, the third student in line from each of the four groups stands up, races around behind the other students in a complete circle, reaches his or her original group, picks up and then slides the team's frisbee toward the pin in an effort to knock it over.

Before the game begins, Peter moves from one end of the line to the other where some boys from his class are seated. He waves his arms in karate-like movements as the teacher gives instructions.

Peter's number was never called, so he did not get to participate directly in the game. He seemed excited while watching his team, but when the teacher announced that the game was over, he acted very disappointed that he did not play. As she asked recap questions about what the students learned about safety during the game, etc., Peter never volunteered to answer any of the questions.

I did not observe anything terribly significant about Peter during this session. His facial expressions made me think that he was almost angry about not being called on to knock the pin down. If he was, though, it was not evident when he returned to class.

His body movements were similar to those I see him making while walking down the hallway or standing in line. Similarly, he fidgets a lot in class, as previously mentioned. I do not see anything very unusual about his movements, but I do think he has a lot of energy that needs to be expelled throughout the day.

Direct Conversation With and Observation of Peter Williams, September 5, 11:45 AM–Noon

A personal confrontation with the subject student precipitated this observation, and to some degree, my reason for choosing Peter Williams as my case study student.

It is routine for all students to frequent the restroom after lunch. They line up in girl/boy lines (one each), and are sent into the restroom in small groups. Today when one other student came out, he said that Peter had hit him. I confronted Peter; he denied the accusation. When I told him to wait in the hall while I located my mentor teacher, he refused. I was not sure at this time what her policy was regarding this type of behavior and because the other boy was hurt and asked to go to the nurse, it was not something that could be ignored. My mentor teacher asked the two boys exactly what happened. Peter said he did not mean to hurt the other boy—the other student insisted that he did. My mentor was severe in her scolding, and took Peter to the office. He returned to class after a short time and seemed to have regained his composure. Neither his behavior nor his performance indicated that his mood was permanently affected. That is, he was not defiant again and he produced the work that he was asked to do.

A summary about this incident as it related to handling Peter in similar situations would probably be premature if made at this time. I will continue to observe how he responds to correction and discipline and will make recommendations should they be warranted at a later time.

Observation During Lunch With Student, September 18, 11:05–11:20 AM

When students in my classroom earn four cones in the lunchroom as a group for good behavior, my mentor teacher gives them the opportunity to eat lunch on the patio. The children seem to really look forward to and enjoy this reward. They have more freedom to talk and the ambiance is very pleasant if the weather is nice. Both my mentor and I eat with the students. Today I chose to sit next to Peter in order to have a direct conversation with him and make this one of my observations.

Peter was very talkative during our conversation. He told me about his two sisters, but seemed to especially like talking about sports. He loves baseball and is evidently a very good player. As noted in the general information about Peter, his mother thinks that he has the talent to be a professional baseball player. He plays in leagues and has won city-wide championships.

The principal thing that I gathered from today's observation was the realization that Peter can be engaged if individual attention is given to him. So often, he seems uninterested in being a real part of the group and he acts as if school is something to be endured rather than enjoyed. Many times he mutters to himself in what seems to be disdain for the authority figure in the classroom and I tend to construe his actions a being indicative of his apparent dislike for school and those in charge. But this student can be reached. When attention is given to him, he responds. The danger in "reading" him is that he does not always respond immediately, so there is a tendency to move on to another student.

But with persistence and encouragement, he can be brought around to enjoying the school setting. He seemed to genuinely enjoy talking with me and has on several occasions brought up baseball to me since this conversation. The topic has become a link between us and I believe he tries harder in the classroom because I have shown an interest in his love for baseball.

Observation During Spelling Dictation, October 9, 11:45 AM–12:05 PM

The following is a tallying observation done on the case study student. The intention of the observation is to determine if the student has special problems in taking down dictation sentences because of specific routine behavior he exhibits.

Dictation tests are administered to students once a week in this class. The final test in spelling is given on Fridays and consists of the words of the week only. Dictation is a midweek test which is returned to the students on Thursday so that they can study directly from it in preparation for the final test on Friday. The purpose for the dictation is to assess the students' ability to listen to a complete sentence and then transfer that information to paper.

Peter has trouble completing the sentences in the allotted time. Even though each sentence is repeated three times very slowly, it seems that he is so deliberate in his writing (presses very hard with the pencil), that he runs out of time. All of the other students finish considerably ahead of Peter on every sentence. He spells the words correctly for the most part. When given ample time, he makes an A on virtually all of his tests.

Because the purpose of the dictation test is not to assess speed, special care should be taken to see that this student has enough time to complete his work. He should either be given more time during the test or should be given additional time after the test. Otherwise, he will become terribly frustrated (as I have seen happen before his problem was noticed). Some testing might be in order if it is determined that his lack of speed is extraordinary. But before this stage is reached, Peter should be coached on how much pressure to put on his pencil and shown how too much pressure causes him to write slower.

Observation During Recess, October 18, 1:45–2:00 PM

Today's observation is being conducted in order to determine how Peter interacts with other students in the least structured environment at school.

It is a beautiful day and the children are thrilled to be outside. Peter is playing on a dome, monkeybar-like piece of equipment. Seven students from our class are also playing here along with children from the other third grade classes.

Peter is rambunctious. He plays with the other boys in a very rough manner but the mood is fun and all seem to be having a great time. One girl from our class is included, but the boys only "roughhouse" with each other. Peter tends to play with boys most of the time and gets along well with them.

Nothing inordinately revealing took place during this observation. Peter seems to be well-rounded in his relationships with other students. He prefers the company of boys, but the for most part gets along well with girls in the classroom setting. As noted during other observations, Peter has a lot of energy. He enjoys doing things that require kinesthesia rather than passive learning. That is, not only during recreational times does he like to move around a lot, but he appears to be much more attentive in the classroom setting when he is physically involved in learning.

Time Line Observation, October 21, 1:05–1:20 PM

The purpose of observing at this time is to determine if what appears to be off-task behavior results in a low test score for the case study student.

1:05   Student fidgets, rubs eyes.

1:06   Student looks around room during lecture; stares at clock.

1:07   Student mutters to himself; appears to be totally off task.

1:08   Student does not watch lesson being presented on overhead projector—continues to look around the room.

1:09   Student's hands cover his face; he plays with his desk tag.

1:10   Student talks to student seated directly across from him.

1:11   Student rests his head on arm, and in turn on his desk like he might fall asleep.

1:12   Student is totally slumped down into his chair and across his desk.

1:13   Student talks with student seated next to him.

1:14   Teacher calls student's name; he quickly straightens up. Teacher asks if he is "with" the group. He nods affirmatively. No direct question is asked of the student, so it is not evident if he is on task.

1:15   Teacher hands out a quiz which will cover what was being presented on overhead projector (short vowel sounds).

1:16   Teacher works sample problem on board. Student is confused—thinks that she is working the first problem on the test.

1:17   Student still seems disconcerted. Has not been paying attention, so he does not know what he is supposed to do. The student who sits next to him gives him directions.

1:18   Student begins working on test. He seems troubled. Brow is furrowed.

1:19   Student continues working on test—seems to be more relaxed.

1:20   End of observation—student diligently working on test.

Test Results

This student produced "A" work on both sides of a worksheet that tested knowledge of short vowel sounds. Obviously, his apparent off-task behavior could be misconstrued as just that. He either already knew the material and was bored and/or restless, or appeared uninterested and still managed to absorb the instruction.

Observation During Language Arts Tutoring Session, October 24, 12:15–12:30 PM

This observation was during a tutoring lesson that the student attended in the classroom along with five other students. The purpose was to note how the student reacts to working with a teacher and small group contemporaneously with being retaught something he did not initially understand.

After approximately ten minutes the student understood the concept and began to present it to another student who was being tutored.

One thing that is puzzling about this student is his attitude. At the beginning of the tutoring session he was sullen and seemed as though he was about to refuse to pay attention or participate in the discussion. Within minutes, however, he proceeded to explain a point about predicates to another student (made a distinction between subjects and predicates). I think caution must be taken when trying to "read" the student by his mannerisms. He often appears to be irritated or bored and then suddenly takes a turn and becomes involved or interested in the discussion.

On the reteach worksheet that these students were given to complete at home, the case study student made 100 percent.

Observation During Retention in Classroom at Recess Time, October 24, 1:45 –2:00 PM

Today at lunch Peter was reprimanded and reported by the lunch monitors for throwing orange peels at another student. Four other students also got into trouble and were reported for various other infractions. All five students were made to stay in at recess for their misbehavior. I did not observe the lunchroom behavior, but I know that Peter gets reported fairly frequently compared to the other students. I have not kept track of how many times he has been in trouble for misbehaving in the lunchroom because I did not know from the beginning of the year whom I would observe.

The purpose of this observation is to attempt to assess how the student reacts when made to miss a part of the day he really enjoys.

Peter's behavior during the time he stayed in during recess was fine. He worked on his homework and seemed to have no problem staying on task.

Misbehavior at certain times of the day does not necessarily mean that Peter will have an entirely "bad" day. As mentioned in previous observations, care must be taken to pull this student back into the fold, because he is capable of "taking a turn for the better" even after having gotten into trouble. He was quite cooperative during this retention period.

Observation During Science—Cooperative Learning Lesson on Light Weights, October 22, 2:00–2:40 PM

The subject student sits at a table (on a daily basis) with three girls who are his team members during a science experiment on light weights. The main objective of this observation was to watch the student interact in a group.

Not long after the group work began, the girls who were Peter's partners requested my assistance. They all told me that Peter was refusing to participate in the experiment and that he would do nothing but disagree with them. He told me that he did not want to do the activity with girls and that I should let him work with boys. I asked them to try and get along because I had already arranged everyone (I also felt that it was premature to move him out of this particular group and wanted to see if they could work through some of their disagreements). In addition, I gave him the right to disagree with their theories. He was instructed to write on the group sheet that he differed with their opinions, tell what he thought, and sign the paper.

Once the experiment progressed to the point where he became physically active in the process, the group coalesced. Peter performed the "comparison drop" portion of the activity and all seemed well from that point on.

This is a point I would like to expand on regarding the subject student. Before I had decided whom I would observe, I noted that hands-on activities are important for inspiring Peter. He seems least engaged during teacher lecture, even though he does not necessarily miss the instruction that is being given. He just seems more captivated (as do most of the children) during those times when they are actively involved in the learning process rather than passively listening to a principally one-way conversation.

In sum, this student must be monitored fairly carefully to ensure that he is "with" the group or following the discussion. At times when he appears to be somewhere else, he is obviously listening. There are frequent occasions, however, when he appears to be off task and is. When called on, he does not know the answer because he has not been following in the book or listening to the teacher. An effort should be made to call on him fairly frequently if long periods of time lapse between times that he raises his hand to respond voluntarily.

Observation During Math, November 4, 8:35–8:50 AM—My Solo Teaching Day

Because Peter's group seemed to be interacting extraordinarily well while working on a group math puzzle, I decided to make an observation during the last fifteen-minute segment of the math period. This is an anecdotal transcript observation which notes his conversations with others in his group.

The first activity of the day was a math test. Students finished at different times, so I had puzzles for them to work on in small groups. Peter and his group worked so harmoniously together, I could not help but take note. I complimented them several times and finally asked if there was something different about today. (They have had problems working together during previous cooperative learning activities). They all said that the girl who was absent argues with Peter, and that they were getting along because she was not there.

At various times, I would walk by the areas in which the students were working. They talked with each other about possible answers and had designated different things each was to do. They checked each other for correctness of addition and Peter colored each square as instructed on the worksheet. They caught a misprint on the worksheet which immediately told me they were working very carefully. There was no dissension among the group. All conversations I overheard were congenial and supportive. Once when the group got loud, I heard Peter tell the girls to be quieter. I had made it known early in the morning that rewards would be given at the end of the day for good behavior. Peter obviously wanted to maintain a good track record and was very conscientious of doing the "right" thing.

The group finished the puzzle and seemed very proud of its work. I continued to comment in front of the entire class on how well this group was working together. Peter was on task all day, volunteered to answer questions, and even came up to the front of the room to perform a rap, which he has never wanted to do. I was impressed and pleased with his behavior and academic performance this day. He seemed to genuinely enjoy himself; his attitude was markedly different. Enabling this student to work with the right combination of people and giving encouragement and recognition are key factors in motivating this student.

Barbara Murray
Pre-Service Student/Intern
San Antonio, Texas

► REFERENCES

Anderson, R. & Freebody, P. (1981). Vocabulary knowledge. In J. Guthrie (Ed.), *Comprehension and teaching.* Newark, DE: International Reading Association.

Anderson, L. W. & Pellicer, L. O. (1990). Synthesis of research on compensatory and remedial education. *Educational Leadership 48*(1), 10–17.

Ascher, C. (1987). *Improving the school-home connection for poor and minority urban students.* New York: ERIC Clearinghouse on Urban Education, I.U.M.E., Teachers College, Columbia University.

Blatt, M. & Kohlberg, L. (1975). The effects of moral discussion upon children's level of moral judgement. *Journal of Moral Education, 4,* 129–161.

Bloom, B. S. (Ed.). (1956). *Taxonomy of educational objectives, Handbook I: The cognitive domain.* New York: David McKay.

Brandt, R. (1993). On teaching for understanding: A conversation with Howard Gardner. *Educational Leadership, 50*(7), 4–7.

Bruner, J. (1960). *The process of education.* Cambridge, MA: Harvard University Press.

Butler, K. A. (1984). *Learning and teaching through style in theory and practice.* Maynard, MA: Gabriel Systems, Inc.

Clay, M. (1993). *The early detection of reading difficulties,* 2nd Edition. Portsmouth, NH: Heinemann.

Colorado Commission on Higher Education. (1992). *What must postsecondary education provide to meet individual student expectations? Colorado Commission on Higher Education Master Plan Background Paper.* Denver, CO: Colorado Commission on Higher Education. Eric Document, ED 351, 933.

Dunn, R. & Dunn, K. (1978). *Teaching students through their individual learning styles: A practical approach.* Reston, VA: Reston Publishing Co.

Elkind, D. (1989). Developmentally appropriate practice. *Phi Delta Kappan, 71*(2), 113–117.

Erikson, E. H. (1968). *Identity, youth, and crisis.* New York: W. W. Norton and Co.

Evangelauf, J. (1992). Enrollment projections revised upward in new government analysis. *Chronicle of Higher Education, 38*(20), A1, 36, Jan. 22, 1992.

Gardner, H. (1983). *Frames of mind.* 10th Anniversary Edition, 1993. New York: Basic Books.

Gardner, H. (1991). *The unschooled mind: How children think and how schools should teach.* New York: Basic Books.

George, P. S., Stevenson, C., Thomason, J., & Beane, J. (1991). *The middle school—and beyond.* Alexandria, VA: ASCD.

Gerald, D. & Hussar, W. (1991). *Projections of educational statistics to 2002.* Washington, DC: National Center for Educational Statistics, U.S. Department of Education.

Gillet, J. W. & Temple, C. (1992). *Understanding reading problems: Assessment and instruction.* New York: Harper Collins.

Gilligan, C. (1984). *Caring: A feminine approach to ethics and moral education.* Berkeley, CA: University of California Press.

Greene, M. (1978). *Landscapes of learning.* New York: Teachers College Press.

Gregorc, A. F. (1982). *An adult's guide to style.* Maynard, MA: Gabriel Systems, Inc.

Harrow, A. J. (1972). *A taxonomy of the psychomotor domain.* New York: David McKay.

Hass, G. & Parkay, F. W. (Eds.). (1993). *Curriculum planning: A new approach,* 6th Edition. Boston: Allyn & Bacon.

Havighurst, R. J. (1953). *Human development and education.* New York: David McKay.

Havighurst, R. J. (1972). *Developmental tasks and education,* 3rd Edition. New York: David McKay.

Heflin, L. J. & Bullock, L. M. (1992). *Exceptionalities in children and youth.* Boston: Allyn and Bacon.

Hetherington et al. (1981). *Cognitive performance, school behavior and achievement of children from one-parent households.* Washington, DC: Families as Educators Team, National Institute of Education. ERIC DOCUMENT ED 221, 780.

Hoot, J. L. & Parmar, R. S. (1992). Normal growth and development in children and youth. In L. J. Heflin & L. M. Bullock (Eds.), *Exceptionalities in children and youth.* Boston: Allyn and Bacon.

Jacobs, H. H. (1986). The interdisciplinary concept model: Design and implementation. *Gifted Child Quarterly,* Winter.

Jung, C. G. (1971). *Psychological types.* (Originally published in 1921). Princeton, NJ: Princeton University Press.

Kohlberg, L. (1970). *Moral education.* Cambridge, MA: Harvard University Press.

Kohlberg, L. (1975). The cognitive-developmental approach to moral education. *Phi Delta Kappan, 56*(10), 670–677.

Kornhaber, M. & Gardner, H. (1993). *Varieties of excellence: Identifying and assessing children's talents.* New York: National Center for Restructuring Education, Schools, and Teaching (NCREST), Teachers College, Columbia University.

Kozol, J. (1991). *Savage inequalities: Children in America's schools.* New York: Crown.

Krogh, S. L. & Lamme, L. L. (1985). Distributive justice and the moral development curriculum. *Social Education, 55*(4), 616–621.

Legters, N. & Slavin, R. E. (1992). *Elementary students at risk: A status report.* Baltimore, MD: Center for Research on Effective Schooling for Disadvantaged Students, Johns Hopkins University.

Leinhardt, G. (1992). What research on learning tells us about teaching. *Educational Leadership, 49*(7), 20–26.

Marzano, R. & Hutchins, C. L. (1988). *Thinking skills: A conceptual framework.* Boulder, CO: Mid-Continent Regional Educational Laboratory.

McCarthy, B. (1980). *The 4MAT system: Teaching to learning styles with right/left mode techniques.* Barrington, IL: Excel, Inc.

Moles, O. J. (1987). Who wants parent involvement? *Education and Urban Society, 19*(2), 137–145.

National Association of Elementary School Principals (NAESP). (1980). *First-year report of a longitudinal study conducted by the consortium for the study of school needs for children in one-parent families.* Arlington, VA: NAESP.

Natriello, G., McDill, E., & Pallas, A. (1990). *Schooling disadvantaged children: Racing against catastrophe.* New York: Teachers College Press.

Newman, F. M. & Wehlage, G. G. (1993). Five standards of authentic instruction. *Educational Leadership, 50*(7), 8–12.

Nyberg, D. (1990). Teaching values in school: The mirror and the lamp. *Teachers College Record, 91,* 595–611.

Oaks, M. M., Worthy, J., & Remaley, A (1993). Confronting our nation's at-risk and dropout dilemma. In Hass and Parkay (Eds.), *Curriculum planning: A new approach,* 6th Edition. Needham Heights, MA: Allyn and Bacon.

Passow, A. H. (1980). *Education for gifted children and youth: An old issue—a new challenge.* Los Angeles: National/State Leadership Training Institute on the Gifted and Talented.

Passow, A. H. (1989). *Curriculum and instruction in chapter I programs: A look back and a look ahead.* ERIC-CUE Trends and Issues No. 11. New York: ERIC Clearinghouse on Urban Education, Teachers College, Columbia University.

Passow, A. H. & Rudnitski, R. A. (1993). *State policies regarding education of the gifted as reflected in legislation and regulation.* Storrs, CT: National Research Center on the Gifted and Talented.

Pearson, D. P., Hanson, J, & Gordon, C. (1979). The effect of background knowledge on young children's comprehension of explicit and implicit information. *Journal of Reading Behavior, 11*(3), 201–209.

Piaget, J. (1950). *The psychology of intelligence.* New York: Harcourt.

Piaget, J. (1955). *The language and thought of the child.* New York: World.

Rumelhart, D. E. (1980). Schemata: The building blocks of cognition. In R. J. Spiro, B. C. Bruce, and W. F. Brewer (Eds.), *Theoretical issues in reading comprehension.* Hillsdale, NJ: Lawrence Erlbaum.

Salend, S. (1990). *Effective mainstreaming.* New York: Macmillan.

Samples, B. (1992). *The metaphoric mind: A celebration of creative consciousness,* 2nd Edition. Rolling Hills Estates, CA: Jalmar Press.

Seligman, M. P. *Learned optimism.* New York: Alfred A. Knopf.

Smith, D. C. & Neale, D. (1991). The construction of subject-matter knowledge in primary science teaching. In J. Brophy (Ed.), *Advances in research on teaching.* Greenwich, CT: JAI Press.

Smith, F. (1988). *Understanding reading.* Hillsdale, NJ: Lawrence Erlbaum.

Tannebaum, A. J. (1983). *Gifted children: Psychological and educational perspectives.* New York: Macmillan.

U. S. Department of Education, Office of Educational Research and Improvement. (1991). *Youth indicators 1991.* Washington, DC: U. S. Department of Education.

U. S. Department of Education Office of Research and Improvement. (1993). *National excellence: The case for developing America's talent.* Washington, DC: Author.

U. S. Office of Education. (1977). Implementation of Part B of the Education of the Handicapped Act. *Federal Register 42,* 42474-42518.

Vygotsky, L. S. (1962). *Thought and language.* Cambridge, MA: Harvard University Press.

Vygotsky, L. S. (1978). *Mind in society.* Cambridge, MA: Harvard University Press.

Witkin, H. & Goodenough, D. R. (1981). *Cognitive styles: Essence and origins.* New York: International Universities Press.

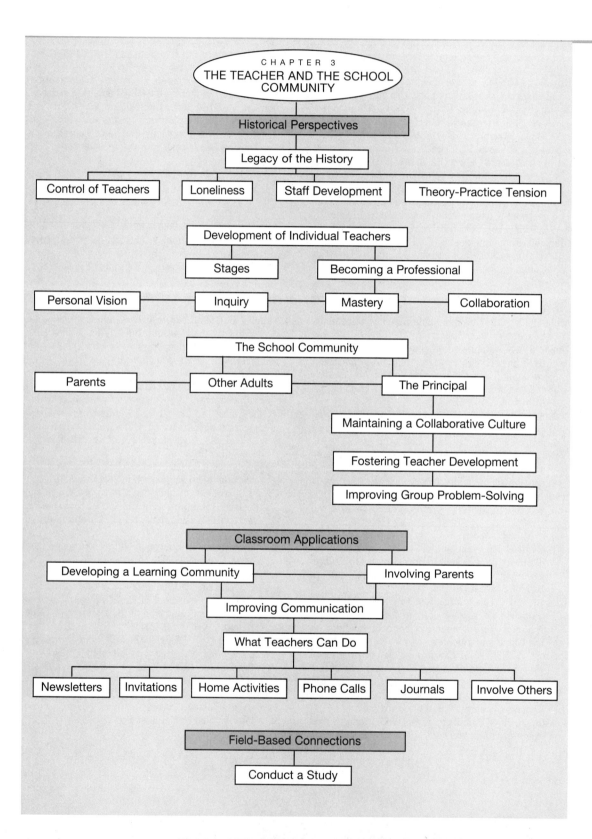

CHAPTER 3
THE TEACHER AND THE SCHOOL COMMUNITY

Historical Perspectives

Legacy of the History

Control of Teachers | Loneliness | Staff Development | Theory-Practice Tension

Development of Individual Teachers

Stages | Becoming a Professional

Personal Vision | Inquiry | Mastery | Collaboration

The School Community

Parents | Other Adults | The Principal

Maintaining a Collaborative Culture

Fostering Teacher Development

Improving Group Problem-Solving

Classroom Applications

Developing a Learning Community | Involving Parents

Improving Communication

What Teachers Can Do

Newsletters | Invitations | Home Activities | Phone Calls | Journals | Involve Others

Field-Based Connections

Conduct a Study

The Teacher and the School Community

Introduction

As a person entering the field of teaching, you are entering a profession with a long and noble history. You probably chose to become a teacher because you had a teacher or teachers who inspired you to learn, and who created a caring environment in which you could practice new skills.

- What makes such a teacher? What have been, and are, the supports and obstacles to a teacher being inspiring, creative, and caring?
- How can you develop into the best teacher that you can be?
- What are the responsibilities of the teacher in relation to the parents of a student?
- How can a teacher involve parents and other community members in the education of their children?

These are some of the questions raised and discussed in this chapter.

▶ THEORY

Historical Perspectives

Teaching in America Before the Common School

Since the inception of public schooling in America, generally attributed to the year 1647, with the enacting of the "Old Deluder Satan Act" in Massachusetts, we have had formal arrangements to provide teachers for our children. This law required a community of fifty households to appoint a teacher to provide instruction in reading and writing.

Communities of more than 100 households were required to establish grammar schools, where the students would study reading, writing, and Latin and "ciphering" as well (Cremin, 1970). Before this law was enacted, it had been the sole responsibility of parents and masters of apprentices to insure that everyone had to at least read the Bible. Spring (1990) asserted that it was not until the parents and masters were unable to fulfill this mission that formal schools were initiated.

Early colonists established what were called Dame Schools to alleviate the educational problems of the colonies. The Dame Schools were schools held in the kitchen or parlor of a local woman. Neighborhood children would gather there for instruction in reading the scriptures, and in piety and conduct. This helped establish teaching, especially of young children, as the work of women in the United States. Attendance at the grammar school was a prerequisite for attendance at college, which usually led to work in the clergy or a position of leadership. Though many grammar school teachers were women, they were barred from attending college until the eighteenth century. This history was to have a profound effect on the formation and perception of the profession, even to the present day (Apple, 1986).

With the birth of the common school in America in the mid-nineteenth century, the role of the female teacher remained surprisingly unchanged. So even though men did become teachers, this was usually viewed as a temporary circumstance until they became ministers or were otherwise gainfully employed. Though the female teacher, or schoolmarm, as she was called, was no longer teaching in her kitchen, she was still teaching the youngest children at the lowest levels; she was required to emphasize reading and writing, and was expected to care for the needs of the children in many basic ways, such as cleaning the schoolhouse and stoking the wood stove for heat before the children arrived in the morning. Her personal life was restricted so that she could devote herself totally to the children of the town. If she married, she was expected to quit her job, and she was, of course, expected to be a model of virtuous behavior in her personal life, so that she could serve as a role model for the children. If she was not, she was simply fired (Apple, 1986). As Spring (1990) put it, these factors, along with the prevailing teaching methods and material of the time, "added the final touches to the portrait of the nineteenth-century schoolmarm as the inexpensive, moral, nurturing, stable, kind, charitable, and subordinate backbone of the common school system" (p. 117).

The Legacy of the History

Teaching is Restricted and Controlled

Apple (1986) asserted that the work of teachers is characterized by a process of de-skilling, the prescribing of techniques to be memorized and applied in a given number of situations. He attributed its easy acceptance to the fact that teaching was women's work, and undervalued by the society as a result. Many materials and practices indicate that there is a measure of truth in Apple's claims. One need only to look at the teacher's manual of a basal reading series to see evidence of this concept. Instructions to the teacher are explicitly given, even to the point of providing the questions to ask and the answers the teacher should expect from the students. This kind of treatment implies that the teacher is incapable of thinking of her own questions. (See Apple, Chapter 2, section on authentic teaching.)

Some evidence of de-skilling may also be found in supervision and evaluation practices. In the typical situation, the teacher is alone with the children in the classroom, whether it is high school or elementary school, for almost every day of the school year. Then, on a Monday, say, in May, the supervisor asks the teacher if it is O.K. if he comes in to observe on Thursday. He comes in with a checklist on Thursday, and checks to see that the lesson contains the seven "essential elements of effective lessons:"

1. Anticipatory Set;

2. Objective and Purpose;

3. Input;

4. Modeling;

5. Checking for Understanding;

6. Guided Practice; and

7. Independent Practice. (Hunter, 1984)

Of course the teacher, knowing that these will be the criteria, has geared the lesson to the seven elements, even though she knows that not all lessons fit this neat formula; and she, in fact, resents the implication that teaching is such a simple affair. The principal, or supervisor, sees the elements, checks the features on the list, and takes it to his office to file it; another duty accomplished in his busy schedule.

This condition is changing. With many principals reflecting on the meaninglessness of such supervisory practices, newer models of teacher evaluation are emerging, just as with newer models of student assessment. One principal, sharing his reflections on traditional supervision, stated:

> After examining our evaluation system, I realized that it was based on several assumptions:
>
> 1. The power to change teacher behavior is inherent in my role as principal.
>
> 2. Teachers are all, in some way, "broken" and need "fixing"...
>
> 3. Clinical supervision is the model for our evaluation system, This done well, requires multiple observations and a coaching relationship—not an evaluative one.
>
> 4. Because a small minority of teachers could be considered "incompetent," the system of remediation is used for all.
>
> 5. The ranking of teachers as Excellent, Satisfactory, and Unsatisfactory in some way relates to improved instruction.

Personally, I subscribed to none of these beliefs. (Rooney, 1993, p. 43)

The principal later went on to tell how she changed her supervision practices to reflect her own beliefs. This is a powerful example of how reflection can cause one to question previously accepted and unquestioned practices and improve them.

Teaching is Lonely

Teaching has been characterized as a lonely profession in which practitioners have little contact with each other or with many other adults, for that matter (Sarason et al., 1966; Lortie, 1975). Teachers are confined with their students for hours at a time, with little interaction with other classes or the outside world. This isolation has helped to formulate some professional norms of teaching that may be characterized as negative and counterproductive to the professional growth and expansion of individuals, to say nothing of the profession itself. An example of a negative norm is closing the classroom door and teaching the way one was taught, or the way one wants to, despite knowing that there may be a better, more effective way (Jackson, 1968; McPhereson, 1972). This is a generally accepted practice in teaching, brought about by the conditions under which teachers have worked for many years. But many in the profession are working to change those conditions in an effort to improve teaching and learning in our schools (Little, 1993).

Staff Development is Inadequate

Although all prospective teachers must attend college and experience some form of teacher education in order to be professionally certified, once they are employed their further education is the responsibility of the local school district. Many districts are ill-equipped to handle such a task, and many administrators, who have more access to newer practices (Firestone, 1993), seeking a "quick fix" for such problems as low standardized test scores, view staff development as an opportunity to seek a quick solution.

Much of the time, staff development consists of "training" in the implementation of the newest model or trend on the educational market. We live in a consumer-based society, and many school administrators fall prey to the society's push for the best "product," and instant gratification. Dewey (1904) saw this problem, and attributed it to a "lack of intellectual vitality among those occupying administrative positions" of his time (p. 321). Some staff development reflects this. Many teachers can tell you about going through training in career education in the 1970s, and being trained in the *essential* elements of instruction, only to have these pass with time.

Another problem with staff development models is that they may be fragmented. As new

ideas gain acceptance, the temptation is to be "the first on the block" to have implemented a writing or thinking skills program, for example. So, a district will call in a consultant with expertise in that area for one day of training; the teachers attend the workshop; the consultant leaves, and the teachers go back to their classrooms to teach as they always have, because there is no follow-up or support for the changes. Many of these isolated workshops may also contain conflicting information or conflicting purposes as well (Little, 1993).

The Tension Between Theory and Practice

There is a long history of tension between theory and practice in teaching (Dewey, 1904). In the 150 years that we have been preparing teachers in the United States, we have had a difficult time coming up with a system that the teachers feel is adequate preparation for being placed alone in a room with twenty-five to thirty-five or more children and expected to educate them (Lieberman & Miller, 1984). Dewey (1904) explained the situation in this way:

> The would-be teacher has at some time or other had to face and solve two problems, each extensive and serious enough by itself to demand absorbing and undivided attention. These two problems are:
>
> 1. Mastery of subject matter from the standpoint of its educational value and use; or, what is the same thing, the mastery of educational principles in their application to that subject matter which is at once the material of instruction and the basis of discipline and control;
>
> 2. The mastery of the technique of class management.

This does not mean that the two problems are in any way isolated or independent. On the contrary, they are strictly correlative. But the mind of a student cannot give equal attention to both at the same time. (p. 318)

The members of the teaching profession have been wrestling with these issues for a long time. However, current reforms show promise in breaking the cycles of repetition in the conditions of teaching (Little, 1993).

Individual Development

In order to best understand yourself as a teacher, it is important that you see that there are general stages of development which most teachers undergo as they enter the profession and develop experience and expertise. Like children moving through the stages of development of Piaget or Erikson, teachers move through these stages at their own pace. There is no set number of years or months for each one.

Field (1979), a fourth-grade teacher, studied a group of teachers, and found that their concerns, especially regarding ten key tasks, could be categorized into stages. The ten tasks were:

- arranging the classroom; planning the entire day;
- planning large group activities;
- diagnosis of student needs;
- record keeping;
- parent conferences;
- free, unstructured time;
- transitions;
- students' behavior; and
- self evaluation.

She described the stages of teacher development as follows:

Stage One. The survival stage. At this stage the beginning teacher is concerned with day-to-day survival in a job which seems impossible. The teacher spends much time and energy worrying about personal performance, rather than that of the children. The children, materials, physical environment, disciplines, and self all seem separate to the new teacher.

Stage Two. This is the inconsistent stage. At this stage the teacher is experiencing some successes, and can articulate them. The teacher is now able to solve some problems based on past experience, and can now also plan for several weeks at a time, rather than day-to-day. There is increased confidence and a feeling that the job is possible.

Stage Three. This is the stage of expertise. The teacher has developed a repertoire of strategies, and can assess situations and children to the degree that this expertise can be applied with regular success. The classroom is seen as a whole system or community, with each member making valuable contributions. The physical and social environments are used to create a positive climate in which the students and the teacher can work. There is increased flexibility and openness and experimentation evident in the teacher's behavior.

It appears that the teacher at Stage One has little time or energy to keep a reflective journal or to risk losing control of the class by experimenting with a new idea. Most veteran teachers will tell you that this is true. However, we urge you to persevere. We believe that, like the students in the previous chapter who were urged on by ideas and behaviors of more sophisticated levels, you will move to the higher stages more quickly.

Becoming a Professional Teacher

There are other things that you can do to be the best teacher that you can be. In Chapter 1, we discussed the philosophical underpinnings for this book and our conception of good teaching. The concept of professional virtue (Sergiovanni, 1992) is one that we hope will be the driving force for you in your work. It is at the heart of what Fullan (1993) calls "moral purpose" in teaching. This is akin to the sense of agency we discussed in Chapter One with regard to reflection. Fullan asserts that teachers, faced with the expectation of engaging in continuous change and improvement, should focus on their moral purpose. He suggests, in conjunction with moral purpose, that teachers view their purpose in schools as change agents, whose goal it is to change schools for their students. "Moral purpose keeps teachers close to the needs of children and youth; change agentry causes them to develop better strategies for accomplishing their moral goals" (p. 12).

Fullan gives four capacities necessary for teachers to become change agents: personal vision-building, inquiry, mastery, and collaboration. Though much of this book is geared to help you to develop those skills, we elaborate on them here because we believe that they are important.

Personal Vision-Building. This is something that is an ever-evolving process. Fullan (1993) states that it "means examining and re-examining why we came into teaching" (p. 13). This process is enhanced as one writes a philosophy of education and reflects upon one's teaching. It is important that you, as a professional teacher, reflect upon your practice, your feelings about your practice, and how your beliefs and feelings are changing. These activities will

help you as a beginning teacher along the road to building a personal vision.

Inquiry. The process of inquiry in teaching involves persistent questioning. This can take the form of questioning one's values or practice, or trying to find better solutions to problems in the classroom. As a teacher, one must also be a learner—someone who is learning about teaching—throughout her career. "The professional teacher, to be effective, must become a career-long learner of more sophisticated pedagogies and technologies and be able to form and reform productive collaborative colleagues with parents, community agencies, businesses, and others" (Fullan, 1993, p. 16).

The professional teacher is a scholar, studying her craft, making sense of theory, and developing a discourse that combines the two. As part of her work as a scholar, she can exercise her moral purpose by speaking out against social and political injustices that affect the children and hinder their ability to learn (Giroux, 1993).

Mastery. Fullan (1993) points out that "people behave their way into new visions and ideas, not just think their way into them" (p. 13). Part of being a professional is working toward expertise by using the strategies that you know; in applying them to the appropriate contexts; and in assessing contexts to determine their appropriateness. You are continuously striving toward mastery in these areas as a teacher.

Collaboration. It is very difficult to practice these skills in a vacuum. It is very important that you are part of a school community which fosters your professionalism and change agentry. Working toward collaborating with colleagues is one of the most important tasks of the professional teacher. Working in a vital school community makes the work of any teacher more rewarding and fulfilling. We will discuss this in more detail in the next section, the school community.

The School Community

The school community is comprised of many people; the professional and non-professional staff of the school, the teachers, the administrators, the parents, other members of the community, and the students. All of these people share the responsibility for educating the students, though some of them are never explicitly aware of that fact.

The Parents

The most important educators in the life of any child are the parents. Children spend the first four to five years of life at home. Many assert that the child's personality is formed during this time (Erikson, 1968). Even after children enter school, the family is as important an educative institution as the school. It is the place to which the child returns every day after interacting with other people and institutions. According to Leichter (1980), it is a mediating institution, one which interprets, criticizes, and creates meaning for the child's educative experiences.

Parental involvement in their children's education has a strong tradition in American education. A problem arises when one looks at which parents are most involved, and which are not. A child from a traditional, white, middle-class home is likely to have parents who are involved in school activities, parents who feel that they are part of the school community. A child from a non-traditional, or racial or ethnic minority, or low socioeconomic family, or a child with parents who did not attain a high level of education, is likely to have parents who feel alienated from the school community (Lightfoot, 1978). A lack of parental interest or involvement in a child's education could help to place that child at risk.

Parents from racial, ethnic, and cultural minorities, especially those of low socioeconomic status, generally tend to feel less affinity for the school than those in the mainstream middle class (Litwak & Meyer, 1974). This alienation has been ascribed to the school's traditional role in the reproduction of the predominant class structure of American society (Katz, 1975; Ogbu, 1977; Tyack, 1981). Low-income, culturally different parents have traditionally been marginalized by the school community through their perceived inability to communicate with schools, and through the inflexibility of the school as an institution. This tradition has fostered the feelings of inadequacy, failure, and poor self-worth that are cited as reasons for low participation of parents from marginalized groups (Liontos, 1991b). The situation is perpetuated and exacerbated by some parents' inability to communicate with the school due to low proficiency in the English language or the economic, emotional, and time constraints placed on low socioeconomic status (SES) parents in the daily struggle to survive (Bastion, Fruchter, Gittell, Greer, & Haskins, 1986). Looking at the profile of the students of the late twentith and early twenty-first centuries, one can see why parent involvement, especially of traditionally marginalized parents would be a concern of teachers and other members of the school community. Concern is greatest for the lack of involvement of parents of at-risk students, who are especially in need of the support of the home environment in their formal schooling.

Children who are at risk are placed in two distinct environments every day: that of the home, and that of the school. They are the students most in need of parent involvement programs because the home and school environments are so different (Liontos, 1991a). If the parents of at-risk children become involved with their children's school, they will be better able to help their children adapt to the differences between the home and school environments. If no involvement exists, there is a good chance that the children will embrace the familiar home culture and reject the unfamiliar school culture (Hamilton-Lee, 1988). Strategies to involve parents will be presented in the section on classroom applications.

Other Members of the School Community

The other members of the school community are important to your goal of establishing an environment in which your students can learn. Such an environment must be one that fosters caring and belonging as well as inquiry and expression. It must reinforce these elements in every way. As part of the restructuring movement, many schools are forming school improvement teams that include members of the school community other than teachers, parents, and administrators. As a new teacher, be aware of the school improvement efforts in your school and the segments of the school community that are represented in those efforts.

The Principal

The administrator with whom you will probably work most closely is the principal. The position of principal was started when schools grew too large to be managed by the teachers who taught in them. Schools appointed a principal teacher to take care of the organizational needs of the school in order to give his/her colleagues time to work with the children. One can see how the job has grown in the intervening years.

The principal's function in the school community varies a great deal, depending on the person and the nature of the school culture, and can exert a positive influence or a negative one (Barth, 1991; Sarason, 1990). However, in all cases, the principal plays a central role of leadership in forming and maintaining a spirit of community in a school (Rudnitski, 1992; Sergiovanni, 1993). Some of the major concerns of the principal regarding the school community are: maintaining a collaborative culture, fostering teacher development, and improving group problem-solving (Leithwood, 1992).

Maintaining a Collaborative Culture. Little (1993) cited norms of collective responsibility and continuous improvement as central to the maintenance of a collaborative professional culture in schools. The principal can be a driving force in this regard by constantly pushing for improvement while supporting the teachers' efforts to improve (Fullan, 1992). Principals can use a variety of strategies to maintain the push and support with everything from covering a teacher's class to observing or planning with another teacher to involving the entire school community in decision-making.

Fostering Teacher Development. The aspect of support is key in this regard. The principal who fosters teacher development is one who helps each teacher set individual goals for improvement, and who helps each teacher reach them. Leithwood (1992) also cites involving teachers in non-routine problems of school improvement as fostering teacher development.

Improving Group Problem-Solving. The principal may improve group problem-solving by involving a broad range of perspectives in the process. This means including individuals who might not have been included in this process in the past. People like school custodians and secretaries should be included in discussions that affect educational decisions, and not just procedural ones. The principal who is a true leader empowers all members of the school community to feel that they can be included in all aspects of decision-making.

Conclusion to Theory

As a teacher, you will be part of a school community, but actually, we are all part of many communities in our everyday lives. As an intern, you are also part of many communities or cultures: the school, the academic community, the elementary or secondary education community, the young adult community, your gender community, racial and cultural communities, the student community (Fox, 1992). Each of these communities affects you and your teaching, but the one that is closest to you and your students is the community or culture of the school you share.

The community of teachers is comprised of your professional peers. As a novice teacher, you will probably be at a different stage of professional development than a veteran teacher. This does not mean that you will not progress, or that you have not achieved an acceptable level of expertise. It is, however, helpful for you to be aware of the different *stages* of development of teachers so that you know that you are not alone in your concerns, and also to know what to strive for in your own development.

Of the many members of your school community, the parents of your students are the most important in terms of helping your students to develop and learn. Parents and teachers are allies in education, and are the people in the best position to be advocates for children. It is important that you use your position as a teacher to advocate for what you believe is right and just for your students, and for what you believe will facilitate their healthy growth and development. It is also important that you share this moral purpose in your teaching with the parents of your students.

It is also important for you to know the characteristics and activities of good school principals. The principal of a school can facilitate learning or hinder it. We presented the characteristics of the principal as a school community leader so that you might choose the site where you will work with this in mind. The principal, rather than being an instructional leader, is really a leader of instructors (Schlechty, quoted in Brandt, 1993).

► CLASSROOM APPLICATIONS

As a teacher, you will be called upon to work collaboratively with your colleagues and others involved in the education of your students in creating visions, making tough decisions, and planning change. These are not easy activities. They take time, and the willingness to listen to the perspectives of others just as they are difficult processes as you experience them. This process will be doubly complicated for you as a beginning teacher, for you will be busy finding your own way. That is a difficult enough task without dealing with the searches of others; yet you must participate. There is much to be learned through the change process in education, and as we stated earlier, school communities dedicated to the education of their children are committed to a process of continuous improvement and experimentation. Change is part of the routine in a school; it is not new, nor is it something that will pass with time.

Developing a Professional Learning Community

Fullan (1993) suggested several actions teachers could take to foster what they called interactive professionalism (cited in Fullan, 1993). Interactive professionalism is their concept of the relationships in a school community that work toward continuous improvement and share a sense of moral purpose in its work. The actions delineated by Fullan serve as guidelines for the discussion that follows.

• Professional teachers in effective school communities have their own inner vision and can articulate it. They try to locate their own inner voice as individuals, and then share it with the others in an attempt to develop a common vision as well. The common vision is negotiated in a professional learning community.

• Professional teachers practice reflection in action, thinking as they teach, and responding to the actions of others thoughtfully. They reflect on their actions as well by keeping a journal, and by sharing reflective thoughts with colleagues, when appropriate. They also reflect about action, considering alternatives and their implications. The actions upon which professional teachers reflect are not necessarily their own action, or even actions in schools. They may be actions of world leaders or other events. These actions affect their teaching, and should not be overlooked.

• Members of a professional learning community develop a risk-taking attitude. Though they are not reckless, they are not afraid to voice and try new ideas. They are also not afraid to share their failures, for they know that they are sometimes the best learning experiences. They also allow they children to make mistakes in the same way that they would like others to allow them.

• Members of a professional learning community respect each other, and view others as whole people, not just as the roles that they play in the school. They get to know their colleagues' interests and hobbies as well as their professional strengths and interests. They invite their colleagues to their classroom to share when they are doing things that they know the colleagues will enjoy, or be able to enhance. They appreciate and accept their colleagues for who they are, and not who they wish they were.

• Members of a professional learning community are committed to working with their colleagues. They do not always shut their doors as teachers did in the past, and when they encounter a colleague who does just that, they encourage that colleague to share as well. This is done through invitations at appropriate times, and sharing when the teacher thinks that the colleague may be interested.

- A professional teacher seeks variety and avoids getting into a rut. Some things work very well, but even they can become stale with time. The professional teacher is a seeker of new ideas and strategies to add to the teaching repertoire. She is committed to her own and her colleagues' continuous improvement and ongoing learning; she supports them and expects their support in return in this regard.

- The professional teacher redefines the teaching role to extend beyond the classroom. Getting involved with the students in activities outside of school, and taking the students into the community for learning and apprenticeships as much as possible is an excellent example of this. There is, of course, danger in this in that the teacher may become too involved, and become nearsighted in work and play. It is for this reason that, in the same breath, we speak of balancing work and life. The professional teacher has interests that are outside of the school community. Though these interests may sometimes relate to the work the teacher and students do in the classroom, they are primarily non-school activities that get the teacher away from work.

- Just as principal leaders push and support teachers in their professional development, it is the responsibility of professional teachers to do the same for principals. Interactive professionalism is just that—interactive.

The development of all members of the professional school community is interactive, and all members should be considered when development and change are planned. This includes parents, students, all adult members of the school community, and the outside community as well.

Involving Parents

As discussed earlier, many parents do not feel that they are a part of the school community. As the person who is in closest contact with parents, it is the teacher's role to invite the parents to the school and make them feel welcome. At the school community level, these strategies have proven helpful. Though teachers may be involved in them, these activities are usually carried out in a school community with the leadership of the principal or other administrators.

Improving Communication

Home Visits. One strategy that works is informal home visits. It is important that the parents do not think that the school is "snooping" on them, and that they and everyone present feel comfortable. One way to insure this is not to wait for a crisis or emergency to make a home visit, but to schedule regular ones. It is a very good idea for a teacher to phone a family the summer before a child is to be in class, and arrange to visit the home before the start of school.

Neighborhood Coffee Klatches or Teas. Another effective strategy to get to know parents is to have a neighborhood gathering. This is a very effective activity in inner cities, where many students might live in the same building or in a housing project. These should also be planned ahead of time, and not arise out of a crisis, but out of a genuine interest in getting to know the parents and involve them in their children's education. Another thought: If several students in the neighborhood speak a language you do not know, arrange for a bilingual parent or other community member to act as an interpreter. This demonstrates that you have placed a value on and have shown an appreciation for the language and culture of these parents and their children, and will help them to feel more welcome in the school community.

Public Information Fair. Arrange an evening or weekend day that does not interfere with the religious observances of any of your students for a community service fair. This would be a good way to provide a needed service for your parent community members as well as to get to know some other members of the community. A fair could be held in the gymnasium, with members of different community services and organizations manning tables and providing information on their organizations. This could also serve as a good warm-up exercise for you and your students for the curriculum-based gatherings and fairs that you will be having throughout the year.

Parent Lounge/Resource Center. Arrange to have a room set aside for your parent members, if you have the space. In schools that have these, the school usually arranges for some parents to take responsibility for a coffeemaker and supplies. Work some money into your budget to buy some resources for the parent center every year. These resources may be child development books and video-

tapes, and guides on studying with children. Many parents appreciate some help in raising their children, and since most have not studied child development or child rearing at all, they need the help.

Regular Before-School Breakfasts. In today's working world, where most parents are in the work force, it is simply insensitive to schedule parent meetings during work hours, or even in the evening, when many parents are tired or busy with their leisure activities. Many schools have had success with early morning, before-school doughnuts or muffins and coffee for parents and their children. Since it is unrealistic to expect parents to leave their children at home or with a baby sitter while they are meeting with members of the professional school community, they should feel that they are allowed to bring their children along; unless the activities or discussion will be sensitive or confidential.

School Informational Videos. A great project for a media class is to make a documentary video on the school. In addition to being a description, it could contain an oral history of the school as well. This video could be signed out of the library or the parent resource room, and could be lent to families who are moving into the district, and whose children will be attending the school. The video could be remade or updated periodically to give other students a voice in the history of the school, and to provide other classes with a good project. One more important point is to be sure that the video is translated or dubbed into every language spoken in your school community.

Family Night. School should be fun, and an activity that can foster this feeling is a family night. This is a night when families can bring in and play board games or Bingo, to have refreshments, and to get to know the school and one another. The night could also be centered around a problem-solving activity such as a scavenger hunt or an interactive murder mystery. Such shared experiences help to foster feelings of community among the members of a professional community.

Parent Handbook. Have a parent handbook available which tells about the school, its norms, rules, and routines as well as its history and anecdotes. Again, it should be available in every language spoken by parents in the school community.

Parent-Student Exchange Day. Arrange two or three days a year when parents may sign up to come to school with their children and attend classes for a morning, afternoon, or the whole day. Parents should have a choice of days, but should only come to school as students for one of the days. This is a fun way for them to see the school through the eyes of their children, and a reminder to all in the school community that they are interested participants in their children's learning.

What Teachers Can Do to Involve Parents

Newsletters. Send home weekly or bi-weekly newsletters with student work or articles, letting parents know what the students are doing. Include curriculum-based activities the parents can do to help their children to learn, and to also familiarize them with what the children are learning. If you teach at the sec-

ondary level, it is just as important to keep parents informed, though the students are more reluctant to see their parents involved. Send home a biology or history newsletter. The parents may be surprised at first, but they will appreciate it.

Make Parents Feel Welcome. Though it seems threatening to many teachers, it becomes a very natural activity, when one has an open-door policy with parents. Invite them to the class frequently, and always let them feel welcome when they come unannounced. If you feel that their presence will be disruptive to the students or to their child, then let them know that, and ask them to wait in the office, parent, or teacher's lounge until a better time that day.

Monthly Achievement Packets. For extra credit, send home packets of activities for students to complete with parents, when appropriate. Students should not feel penalized if their parents do not have the time to complete the activities with them, but should also feel that it is good to share their learning in school with those at home.

Regular Phone Calls. The worst phone call from the teacher is the only phone call the parent usually receives. Do not wait for a crisis. Call the parents of your students regularly to chat about their children, and to let them know some good news about them. A phone call once a month in the school year will help that year to stand out in the parents' and the students' minds as a year of exceptional communication.

Dialogue Journals. These should be used judiciously with parents, for they may cause some parents embarrassment. Many adults do not have the reading and writing skills in standard English that one might expect. Be cautious in the use of dialogue journals with parents, but use them if, in your professional judgment, they are appropriate.

Involving the Principal and Other Members of the School Community

It is good professional practice to invite all members of the school community to your classroom periodically, especially when your curricular activities may be of interest to them. If your first grade is making a food to go along with the reading of a book, or to augment the study of a holiday, invite the cafeteria staff to join you. Ask their advice on increasing or decreasing recipes. Invite them in as experts when doing a unit on nutrition. If you teach high school biology, you might also invite the cafeteria staff to view the exhibitions and culminating activities of your curriculum units.

Think of the professional staff of your school as individuals as well, and do not always associate them with their jobs. A school custodian may be an expert hunter or orienteering expert. The principal may play the violin or the banjo. A maintenance person may be an expert pilot. Get to know the members of the school community well enough to know when to invite them to your classroom. This kind of thinking, and these kinds of activities, makes the difference between the exceptional professional teacher and the ordinary one.

▶ FIELD-BASED CONNECTIONS

Guidelines for Interns

Conduct a Study

Do a study of the parents of the students in your classroom. Center the questions around what they think are the characteristics of a good school, and what they think makes a good teacher. Ask them what they think they should do to help their children do well in school. After you have analyzed the data, share your findings with them. This could be a very interesting, informative experience. You may want to do this every year, for the parents and their perceptions and needs change every year.

Interview The Principal. Interview the principal of your school. If there are several interns in the school, conduct a group interview: Why did you become a principal? What do you view as your role in the school community? What about your professional goals? What do you envision for yourself ten years from now? What do you think that schooling will look like in the year 2020? Let the principal ask some questions of you. What do you want to know about being a principal?, for example.

Interview Each Other. As part of the above activity, interview another intern, and ask similar questions.

Interview Yourself. Write in your reflective journal, using the above interview questions along with the questions you created as guides. Will you be teaching in the year 2020?

▶ CHAPTER CLOSURE

Summary

In this chapter, we focused on the adult members of the school community. The teachers are the adults who have the closest contact with the students, and who are the primary mediating agents between the students and the curriculum, and between the students and other members of the school community. Teachers, like students, go through stages of development at their own rate and in their own ways.

Another important adult professional member of the school community is the principal. The principal is the person closest to the teacher, and is a mediating agent between each classroom and the school community as a whole. As the adult with "the big picture," the principal plays a central role in the development of a positive climate for students and teachers.

Parents are a very important link in the educational process. When parents are involved in their children's education in positive ways, the children are more successful in that education. It is the teacher's responsibility to involve parents in the educational process. Many suggestions for doing this were described in this chapter.

Educators often overlook non-professional staff and other adult members of the school community who are involved with students in schools. These people can be helpful resources for curriculum units, bringing their expertise to bear in areas related to their jobs and hobbies. They often form personal relationships with students and are a valuable asset in forming positive relationships in the school environment. They are included in this chapter in order to emphasize their importance in the school.

Chapter Discussion Questions

1. It is said that we do not value our children in this society, and therefore we do not value their teachers. It seems that the younger the children, the less respect the teacher receives. Do you think that this is still the case? Why? If you do think that this is true, what do you suggest to change the attitudes?

2. You are in the process of developing a personal philosophy of education. Part of that philosophy includes your conception of what a good teacher does. What is an effective teacher? How do you think principals should evaluate teacher effectiveness? How does the community evaluate teacher effectiveness? Is there a better way?

3. When you are teaching, how do you intend to keep up with the latest innovations and ideas in the profession? Will you expect your school district to provide all of your inservice development, or will you choose your own? What would you choose, and how will you account for the changes you make in your practice as a result of what you learn? How will others know that you have learned something?

4. Ask a friend or someone in the class who is a parent of school-age children what they think a good teacher does. How does this compare with your description of an effective teacher?

The case study examples can be used for analysis in small or large groups. Questions follow each case study as suggestions for discussion.

CASE STUDY 3-1: by Eleanor Levine, Teacher, Scarsdale, New York

Read the following vignette of a first-grade classroom before the start of the school day.

A Day in First Grade

It is 8:55 AM and the children stroll in. "Good morning, Kira." "Good morning, M.L. (Mrs. Levine)."

Our school is collecting pennies for the starving children in Somalia. Martin has emptied (with permission) his father's piggy bank, and Ayumi and Andrew help him make many piles of ten pennies all over their desks. Later, the children will tell how they earned the pennies they are giving: David raked the lawn for the pennies he brings, Kim made her bed, Trina folded laundry, and Richard gave some of his allowance.

We are reaching outside our classroom to sense the needs of others and, as we are helping with our few pennies, we feel that we are making a difference. Nyberg (1990) says that "the most important moral skill . . .is to think seriously about and try to persistently feel what it is like to be somebody else." He believes that it is important that we know that the "pain in our neighbors throbs the same as pain in ourselves." Nyberg said that when you understand the pain of others you "begin to know your moral duty, which has a lot to do with the way we respond to human suffering."

Robyn is busy at the puppet stage where Trina, Kira, and she are preparing for a puppet show for the class. Greene (1978) believed "there is a need to externalize through various kinds of action their own imaginings." She spoke of the need for interest and wide-awakeness . . .the direct opposite of the attitude of bland conventionality and indifference" which suggests a lack of care and absence of concern.

Kim, Haruka, and Malea are sprawled on the floor with their colored markers, busily illustrating the giant chart story that the teacher wrote about Kim yesterday. Ashely S. is working at the easel, painting her version of Goya's portrait of *Don Manuel*. In June, our class will visit the Metropolitan Museum of Art to see the original painting. We are reaching outside our class to the greater society, and reaching back into history to appreciate a work of art.

Matthew and Richard are working feverishly with Lego pieces. At Matthew's side are his coat and backpack which, as usual, he has forgotten to hang up. Everybody is active. Everybody is busy and learning.

Michael L. and David work in the block corner. They are building a wall for a puppet show. This is the first time we have ever seen a puppet show being prepared in the block corner. What a great idea! Dewey (1916) said that since "a progressive society counts individual variations as precious (and) the means of its own growth, it must allow for intellectual freedom." Creativity, new ideas, and acceptance of these new ideas gives the children confidence and the incentive to be even more creative.

Sara lost a tooth and she colors a box on the tooth chart, while Catherine and Ashely L. huddle over the checker board. After Dylan, our class chess-master, waters the plants, he will look for a chess pupil. Matthew wants to learn. We are friends in this community and we teach others what we know.

Our Christmas cactus is blooming at Thanksgiving time again, and we carry it into the hall to display it. Michael F. writes a sign to tape near it. It is our classroom, and we are all responsible for it.

The teacher sits at the reading table, and she calls up those children who need to correct yesterday's work, or need to read and edit their journals. Kira is making a book about her family. Trina is finishing the illustrations on her book about Bill Clinton. Perhaps we should send it to him. A light tinkle of the bell and the children stop, look, and listen. The teacher calls up more children and the others bend over their projects again.

There is order in our day. There is a measure of freedom co-mingled with discipline. It is a safe place to be, a good place to learn. Dewey (1916) said that "the inclination to learn from life itself and to make the conditions of life such that all will learn in the process of living is the finest product of schooling."

At 9:30 AM the bell rings to end activity time. The children's projects are discussed and praised, and we clean up and prepare for our daily meeting.

Case Study Discussion Questions

1. Discuss in your journal other ways that the teacher could foster a sense of community and to reach outside the classroom.

2. Does the teacher feel a sense of moral purpose? How do you know? Does she view herself as a change agent?

Case Study References

Dewey, J. (1916). *Democracy and education.* New York: Macmillan.

CASE STUDY 3-2: by Beverly Woods, Teacher, Newburgh, New York

Read the following rationale for becoming a teacher, written by a veteran teacher in an inner-city school.

Although my teaching career started about ten years ago in the private sector and approximately five years ago in the public school system, I feel as though I have been involved in the education of others for many more years. I was brought up in a suburban middle-class town where I attended elementary school in the late 1960s. I suppose that this is not an atypical experience for a majority of today's teachers. There is, however, a significant difference: I am black.

For many of the students and teachers with whom I spent my elementary years, my sister and I were their first experience with black people. From the moment that I began to attend school, I began to teach: All blacks are not low achievers, all blacks are not from low-socioeconomic backgrounds, all blacks are not behavior problems with little or no interest in education. At six years old, I began my crusade against ignorance and hate.

Although I do not remember specific things said in my home, I imagine my parents were very supportive through these years. The late sixties were quite turbulent and I am sure that my sister and I could have just as easily grown up full of hate and anger. There were plenty of incidents of prejudice, discrimination, and blatant namecalling. My parents, particularly my mother, made it clear to us that it was ignorance and not skin color that caused people to act this way. My mother was also very aware of the value of education and taught us that our only limits were those that we imposed on ourselves.

More than twenty years later, my crusade has not ended. I am still unteaching stereotypes, now to inner-city and suburban children, who seem bound by their unquestioning belief in what society tells them about themselves. I have found that, just as important as the content that we teachers are required to teach, an understanding, acceptance, and love of self and others should be first on the agenda. Once this has begun, the educational process is enjoyable for teachers and students.

The task of teaching children, any children, is not a simple one. I have my moments when I consider other professions which are more financially rewarding and respected. Yet, the rewards one receives as an educator, though not always quantifiable, far outweigh money and power. I love learning, I love teaching, and I love my children.

Case Study Discussion Questions

1. What personal and professional commitments does this teacher express?
2. How do you think her philosophy is manifested in the classroom?

▶ REFERENCES

Apple, M. W. (1986). *Teachers and texts: An economy of gender relations in education.* London: Routledge.

Barth, R. S. (1991). Restructuring schools: Some questions for teachers and principals. *Phi Delta Kappan, 73*(2), 123–128.

Bastion, A., Fruchter, N., Gittell, M., Greer, C., & Haskins, K. (1986). *Choosing equality: The case for democratic schooling.* Philadelphia: Temple University Press.

Brandt, R. (1993). On restructuring roles and relationships: A conversation with Phil Schlechty. *Educational Leadership, 51*(2), 8–11.

Cremin, L. (1970). *American education: The colonial experience 1607–1783.* New York: Harper and Row.

Dewey, J. (1904). The relation of theory to practice. In *National Society for the Scientific Study of Education,* Third Yearbook, Part I. Chicago: University of Chicago Press.

Erikson, E. H. (1968). *Identity, youth, and crisis.* New York: W. W. Norton and Co.

Field, K. (1979). *Teacher development: A study of stages in the development of teachers.* Brookline, MA: Teacher Center.

Firestone, W. A. (1993). Why professionalizing teaching is not enough. *Educational Leadership, 50*(6), 6–12.

Fox, D. L. (1992). *The influence of context, community, and culture: Contrasting cases of teacher knowledge development.* Paper presented at the Annual Meeting of the National Reading Conference, San Antonio, TX.

Fullan, M. G. (1992). Visions that blind. *Educational Leadership, 49*(6), 19–20.

Fullan, M. G. (1993). Why teachers must become change agents. *Educational Leadership, 50*(6), 12–17.

Giroux, H. A. (1993). Teachers as transformative intellectuals. In S. V. Shapiro and D. Purpel (Eds.), *Critical social issues in American education.* New York: Longman.

Hamilton-Lee, M. (1988). *Home-school partnerships: The school development program model.* Paper presented at the Annual Meeting of the American Psychological Association, Atlanta, GA. ERIC Document 303, 923.

Hargreaves, A. (1992). Time and teachers' work: Teacher preparation time and the intensification thesis. *Teachers College Record, 94*(1).

Hunter, M. (1984). Knowing, teaching and supervising. In P. S. Hosford (Ed.), *Using what we know about teaching.* Alexandria, VA: ASCD.

Jackson, P. W. (1968). *Life in classrooms.* New York: Holt, Rinehart and Winston.

Katz, M. B. (1975). *Class, bureaucracy, and schools.* New York: Praeger Publishers.

Leichter, H. J. (1980). *The public school and the family.* New York: The Pilgrim Press.

Leithwood, K. A. (1992). The move toward transformational leadership. *Educational Leadership, 49*(5), 8–13.

Lieberman, A. & Miller, L. (1984). *Teachers, their world and their work: Implications for school improvement.* Alexandria, VA: ASCD.

Lightfoot, S. L. (1978). *Worlds apart: Relationships between families and schools.* New York: Basic Books.

Liontos, L. B. (1991a). *Involving at-risk families in their children's education.* ERIC Clearinghouse on Educational management: Eugene, OR. ED 326, 925.

Liontos, L. B. (1991b). *Involving the families of at-risk youth in the educational process.* ERIC Clearinghouse on Educational Management: Eugene, OR. ED 328, 946.

Little, J. W. (1993). *Teachers' professional development in a climate of educational reform.* New York: National Center for Restructuring Education, Schools, and Teaching (NCREST), Teachers College, Columbia University.

Litwak, E. & Meyer, H. J. (1974). *School, family, and neighborhood.* New York: Columbia University Press.

Lortie, D. C. (1975). *School teacher: A sociological study.* Chicago: University of Chicago Press.

McPhereson, G. (1972). *Small town teacher.* Cambridge, MA: Harvard University Press.

Ogbu, J. (Ed.). (1977). Racial stratification and education: The case of Stockton, California. *IRCD Bulletin, 12*(3).

Rooney, J. (1993). Teacher evaluation: No more "super"vision. *Educational Leadership, 51*(2), 43–44.

Rudnitski, R. (1992). *Through the eyes of the beholder: Encouraging participation of minority parents in school.* Paper presented at the Annual Meeting of the American Educational Research Association, San Francisco, 1992.

Sarason, S. B., Levine, M., Goldenberg, I., Cherlin, D., & Bennett, E (1966). *Psychology in community settings.* New York: John Wiley and Sons.

Sarason, S. B. (1990). *The predictable failure of school reform.* San Francisco: Jossey-Bass.

Sergiovanni, T. J. (1992). *Moral leadership: Getting to the heart of school improvement.* San Francisco: Jossey-Bass.

Sergiovanni, T. J. (1993). *Building community in schools.* San Francisco: Jossey-Bass.

Spring, J. (1990). *The American school: 1642–1990.* New York: Longman.

Tyack, D. B. (1981). Governance and goals: Historical perspectives and public education. In D. Davies (Ed.), *Communities and their schools.* New York: McGraw-Hill.

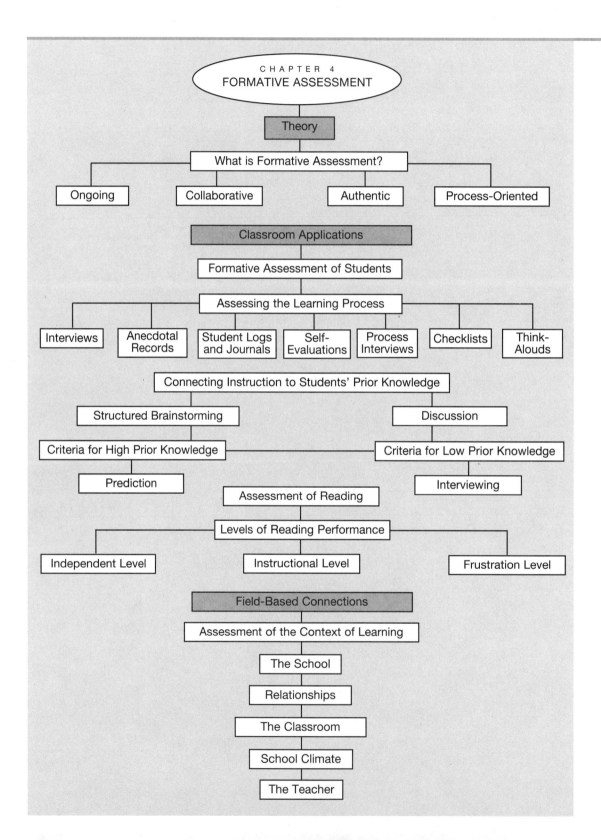

CHAPTER 4
FORMATIVE ASSESSMENT

Theory

What is Formative Assessment?

Ongoing   Collaborative   Authentic   Process-Oriented

Classroom Applications

Formative Assessment of Students

Assessing the Learning Process

Interviews | Anecdotal Records | Student Logs and Journals | Self-Evaluations | Process Interviews | Checklists | Think-Alouds

Connecting Instruction to Students' Prior Knowledge

Structured Brainstorming   Discussion

Criteria for High Prior Knowledge   Criteria for Low Prior Knowledge

Prediction   Interviewing

Assessment of Reading

Levels of Reading Performance

Independent Level   Instructional Level   Frustration Level

Field-Based Connections

Assessment of the Context of Learning

The School

Relationships

The Classroom

School Climate

The Teacher

4

Formative Assessment

Introduction

When a person walks into a room, there is an immediate assessment of the situation done by that person, while those already in the room concurrently assess that person. Assessment, both formal and informal, is not only a fact of life, it is a natural part of life. We will be assessed in one form or another or for one reason or another every day of our lives, both by others and by ourselves.

Chapter 10 is entirely devoted to the assessment of students, and deals with the concept in depth. This chapter is meant to provide you with the means to assess the prior knowledge of your students and their progress over time during your teaching. The chapter ends with a section designed to help you to get to know your school community and the culture in which you have decided to work. This activity will help you to discern what you believe to be the ideal school culture.

▶ THEORY

The terms assessment and evaluation are used interchangeably in this chapter. Though assessment generally refers to the appraisal of individuals and evaluation refers to programs, curricula or institutions, the term assessment has also come to mean a broad range of non-standard techniques used to gather information in educational settings, while evaluation is used to denote tests and program evaluation (Madaus & Kellaghan, 1992). Since the meaning of the terms have been merged so often in common usage, we have merged them here to avoid more confusion.

What is Formative Assessment?

Formative assessment is ongoing, and provides feedback and information on *processes*. Formative assessment also provides information on development over time. It differs from summative assessment in that summative assessment provides feedback on *products* and occurs at the end or summation of an activity.

Formative assessment is also used to assess situations and contexts that have purposely been formed to serve a function or have been formed with a goal in mind. A school is such a context. Other examples include classrooms and lessons or learning experiences. If you can assess important aspects of a school culture before you get involved, it helps you to decide if you want to become part of that culture. A formative or pre-assessment of a context also may be easily converted into a needs assessment, in which areas needing change or improvement are delineated and prioritized.

Formative assessment in the classroom provides educators with information for determining students' instructional needs and interests. Through systematically recorded formative assessment, one can keep track of a student's progress over a long period of time. Through informal and formal formative assessment, the teacher can learn much about the students' prior knowledge of a curricular topic or the students' personal theories of how the world works.

A teacher may also use formative assessment to reinforce standards in the classroom. Periodic checks can serve as reminders to students of what is expected of them, and help the teacher to determine the progress of each individual student. Because it is ongoing and process-oriented, formative assessment is inextricably tied to instruction. As such, it will be treated in this chapter as a series of field-based activities. In this way, you will be able to tie your class instruction, reading, and discussions to the field through this text.

Remember that the ultimate purpose of formative assessment is to facilitate teaching and learning. It should be ongoing, positive, and dynamic. The atmosphere in which the assessment takes place is critical to its nature and effectiveness. An atmosphere of criticism and judgment will most likely cause negative responses to the assessment. An atmosphere of acceptance and expectation will most likely encourage positive attitudes and growth. Positive formative assessment can provide students with a sense of accomplishment and anticipation that they are getting better over time, and is progressing toward valued goals.

Some general guidelines for formative assessment in the classroom are:

- It is not necessary to assess everything that each student does;
- Use both qualitative (interviews and journals) and quantitative (multiple-choice tests and other standardized assessment techniques);
- Assess both the process and the product;
- Use peer and self-assessment when appropriate;
- Involve parents and other community members in assessment when possible;
- Include students in decisions, including decisions as to what will be assessed;
- Be systematic, but keep your record-keeping system as simple and flexible as possible; and
- Share your findings with students and their parents. You have nothing to hide.

Conclusion to Theory

Formative assessment is generally authentic and tied to the curriculum goals and objectives. Since the curriculum is developed by the teacher, formative assessments should be designed and developed by the teacher as well. They are simple, and easy to construct, and therefore cost-effective. They are also designed with specific students in mind, and are therefore "student specific" and accurate when done well. The following sections give several applications for formative assessments of students.

CLASSROOM APPLICATIONS

Formative Assessment of Students

Assessing the Learning Process

Some of the most common forms of assessment of student progress are quizzes during the process of instruction, and tests at the end of each unit, with a final examination at the end of a series of smaller curriculum units. Though these are helpful, they do not necessarily provide an authentic picture of each student's work, or the nature of the classroom tasks that the student performed during the course of the unit. They work best in large-scale situations, where cost is a prominent factor in the choice of assessment methods (Popham, 1993; Worthen, 1993).

In the past few years, alternatives to these types of tests have become more popular in classrooms, and have grown in acceptability as viable and valuable indicators of student progress. Some of the more common forms of alternative assessments at the formative stage are:

1. Individual interviews;

2. Anecdotal records of behavior observed in a variety of situations;

3. Student learning logs and journals;

4. Student self-evaluations: both oral and written;

5. Debriefing and process interviews after and during student projects, exhibitions, and demonstrations, in which the students describe what they did, why they did it, how they performed the task, and reflect on possible changes and improvements for the project;

6. Behavioral checklists; and

7. Student think-alouds in conjunction with work and performances, including tests (Herman, Aschbacher, & Winters, 1992).

Individual Interviews. Interviews with students, their former teachers, and the students' parents can provide valuable information on the student' out-of-school background, interests and talents, and previous activities and achievements. There are several published checklists designed to determine student interests and preferences in reading (Eberwien, 1973), but interviews can provide a more personal forum for discovering students' interests.

In an interview, the teacher is able to probe more deeply into areas of interest, and can determine if a student is simply saying what he/she thinks that the teacher wants to hear. There is also an affective element to an interview that is difficult to achieve with a checklist or questionnaire. Taking the time to interview students shows the students that you care what they think. Interviews are a way for the teacher to demonstrate a personal commitment to getting to know each student as a unique individual.

Constructing an interview is a goal-directed task. First, one must determine what it is that one wants to know and accomplish through the interview. Since interviewing is an ongoing assessment tool, the teacher need not feel pressured to gather all the necessary information in the initial interview. Regular, short conferences with students, in which each one is systematically interviewed, should be part of the classroom routine. Recording each student's answers to a set of questions geared to gather specific information is a valuable type of formative assessment, and should be a part of a teacher's routine activities. In order for the assessment to be worthwhile, the answers are not only used for class records, but they also affect curriculum and instruction in terms of content, process, and teaching methods. In this way, the culminating test is not the only assessment that drives what is taught and how it is taught. Formative assessment of this nature can be a way to have your students connect with and affect the curriculum.

Anecdotal Records. An anecdotal record of each student's observed behavior is another valuable type of formative assessment of students in a classroom setting. Teachers have been doing this on an informal level for centuries, but only recently has this method been accepted as a practical tool for keeping track of student development, and for assessing the effectiveness of one's own planning and instruction. One of the goals of this "kid watching" (Goodman, 1986) is to determine the needs and responses of the students in order to adjust one's curriculum to better align with those needs and responses.

Anecdotal records are currently used extensively by teachers who are gathering data to support their referral of students to special education programs, but all students deserve to be watched by their teacher. Examples of anecdotal records are contained in the case study in Chapter 2. These may be studied to get a sense of their form and purpose. As with interviews, it is important to keep one's goals in mind. What are you looking for? Why? These questions should guide all structured observations of students.

A good method for keeping anecdotal records in the classroom is the clipboard method. Thoughtful teachers keep a clipboard on which they have a sheet with the names of all the students in the class. A master sheet can be made at the beginning of the year, and copies made on a weekly basis to adjust to student mobility in and out of the class. On this sheet, the teacher writes something about each student every day. In that way, the teacher has a record of each student's behavior over time. If a student's behavior demands more attention, then the teacher may want to keep more in-depth anecdotal records for that student, but the clipboard system insures that all students receive attention every day. Once part of a teacher's routine behavior, it is as simple as it sounds.

Anecdotal records are used for more than classroom management. They may also be used to record learning behaviors. As such, they must be based on the teacher's knowledge of the appropriate learning behaviors for a given situation and a good knowledge of *how* students learn. For this reason, the teacher must have a definite idea of what to look for. It is also important that these records be kept frequently over a period of time, to establish patterns of behavior, and not just isolated incidents. It is from the patterns that the teacher assesses the student's development and depth of understanding.

Student Learning Logs and Journals. Student learning logs and journals are a very personal way for a student to communicate his/her understanding and learning processes to the teacher. It is essential that students have direction in their writing of learning logs and journals so that they know what is expected of them in those journals. Many teachers find the use of short "journal starters" to be useful. Incomplete sentences such as "I would have made the same decision [as the main character in a piece of literature] because _____"; or "Photosynthesis is like a person eating because _____; it is different in these ways _____;" can help to elicit specific information from students without placing them in artificial testing situations. They can also help the teacher to dispel any misconceptions that the student may have.

Student Self-Evaluations. Effective assessment at any time during the learning process involves the student. The teacher can learn much about a student's perceptions of self, as well as of personal learning through guided self-assessment. Guidance also can help students to see the positive side of evaluation, and to view it as a part of the process of growth rather than as a judgment pronounced by some outer force on their capabilities as students, as it too often is.

Guidance for self-evaluation by students can take the form of simple questions adapted to specific situations, activities, and subjects. Questions like: "How do you feel you are doing with this project?" "What are your strengths in science?" and "What do you feel you need to do to improve your performance in language arts?" can be used in interviews, in conferences, as guides in journal writing or as part of a questionnaire. No matter what the form, self-evaluation should be as frequent as evaluation by the teacher and any other person.

Debriefing and Process Interviews. Debriefing interviews are really a form of summative assessment, but are included here because they are part of an entire, ongoing process of assessment, of which formative assessment is the initial step. It is from debriefing interviews that teachers obtain the information which helps them to improve a project the next time they use it in the classroom. They also help students learn what they might do differently next time. However, if the student and teacher have been communicating throughout the project, the debriefing interview should hold no surprises for anyone.

Process interviews help teachers to know what the students are thinking as they go through the learning process. They give valuable insight into metacognitive processes and help the students to think about their thinking. Process interviews have been applied to the field of reading frequently (Paratore & Indrisano, 1987). Asking students what they do when they come to a word they do not know can let the teacher know their strategies for constructing meaning from text. This has also been applied informally in the field of mathematics. Asking students how they arrived at an answer lets the teacher in on the hidden or metacognitive processes at work and reveals insights the students have, as well as any flaws they may have, in their thinking.

Behavioral Checklists. Behavioral checklists may be developmental, and are meant to assess a student's developmental level in a given area (Cockrum & Castillo, 1991). Other checklists may be constructed by the teacher to determine student progress through a curriculum, or to help the teacher observe behavior over time. In a behavioral checklist, the desired behaviors become the criteria—what the teacher is looking for. In order to construct such a checklist, one need only define the desired behaviors, such as "accurately retells stories from text," or "independently applies SQ3R strategy in context," and look for them as the students go about the daily business of school work. As with other types of formative assessment, behavior checklists can be a natural part of a teacher's daily routine without becoming an overwhelming task or a burden to carry out.

Some guidelines for constructing checklists are:

- Keep the checklist as short and simple as possible;
- Form the checklist to align with short- and long-term curricular goals;
- Include quantitative as well as qualitative information on the checklist; and
- Be specific, and do not try to do too many things on one checklist.

Student Think-Alouds. Like process interviews and, to some extent, self-evaluations and journals, student think-alouds are a way to view the students' metacognitive processes. These occur as the student is solving a problem, conducting an experiment or carrying out a task. Teachers model think-alouds frequently during the course of their teaching day, making this an assessment activity that is relatively easy to implement. Simply ask the student to explain aloud what is being done and the thinking that is taking place while performing the task you wish to assess. Have the student take the teacher through the process, step by step. This illuminates how the student is thinking.

Connecting Instruction to Students' Prior Knowledge

There are several ways to assess students' prior knowledge. We will discuss the following methods: structured brainstorming; discussion; prediction and hypothesis formation; and interviewing.

Structured Brainstorming

When introducing a new topic, a teacher may ask the students what they already know about the subject. As they brainstorm what they already know, the teacher writes their responses on the board, placing them in general categories. For example, if the topic is bridges, the teacher might write all the information expressed about suspension bridges in one column, place information on wooden bridges in another, and so on. This helps the teacher and the students to discover what they know and what they do not know—where there is a foundation, and where there are gaps. It also helps the teacher and the students to connect across categories and to create inner frameworks for concepts they will learn later.

Discussion

An informal discussion is also a good way to determine students' prior knowledge. As the class discusses the topic, the teacher looks for the following criteria in their statements and questions. The same criteria apply to structured brainstorming.

Criteria for High Prior Knowledge

- Many associations;
- Use of correct terminology or vocabulary;
- Definitions of words that come up in discussion;
- Mention of related topics and concepts;
- Spontaneous categorization of concepts and terms;
- Placing the content in correct sequence; and
- Connecting previous content to the new material.

Criteria for Low Prior Knowledge

- Few associations;
- Incorrect associations;
- Sound-word relationships stressed rather than meaning-word relationships; and
- Few answers or nothing to say.

If the students exhibit a low degree of prior knowledge, then the teacher must help them to build knowledge of the subject. The formative assessment gives the teacher an idea where to start.

Prediction

Students need some prior knowledge to make predictions. Predicting may be used as a motivator to get students interested in a topic. It helps for the teacher to prepare an anticipation guide when introducing new material. An anticipation guide may be structured around a broad statement related to the topic. Such a statement before reading O. Henry's (pen name [pseudonym] for the author William Sydney Porter) *Gift of the Magi* might be: "The best laid plans don't always work out the way they were meant to be." Students then predict the main idea of the story based on that statement and what they know about the work.

Interviewing

One may also interview students to determine what they know about a given subject or topic. It is also sometimes useful to have students interview each other. Whichever method is used, it is important that there be a purpose set for the interview; the teacher and the students should create the criteria and plan the questions they will ask before the interview is actually conducted.

Assessment of Reading

Much of the information that students use in their projects and curriculum activities are obtained through reading. How can a teacher assess what a student is learning from reading? There are two main ways: The teacher can ask the student to read the material aloud;

if the student is uncomfortable reading aloud, the teacher may ask for the story to be told in the student's own words. The student can also be asked questions about the content to determine if the reading was understood. The following discussion should serve as a guideline in your assessment of student comprehension and reading. It is suggested that, if the reader is interested in assessing students' reading through informal reading inventories, the book, *Informal Reading Inventories*, by Johnson, Kress, and Pikulski (1987) be referred to. It is available from the International Reading Association, 800 Barksdale Road, Newark, Delaware 19714, and offers a more comprehensive look at this assessment method, presented only briefly here in spite of its importance and value.

The teacher chooses the text for an informal inventory of a student's reading. It should be something that the student is reading in class or is reading as part of research. Both the teacher and the student should have a copy at the time of the assessment. The teacher needs to have a copy of the text that can be marked.

Before administering an informal inventory, the teacher should ask the student questions related to the main idea in the text passage to determine if the student has any prior knowledge of the topic. Students comprehend at higher levels when they have prior knowledge of the ideas and topics of the text.

During the reading, the teacher marks any miscues that the student makes by marking a slash through a word read incorrectly. If the student substitutes another word for the one written in the text, the teacher writes the word above the one that it replaced. If a word is omitted, a circle is placed around that word. When the student repeats a word or phrase, it is underlined. When a student makes a miscue, but goes back and self-corrects, the teacher writes S.C., and does not count it as a miscue. A substitution that means the same thing as the word it replaced also does not count as a miscue.

Independent Level

Oral Reading. If, when the student reads the material aloud, it is read with 99 percent grammatical accuracy and in a fluent, rhythmical manner, that student is probably able to read the material independently.

Readers who are having difficulty with their reading (or retelling), exhibit certain behaviors: they might "line" (follow the text with their finger); they might pause in their reading because they are trying to figure out how to pronounce a certain word; some fidgeting might be seen—while either sitting or standing; their voice might "fade" in or out as they read; or the book might be held too close to the face or held tensely. These are only some signs, but they all point to the student's discomfort with what they are reading (or telling).

Comprehension. If the student answers the "story specific" questions or retells the story with at least 90 percent accuracy, reflecting good understanding of the material, he/she understands it at the independent level. Retellings should reflect the organization of the original text, and students should demonstrate some integration of prior knowledge with the new knowledge for it to be at their independent level.

If the material is at the student's independent level, the teacher does not have to supplement it with instruction, but must be aware that the student may need more challenging material. Supplementary reading should be available for students who want to go further than the reading of the basic material, or who finish with it quickly.

Instructional Level

Oral Reading. Reading at this level is also fluent and rhythmic, with 95–98 percent accuracy. There are few deviations from the print, or they are corrected by the reader. There are few behaviors associated with reading difficulty apparent, and rereading improves the reader's performance.

Comprehension. The student answers questions or retells the story with 75–89 percent accuracy. Answers reflect good understanding of the material, with some connection to prior knowledge. Retelling reflects the organization of the original text, somewhat.

If the student is at the instructional level with the material, it is important that the teacher supplement it with instruction and other material. The teacher provides more guidance when the student is working with material at this instructional level. The student's comprehension is monitored closely through questioning and discussion.

Frustration Level

Oral Reading. The oral reading of the material is labored and not fluent. The reader exhibits behaviors associated with difficulty: finger pointing, squinting, lip biting, movement of head from left to right. Oral rereading does not improve over reading at sight. Accuracy is 90 percent or less.

Comprehension. The student answers questions or retells the story with 50 percent or less accuracy. Discussion reveals little prior knowledge of the subject.

If the student is at the frustration level with reading material, the teacher must either make adaptations, such as tape the material or finding material at a more appropriate level for the student. The teacher may also find alternative methods to convey the information to the student—graphic organizers, videos, pictures, role plays.

It is important to keep running records of students' reading in the elementary grades when literacy skills are developing at a very fast pace. It is especially important to do informal reading inventories with students whom you feel are having difficulty reading. They become part of your records and may be used in referring those students for special programs, another common use for formative assessment techniques.

Portfolios

Though portfolio assessment is covered in depth in Chapter 10, it should be mentioned here as a form of formative assessment. A formative portfolio, like all types of formative assessment, has a purpose. If it has no goal, a portfolio may end up looking like a folder of student work. A process portfolio can be a motivator for students, a source of pride in their work, and growth over time. The student should have a voice in deciding what goes into the portfolio, and should also give a rationale for the choices made. Each portfolio can be highly individual and unique, yet adhere to a common set of standards for evaluation. The key is to have the criteria match the goals and content of the portfolio. All of the assessment measures just discussed may be included in a student's portfolio along with work produced by the student in order to give a picture of the whole person.

Summary of Formative Assessment of Students

Formative assessment of students should be a collaborative endeavor between the student and the teacher. It is ongoing, and is the basis for some choices that the teacher makes in curriculum and instruction. It should give the student a positive sense of progress over time, should be natural and authentic, and not conducted under artificially constrained conditions. Formative assessments should be kept in a folder for each student in order to give a picture of that student over time. Each one should have a purpose, and be guided by that purpose, and clear criteria should be set according to the purpose.

► FIELD-BASED CONNECTIONS

Contextual Assessment

The first three chapters of this book were devoted to providing you with enough background knowledge to assess your school placement as an intern. In this chapter, you will be provided with three activities to help you to reach a deeper level of understanding of your context.

The School

Rationale

The school consists of a physical plant and people. They exist and work together to help form the culture of the school. It is important that the intern teacher have:

1. a means of assessing the physical aspects of the school building;
2. the relationships among the people as a means of understanding them; and
3. the impact that they have on curriculum and instruction.

We will use a variety of methods and a variety of sense to collect our data and form our impressions.

Activities

Take a walk around the school building in which you are serving your internship. Ask in the office for a map of the school and test it for accuracy. What would you change? How would you lay it out on the page to make it more appealing to you? Do you think that whomever made the map pondered that question? Note places of particular interest to students. Is there a bulletin board where they tend to congregate? Is there a courtyard? Make your own map of the school. Try to make a map that reflects your values and conception of what a school should be. Share and compare your map with another intern.

Take another walk around the school. This time, take the time to jot down all the sounds that you hear as you travel around the building. Do not focus on transient sounds such as passing children or conversations.

Focus on building sounds: the hum of the furnace or air conditioner or the clanking of the dishes in the cafeteria. Are there bells? When do they ring? Are they a distraction, or does everyone ignore them? Make a copy of your first map and fill in the regular building sounds that you heard on your walk. Place them on the map at the places you heard them. Do you think that any of these sounds might affect teaching and learning in the school? Share your map with another intern who has done the same exercises. Are they similar? Discuss the implications of the sounds of the building for instruction and school climate.

Now that you have been in the school for a couple of weeks, and have purposely experienced it, what would you change about it? What would make it more user-friendly? What would make it a more pleasant place to be, or a more effective setting for learning?

These questions are meant to aid you in the formulation of criteria by which you may assess other school buildings, especially when you are deciding where to apply for work. If, for example, physical comfort is very important to you, and the part of the building in which you work is cold or noisy, you might be uncomfortable and unhappy in your work as a result. If the physical layout of the building hinders the ability of the faculty to get to know one another and you are very gregarious and collaborative, you might not like it. This would be especially true if you were committed to being a professional teacher who is a member of a professional learning community in that school building. Think about what is most important to you. How does your school compare to your ideal? Write a short description to accompany your maps.

The Personnel

List all the people who work in the school. If necessary, place them in their rooms or offices on the map. Write a brief description, in your own words, of what each one does for a job. If there is a school handbook, look for written descriptions of each job. How do the formal descriptions compare with yours? Place the people into these four categories: administration, professional staff, support staff, students.

Try to determine the power relationships between personnel in your school district. Make a chart of the power relationships, placing the most powerful person(s) at the top of the chart and the least powerful at the bottom. Who is at the top? Who is at the bottom? How does this affect learning and instruction in the school? Write a short vignette to accompany your chart of the personnel in the school district.

The Classroom

Look at your own classroom. How are the desks arranged? Where is the teacher's desk? What is on the walls? Are there any nooks where a student can sit in private and read or do independent work? Make a map of the room. Figure 4–1 shows an example of such a map.

Devote one day to observing children in the room. Look at their traffic patterns: where they walk most frequently, where they stop most frequently. What are the norms and regularities of their movements about the room? On the map you made of the room, chart the students' use of it. Are there areas that are utilized very frequently? Are there areas that are

FIGURE 4–1 Classroom Map

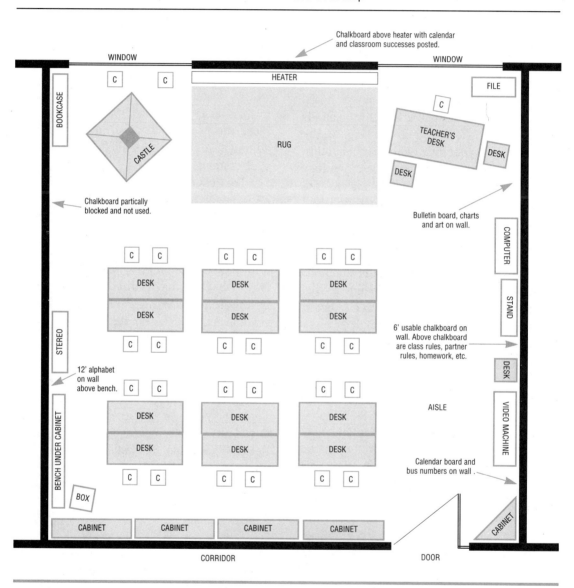

not utilized at all? How could the room be used more efficiently? Write a short description of the students' typical movements in the room to accompany your map.

Devote one day to observing the teacher's movement about the room. Where does the teacher stand when lecturing? How about seat placement when reading aloud or when grading papers? What are the norms and regularities of the teacher's movements around the room? On your map, chart the teacher's use of the room. Write a short vignette about the teacher's typical movements around the room to accompany your map.

The School Climate

There are many factors that make a school a comfortable place to learn. There are also many opinions as to what comfort is, and whether it is a necessary element of school culture. We have taken a particular point of view in this book, and based the following guidelines for assessing school climate on that point of view.

Value for Diversity

1. Do all students, male and female, of a diversity of racial, social, cultural, and ethnic groups have access to and actually experience an equal opportunity to learn in school?

2. Do students and other members of the school culture, including parents, show positive attitudes toward different cultural, racial, ethnic, religious, and gender groups?

3. Are the students involved in important decision-making? Do they serve on planning teams and committees? Do they have input into curriculum, instruction, and assessment?

4. Are students involved in peer mediation and in resolving their own conflicts through peaceful non-violent means? (Adapted from Banks, 1989)

High Academic Standards

1. Do students value good grades, or do you hear terms like "nerd" and "dweeb" used to describe those who achieve well in school?

2. Do students say that they feel challenged by the curriculum, or do they say that school is boring and not hard enough?

3. Is student work displayed in showcases in rooms and hallways? Does the faculty express pride in the accomplishments of students?

4. Are students in classrooms actively engaged in learning tasks, or are they passively listening to the teacher lecturing and talking *at* them?

Professionalism

1. Do teachers in the teachers' room talk about professional activities and their teaching as well as their personal lives?

2. Do they speak of the students in a caring, professional manner, or do they gossip about them?

3. Is there a professional library at the school? Is it or the materials in it used often?

4. Are there current professional journals in the teachers' lounge and library?

Value for Creativity

1. Is there a vital arts program in the school?

2. Where student work is displayed, is it all on the same theme, in the same format or is there a variety?

3. Do criteria for evaluation of student projects and performances include criteria related to originality?

Caring

1. Do you see teachers spending time with students after school, giving extra help, coaching teams or lending an ear?

2. Is there a community service component to the overall school program?

3. Are adult members of the school community visible in the hallways, and interacting positively with students—not just telling them to behave or to be quiet or disciplining them most of the time?

4. Do the students treat each other, and speak to each other, respectfully in the hallways, the classrooms, and on school grounds?

The Teacher

Throughout the course of the year, you will get to know your mentor teacher very well. For this activity, observe the teacher for one day, focusing on the following:

Beginning of the Day/Lesson

- How is the day begun?
- What does the teacher do?
- What preparation is made for the start of the day?
- How is a new lesson begun?
- What is written on the board or elsewhere to start a lesson?
- How is the students' attention focused?

Teacher Style

- Where does the teacher habitually stand or sit?
- What is the primary tone of voice used in instruction?
- What is the primary tone of voice used in talking with students about their work?
- What tone of voice is used when disciplining the class?
- How often is eye contact made with the students?
- Does the teacher call on boys or girls more often, or is everyone called on equally?
- Is the teacher business-like or informal in interactions with the students?

Introducing New Material

- How is a new concept or new material introduced to the class?
- Are questions asked of the students?
- What is the general climate in the room when new material is being presented?

End of the Day/Lesson

- How does the teacher wind down at the end of the lesson?
- Is the material reviewed or summarized?
- Does the tone of the class change toward the end of the class/day? If so, how?
- Does the teacher model the use of the material presented in the lesson before it ends?
- What is the teacher's response to the ringing of the bell? The students?

Theories in Use

- Based on what you observed, what do you think the teacher's philosophy of education is?

- How do you think the teacher views the students?

- What is the most important concept to teach, according to this teacher's philosophy, based on your observations?

- If you asked the teacher what was most important to teach, do you think it would be the same thing that you deduced from the observations? Why or why not?

Using the preceding information, write a short vignette of your mentor teacher. If you feel that you can, share it with the teacher. Is there agreement with your assessment or disagreement?

Portfolio Activities

1. Ask your mentor teacher the schedule for introducing a new topic or concept. Ask if you can conduct a pre-assessment and do a structured brainstorm or discussion with the class or with a small group of students. Now, with the teacher's permission, assess their prior knowledge and set some goals for instruction according to your assessment. Go over these goals with your mentor teacher, and see if there is agreement.

2. While the class is involved in reading a story or textbook, choose a student in the class and assess the child's level of oral reading and comprehension. Try to do this during a conference time or other time when it will not stand out as an unusual experience.

    Once you have found the student's level, write a plan for what you think the student needs to do to reach a deeper level of understanding of the material. Again, share this with your mentor, and ask for more suggestions.

3. Make a final draft of the case study of your context; include your maps and description of the building, the chart and description of the school personnel and the power relationships between them, the classroom description and map, the vignette of your mentor teacher, and your description of the school climate. Place these in your portfolio.

▶ CHAPTER CLOSURE

Summary

This chapter provided a brief overview of authentic assessment and the kinds of assessments you might use early in your field placement. These assessments are useful when working with students and in the school context. They can be applied to any situation, but must be developed by you to meet that situation. These assessments are not one-shot, like many tests, and they are not meant to compare one student to another, or one school to another. They are to help you get to know your students and your school. Through this quest, you will also get to know yourself as an emerging educator.

Chapter Discussion Questions

1. Reflect on your own educational experiences. Discuss the methods of formative assessment used when you were in school.

2. Do the assessments of students included in this chapter reflect what you want to know about your students? How would you change them?

3. Do the assessments of the school and school culture reflect your priorities? Discuss the ways that you would change them.

▶ REFERENCES

Banks, J. A. (1989). Multicultural education: Characteristics and goals. In J. A. Banks & C. A. McGee Banks (Eds.), *Multicultural education: Issues and perspectives*. Boston, MA: Allyn and Bacon.

Cockrum, W. A. & Castillo, M. (1991). Whole language assessment and evaluation strategies. In B. Harp (Ed.), *Assessment and evaluation in whole language programs*, 73–86. Norwood, MA: Christopher-Gordon.

Eberwien, L. (1973). What do book choices indicate? *Journal of Reading, 17,* 186–191.

Goodman, K. (1986). *What's whole in whole language.* Portsmouth, NH: Heinemann.

Herman, J. L., Aschbacher, P. R., & Winters, L. (1992). *A practical guide to alternative assessment.* Alexandria, VA: ASCD.

Johnson, M. S., Kress, R. A., & Pikulski, J. J. (1987). *Informal reading inventories,* 2nd Edition. Newark, DE: International Reading Association.

Madaus, G. F. & Kellaghan, T. (1992). Curriculum evaluation and assessment. In P. W. Jackson, (Ed.). *Handbook of research on curriculum.* New York: Macmillan.

Paratore, J. R. & Indrisano, R. (1987). Intervention assessment of reading comprehension. *Reading Teacher, 40,* 778–783.

Popham, W. J. (1993). Circumventing the high costs of authentic assessment. *Phi Delta Kappan, 74*(6), 470–473.

Worthen, B. R. (1993). Critical issues that will determine the future of alternative assessment. *Phi Delta Kappan, 74*(6), 450–454.

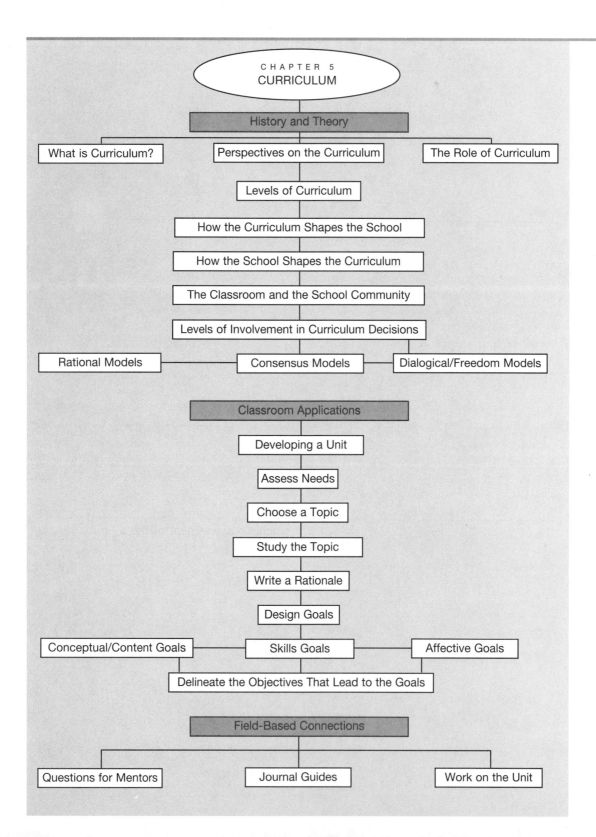

CHAPTER 5
CURRICULUM

History and Theory

What is Curriculum? | Perspectives on the Curriculum | The Role of Curriculum

Levels of Curriculum

How the Curriculum Shapes the School

How the School Shapes the Curriculum

The Classroom and the School Community

Levels of Involvement in Curriculum Decisions

Rational Models | Consensus Models | Dialogical/Freedom Models

Classroom Applications

Developing a Unit

Assess Needs

Choose a Topic

Study the Topic

Write a Rationale

Design Goals

Conceptual/Content Goals | Skills Goals | Affective Goals

Delineate the Objectives That Lead to the Goals

Field-Based Connections

Questions for Mentors | Journal Guides | Work on the Unit

5

Curriculum

Introduction

The teacher acts as a mediator between the curriculum and the students, negotiating between the written document and the human needs of the individual learners (Bolin, 1987). Much of the time the professional teacher develops the written curriculum itself, negotiating between that document and the students. Notice that there is a distinct difference between planning day-to-day or week-to-week in a lesson plan book (short term) and developing curriculum (long term). The teacher who develops curriculum units plans with long-term goals and outcomes in mind. Deciding on goals and outcomes focuses the teacher's curriculum and instruction and fosters a deep understanding in the students. Deep understanding is the ability to use a knowledge base of facts and information to suit one's needs. For example, in preparing for a debate, a student needs to research both sides of the issue while honing the skills of logical argument.

The teacher uses creative thinking skills, writing skills, problem-solving skills and assessment, and evaluation skills in developing curriculum for a specific classroom community and setting. The skills involved in curriculum development are higher order thinking skills, and the enactment of the curriculum, with an act of creative performance, and with some improvisation, are based on the teacher's assessment of the attendant conditions. Compare all of these to the teacher who strictly follows a textbook, has the children read and answer the questions at the end of each chapter, and presents the material in a lecture format for reinforcement. The latter process can be likened to following a recipe. Some research has shown that in a majority of classrooms in the United States, especially at the secondary level, this is still the prevailing method of instruction (Goodlad, 1979, 1984; Sizer, 1984). As a professional teacher committed to practice in an exemplary way, part of your charge is to develop curriculum that is appropriate and beneficial for both you and your students. Knowledge of curriculum issues, theory, and development is the nucleus of your professional knowledge base as a teacher (Zumwalt, 1989). For this reason, the curriculum chapters form the core around which all of the other chapters of this text revolve.

▶ THEORY

What is Curriculum?

The word curriculum comes from Latin, originally meaning the course to run in a race. We still use the word "course" as a metaphor to symbolize one definition of curriculum. The concept of the school curriculum can best be exemplified in the ways that schools answer nine guiding curriculum questions:

1. What should be taught?

2. To whom should it be taught?

3. Why should it be taught?

4. How should it be taught?

5. When (for how long; and in what order?) should it be taught?

6. How shall we know that learning took place?

7. What resources will be used (textbooks, materials, videos, laser disks, etc.)?

8. Under what conditions will the curriculum be enacted? What groupings (cooperative, homogeneous, individual) will be used?

9. What aspects of the classroom environment (desk arrangements, classroom ecology) will be featured in the curriculum?

What the curriculum turns out to be is based on a series of choices made in choosing answers to these questions.

Until the twentieth century, curriculum was primarily viewed as content and evolving subject matter; the "what" of schooling. It really wasn't until the rise of the progressive and behaviorist movements in the late nineteenth and early twentieth centuries that other factors, such as student diversity, societal needs, and even instructional strategies were included in the prevailing conception of curriculum (Kliebard, 1992). There are many definitions of curriculum. They can be placed on a continuum from the narrowly focused to the broad. For instance, a narrow focus is one which defines curriculum as a plan for disciplined study in five academic subject areas: English, mathematics, science, history, and foreign language (Bestor, 1956). This kind of definition leaves no room for the nuances added to that plan by the teacher and students in a classroom setting. An example of a broad definition would be the one put forth by Giles et al. (1942), "the *total* (author italics) experience with which the school deals in educating young people" (p. 293). This, of course, could include recess, lunch, and extra-curricular activities. In fact, several studies have determined that the extra-curriculum, depending on the type of activity, exerts a significant influence on students (Dressel & Lehmann, 1968; Spady, 1971; Rudnitski, 1993; Berk, 1992).

Definitions of curriculum may be as simple as the terms we use to describe it, and may range from those based on the perspective of the society, to the locality, to the school, to the classroom, and to the individual (Figure 5–1).

FIGURE 5–1   Word Map Definition of Curriculum

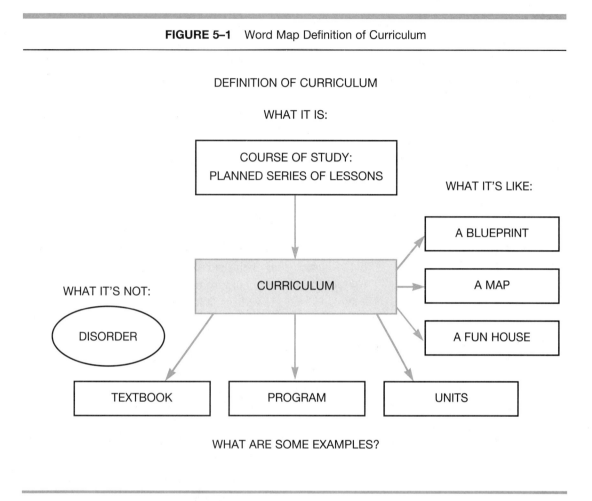

Reprinted with permission, R. M. Schwartz and T. E. Raphael (1985), "Concept of Definition: A Key to Improving Students' Vocabulary," *Reading Teacher*, November, 198-203.

Twentieth century definitions of curriculum depend more on the perspectives from which they are derived than on their place in history. For example, Franklin Bobbitt, in the first text on the subject in 1918, took a rather broad view of the curriculum in his two-sided view:

(1) The entire range of experiences, both undirected and directed, concerned in unfolding the abilities of the individual; or (2) it is the series of consciously directed training experiences that the schools use for completing and perfecting the unfoldment.

Bobbitt's broad conception of the curriculum first cited was based in the perspective of fostering individual development through all experiences and through planned school experiences. Other conceptions take different perspectives based on other needs.

Though John Dewey (1902) once defined curriculum in rather narrow terms as "the course of study met in school [emphasis mine] [which] presents material stretching back indefinitely in time and extending outward indefinitely in space" (p. 5), he saw the curriculum as being derived primarily from the needs of society. Two years before Bobbitt's book, Dewey (1916) wrote, "The scheme of a curriculum must take account of the adaptation of studies to the needs of existing community life; it must select with the intention of improving the life we live in common so that the future shall be better than the past" (p. 125). This is not to say that the needs of the individual were ignored by Dewey. His primary perspective, however, was social reconstructionist, one which places the needs of society as the primary motivating force in curriculum and teaching in schools.

Perspectives on the Curriculum

In his classic book, *Basic Principles of Curriculum and Instruction,* Ralph W. Tyler (1949) stated that the first step in the thorough study of curriculum and instruction, whether on a global level or on the school or classroom level, is to ask the question, "What educational purposes should the school seek to attain?" (p. 1). Each curriculum developer answers this question from a certain perspective based primarily on the needs of each of the levels of curriculum: the society, the subject matter, the learner, the skills to be taught, or the curriculum itself, when answering the nine basic guiding curriculum questions. This perspective is reflected in every aspect of the curriculum: from the goals and objectives to the activities and instructional strategies to the evaluation plan.

Kliebard (1986) asserted that in the development of the American curriculum in this century there have been four interest groups, each with its own curriculum perspective. He concluded that the prevalent curriculum in America is actually a loose conglomeration of all of the perspectives, based on an unarticulated compromise between the four points of view. It is important to consider this point when developing one's own curriculum units. Almost all curricula represent some form of compromise between the perspectives and is not a one-sided view, though one perspective may dominate.

Eisner and Vallance (1974) delineated "five orientations" in viewing curriculum, which serve as guides in our exploration of the topic: the development of cognitive processes, academic rationalism, personal relevance, social adaptation and social reconstruction, and curriculum as technology. Other terms used to describe them are perspectives on, or conceptions of, the curriculum—or curriculum paradigms. Each of these perspectives influences the curriculum by serving as a value framework for the choices made when answering the nine guiding curriculum questions. Each perspective does this by placing more value on one aspect of the curriculum than others (Figure 5–2).

Each of Eisner and Vallance's perspectives on the curriculum is explained in the following:

FIGURE 5–2 Emphases of Five Perspectives on the Curriculum

PERSPECTIVE	EMPHASIS
COGNITIVE PROCESSES	Processes, Skills, Learning
ACADEMIC RATIONALIST	Disciplines Subject Matter
PERSONAL RELEVANCE	Individual
SOCIAL RECONSTRUCTION	Society
CURRICULUM AS TECHNOLOGY	Science of Curriculum Development

Derived from E. Eisner and E. Vallance (Eds.) (1972), *Conflicting Conceptions of the Curriculum,* Berkeley, CA: McCutchan.

Cognitive Processes

Cognitive processes is the orientation which places cognitive skills at the center of importance. The purposes of the school implied in a cognitive process curriculum are "(1) to help children learn how to learn and (2) to provide them with the opportunities to use and strengthen the variety of intellectual faculties they possess" (p. 62). This curriculum perspective emphasizes *process* over *content*.

The kinds of programs based on the cognitive processes perspective are creative problem-solving programs, thinking skills programs, or programs based on the actual modes of inquiry of a discipline. Bloom's Taxonomy provides a guideline for this perspective and for the cognitive aspects of any curriculum. First published in the book, *Taxonomy of Educational Objectives: Handbook 1, The Cognitive Domain* (1956), the taxonomy presents a hierarchy which moves from lower levels of cognitive functioning to higher, more complex processes. The levels of cognition delineated by Bloom and his colleagues, from lowest to highest are:

- Knowledge: the recall of content (information, concepts, skills, principles);

- Comprehension: the understanding of content;

- Application: use of content in planned classroom experiences;

- Analysis: study through breaking down content to its component parts;

- Synthesis: seeing relationships within content, processes, affect or among different areas and/or aspects of study and combining them; and

- Evaluation: judging the value of content, processes, and ideas through establishing criteria and standards.

Many have correlated Bloom's Taxonomy to verbs used to write behavioral objectives for students and to products and activities to be produced by them through experiences in the curriculum (Figure 5-3).

These charts help teachers to plan a variety of effective learning experiences and, when appropriate, sequence them from the lower levels to the higher levels. That has been shown to be the appropriate sequence for most curricula, because it models much of our own thinking a good deal of the time. When the curriculum models natural ways of thinking it helps the learner to process information more efficiently and enhances understanding (Taba, 1962). Bloom's Taxonomy is used as a tool in designing curriculum for that reason.

It is important to note that Bloom's Taxonomy was part one of a two-part handbook. Krathwohl edited the second volume, which dealt with the affective domain. This is the domain which involves values, beliefs, and feelings. Since schools do not generally emphasize these aspects of individuals, Krathwohl's taxonomy has been largely ignored by curriculum developers. Though this is changing, we are far from fully integrating these issues into curriculum goals. The affective domain would almost certainly not be included by a cognitive processes curriculum developer (Figure 5-4).

Academic Rationalism

Academic rationalism is one of the oldest perspectives on the curriculum. It is epitomized by Mortimer Adler's *Paideia Proposal* (1983), a philosophical treatise on education in which he advocates the same traditional, academic course of study with the same goals for all. It embodies what is essentially a classical education.

The academic rationalist views the curriculum as the means of transmitting the great ideas and the great works created by humankind. A primary objective of an academic rationalist program is the development of rational thought through the study of the great products of Western civilization. This kind of education was once reserved only for those in the upper-socioeconomic classes. Having the same goals for all insures that those who would normally not be eligible for such a program receive access to the same high level of knowledge. Thus, the rationale for this perspective, though it centers on the disciplines, is social democracy.

Personal Relevance

Personal relevance is the orientation that focuses on the perceived needs and interests of the individual student. Without the direct input of the student, the curriculum seems to be an imposed plan based on someone else's conception of what is important. It is therefore irrelevant to the learner.

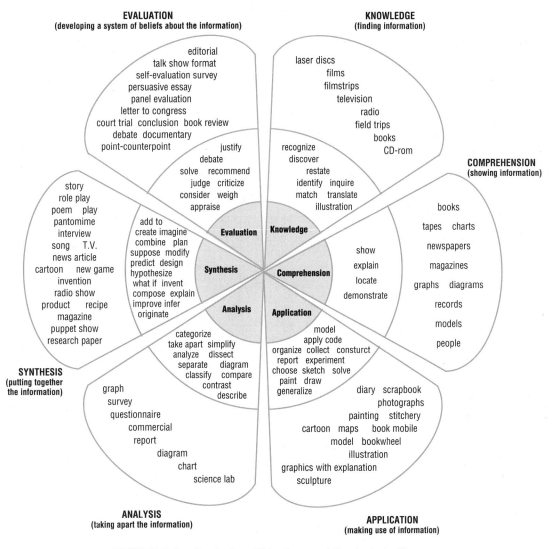

FIGURE 5–3   Curriculum Objectives and Products in Bloom

In a curriculum based on the personal relevance point of view, and speaking theoretically, the teacher and student relate in ways which bring forth the needs of the student to the teacher. Once the student's needs have been identified, the teacher's role is to connect the student with the best materials in order to help the students actualize their potential.

This perspective has been criticized for its emphasis on "felt" student needs. How do young children know their needs? In articulat-

---

FIGURE 5–4 The Affective Domain Taxonomy

RECEIVING

- Awareness
- Willingness to receive
- Controlled or selected attention

RESPONDING

- Acquiescence in responding
- Willingness to respond
- Satisfaction in response

VALUING

- Acceptance of a value
- Preference for a value
- Commitment (Conviction)

ORGANIZATION

- Conceptualization of a value
- Organization of a value system

CHARACTERIZATION BY A VALUE OR VALUE SYSTEM

- Generalized
- Character

Adapted from D. Krathwohl et al. (1956). *Taxonomy of Educational Objectives, Handbook II: The Affective Domain,* New York: David McKay.

ing this type of curriculum, the teacher, assessing the needs of the children through interaction, focuses on the present most of the time. This makes long-term planning very difficult and frequently leads to a fragmented curriculum. Schools ascribing to a personal relevance perspective are called "free schools." A. S. Neill's *Summerhill* (1960) was probably the most famous example of this type of school.

Social Adaptation/
Social Reconstruction

Social Adaptation. Social adaptation places the needs of society at the center of determining the purpose of the school. The first, social adaptation, views society as needing little change. The student must change and adapt to the norms and needs of the larger group. In this curriculum view, the school is a vehicle for reproducing the society and basically maintaining the status quo.

The Social Reconstructionist. The social reconstructionist views the school as a vehicle for improving society. This implies a basic dissatisfaction with the dominant society. Peace education programs and community service projects directly exemplify a social reconstructionist perspective. The perspective, however, may be imbedded in what appears to be a traditional curriculum. The problems of society may be addressed through the disciplines of the curriculum, which is used "as a tool for dealing with what is socially significant" (Eisner, 1979, p. 78).

Curriculum as Technology. Curriculum as technology is a view of curriculum that is quite widespread in practice. In this paradigm, the curriculum is developed to actualize predetermined ends: goals or outcomes and behavioral objectives. Behavioral objectives are statements describing ways in which students' behavior will be changed through the learning experiences in the curriculum. Goals or outcomes, behaviors which will be exhibited by all students, are decided upon before one writes the curriculum. What is decided upon is heavily couched in the writer's "conception" of the purpose of the school. The writer is usually a curriculum- or subject-area expert who is far removed from the actual classroom context in which the curriculum will be articulated, and not the teacher who is in it. This leads to standardization of the curriculum.

According to Eisner, this is the predominant curriculum paradigm, and several of its proponents who have influenced curriculum theory have been cited here: Bobbitt, Tyler, Taba, Bloom. Eisner (1979) includes John Dewey in the list. We do not, since Dewey argued different positions at different times, advocating a perspective balanced between all levels of influence, with an emphasis on society.

It is clear that one's perspective on the curriculum affects the nature of the content and the types of materials and instructional strategies the teacher uses. It is therefore important that the teacher has a clear personal perspective on a curriculum in order to provide a varied, balanced program of curriculum and instruction. Choosing to follow one view, all or most of the time, would not be in the best interest of the diverse population of students. Figure 5–5 presents perspectives correlated with instructional strategies chosen most often for each point of view.

How does a teacher determine personal perspective on the curriculum? The answer is that this is done through continuous, personal reflection on one's practice and feelings. This is why the reflective journal started in Chapter One is so important. A teacher who does not reflect may not even be aware of having a perspective. This lack of awareness could lead to less intentionality in instruction and a hidden curriculum that the teacher does not want, over which the teacher has no control.

FIGURE 5–5 Instructional Strategies Correlated with Curriculum Perspectives

STRATEGIES	PERSPECTIVES				
	Cognitive Processes	Academic Rational	Personal Relevance	Social Reconstruction	Technical, Scientific
Direct Instruction	X	X	X	X	X
Lecture		X			X
Modeling	X		X	X	X
Textbook		X			X
Seatwork	X	X			X
GROUP					
Discussion		X	X	X	X
Coop. Learning			X	X	
Role Play			X	X	
Learning Centers	X		X		
Projects	X		X	X	
INDIVIDUAL					
Inquiry	X		X	X	
Learning Styles	X		X	X	
Decision-Making	X		X	X	
Problem-Solving	X		X	X	

X = Very Suitable

The Role of the Curriculum

One problem with a heavily technical or scientific view of curriculum development is the tendency to lead to standardization, frequent testing at low levels of cognition (multiple choice or true/false tests of knowledge, for instance), and an emphasis on the outcomes and not the processes of learning. It creates a "hidden" curriculum which teaches students that tests (light learning) and not knowledge (deep learning) are important. Another danger of this curriculum view is that it takes control away from the teacher and students for whom it was written. The curriculum could be perceived as being depersonalized and irrelevant, routine, and low level. The teacher, relying on experts, could view the curriculum as a *prescription* rather than a guide—which is loosely followed or not follow at all—depending on the needs of the micro-society in the classroom.

The hidden meaning in classroom interactions gained prominence in the 1970s (e.g., Jackson, 1968; Rist, 1970; Vallance, 1973–74). As the curriculum field has evolved, the concept of "layers" of curriculum has gained acceptance. It was a theme running through almost every chapter of the 1992 *Handbook of Research on Curriculum* (Berk). The terms for the layers of curriculum (Figure 5–6) used here will be:

- Intended
- Expressed
- Hidden
- Experienced

The Intended Curriculum

The "intended" curriculum is the written curriculum document. On a societal level, it can be a national curriculum or a state syllabus. At the local level, it can be a school district's curriculum guides, textbooks or even a teacher's lesson plan book. It is what is intended to be taught, how it is intended to be done, and under what intended circumstances. The intended curriculum is rarely followed exactly by a teacher. The teacher adds personal style, best tried and true methods, and personal anecdotes. For this reason, the next layer of curriculum is called the expressed curriculum.

The Expressed Curriculum

The "expressed" curriculum has been called the enacted or manifest curriculum elsewhere (Erikson & Schultz, 1992). We use the term expressed because we feel that teachers express themselves through the *enactment* of the curriculum in their teaching. The teacher who has a good sense of humor will make jokes, while the teacher who chronically barks orders will express the intended curriculum in just that manner. The words "expressed curriculum" give personal meaning to the articulation of curriculum.

The Hidden Curriculum

The hidden "curriculum" is the curriculum that is invisibly taught by the interactions of the teacher with the students. The teacher who always sets the agenda for the class, who always decides what and how they will do things is modeling a mistrust of the students' judgment. The teacher who holds lower expectations for children who are on free lunch or who are more proficient in a language

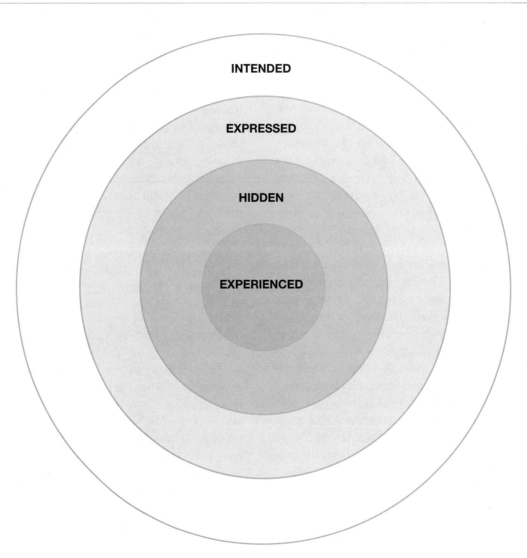

FIGURE 5–6 Layers of Curriculum

other than English is also expressing a hidden curriculum. These interactions teach students just as much as the intended curriculum intended to teach, and some of these hidden lessons may have more long-lasting and pervasive effects.

The Experienced Curriculum

The experienced "curriculum" is the students' actual experience in the classroom. There has not been a lot of research done in this area, though curriculum specialists view it as needed for the development of the field (Erikson & Schultz, 1992). This is the meaning the students actually derive from the combination of layers of curriculum to which they are exposed. Though students rarely actually *see* the "intended" curriculum, they experience it through the "expressed" curriculum. As the teacher articulates what has to be done, the intended curriculum is shared with the students. "We have to cover the Middle Ages before spring break or we'll be behind." "For the next three weeks, we will be preparing for the district-wide testing. The principal will be sending home a message to your parents with tips to help you be successful." "Be sure to eat breakfast the morning of the test." These statements express values, even though they may not reflect the actual values of the teacher.

In the "expressed" curriculum, the students also experience the teacher's values. "The standardized tests are coming up, but I want to finish our projects so we can start something new. We'll go over test-taking skills in the period before lunch sometime this week." This expresses the value the teacher places on both the projects *and* the tests. Students learn from this curriculum as well.

Students experience the "hidden" curriculum throughout the day in all their interactions and relationships in school. An entire school may have a hidden curriculum expressed in not-so-subtle ways. I once asked a teacher in an inner-city high school with a history of violence what adaptations were made for the gifted. He said, "No one thinks any of the students in my school are gifted." The hidden curriculum had been internalized by everyone.

On an individual level, a student may feel like a failure because of trouble with reading and is reading "several grade levels below everyone else in the room." The teacher may have made that statement to both student and parents, and may require a "remedial reading" class where students describe themselves in terms of "I can't read." Look at the all the negative statements in quotations in this paragraph. What would you have felt about yourself if you had been that student?

Thus, the experienced curriculum is the sum total of the intended, expressed, and hidden curricula, and is different for each and every student. Students bring their own personalities, background knowledge, and "baggage" to every learning experience. Each interprets the three outer layers of the curriculum in a very personal way. Though the experienced curriculum may be similar to that of others, the student described in the previous paragraph derives an individual sense of meaning from those experiences. Another student encountering the same experiences might react with anger and increased motivation and learn to read at all costs.

How the Curriculum Shapes the School

It has also been asserted that the traditional curriculum view leaves those who are not in the mainstream of society by the wayside (Apple, 1979, 1986; Giroux, 1981); disenfranchises teachers and students (Apple, 1986); and marginalizes certain subject areas and fields of knowledge (Eisner, 1992). We have discussed some of these issues in the chapters on parents and community and the school culture.

The traditional curriculum marginalizes some subject areas in very subtle, almost invisible ways. For example, the arts are not required throughout high school, and when a student takes an art course, it is typically for a once- or twice-a-week class, and thus given less time (and therefore less importance) in the schedule. The arts are also the subjects most readily cut from the budget when monetary choices are made. The implicit message in these actions is that the arts are not an important or valued part of the curriculum. That message, or lack of value, though unarticulated, has a tremendous impact on the nature of the curriculum, teaching, and the types of knowledge that it implies are the *most* valued.

When a narrow conception of valued knowledge dominates the curriculum, those who learn it most easily and in the most valued ways (usually demonstrated through testing) are implicitly esteemed as the "elite." Until very recently, they were put into upper "tracks" in schools, given the best instruction, and afforded opportunities for enrichment. Those for whom learning the *valued* knowledge is difficult are relegated to the lower tracks, where instruction is "basic skills" and primarily at the lowest levels of cognition (Oakes, 1985). This practice of tracking students denies those who are in the lower tracks equal access to the valued knowledge (Oakes, Gamoran, & Page, 1992; Passow, 1988). Particularly in the first half of this century, tracking helped to create a virtual student caste system within the school (Ogbu, 1978). The lower tracks were assigned to the most demoralized teachers who, in turn, viewed the students with little hope and communicated this through their curriculum and teaching expectations (Rist, 1970). The low-achieving students were essentially told that they would not succeed; a self-fulfilling prophecy (Rosenthal & Jacobson, 1968).

What does this have to do with you as a beginning teacher? Many vestiges of this history continue to exist in schools. As a new teacher with no seniority, you may be assigned to a class or school that more senior teachers did not want because they viewed it as too difficult or demanding. It is important that you are aware of the larger forces that may be influencing your situation, and that you maintain high expectations for all your students, even though others may sometimes try to get you to do otherwise.

Tracking and its accompanying ills will not affect you and the students in your classroom if you follow these basis ideas: maintain high expectations, use a wide variety of groupings, and differentiate your curriculum and teaching for a variety of factors. Maintaining high expectations for all your students means to literally expect that they *will learn*. An idea which helped to revolutionize the field of reading was the concept that we expect all babies to learn to talk (and the vast majority eventually do); but when children are in school, there are some who are not expected (for example) to learn to read (Butler & Turbill, 1987; Cambourne, 1988). Communicate the expectation that all your students will learn through both the explicit and the hidden curricula as well as through your teaching.

By using a wide variety of grouping patterns, the impact of homogeneous grouping is lessened. You can group children according to the projects they choose to do, the guiding questions they choose to work on answering, where they want to sit. You can even group students together with friends. Who says that friends do not learn from one another? Do remember, though, that the occasional homogeneous group is fine if it will enhance the students' learning.

The reasons to differentiate curriculum and teaching vary. You may want to differentiate for learning style, interest, strength of mind or one of the multiple intelligences (Gardner, 1983), and for the cultures represented in the students in your class.

These issues are discussed in depth in Chapters 3 and 8.

How the Curriculum is Shaped by the School

The system of tracking was designed as an adaptation for the convenience of (1) teachers: who generally insisted that they could not teach to groups with a wide range of abilities, and the convenience of (2) the school: which could schedule tracks easily and assign texts at the appropriate levels. Tracking also served to sort students into groups of "winners" and "losers," with specific cultural, racial, ethnic, and gender groups fitting neatly into each category. (See Chapter 3.) It has its roots in the social efficiency movement at the turn of the century which affected the prevailing conceptions of curriculum for much of the rest of this century (Franklin, 1974; Spring, 1976). Educators are more aware than ever of the mechanisms which sort students, and practices are changing rapidly to address these issues.

One thing that has taken hold is the idea that the philosophy of the school drives the rest of the activities of the school. Many schools have developed statements of philosophy and "mission statements." These statements of philosophy also guide curriculum and teaching, and affect the philosophy statements and rationales for all curricula developed by the school.

A school placing high value on standardized test scores will gear its curriculum and instruction toward success on that type of test (Darling-Hammond & Snyder, 1992; Madaus & Kellaghan, 1992). One curious aspect of this is that the high value for those tests might not be expressed in the school's philosophy or mission statement, but could be expressed in the hidden or implicit curriculum enacted on a daily basis. It is for this reason that it is essential that one carefully observe the curriculum expressed by the teachers through their choices of materials and instructional strategies. In Chapter 8 there is a guide for observing mentors and other teachers when looking for the expressed curriculum.

The Curriculum and the Classroom Community

Each classroom is a microscopic version of society, and since the teacher is largely responsible for shaping the classroom and curriculum, the teacher's philosophy is extremely important. One way to insure that your classroom is a model of democracy and not a factory or, worse, dictatorship, is to involve your students in many of the decisions made on a daily basis. (See Chapters 3 and 4). These decisions run the gamut from deciding where to put up the list of classroom helpers to directions the curriculum will take. (For comprehensive descriptions of classrooms where students take part in curricular decisions, see Stratemeyer et al., (1948), *Developing a Curriculum for Modern Living*.)

Children know that some decisions are more important than others and it is therefore critical that the teacher involve the students in making some of the more important decisions. Deciding the order in which to experience a series of activities in a curriculum is a much more important decision than who should collect the test papers, for instance. It is more meaningful for students and increases the value of their learning if they are involved in curricular decisions. The hidden curriculum in this case is that their ideas matter, and they have some control. This is a consensus model of curriculum development.

Levels of Involvement in Curriculum Decisions

We have discussed the effect of the standardization of curriculum and teaching on groups of students, the role and expectations of the teacher, and on the curriculum itself.

Rational/Control Models

The rational/control models of curriculum development are the most common in schools today (McNeil, 1985). Rational curricula are defined and developed by experts in subject areas and by curriculum specialists. Most school districts prescribe curricula and reinforce their use through standardized testing and standardized evaluation of teachers (see Chapter 4). In many districts, the teacher must write the aim or objective of the lesson on the blackboard so that the children know what is expected of them (and so that a visiting administrator may see it). This specification of a teacher behavior exerts control over the curriculum and leads even more strongly toward a *control model* of curriculum and teaching.

Consensus Models

Consensus models of curriculum are more democratic in nature and involve the students in the decision-making (McNeil, 1985). The level of consensus, like the level of control, can occur by degree from very little to very active involvement. The difference is essentially in the number of decisions in which students are invited to participate and the nature of the decisions. If a class is planning to do a thematic unit based on an organizing theme and helps to choose the theme, that is active involvement. They are not as involved when the teacher chooses a theme and asks the class to choose between two possible novels related to the theme.

Dialogical/Freire Models

In dialogical/Freire models, the students actually let the teacher know what they want to learn through an ongoing dialogue. This is a common model in enrichment programs where students define independent study projects based on talents and interest. It is also an appropriate model for social reconstructionist curricula (McNeil, 1985). In this model, there is little concern for curriculum mandates imposed at the state, local or national levels. The main concern is for the needs and desires of the student, who is considered to be expert enough to delineate scholastic needs.

The Roles of the Student and the Teacher. As one moves from the control models to the least controlled models, the roles of the student and the teacher change dramatically. In the rational/control model, the teacher is viewed as the source of knowledge and direction. The teacher here is the "sage on a stage." The control model teacher primarily uses frontal methods of teaching and objective methods of testing. This teacher relies on textbooks and other prepared materials provided by the district.

The student in the control models, on the other hand, is placed in a very passive role. This is an ancient model which assumes that the student is an "empty vessel" waiting to be filled. Freire (1970) called this the "banking concept of education." Teachers make deposits of information into the students who accumulate an education much in the same manner that one amasses a fortune.

In the consensus models of curriculum, the role of the teacher is one of "guide by the side." In this case, the teacher is there as a resource for the students, connecting them with the appropriate materials, and helping them to derive meaning from the curriculum. The student in this model is an active participant in the curriculum choices made, with the strong advisement of the teacher.

In dialogical/Freire models, the student takes the lead in asking for help, be it in the form of information or resources. The teacher observes the student and advises, but does not take the initiative unless the student asks for it. Dialogical/Freire models are difficult to implement in the typical American classroom, though they work in guiding students in curriculum-based projects and special programs. Students must be familiar with decision-making and participation in the process of curriculum development, or they will need to develop the skills as part of the required prior knowledge for such a curriculum.

Across the continuum of involvement, the teacher is the acknowledged expert in curriculum. The difference is not in expertise on the

part of the teacher, but in the actual level of control exerted on the curriculum by outside forces. In fact, the less outer control, the more expertise demanded on the part of the teacher.

Conclusion to Theory

In this brief introduction to the history-rich field of curriculum studies, we attempted to give a sense of how theory and our past affect the curriculum and instruction in our classrooms today. We have seen that curriculum decisions are made at several levels, and that the farther away they are from the classroom, the less control is exerted on the curriculum by the teacher and students, the people for whom the curriculum is intended.

In a sense, we are the victims of our collective past, and many practices which may have fostered inequality in classrooms have lingered to today. The first step in addressing the mistakes of the past is being aware of them. It is only through awareness and then caring that the teacher can make conscious decisions to improve practice and to make a commitment to professional virtue.

We have also seen that curriculum is many things to many people. One's view of curriculum depends not only on one's place in the school culture, but also on one's philosophy and point of view. If one believes that the curriculum is meant to convey the great works of Western civilization, then one probably espouses accompanying classic instructional strategies as well. If one believes that the curriculum should teach students how to think, then the view of curriculum and instruction changes.

The point is *not* that one has a static perspective on the curriculum, but rather that it is fluid. Most teachers in the course of the day exhibit several perspectives, depending on the subject matter taught and the instructional strategies used.

▶ CLASSROOM
▶ APPLICATIONS

A Rational Model of Curriculum Development

Curriculum development is a process. It is like the writing process in that one retraces one's steps in re-reading, editing, and revising. It is also like riding a bicycle in that one is really doing all the steps in the process at the same time. If we thought of riding a bicycle only in terms of balance, we would never get it to go anywhere. Yet if we thought of riding a bicycle only in terms of pedaling, we'd fall over.

Developing a Unit

Assess Needs

The first step in developing a unit is to assess one's needs. If you are required to teach your state's history in fourth grade, then that is a need. If you have a passion for your hobby of making and launching model rockets, you might want to incorporate that into your science curriculum. That is a need. If the president suddenly declares that we will be sending troops to the Persian Gulf to fight a war, and your students can't stop talking about it, that is a need.

If one of your students has a passion for sharks (see the accompanying case study), then that is a need; perhaps for just that student though. A lot depends on your judgment in *assessing* and *prioritizing* needs. The key here is to prioritize.

Guiding questions to ask while assessing needs are:

- *What am I really teaching?* Go over your plan for the year. If you are currently an intern, ask your mentor teacher to make a curriculum map with you so that you can both see what is really taught in your room.
- *How important are the state and federal requirements to me at this time?* Perhaps you and your students have covered most of the required curriculum and can now follow your interests more closely.
- *What do my supervisor and/or principal expect of me?* If you are expected to follow the lesson cycle in every lesson, you may have little room in your curriculum for free exploration activities.
- *What are the needs and interests of my students?* You will want to address the strongest needs first. The child who is obsessed with learning about sharks really needs the opportunity to find out about them.
- *What resources are available?* If you love to make and launch model rockets, but find that it will cost $10.00 per child to do a project with them, that might color your decision.

Choose a Topic

View the list of needs as a problem to be solved. Which needs are the most important? How many can be addressed at one time?

What subject areas and/or topics will be included in the unit? What model of curriculum development fits it most closely?

When brainstorming solutions to the curriculum needs problem, it sometimes helps to list all ideas in columns labeled highest, medium, and lowest in order to refine prioritizing. At other times it helps to make what is sometimes called a mind map. This is a method of connecting thoughts and ideas while brainstorming. It helps to see relationships and generate related ideas and may lead to an integrated curriculum unit rather than a subject area-based one. (Also see Chapter 6.)

If you choose a consensus model, you might share this process with the students. It is sometimes surprising how many ideas students will have that you might not. I can remember a "bridges" curriculum in which a first grader asked the question, "What was the first bridge?" This might not have been covered in the curriculum if she had not asked the question.

If you choose to do this step with students, you will be brainstorming at the blackboard. Once a long list of ideas is on the board, ask the students if anyone needs clarification. In this part of the process, there is even more refinement. What does this idea mean? Are these two very similar? Do we want to combine them? This helps to narrow down the options. Always keep in mind that the problem to solve is: which is/are the best idea(s) for a curriculum at the time you want to do it, with the students you have, and which ideas might combine easily. With combined ideas, you might be able to essentially do two things at once.

After clarifying, take a preliminary vote. Ask students to choose the three ideas they like the best and vote for them. Next, erase the ideas receiving the least number of votes or no votes at all. This creates the short list.

You can cut out the above steps if, after your needs assessment, you have narrowed the list down by priorities and needs. You can start with the short list by placing five possible ideas for unit topics on the board and asking the class to choose. Sample ideas are given below for a New York State fourth-grade social studies class: (All examples in this chapter are for the fourth-grade level.)

The Big High Five NYS Cities

The Erie Canal/Clinton's Folly?

The Big Apple: Rotten, But How Sweet It Is!

New York Governor: Route to the Presidency?

The Iroquois Federation: Roots of Democracy

Upstate Women: Emma Willard, Sojourner Truth, and the New York women on whose shoulders we stand

Who Do You Think I am? Rockefeller?

This is another decision-point in the process.

Criteria for choosing a topic are:

1. The topic is one that has to be done at this grade level.

2. The topic illuminates a traditional subject area for the learners.

3. The topic is important globally, and/or its study will help the students to develop into better citizens of tomorrow.

4. The topic should be done this way and not in an integrated unit or combined with other topics. (If it would be more suited to integration or in combination

with others, then do not choose it for this type of curriculum.)

5. Through the deep understanding of this topic that the students will develop in this unit, the students will better understand related universal principles, concepts or generalizations.

Sometimes the entire short list of topics is good. Some students like some ideas more than others, but generally, you would probably like to do them all. If that is the case, then you can park at this step for a while and have students choose the topic they would most like to investigate. This will be a natural way to form small groups for problem-solving and investigation. Once groups have chosen their topics, skip to writing the rationale. Each group will have a different rationale for its topic.

Once the short list is on the board, the next step is to lobby. Students may lobby for any ideas that they like, but they may not lobby *against* any ideas. Try to avoid negativity at all times. As they lobby, students are not only practicing a useful skill, they are also giving reasons why the topic for which they are lobbying is important. This further refines the prioritizing process and starts directing the students toward the rationale. (Keep notes on the ideas expressed during lobbying. They will be useful later.)

After lobbying, take the final vote and go with the topic chosen by the group.

You might find this process difficult at first. Just keep trying; like shooting baskets, it takes practice. You need to find the way to do this that's most comfortable for you. A major pitfall, though, would be to seek too much comfort too often. Don't seek comfort so much that you are never challenged. It is a mark of a true professional teacher to meet challenges and to try new things.

This *is* new to most people. When did anyone ever ask you to make a plan for your own learning? We have been subjected to a rational/control curriculum for most of our own school careers. We are used to being told what to do in school, and not used to making our own decisions. This is a challenge to you now, but think of it this way: if you practice consensus curriculum development, it will be easier for you next time, and easier for the next generation of teacher interns, some of whom may be your students now.

Study the Topic

Once a topic is chosen, it is very important that the teacher and students do a preliminary investigation. If this is not done at this point, you could find, after much work writing and revising, that you do not have enough resources to complete a thorough study or that the topic wasn't nearly as suited to your needs as you thought.

The preliminary investigation is where the encyclopedia is used most in the pedagogic classroom. Encyclopedias are good sources of general information on a topic, but they are secondary and tertiary sources. When at all possible, you want your students to be able to find whole books, magazine articles, pamphlets, and other sources of information for their use in the unit itself. Students need more direct contact with the topic or people associated with the topic than an encyclopedia can provide. They also need to know that there are other sources of information to use. Perhaps they were sources used in writing the encyclopedia!

Write a Rationale

A rationale for fourth-grade students who are involved in curricular decisions is that they are practicing a lifelong skill that is neglected in the current curriculum. We want to produce lifelong learners who know how to choose their own topics of study and to plan their own course of study: "their" curriculum.

We will be preparing students for the future by using a consensus model. The brainstorming process described is similar to the model used in many institutions utilizing shared decision-making techniques. Making curriculum decisions as a group, the students are also experiencing group process in the context of planning learning. In experiencing this process, students are learning a very useful skill in this regard because it is likely that they will someday be called upon to use it in the workplace.

The average student today will change jobs seven times in her lifetime. This change will necessitate lifelong learning skills. These students will not only be required to learn new tasks, they will be required to define the areas they will study. They may be compelled to create their own jobs and courses of study. It is important that they have experienced this before and that it is not something new that they encounter as adults.

Involving students in curriculum development, even on a peripheral level, is developmentally appropriate for this age group. Students in grade four are entering the "middle school" years, ages ten to fourteen. As early adolescents, they are ready to become more independent in decision-making, and want to attempt things on their own. The process of curriculum development, under the careful guidance of a teacher, is a meaningful activity through which they can exercise their autonomy as learners.

Early adolescence also initiates the time of life when students start to organize a personal system of values (Nielson, 1987). Involvement in making the value-laden decisions inherent in developing curriculum will facilitate these students in developing their own system of values. It will also help them value their learning because they will have taken part in its planning.

The above section is an example of a short rationale for consensus curriculum development. It provides reasons for undergoing an investigation of a topic, subject area or concept. In writing a rationale, you are developing your reasoning skills. If you involve your students in the process, you are helping them to develop their reasoning skills as well. (Other examples of rationales actually written by teachers and students are included in the appendices.)

Guiding questions for an effective rationale that presents a strong case for a curriculum topic and methods are:

1. Start at the societal level. Why is this good for society?

2. Why is this an important topic for the community and the learners?

3. Why are the topic and methods appropriate for the students who will experience the curriculum?

Criteria for a good rationale include the criteria for any good piece of persuasive writing:

1. The arguments are clear.

2. The points are logically sequenced and make sense.

3. There is a system of organization to the rationale: a beginning, a middle, and a strong conclusion.

4. All possible reasons are explored in the rationale. Nothing is missing.

5. The writing is rich, descriptive, and in active rather than passive voice.

6. The writing follows conventions of grammar, punctuation, and spelling developmentally appropriate for the writer(s).

Design Goals and Objectives

Do you remember Ralph Tyler's first curriculum question? "What educational purposes should the school seek to attain?" This is the step in which the curriculum developer answers that question with regard to the curriculum unit under development. Although the overall purpose of the school in which the curriculum will be articulated affects the curriculum, the unit needs a statement of purpose as well.

Statement of Purpose. The statement of purpose can be one paragraph. It is a general, overall umbrella statement on why the curriculum was developed. In this statement, you should not be too specific, but give an overview of the purpose. This is akin to the mission statement of a school on a smaller scale, and reflects one's perspective on this particular unit.

Much of the work in writing the statement of purpose has been done in brainstorming and writing the rationale. As you went through the process of decision-making and narrowing your choices, many of the ideas voiced during those discussions will be useful here.

Remember: **The main criterion for a good statement of purpose is that it reflects the rationale.**

Integrity in the Curriculum

The term "unit" implies a unity which can only be borne out through integrity. This curriculum integrity is achieved through coherence between the rationale and the rest of the unit.

It is very important that every part of the curriculum reflect the rationale. In choosing to become a teacher, you have committed yourself to exemplary practice and an ethic of caring. Exemplary practice is embodied in practice with integrity. Practice with integrity depends on actions based on one's expressed beliefs. There is also a hidden curriculum involved in this aspect of curriculum development. Students know when a teacher does not model what she professes to believe. It is a form of honesty to model integrity in one's curriculum writing. It is also a form of caring for your practice, the profession, and your students, who will know that you care enough for them to be honest.

You have explicitly stated your beliefs in the rationale. Now every part of the plan to enact those beliefs must reflect that. If you feel that you must include something in the design which was not covered in the rationale, then you should simply go back and adjust the rationale so that it does reflect what you have planned to do. Here you can see first-hand why curriculum writing is not a linear process. We go back and revise and edit as we go forward.

Determining Goals and Objectives

Goals are short statements of purpose in four general areas: content or conceptual; skill; affective; and process (Figure 5–7). They are large steps (goals) to the end purpose of the unit. If one purpose of the unit is to help students to develop a sense of citizenship in your state, then a content goal might be: The students will compare the New York State system of government to the national system.

Objectives are the small steps which must be taken in order to reach the large goals. Objectives which might be included under the above goal could be:

- The students will read daily newspaper articles on the current activities of the state legislature.

- In the first lesson, the students will read the legislative section of the state constitution and write it in their own words. In the next lesson, the students might choose or be assigned to roles in the legislature and study their respective roles.

- In the next lesson, the students might create a role-play simulation of a legislative session in which someone proposes a piece of legislation and they debate it.

FIGURE 5–7 Curriculum Goals and Questions

CONTENT GOALS	**SKILL GOALS**
WHAT ARE WE GOING TO LEARN?	WHAT ARE WE GOING TO BE ABLE TO DO?
WHAT ARE WE GOING TO KNOW?	WHAT DO WE WANT TO BE ABLE TO DO?
WHAT DO WE WANT TO KNOW?	
AFFECTIVE GOALS	**PROCESS GOALS**
WHAT WILL WE BELIEVE?	HOW ARE WE GOING TO LEARN?
HOW WILL WE FEEL?	HOW WILL WE PRACTICE OUR SKILLS?
WHAT DO WE WANT TO BELIEVE?	

These objectives lead to the larger conceptual goal stated above.

The students in this unit will obviously be very involved in the processes of the state government and experience authentic experiences through simulations. Authentic experiences and simulations give students an opportunity to approximate expertise in the area they are studying. These experiences are useful in that, in order to design them, one must extract the essence of each experience and recreate it in the classroom if one cannot provide a truly authentic situation in which the students can practice the skills. Determining the essence of an experience is the first step in designing an authentic assessment, so you have a head start on assessing student learning when you design authentic experiences and simulations. (See Chapter 10.)

Conceptual/Content Goals. Conceptual/content goals are those which answer the question, "What are we going to *learn* by the end of this unit?" or "What are we going to *know*?" This is an easy formula to remember. Simply translate the goals of the unit into large questions, and the concept of goal-setting will become comprehensible to the students.

Skill Goals. Skill goals are those which answer the question, "What are we going *to be able to do* at the end of this unit?" It may take several weeks of practice for each student to develop a skill, but the actual skill is what is contained in a skill goal. Each objective will encompass a part of the skill.

Affective Goals. Affective goals are those which answer the questions, "What are we going to *believe* about this topic at the end of this unit?" and/or "How are we going to *feel* about this topic at the end of this unit?" In this and all areas of goal-setting, we must remember the developmental stage of each of the learners.

Process Goals. Process goals may concern two different areas. They may describe the processes the students will use in their investigations and activities, or they may describe the skill processes that the curriculum unit is designed to develop. In that case, they would either be optional or replace the skill goals because they would essentially duplicate them. Process goals answer the question, "How are we going to *find out* what we want to know, or practice what we want to be able to feel, or explore ways that we could feel about this subject?"

Set Priorities

Once the goals have been established, check to see that they reflect the rationale. If they do not, then you need to ask yourself: What is most important to me? What are the highest priorities for this unit? Priorities may not match what is important to you. However, it may be a more important priority to finish the state social studies mandates rather than to study model rockets. Use your professional judgment and set realistic priorities. Then, revise the rationale to reflect any changes, and prioritize the goals into three categories: must accomplish; should, if we have time; and optional, for any students who accomplish the musts and shoulds in the time allotted.

It is also here that you should be looking at the amount of time you will have to do the

FIGURE 5–8 Sample Lesson Format

OVERALL GOALS ADDRESSED IN THIS LESSON:

1. _____

2. _____

LESSON TITLE:_____

TAXONOMY LEVEL:_____

FRAMES OF MIND ADDRESSED:_____

CURRICULUM MODALITY: _____

TIME FRAME: _____

RESOURCES AND MATERIALS:_____

_____

_____

OBJECTIVES: _____

_____

PROCEDURE: _____

_____

QUESTIONS TO BE ASKED TO GUIDE
INVESTIGATION AND THINKING: (IN ORDER)_____

_____

_____

_____

CONCLUSION: _____

_____

EVALUATION: _____

_____

REFLECTION: _____

_____

unit. How many weeks will it take? How often will we work on it, and for how long? You need to have some of this in your mind as you set the goals and prioritize. This will keep you on target in terms of how many goals are musts, and which are the highest priorities.

Devise Objectives

After making the necessary adjustments, then devise objectives which lead to each goal. The chart in Figure 5–3 (p. 109) should help you to determine verbs to use in writing objectives. They should be active and measurable in some way. The unit will be evaluated on the basis of whether goals are achieved. The learning experiences are evaluated on the basis of the objectives achieved. (See Chapter 10, Summative Assessment and Testing.)

Once the objectives have been determined, it is easy to brainstorm activities which help the students to perform the actions. Actually, you have probably been thinking in terms of things the students will be doing all along. This is the time to finalize those activity ideas. There is a sample format for lesson plans in Chapter 8. A rational model is given here (Figure 5–8).

It is also important to remember that you cannot possibly do all the activities that you can think of. One of the hardest things about writing a unit is deciding what you are not going to do. Remember your priorities. It takes self-discipline and thought to reign in and make a final decision. You can see that if you involve your students in these decisions, they will learn these skills along with the content of the curriculum.

► FIELD-BASED CONNECTIONS

Guidelines for Interns

Most mentor teachers have been teaching for several years, and may not have heard of consensus models of curriculum development. Yet, many teachers at the elementary level employ consensus practices in their curriculum and teaching. Observe your mentor and write down examples of consensus-building activities, whether they are curriculum-related or not, which are initiated during a day. Both of you may be surprised at the large number of activities you find.

Share the consensus model and ask your mentor to try it to develop a short pilot unit on a specific topic. Encourage the teacher to take a risk. There is little to lose in a short unit, and a great deal to gain if it is successful. Share your anticipation with the students, and tell them they are involved in a pilot project with you. Encourage their suggestions for solutions when you feel stuck. You will be modeling risk-taking, a characteristic behavior of creative people. You will also be creating a unit.

Journal Guides

Some questions to guide your reflection in the journal might include the following:

• Did you ever experience a feeling of exclusion in terms of the curriculum in school? Did you ever feel a tension between the teacher and the subject matter? In what grade? What was the teacher like?

- Remember a time when you felt very alive and excited during a lesson as a student. What was happening? How could you create a similar situation in your own classroom?

- How do you feel about the amount of work it takes to create a coherent unit? Does it seem too hard? What would make it easier? What stands in the way of your making it happen?

▶ CHAPTER CLOSURE

Summary

Though the rational model of curriculum development has been criticized as being too linear (Kliebard, 1970), it continues to be the prevalent model espoused in American schools. In order to be conversant in the dominant method of curriculum development, you, as an intern in the profession, must be familiar with the rational method. We have modified and modernized the rational model substantially by adding a consensus component and by placing it within the pedagogic point of view.

The rational model of curriculum is a strong model and deserves to be used in most contexts some of the time. A problem arises, however, when a school or an individual teacher relies on only one model. Some children will do very well with this model; others will not. It is therefore important that the teacher utilize several models and balance the classroom curriculum and instruction between them.

We have not gone deeply into the formulation of a scope and sequence, and evaluation and assessment here because they are common to all curriculum development processes. Scope and sequence and evaluation are discussed comprehensively in the next chapter on integrating the curriculum.

Chapter Discussion Questions

1. Obtain copies of several curriculum guides and study them. What elements do they have in common? How are they different? Which ones would you use? Why?

2. Obtain copies of all the curricula for every subject in your grade level and make a curriculum map of the year. Making such a map is easy. Just make a chart with a box for each month of the school year. In each box, write what the students do or study during that month in each subject. What do they study in math, English/language arts, science, social studies, art, music, and physical education in September, October, etc. Just write down the major concepts covered during that time.

3. What do you know about United States history in the twentieth century? Compare the history of the country to the history of the curriculum. Where are there parallels?

4. What trends do you see in education today, and how can you address them in the curricula you develop?

5. What was your favorite subject in school? Try to brainstorm topics in that subject to write units for the grade level you want to teach.

6. What was your least favorite subject in school? Try to brainstorm topics in that subject.

► REFERENCES

Adler, M. (1983). *Paideia proposal*. New York: Macmillan.

Apple, M. W. (1979). *Ideology and curriculum*. London: Routledge and Kegan Paul.

Apple, M. W. (1986). *Teachers and texts: A political economy of class and gender in relations in education*. London: Routledge and Kegan Paul.

Berk, L. E. (1992). The Extracurriculum. In P. W. Jackson (Ed.), *Handbook of research on curriculum* New York: MacMillan.

Bestor, A. (1956). *The restoration of learning*. New York: Alfred A. Knopf.

Bloom, B. S. (Ed.). (1956). *Taxonomy of educational objectives, Handbook I: The cognitive domain*. New York: Longman.

Bobbitt, F. (1918). *The curriculum*. Boston: Houghton Mifflin.

Bolin, F. S. (1987). The teacher as curriculum decision maker. In F. S. Bolin and J. M. Falk (Eds.), *Teacher renewal: Professional issues, personal choices*. New York: Teachers College Press.

Butler, A. & Turbill, J. (1987). *Towards a reading-writing classroom*. Portsmouth, NH: Heinemann.

Cambourne, B. (1988). *The whole story: Natural learning and the acquisition of literacy in the classroom*. New York: Ashton/Scholastic.

Darling-Hammond, L. & Snyder, J. (1992). Curriculum studies and the traditions of inquiry: The scientific tradition. In P. W. Jackson (Ed.), *Handbook of research on curriculum*. New York: Macmillan.

Dewey, J. (1902). *The child and the curriculum*. Chicago: University of Chicago Press.

Dewey, J. (1916). *Democracy and education*. New York: Macmillan.

Dressel, P. L. & Lehmann, I. J. (1968). The impact of higher education on student attitudes, values, and critical thinking abilities. In O. Milton and E. J. Shoben (Eds.), *Learning and the professors*. Ohio: Ohio State University Press.

Eisner, E. W. (1979). *The educational imagination*. New York: Macmillan.

Eisner, E. W. (1992). Curriculum ideologies. In P. W. Jackson (Ed.), *Handbook of research on curriculum*. New York: Macmillan.

Eisner, E. W. & Vallance, E. (Eds.). (1972). Conflicting conceptions of the curriculum. *National society for the study of education series on contemporary educational issues*. Berkeley, CA: McCutchan.

Erickson, F. & Shultz J. (1992). Student's experience of the curriculum. In P. W. Jackson (Ed.), *Handbook of research on curriculum*. A project of the American Educational Research Association. New York: Macmillan.

Franklin, B. M. (1974). *American curriculum theory and the problem of social control, 1918–1938*. Paper presented at the Annual Meeting of the American Educational Research Association, Chicago, April, 1974. ERIC Document Number ED 092, 419.

Freire, P. (1970). *Pedagogy of the oppressed*. New York: Seabury.

Gardner, H. (1983). *Frames of mind*. New York: Basic Books.

Giles, H. H., McCutchen, S. P., & Zechiel, A. N. (1942). *Exploring the curriculum*. New York: Harper and Row.

Giroux, H. (1981). *Ideology, culture, and the process of schooling*. Philadelphia, PA: Temple University Press.

Goodlad, J. I. (1984). *A place called school*. New York: McGraw-Hill.

Jackson, P. W. (1968). *Life in classrooms*. New York: Holt, Rinehart and Winston.

Kliebard, H. M. (1970). Reappraisal: The tyler rationale. *School Review, 78*(2), 259–272.

Kliebard, H. M. (1986). *The struggle for the American curriculum: 1893–1956*. London: Routledge and Kegan Paul.

Kliebard, H. M. (1992). Constructing a history of the American curriculum. In P. W. Jackson (Ed.)., *Handbook of research on curriculum*. New York: Macmillan.

Krathwohl, D. R., Bloom, B. S., & Masia, B. B. (1964). *Taxonomy of educational objectives, Handbook II: Affective domain*. New York: David McKay.

Madaus, G. F. & Kellaghan, T. (1992). Curriculum evaluation and assessment. In P. W. Jackson (Ed.), *Handbook of research on curriculum*. New York: Macmillan.

McNeil, J. D. (1985). *Curriculum: A comprehensive introduction*, 3rd Edition. Boston: Little, Brown and Co.

Neill, A. S. (1960). *Summerhill*. New York: Hart Publishing Co.

Nielson, L. (1987). *Adolescent psychology: A contemporary view.* New York: Holt, Rinehart and Winston.

Oakes, J. (1985). *Keeping track: How schools structure inequality.* New Haven, CT: Yale University Press.

Oakes, J., Gamoran, A., & Page, R. (1992). Curriculum differentiation: Opportunities, outcomes, and meanings. In P. W. Jackson (Ed.), *Handbook of research on curriculum.* New York: MacMillan.

Ogbu, J. (1978). *Minority education and caste: The American system in cross-cultural perspective.* New York: Academic Press.

Passow, A. H. (1988). Issues of access to knowledge: Grouping and tracking. In L. N. Tanner (Ed.), *Critical issues in curriculum.* Eighty-seventh Yearbook of the National Society for the Study of Education, Part I. Chicago: University of Chicago Press.

Rist, R. (1970). Student social class and teacher expectations: The self-fulfilling prophecy in ghetto education. *Harvard Education Review, 40*(3), 411–451.

Rosenthal, R. & Jacobson, L. (1968). *Pygmalian in the classroom.* New York: Holt, Rinehart and Winston.

Rudnitski, R. A. (1993). A generation of leaders in gifted education. In K. Arnold and R. Subotnik (Eds.), *Beyond terman: Longitudinal studies of the gifted.* NJ: Ablex.

Sizer, T. (1984). *Horace's compromise: The dilemma of the American high school.* Boston: Houghton Mifflin.

Spady, W. G. (1971). Status, achievement, and motivation in the American high school. *School Review, 79*(5), 384–385.

Spring, J. (1976). *The sorting machine.* New York: Longman.

Stratemeyer, F. et al. (1948). *Developing a curriculum for modern living.* New York: Bureau of Publications, Teachers College, Columbia University.

Taba, H. (1962). *Curriculum development: Theory and practice.* New York: Harcourt Brace Jovanovich.

Tyler, R. W. (1949). *Basic principles of curriculum and instruction.* Chicago: University of Chicago Press.

Vallance, E. (1973–4). Hiding the hidden curriculum: An interpretation of the language of justification in nineteenth century educational reform. *Curriculum Theory Network, 4*(1), 5–21.

Zumwalt, K. (1989). Beginning professional teachers: The need for a curricular vision of teaching. In M. C. Reynolds (Ed.), *Knowledge base for the beginning teacher.* Oxford: Pergamon Press.

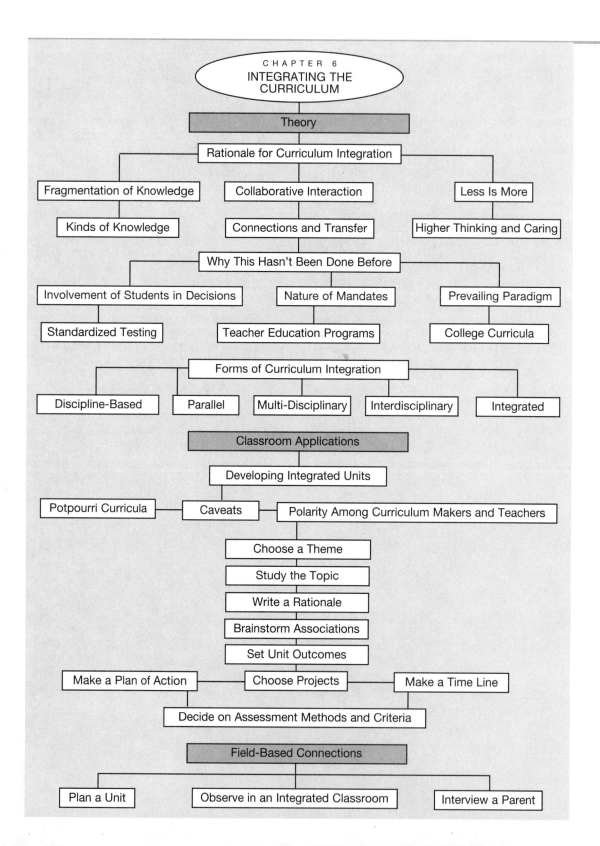

CHAPTER 6
INTEGRATING THE CURRICULUM

Theory

Rationale for Curriculum Integration

Fragmentation of Knowledge

Collaborative Interaction

Less Is More

Kinds of Knowledge

Connections and Transfer

Higher Thinking and Caring

Why This Hasn't Been Done Before

Involvement of Students in Decisions

Nature of Mandates

Prevailing Paradigm

Standardized Testing

Teacher Education Programs

College Curricula

Forms of Curriculum Integration

Discipline-Based

Parallel

Multi-Disciplinary

Interdisciplinary

Integrated

Classroom Applications

Developing Integrated Units

Potpourri Curricula

Caveats

Polarity Among Curriculum Makers and Teachers

Choose a Theme

Study the Topic

Write a Rationale

Brainstorm Associations

Set Unit Outcomes

Make a Plan of Action

Choose Projects

Make a Time Line

Decide on Assessment Methods and Criteria

Field-Based Connections

Plan a Unit

Observe in an Integrated Classroom

Interview a Parent

6

Integrating the Curriculum

Introduction

We have described a process of curriculum development that may be used by the teacher to develop curriculum suited for any classroom situation. This generic process overlaps with the process of developing integrated curriculum: curriculum that integrates a number of disciplines through content, skills, and affective goals. This distinguishes integrated curriculum from interdisciplinary curriculum in two ways: (1) in that more than overlapping content is considered when the planning takes place and (2) in the major purposes of the curriculum. In contrast to a subject-centered curriculum, a main purpose of an integrated curriculum is to integrate a number of curricular and instructional elements across disciplines. Since the purpose of a curriculum and its goals for students are directly linked, it naturally follows that the goals of instruction are the focal point for the integration. For that reason, we begin the discussion on curriculum integration at the goal-determination step of the

process of curriculum development. In this chapter, we will take the process of curriculum development to its completion.

▶ THEORY

Rationale for Curriculum Integration

Fragmentation of Knowledge

There are several reasons for integrating the curriculum. In fact, many of them were delineated a century ago by Francis W. Parker in his book, *Talks on Pedagogics* (1894), and later by John Dewey (1933, 1938). A major reason proposed by these philosophers for the integration of subjects in instruction was that in life, most problems and experiences are interdisciplinary in nature; and we use a multiplicity of skills to learn from experiences and to solve everyday problems, no matter how simple or complex they may be. The emphasis in school on subject matter serves only to make school irrelevant to students, who see little connection between what they learn in school and what they do outside of school. Thus, an integrated curriculum is more relevant to the lives of the students. This should help them to relate closely to the content and provide more intrinsic motivation for them than a traditional subject-centered curriculum. Alfred North Whitehead saw the irrelevance of the traditional curriculum as a problem for which integration was a possible solution. In his classic treatise, *The Aims of Education* (1929), Whitehead asserted:

> The solution which I am urging, is to eradicate the fatal disconnection of subjects which kills the vitality of our modern curriculum. There is only one subject-matter for education, and that is Life in all its manifestations. Instead of this single unity, we offer children—Algebra from which nothing follows; Science from which nothing follows; History from which nothing follows; a Couple of Languages never mastered...Can such a list be said to represent Life, as it is known in the midst of living it? The best that can be said of [the curriculum] is, that it is a rapid table of contents which a deity might run over in his mind while he was thinking of creating a world, and had not yet determined how to put it together. (p. 18)

Collaborative Interactions

Early in the twentieth century, the distinctions between the disciplines were a reflection of the styles of interaction in problem-solving in the sciences, and in manufacturing in industry. Each field had its method of inquiry, and

its own problems to solve. In factories, each worker had a definite job to do that might have been a piece of a larger task. Though this can still be the case, today's problems tend to be more interdisciplinary in nature, and call for collaborative teams from several disciplines to investigate. As members of the work force, students will be called upon to work on multidisciplinary teams in most of their work settings. This is as true for future teachers as it is for other professionals.

Less is More. Another reason to integrate the subjects is that it is a more efficient way to teach. With the addition of many subjects and problems to the elementary and secondary curriculum such as AIDS education, sex education, character education, SAT preparation, and drug and alcohol education—especially in the past twenty years—little time is left in the school day for the development of essential learning skills in the academic subjects. Integrating two or more subjects, and centering instruction around a theme, when appropriate, places the emphasis on skills development rather than coverage of subject matter. This emphasis, the essence of one of the Nine Common Principles of the Coalition of Essential Schools (Sizer, 1992), is a key element in the restructuring of the secondary curriculum. The integration of subjects in the curriculum is a more efficient use of precious instructional time.

The Tension Between Practical and Abstract Knowledge

The elements that characterize a field as a discipline can restrict one to a view of knowledge that is abstract. The major characteristic of a discipline is that it has a nucleus of content and concepts, what Petrie (1992) defines as a set of core metaphors. These metaphors are the basis for the field's methods of inquiry and view of the world, and are not necessarily tied to everyday practical problems. With discipline-based studies focused on concepts and principles, and interdisciplinary studies focused on problems and projects and practical concerns (Petrie, 1992; Tanner, 1989), educators interested in engaging all types of learners should strive for a balance between the two. Some learners think in abstract terms, others think in terms of practical problems. There is room for both in the curriculum.

Connections and Transfer

A fourth reason to integrate the curriculum is that it is brain-appropriate (Caine & Caine, 1991). What this means is that our brains are made to search for patterns in, and connections between, ideas. The focus in an integrated curriculum on relationships between the disciplines on all levels, ideas, skills, and attitudes or beliefs, makes it easier for the students to see the patterns and connections. These patterns of information become what are called schemata (Rumelhart, 1980), or frameworks of concepts in our brains. Schemata are the system of organization that we use to "file" knowledge. An integrated curriculum helps students to create these files, and thus promotes more connected, organized, and deeper understandings of the concepts being taught, and the transfer of understanding from one context to another.

Higher Levels of Thinking and a More Caring Atmosphere.

There is a fourth advantage to integrated/interdisciplinary curricula that is not so apparent on the surface: the methods of teaching that go along with an integrated curriculum. Usually, an integrated curriculum is taught in a different way than a traditional, subject-based curriculum. The primary level of an integrated curriculum, which focuses on problem-solving or projects, is application (Jacobs, 1989). This places the teacher in the position of coach rather than "depositor of knowledge" (Freire, 1974). With the teacher acting as a "guide by the side," rather than a "sage on the stage," the atmosphere in the classroom is transformed to one of caring and nurturing. Jacobs (1989) reported higher levels of attendance, and greater satisfaction on the part of the students and the teachers when an integrated curriculum was employed. Caine and Caine (1991) also cited a more caring atmosphere in classrooms that emphasized thematic or interdisciplinary curriculum and instruction. Students, many of whom come to school under stresses induced by the social and economic conditions of their home lives, need to have a caring atmosphere in school in order to break through the shut-down that occurs in the brain when they are under stress (Caine & Caine, 1991; Clark, 1986). Though some educators advocate stress-reduction techniques as well as integrated curricula (Clark, 1986), an integrated curriculum in a more traditional classroom can do a lot to alleviate the stresses of the outside world, and to encourage students to derive joy and fulfillment from their learning (Barell, 1991).

More Involvement of Students in Decision-Making

An interdisciplinary approach that integrates the content, skills, and affective elements is also more conducive to involving students in the curriculum development process. Such a curriculum can loosely follow an expanded version of the K-W-L model (Ogle, 1986), initially designed to develop active reading of expository text and to enhance reading comprehension. In this model, the students and teacher initially brainstorm what they already know about a topic or integrative theme. As they do this, they categorize their knowledge, and find where there are gaps or where they may need to know more. They then pose questions, asking what they want to know. After they have gone about answering the questions, they list what they have learned. A more structured, curriculum-based model for fostering this involvement was described in Chapter 5, and will be imbedded in the process in this chapter as well. Basically, a curriculum that fosters deep conceptual understanding employs the same techniques as K-W-L does to deepen understanding of text.

Why Integrated Curriculum Hasn't Worked Before

Lack of Textbooks and Materials. Since almost all textbooks and materials written until now were subject area centered, there was little interdisciplinary information available to teachers. This is changing, with many textbook companies scrambling to publish integrated packages, particularly at the elementary level. Though most of these programs are meant to focus on language arts, newer ones are centered in other subjects. The standards set by professional organiza-

tions in math and science call for conceptual integration of those subjects with the others (ASSA, 1989; NAS, 1994; NCTM, 1991).

The Nature of Mandates. The forces working against interdisciplinary curricula have historically been amplified by state, local, and federal mandates and programs that are categorized according to the disciplines. Indeed, many state departments of education are still structured in terms of subject area offices. However, this situation is rapidly changing. There is a trend toward a more interdisciplinary view of education, even in state bureaucracies. In 1992, the New York State Education Department was restructured into interdisciplinary teams in order to foster more connections between the disciplines in that state's educational policies. Widespread acceptance of setting integrative outcomes as state standards has also begun to have an effect on the types of problems posed in classrooms.

The Strength of the Prevailing Traditional Paradigm

Many parents of secondary students express concerns in high schools where interdisciplinary curricula are being implemented. They are afraid that their children will not be sufficiently academically challenged by curricula that are not discipline-based and centered on facts. They also fear that non-standard curricula will work against their children getting into high caliber colleges with rigorous standards. They associate interdisciplinary work with a lowering of standards (Rudnitski, 1994).

Remember that they formed their conceptions of school in traditional school settings. Though interdisciplinary curriculum at the secondary and even tertiary level of education is not a new idea, it is not one that has enjoyed widespread acceptance. When it has been tried and done well, it has worked beautifully. In a nationwide study of thirty secondary schools, many of whom decided to implement interdisciplinary curricula in the 1930s and '40s, these were the major findings:

- The students attending these schools earned higher grades and mastered deeper content than comparable age peers at other schools.

- The students who attended the thirty high schools went to good colleges, had higher grade point averages, received more academic honors, and habitually employed higher levels of thinking and reasoning than comparable age peers who had attended traditional high schools.

- The students who attended the six most experimental schools achieved significantly more than those who had attended the others. (Aikin, 1942)

Though these findings should have revolutionized high school education in America, they had little effect. Many have speculated that the onset of World War II obscured the *Eight Year Study,* as it was called, and lessened its effect (Tanner & Tanner, 1980). Whatever the reasons, we continue to live with the lack of impact of this research on secondary practice.

The Nature of Standardized Tests

Another obstacle to interdisciplinarity that seems to be slowly fading is standardized tests that focus solely on recall of information. Many states have developed performance assessments in writing, mathematics, and science. Connecticut, California, Maryland, and New York are a few examples of states that have implemented extensive authentic and performance-based testing programs for their students. These tests aim primarily at the application level of Bloom's Taxonomy, and examine the students' ability to pose problems and generate solutions. They focus on the process and not just on the answers.

Traditional Teacher Education Programs and College Curricula

Most teachers have not had much practice at viewing the curriculum from an interdisciplinary perspective. They have attended traditional schools, from kindergarten to grade twelve, with discipline-based curriculum and instruction. The college curriculum is even more fragmented, with professors hardly ever co-teaching, sharing or connecting their classes in other ways. Though several schools of education have integrated some of their subject area methods courses, most have not (Goodlad, 1990). In addition, the majority of the undergraduate curriculum experienced by prospective teachers in all other subjects is discipline-based. They have had little opportunity to form connected schemata of their own, which makes it difficult for them to point out relationships in order to help their students connect their learning. When they do, they tend to do it informally, and not in depth or with purpose (Jacobs, 1989).

Forms of Integration

Jacobs (1989), in her definitive book on developing interdisciplinary curriculum, delineated five "options for integration":

- discipline-based, the traditional focus on subjects;

- parallel, when two subjects are studied through concurrent events, such as reading a book from the time period students are studying in history; multi-disciplinary, when several subjects are taught separately through a theme;
- interdisciplinary, when several subject areas are integrated through the lens of a theme; and
- integrated, the integration of subjects and content, skills, processes, and affective goals and activities.

Petrie (1992), in a more philosophical work, used the terms defined at the First International Conference on Interdisciplinarity in the conference proceedings, *Interdisciplinarity: Problems of Teaching and Research in Universities,* in 1972. These terms were:

- disciplinarity, the traditional focus on the disciplines;
- multi-disciplinarity, a number of disciplines focused on a problem; interdisciplinarity, when key elements of the disciplines, such as terminology and method, change; and

- transdisciplinarity, when issues force a unified view of knowledge.

Fogarty (1991) delineated ten possible options for integrating curriculum. This unique set of options specifically focuses on the perspectives taken by the teacher and the learners, and the manner in which the subjects are connected. The ten "views" lend themselves to visual presentations of the different options, and offer teachers a way to graphically represent the integrative goals of the unit.

Since the focus of Jacobs' options was very practical and clearly defined and stated, an adaptation of her terms and levels of integration are better suited to our purposes, and will be used as a framework for our discussion (Figure 6–1).

Discipline-based

Most of the instruction in schools, from kindergarten to grade twelve, is based in the disciplines—the separate subject areas. Although the subjects are separated more explicitly as students progress from elementary to sec-

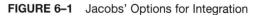

FIGURE 6–1   Jacobs' Options for Integration

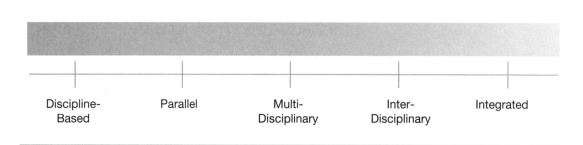

Discipline-Based   Parallel   Multi-Disciplinary   Inter-Disciplinary   Integrated

Adapted from H. H. Jacobs (Ed.) (1989), *Interdisciplinary Curriculum: Design and Implementation,* Association for Supervision and Curriculum Development.

ondary school, one need only to look at the daily schedule to find evidence of discipline blocks, even in kindergarten. The disciplinary categories are reinforced at the secondary level by teacher certification, majors, and departmental structures in schools. There would be no problem with such common and convenient arrangements if schools would acknowledge and allow room for some of the others. If the continuum in Figure 6–1 were a scale, it would be tipped very heavily to the left, with the discipline-based curricula at the heaviest end (Figure 6–2).

It is the lack of balance across the options that causes problems for students and for teachers who would like to integrate their curricula to varying degrees.

Problems for students locked into curricula that are totally discipline-based arise when the perceiving of relationships between the disciplines is needed. This is becoming a common phenomenon outside of schools, where many problems are interdisciplinary in nature. Economic problems, for example, have social, political, and scientific dimensions. Economic status is closely tied to racial issues, which include conceptions of literacy, intelligence, and valued knowledge. These issues must be perceived in order to be addressed, but they might not be in a curriculum centered totally on economics. Students are not exposed to several perspectives on an issue unless they experience some interdisciplinary work.

Problems arise for teachers who want to break out of the disciplinary mold basically because very few textbooks have been written to reflect an interdisciplinary perspective; and with the textbook used as the basis for the

FIGURE 6–2   The Curriculum Scale

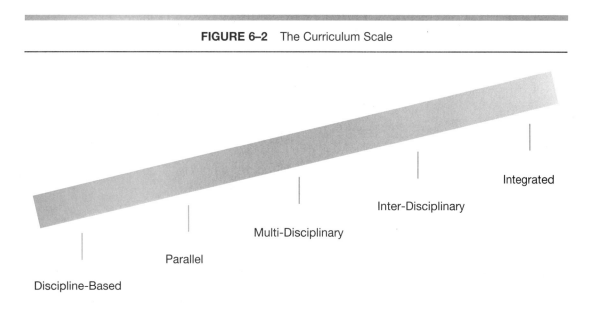

Adapted from H. H. Jacobs (Ed.) (1989), *Interdisciplinary Curriculum: Design and Implementation,* Association for Supervision and Curriculum Development.

majority of the curriculum in schools (Goodlad, 1984), this poses serious planning problems for teachers who rely on them. Since teachers who practice pedagogic principles develop their own curricula and use textbooks primarily as resources, this is less of a problem for them.

Parallel

In parallel curricula, a theme that is concurrent in two subjects is the glue that holds them together. This is a common practice when a piece of literature is used as the organizing center of a curriculum unit. Something is usually done in social studies that relates to it. For example, reading Lois Lowry's *Number the Stars* (1989) might generate a study of the holocaust, but not spark a related study in science or mathematics. This would be considered to be a parallel curriculum.

A problem with parallel curricula is that their level of integration is not deep, and they do not include very many subjects. Though students must experience a parallel unit occasionally, they should also experience units with a deeper level of integration. There are other options and forms of integration available to educators.

Multi-disciplinary

Multidisciplinary units are those in which several subject areas center their content around a theme. This type of curriculum unit is best suited for middle school teams who are grounded in a traditional schedule. Teams following a forty to forty-five minute period schedule, and teaching each class as a sepa-

rate unit, can adapt their planning to a multi-disciplinary approach relatively easily. It takes little common planning time to decide on a theme and to teach each subject using the theme as a lens.

A good practice for a middle school team that is employing a multi-disciplinary approach is to have all of the teachers on the team read the literature that the students will read for the unit, and for the language arts teachers to be familiar with students' texts in other subjects. That is, the teachers in every other subject area can refer to the books the students are reading in language arts as they relate to *concepts* in the disciplines; and the language arts teachers can refer to the textbooks to find comparatives. Students are used to their teachers' not knowing what is going on in their other classes; thus they are often amazed to find that their science, social studies, and music teachers have read "their" books; and that the language arts teacher knows the textbooks in the other subjects. This is indicative of how ingrained the traditional schedule has become, and how much it fragments knowledge. It also suggests that the students in a traditional setting at the middle and high school levels are usually the only individuals in a school who have a view of the entire expressed curriculum (see Chapter 5). The teachers are rarely afforded the opportunity to obtain a similar view.

Interdisciplinary

Jacobs (1989) describes interdisciplinary curricula as periodic units or courses of study that reflect the perspectives of a full array of disciplines. This definition sets forth two criteria:

that interdisciplinary curricula engage all, or most of the subjects, and that the students experience them as part of an overall variety of options on the integration continuum.

This makes sense, especially if one is aware of the possible hidden curriculum involved in teaching only discipline-based and parallel curricula, for example. If those two options were the only ones available in a school, the hidden curriculum would be that relationships exist only between two subjects at a time, and that the basis for connections is *concurrence in time*.

If the only available options were discipline-based and multi-disciplinary, then the hidden message might be that, though there are connections between the disciplines, they are *perceived by chance*, and not purposely.

Also, in each of these designs, teachers do not model their collaboration for the students. They continue to teach separately, emphasizing each separate subject rather than the connections between them. In these ways, interdisciplinary curricula address the hidden messages that the subjects are not deeply related, and that teachers do not share professional activities. Interdisciplinary curriculum units should be team taught in long time blocks, which allow time for the students to engage with the content as they solve problems or work on projects.

Integrated

Though Jacobs uses *Summerhill* as the model for an integrated curriculum, we have created our own definition, which we feel is more feasible to implement in American public schools. For pedagogics, combined curricula are those in which the subjects are integrated conceptually, through skills, and through affective relationships. They are essentially interdisciplinary curricula in which skills and affective goals that relate to each other are included as they relate to the integrated content.

In addition to the just mentioned advantages of interdisciplinary curricula, an integrated curriculum addresses a diversity of learners more naturally. With the integration of diverse content, skills, and attitudes and beliefs, there is more variety in instructional strategies and increased possibilities for new connections to be made. Students with particular strengths of mind may choose to work in their strong areas to learn the content. For example, a group of students might take the concept of change and choose to demonstrate it through movement; while another group might choose to represent it through mathematical theories. Samples (1992), in an article on curriculum modalities, showed how this might work in a conceptually centered lesson on freedom. He asked a sixth-grade student who was a frequent discipline problem to demonstrate the meaning of freedom:

> After some hesitation, a tall student stood and walked heavily forward to the front of the room. I heard the audible reaction of the other students and saw the look of dismay on the teacher's face. The student stopped, stood straight, and announced that he was about to demonstrate Freedom! He began to take a long stride across the room. Halfway through the stride he came to a shattering stop. A look of panic crossed his face, and, for all purposes, his right foot was riveted to the floor. His body lurched forward, them

backward, but his right foot stayed locked to the floor. He jerked and lunged, but the foot wouldn't budge. He tried to pry the foot loose with a nearby chair—he commandeered a broomstick, which also failed to move the foot.

We were all transfixed by the performance. Then his entire body relaxed. He smiled widely at us all, bent over, and deftly slipped his right foot out of its shoe and walked away with a lilt—leaving the "anchored" shoe behind. The class broke into applause, the teacher relaxed, and the student took several bows and returned to his seat. I asked if he could tell us what his movements told us about what freedom means. He said, "Sometimes you have to give up something that matters to you so that you can have it [freedom]." (65)

This example demonstrates that one can use students' strengths (in this case, kinesthetic intelligence) to express levels of understanding that they might not have the linguistic skills to express in writing, the main mode of expression in the typical school. When one is integrating skills development into the curriculum, one may more readily attend to the diversity of modalities available in one's classroom, especially if the content is broadly conceptual. When one is working in one discipline, the primary language and methods of that discipline prevail over the natural modalities of the students.

Conclusion to Theory

Integrating the curriculum is not a new idea. However, with the increased need to see relationships between ideas, and the increasing need to work in diverse groups in many contexts, it is a very appropriate method of orga-

nization for today's students. Since integrated curricula are naturally geared toward the application level of Bloom's Taxonomy (see Chapter 5), facts are put to use, rather than memorized as content. When *facts are tools* for solving problems or doing projects, their position as central to the curriculum and the goals of the learner is recast. This is an advantage in many fields, where the growth of knowledge is so great that the facts cannot be taught as the focus of the curriculum. Also, new knowledge in the field of cognition leads us to believe that relating material is a brain-appropriate method of organization, and enhances learning.

There are many levels of integration that are possible to use in developing curriculum. It is important you choose one that works best for your context. If you are in a middle school with a traditional schedule, and are teaching on a team, a multi-disciplinary curriculum would probably best suit your needs. If you are an elementary teacher in a self-contained classroom, with awareness and planning, you can provide a balance of curriculum options for your class throughout the year. If you are teaching at a high school, in a departmentalized situation with a traditional schedule, mostly disciplinary curricula would be best for you, with an occasional interdisciplinary unit planned with colleagues. This unit could be team-taught with a teacher who shares your students, and whose class is scheduled back-to-back with yours. You could also prepare several parallel units with a willing colleague who shares your students, and who teaches a related subject area. One can see that the many possibilities depend on the context and on the relationships between colleagues in each setting.

CLASSROOM APPLICATIONS

Developing Integrated Units

The development of an integrated unit begins in much the same way as any curriculum. In the rational model, one assesses one's needs in order to determine what is important enough to teach. In determining an appropriate theme, the needs assessment is done through a curriculum map. A curriculum map (Figure 6–3) is simply a graphic representation of the major topics and concepts in each subject that you currently emphasize each week or month of the school year. It is a true map of what you do; not what you think you should be doing or want to do.

Once the curriculum map is done, it is easy to see redundant topics in the curriculum, especially if an entire school participates in the development of the map. Teachers will immediately notice that they repeat the study of Thanksgiving in first and second grades after they have done it in kindergarten. Once this has been noted, it is easy to go into greater depth each successive year: change the topic, or at least view it from another perspective. Teachers who conscientiously make maps of their curricula hear, "This is boring," much less frequently after they have eliminated redundancies.

Another purpose of the curriculum map is to discern topics that relate well across the curriculum. From the curriculum map in Figure 6–3, we can see that the concept of "celebrating change" can tie together much of the first-grade curriculum in November. In social studies, it can be tied through the seasons and Thanksgiving, and how our celebra-

tion of both has changed over time. In science, it can mean the changing seasons, and how they affect our lives now in comparison to how they affected the lives of early Americans—both native and settlers. In math, the students could make change, perhaps through a classroom grocery store, where they might buy the ingredients for a Thanksgiving feast. Some of their language arts reading might be of journals of pioneers and the hardships that they endured in order to settle in a land where they would not have to face religious persecution.

Some Caveats

Potpourri Curriculum. The above examples illustrate more than ideas that might connect. They also show how a curriculum developer might get carried away with many ideas, without enough to tie them together. Jacobs (1989) called this the "potpourri" problem. A potpourri curriculum is one that is fragmented despite having as its central purpose the integration of learning in several subject areas. The curriculum developer can follow a process that contains "checks and balances" to assure that the curriculum is coherent and not fragmented. They will be discussed as we go through the process.

Polarity Among Curriculum Makers and Teachers. A problem that is more common at the secondary level than the elementary is the "polarity" problem (Jacobs, 1989). At this level (grades seven through twelve), the teachers are certified in subject areas and teach their subjects separately. They are also grouped within a subject area department on the faculty of their school buildings, which fosters a

FIGURE 6–3 Sample Curriculum Map

FALL

GRADE ONE

	September	October	November
SOCIAL STUDIES	Families Family Tree Grandparents Day	School Map of School Columbus Indigenous People Halloween	Community Social Organizations Thanksgiving Pilgrims Native Americans

LANGUAGE ARTS	Shared Reading
	Shared Writing
	Dictated Stories
	Vocabulary
	    Development
	Library Experiences
		Big Books
		Picture Books
		Genres of Liturature
		More Vocabulary
		Intoduction to
		    Poetry
		Book Sharing
			Guided and Shared
			    Reading
			Independent
			    Reading
			Role Play

MATH	Review of Numbers	Addition
		Place Value
			Expansion of
			    Addition to
			    Columns
			Introduction to
			    Subtraction

SCIENCE	Observation of Nature Nature Walks	Plant Identification Hands-on Experiences	Seasons Nutrition
ART	Two-dimensional	Masks	Native Americans
MUSIC	Group Singing	Holiday Songs	Instruments

strong sense of disciplinary affiliation among them. To make matters worse, the subject matter becomes more difficult at the secondary level, causing the teachers to be less willing to allow colleagues entry into their disciplinary territory. Many teachers at this level feel that others could not possibly teach their subject matter.

The curriculum development process cannot balance out polarity among the disciplines. It takes time and the awareness of the potential pitfalls. Polarity can be overcome by individuals working together toward common curricular goals as they acknowledge the expertise of colleagues. Certification is not the sole indicator of expertise. Colleagues can be experts in hobbies and other interests they have outside of school, just as students can. Every teacher can tell stories about students who were great at athletics or the arts, or who were great mechanics, but were academic failures. Many teachers are not only expert in their academic fields, but in other areas as well. Planning an interdisciplinary unit as a team brings out things that colleagues never knew about each other. Teachers who work in interdisciplinary teams value their collective and individual expertise more deeply than teachers who do not work in teams (Jacobs, 1989).

Choose a Theme

Once the conceptual connections have been discerned, the team or individual teacher should then brainstorm themes and topics that relate best. This is a kind of guided brainstorming, done after studying the situation. This insures that the ideas will be more "doable" than if they were simply brainstormed without study or direct knowledge of what is being taught and what is expected to be taught at any grade level.

A theme can be a broad concept. It can also be a topic or issue. Hilda Taba (1962), a great curriculum theorist and developer, called these "curriculum foci organizing centers." Though organizing centers of a curriculum may be specific, they can work if they are connected to a limited number of broad concepts or universal principles such as change, democracy, exploration, and patterns. In fact, the linking of any curriculum to a limited number of overarching concepts or key understandings is a major characteristic of good curriculum and teaching in any subject area (Brophy, 1992).

Study the Topic

In Chapter 5, we discussed studying the topic to be taught as a step in the curriculum development process. Please refer to that section for a review of this step. The difference in this context is that the study of the topic is done through the lens of the chosen concepts, key understandings or principles on which you decided to focus. If you chose a conceptual theme, then you must study the subject-area topics you will cover with that theme as a guiding factor. If you chose a topic or issue, you should decide on a few key understandings and concepts for your focus. In effect, your study of the topic is driven by the concepts and principles so that you relate your curriculum topic to them as much as possible.

Write a Rationale

As described in Chapter 5, the rationale section of a curriculum serves not only to justify the topic and concepts chosen, it also serves as a check and balance during the process of developing the unit. If one cannot write a rationale for the topic or concepts, then one should change the topic or concepts without wasting any more time on the unit.

The same standards for a good rationale hold for an integrated unit as they do for any model. The rationale should be written clearly, and should provide examples and citations from educational research and theory to back up the decisions that the curriculum developers made. It is a piece of persuasive writing that convinces us that the topic is important for society, appropriate for these students, and that the choice of model for organization is appropriate. In an integrated unit, since one of the reasons for the unit is the integration of subject areas and content, skills, and affect, that is also written as part of the rationale. This piece of the curriculum answers the question: "Why is it important that the curriculum be integrated?"

Brainstorm Associations

Jacobs and Borland (1979) described a process of brainstorming around an organizing center to facilitate the recognition of relationships among ideas and activities in a variety of subject areas. Their "interdisciplinary concept model" has become the basis for most initial planning of integrated curricula at all levels; especially since it gained popularity among whole language educators at the elementary level, who use it to form "theme webs." Although the interdisciplinary concept model is an excellent graphic organizer, any visual model that enhances the ability to perceive relationships may be used by an individual teacher or a team. For example, in a parallel model curriculum, a Venn diagram (Figure 6–4) might serve as an appropriate model, helping the teachers to conceptualize

the shared issues and concepts their subject areas hold, and the content that they will teach that must be taught separately.

Fogarty (1991) delineated ten different models of integrated curriculum, with ten different graphic organizers. From the vast number of possibilities, one can see that the model and graphic that works best for the given context is the one that should be used.

Set Outcomes for the Unit

This is the point at which an integrated unit diverges from a strictly discipline-based one. While in that model (see Chapter 5), one must set goals in the areas of content, skill, and affect; in this type of unit, one sets integrative outcomes that answer the questions, "What will the students know at the end of this unit?" and "What will the students be able to do at the end of this unit?" They are broad-ranging and may include content and skills in one outcome. They also depend on the values of the community and the teacher—what they believe is valuable—and the needs of the students and society, all of which is included in the rationale. Here we can see how the rationale drives the rest of the curriculum.

Examples of outcomes for a high school unit on civil rights might be:

- The students will demonstrate deep understanding of the American concept of rights as delineated in the Constitution and Bill of Rights.

- The students will demonstrate deep understanding of the changes in American society brought about by the civil rights movement.

- The students will demonstrate mastery of written communication and critical thinking

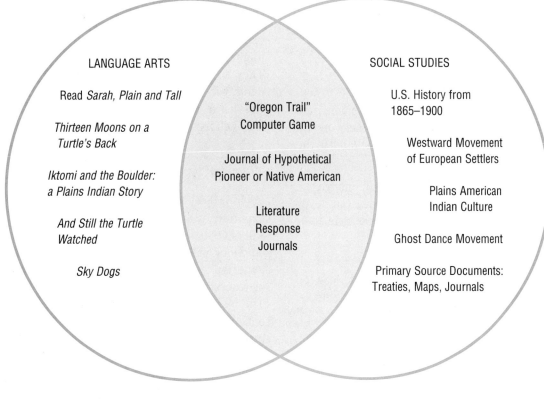

KEY UNDERSTANDINGS:
CHANGE
POINT OF VIEW
APPRECIATION FOR DIVERSITY
ARGUMENT AND EVIDENCE

LANGUAGE ARTS

Read *Sarah, Plain and Tall*

*Thirteen Moons on a
Turtle's Back*

*Iktomi and the Boulder:
a Plains Indian Story*

*And Still the Turtle
Watched*

Sky Dogs

"Oregon Trail"
Computer Game

Journal of Hypothetical
Pioneer or Native American

Literature
Response
Journals

SOCIAL STUDIES

U.S. History from
1865–1900

Westward Movement
of European Settlers

Plains American
Indian Culture

Ghost Dance Movement

Primary Source Documents:
Treaties, Maps, Journals

FIGURE 6–4 Venn Diagram Showing Shared and Separate Content

and problem-solving skills with regard to their own rights, or the human rights of others.

Choose Projects

After defining the outcomes of the unit, it is relatively easy to complete the unit in a coherent fashion. Before going further, though, you should look at the outcomes and see that they reflect the rationale in every way to insure that the curriculum has integrity. If they do not, then you must change them (or the rationale) so that there is congruence between the two sections.

When the adjustments have been made, then you should look again at the outcomes and ask yourself these questions, which will help guide you in choosing options for projects. Again, as described in Chapter 5, you should include the students in this process, having them ask the questions as well. They could come up with projects that are more closely suited to their interests than you can as an adult. The guiding questions are:

- What kinds of exhibitions, projects, or demonstrations will help our students to demonstrate that they have mastered the content and skills we plan to include in this unit?

- In what ways can students demonstrate their attitudes, feelings, and beliefs regarding the concepts and content included in the unit?

- What kinds of experiences will engage the students in activities where they can develop the skills needed to demonstrate their knowledge and expertise?

With these questions in mind, let's go back to the high school unit on civil rights.

1. A group of students could do an oral history of members of the civil rights movement, and how it changed their individual lives.

2. Another group could make a hypertext program on the *Universal Declaration of Human Rights* adopted by the United Nations. (Dillner (1993) described a similar program on *The Bill of Rights* by a teacher for her high school social studies class.)

3. Another group could propose a bill on student rights to the student council.

4. Another group could research the origins of the American concept of rights, and make an educational videotape to report their findings.

5. Another group could simulate a conversation between Ghandi and Martin Luther King, Jr.

6. Still another could simulate a debate between Dr. King and Malcolm X.

All of the above projects are examples of experiences through which the students might demonstrate mastery of the content. They are also means through which the students will be sharing their knowledge. They will learn from each other's projects—*and* they will have fun doing it!

Make a Plan of Action

Each project will require different learning experiences in order to be completed, so each will have its own action plan. However, all the students will have to share some learning experiences, and encounter some direct instruction in order to master the material. The lessons that all the students will experience should be written along with the action plans for all the projects that will be completed for the unit. (Sample lesson plans are included in Chapters 5 and 7). Though most of the lessons and shared experiences, like field trips, may occur at the beginning of the unit, the groups should converge periodically for more shared learning and to share each other's progress. It is important that the lessons and action plans, combined, provide the students with enough of a knowledge base to successfully complete their projects. The teacher can check on this before implementing the curriculum by looking at the levels of cognition of the lessons, using Bloom's Taxonomy as a guide.

When the groups of students converge for shared lessons and progress checks, they can act as support systems for each other as well as give advice and constructive criticism to each group. This kind of activity, in addition to helping meet the content, skill, and affective outcomes of the curriculum, is excellent preparation for the work world; where they will be called upon to participate in groups such as quality circles and shared decision-making teams in a variety of settings.

Make a Time Line

Once the lessons and plans of action have been made, the curriculum developer then prepares a time line. A time line is just that: a day-by-day, week-by-week depiction of what is occurring in the unit. It is helpful to co-develop the time line with the students, and also to write it on chart paper and post it in the classroom. This helps to remind the groups (and the teacher) of the decision points and the deadlines for various aspects of their projects. At the end of the time line, there is always a celebration and sharing of the projects with the community and the rest of the school.

Decide on Assessment

Each project should have its own set of criteria for successful completion. The debate, though grounded in the same knowledge as many of the others, is a demonstration of specific skills of argument and public speaking that are not apparent in the computer project. Both would have different criteria by which they would be assessed.

Formative Assessment. For formative assessment, it is helpful if each group keeps a project portfolio, and each individual keeps an individual journal or learning log. These can be periodically reviewed by the teacher, who can make suggestions and provide support (see Chapter 2).

Summative Assessment. For summative, authentic assessment, each group should be involved in determining the criteria for performance. The students should also be involved in judging their performance and those of others. For sample criteria and rubrics for assessment, see Chapter 12. Many teachers involve experts and community members in the assessment of student projects, in the same vein as judges for science fairs. It is up to you and your students to decide if you want to involve others in their assessment.

Evaluation of the Curriculum

How does one evaluate a curriculum? First, you should set some criteria for performance of the unit that you wrote. An example of a set of criteria by which curriculum units may be assessed is included (Figure 6–5). Your criteria may look very different from these. They should reflect your own standards and context.

Another good curriculum assessment technique is to use questionnaires and personally interview as many of your students as you can. The students may have perceived the curriculum in a totally different way than you did. This activity not only helps you to see your teaching through their eyes, but is a much needed perspective in curriculum research (Erickson & Schultz, 1992).

As we discussed in Chapter 1, the pedagogic teacher keeps a reflective journal. It is a good idea to reserve a portion of each entry to focus on curricula that you develop. This

FIGURE 6–5 Sample Evaluation Criteria for Curriculum Units

The following criteria were used to evaluate the degree of skills demonstrated in your curriculum unit in the delineated areas.

The scale used to assess the degree to which the criteria were met was:
    5 = to the highest degree
    4 = to a great extent
    3 = somewhat
    2 = to a limited extent
    1 = not at all
N/A = not applicable

The above scale was used in conjunction with specific comments found in each section and in the ending section for comments in determining a wholistic grade.

INTRODUCTION

_____ 1. The title of the curriculum is appropriate and captures the spirit of the work.

_____ 2. The Table of Contents is clear and demonstrates that the curriculum is logically organized.

_____ 3. The theme of the curriculum is appropriate for the chosen target population.

_____ 4. The theme or focus of the curriculum provides a good lens through which the curriculum may be viewed.

RATIONALE

_____ 5. Reflects a cogently stated philosophy.

_____ 6. Makes a strong case for the chosen theme.

_____ 7. Includes the needs of the students and society in its case.

_____ 8. Substantiates arguments with citations to research and educational literature.

_____ 9. Reflects a logical plan of organization as a piece of writing.

_____10. Is written following conversation of mechanics in the appropriate language.

GOALS/GUIDING QUESTIONS

_____11. Support or extend the intentions stated in the rationale.

_____12. Goals/large questions are over-arching and broad.

_____13. Goals/questions encompass categories corresponding to conceptual, skill, and affective.

_____14. There is coherence between the goals and objectives or large and small questions.

FIGURE 6–5   continued

CONTENT OUTLINE

_____15. Main components are clearly stated and defined.

_____16. There is evidence of driving themes from the rationale.

_____17. The elements of the curriculum are sequenced in a logical, meaningful way.

KEY CONCEPTS AND TERMS

_____18. There is a complete and comprehensive list of key concepts and vocabulary related to the concepts and goals of the curriculum.

_____19. The concepts and vocabulary are appropriate for the target population of the curriculum.

IMPLICATIONS FOR PRACTICE

_____20. Classroom environment issues are taken into consideration.

_____21. Differentiation for individual differences of learners is evident.

_____22. Sensitivity to the cultures of the students is evident.

LEARNING EXPERIENCE

_____23. Support the rationale, purposes, and goals of this curriculum.

_____24. Coherent with the goals of the curriculum.

_____25. Well-written and thorough.

_____26. Develop deep understanding of each concept in the order and manner in which they are presented.

_____27. Logically and meaningfully sequenced.

_____28. Follow a model of cognition.

_____29. Show evidence of a variety of styles of presentation.

_____30. Show evidence of a variety of groupings.

_____31. Allow for individualization and differentiation.

RESOURCES/MATERIALS/BIBLIOGRAPHY

_____32. Reflect the philosophy stated in the rationale and the curriculum design.

_____33. Resources are provided for the student.

FIGURE 6–5 continued

_____34. Resources are provided for the teacher.

_____35. A variety of media—not just text materials—is given.

TIME LINE/SCOPE AND SEQUENCE

_____36. Sequenced in a meaningful way for the learner.

_____37. Lead to higher levels of thinking rather quickly.

_____38. Provides for creativity and input from the learners.

_____39. Demonstrates how the curriculum is a model of thinking.

EVALUATION PLAN

_____40. Evaluation of learning experiences provides meaningful feedback to students.

_____41. Criteria for assessment are clearly and logically stated.

_____42. Methods of evaluation are coherent with the curriculum and philosophy presented.

OVERALL COMMENTS

_____

_____

_____

_____

_____

_____

_____

_____

_____

_____

may be the most important component of your evaluation of any curriculum unit. It is here that you will discuss your plans for revision, and the many curricular decisions you make based on each day's experiences. This is another of the many uses you will find for your reflective journal throughout your career. Excerpts from the curricular portions of a teacher's reflective journal, focusing on curriculum integration, are included in the Field-Based Connections portion of this chapter.

FIELD-BASED CONNECTIONS

Guidelines for Interns

Plan a Unit

Plan an integrated unit with your mentor teacher, using the process included here. Try to involve the students in the entire process. Throughout, keep a class curriculum dialogue journal as a means of formative assessment. Each person writes in the journal every day. An entry might be about the classroom inter-actions or a learning experience, or a response to someone else's entry. Students, intern, and teacher may carry on multi-layered dialogues focused on classroom experiences through this journal.

Observe a Class Where Integrated Curriculum is Happening. Ask your mentor what other teacher is doing integrated curriculum in his/her classroom, and spend a few days observing there. Look at how the students and teacher relate to each other, and at the multiplicity of relationships in such a class-

room. How are they different from the relationships in a traditional class? Do the students spend the majority of their time engaged with the content and each other, rather than listening to the teacher? What kinds of student products do you see being produced in this classroom, and how do they differ from those produced by students in a traditional setting?

Interview a Parent. If your mentor teacher is committed to integrated curriculum, and does units of this type, ask for permission to interview the parent of one of the children in the room regarding their knowledge of the curriculum and the effects on their child. Make up an interview schedule (the list of questions) ahead of time, and practice your interviewing techniques on a friend, preferably another intern, who might help you to revise the interview. This is called pilot testing the interview. Some questions you might consider are:

1. What kinds of activities does your child talk about when talking about school? Are they mostly group-oriented or individual?

2. Does your child bring home many worksheets? If not, what typifies the work you see coming home?

3. Have you ever visited your child's classroom? If so, what aspect of learning struck you as most important in the class? Were the students doing a lot of investigating and testing of their own hypotheses, or were they engaged in other types of activities?

4. Does your child talk about how ideas in different subjects relate to each other?

5. Does your child talk about working on projects?

6. Have you ever been invited into the class for a celebration or fair centered around the curriculum and not a holiday?

7. What was (use whatever grade level in which you are placed) like when your went to school? What do you remember most about that year?

8. What do you think your child will remember the most about this year?

9. If you could change anything about the curriculum in the class right now, what would it be?

Answers to questions like these will help guide you in your choices when you have a class of your own.

▶ CHAPTER CLOSURE

Summary

We have focused on the process of developing integrated curriculum: curriculum that integrates the content, skills, and affective goals of a number of subject areas. The process, though presented in a sequential way, is more circular than linear, with many steps back to check and rethink decisions made earlier. The most important aspects of the process are:

- that the decisions made by the teacher reflect the needs of the students and the philosophies of the teacher and the community as much as possible;

- that the projects are true demonstrations of the knowledge, skills, and attitudes you were fostering in the unit;

- that the assessments truly measure what the students learned and did in the projects;

- that the unit has coherence, and can be understood by all members of the community so that you may be accountable for all aspects of it; and

- that the unit is a model of thinking, in that it follows a logical sequence to a logical conclusion.

Chapter Discussion Questions

1. Which option for curriculum integration do you feel is implemented least effectively at these three levels of schooling: elementary, middle, secondary? Why?

2. Do you think that you would have done better in high school if you had experienced a more integrated curriculum? Why?

3. Give examples of what a lesson on the Civil War might look like in each of the options for integration.

4. Do a study of the progressive education movement in America. What was it? Why did it die? Be prepared to discuss it in class.

5. Take a series of lessons from a published program used in your classroom. Analyze them and determine at what level of Bloom's Taxonomy each is aimed. Do they progress from lower levels to higher? Do they stay the same? What do you notice?

6. Invite a retired teacher to come to speak to your class. It would be best if you are lucky enough to be in a rural area and the teacher taught in a one-room schoolhouse. Ask that teacher about the curriculum was taught. Ask if the teacher had heard of the progressive education movement.

The case study example can be used for analysis in small or large groups. Questions follow the case study as suggestions for discussion.

CASE STUDY 6–1: A High School Art Teacher Integrates Her Curriculum

Martha has been teaching art in this small high school in New England for several years. She has been part of a core group of teachers committed to the best practice available to them. Three years ago, the high school changed its schedule to a semester configuration, with ninety-minute time blocks for each class. This year, this core staff has made a commitment to deepen the level of integration between their subjects by planning one unit on a significant local historical event, focusing on the concept of change.

Though the unit will not happen until the spring, Martha has decided to start making artifacts for the unit in her fall semester pottery class. The curriculum portions of her journal are excerpted here.

Sept. 1–3

This is a short week, but I feel like I got a good start with the new slant to my curriculum. I feel comfortable talking to the students about change because it is a topic that comes up every year. We talked about their perceptions of [the high school] and how it has changed; why it has changed; and how fast. When we went over the syllabus for the pottery class, I told them how I have changed the expectations, projects, and even the way I deliver the course. I need to discuss the idea of student-as-worker and teacher-as-coach with them. That is the way I am now, and no one complains that much. The difference is that now I am explaining to them why I teach that way and I get their feedback.

Sept. 7–10

I think the class is having fun making primitive artifacts for its exhibition. The trip to the library was good, but I was amazed that only one or two kids bothered to read any text. I was lucky if they read the caption under the picture. When I have them go to the library to look for Indian pottery shapes, artifacts, and decorative patterns, I will have them also write down what it is so they can make labels. I have pointed out the fact that they miss out on a wealth of information if they do not read.

I must be doing something right. In the past, I have been "accused" of teaching science in pottery class. This year, they are asking, "What is this, history?"

Sept. 13–17

I found a passage in a North American Indian crafts book that helped in the transition from pinch to the coil method. I read it aloud as a story while they worked. Both classes responded well. The story illustrates how man has always changed and will always change. The second trip to the library was easier than the first trip. The kids saw why they needed to sketch shapes and decorations of the pottery of the time and culture. This time, they were required to write down what the piece was, what tribe of Native Americans it came from, and any other information we could use for labeling purposes. I wish the exhibit was up already. It should be great.

Sept. 20–24

I can't wait to see the first firing of oxide glazes on the primitive pottery. I did not label them after firing color on every oxide. I told them that was so they could experiment and discover as their ancestors did. I also reviewed the periodic table symbols for the oxides we were using. Some kids remembered from junior high and they had not taken chemistry.

It would be so beneficial to have the same grade level in one class. Connections to other subjects could be heightened in more depth because all the students in the class are studying the same thing (concepts and material).

Sept. 27–Oct. 1

This was a rewarding week. We completed the primitive pottery display and the kids are getting many compliments. Both pottery classes are busy creating coil pottery in the style of the Native Americans. Because of the use of the press molds to start, the coil pottery is much larger in most cases. The paddling gives the work a smoother surface to glaze with designs. I have one kid in the class who is repeating because he failed it in the ninth grade. He is a senior now. He made a comment about the difference between the way I taught the class the first time and now. He likes it better but he sometimes feels like his creativity and freedom are stifled when he has to stick to the style of another people. He did agree that it was the best way to learn about art history—by doing. He also remembered that I have told them their work should be "in the style of" not necessarily a copy. He agreed that this allowed him more freedom.

Oct. 4–8

I went to Mystic Seaport this weekend to begin my research on authentic colonial pottery and crafts. I took some pictures and also purchased three slides and six books. Not only does this extra research use time, but also money. I must admit I am enjoying what I am learning, so I guess the money is worth it.

Oct. 25–29

This week I was thinking about how I would write up lesson plans for the theme of change. Much of what I am doing comes out of class discussions about questions I present to them. Have any of you had any big changes in your lives? What caused the change? Was it a positive or negative change? What changes in lifestyles have come about from ancient times to now? Why is there change? Is change good/bad? Changes in pottery—changes in the school—changes in education across the USA. How is your life different from your parents? Much of the way that I teach comes from the kids I am teaching.

Nov. 1–5

Now that my pottery classes are on the potter's wheels, I am having trouble getting their attention to teach them anything new. I guess I have to *reserve* time to talk and research about the theme. Fridays would be good because the kids should not start anything new, just trimming, glazing, decorating. I still need days for them to research colonial pottery on their own. When I go away for Thanksgiving vacation I will have a sub for two days after vacation. I have arranged to have J.B., a local potter, come in to sub for me. She will demonstrate slip glazing, which is a colonial method used during the period of our general store (the integrated project she is planning to do in the spring with an interdisciplinary group of teachers).

I spoke with the two classes about using Fridays to talk for half the period. The second half will be used to foot and glaze their pottery. They agreed that on Fridays they should not start anything new or it will dry too much over the weekend. I now have a time to work the interdisciplinary theme in for the rest of the semester. I found a long article in *U.S News and World Report* that starts out "If everyone says change is the only constant, then talking about it is a close second." The article covers the years 1933–1993 and highlights major changes occurring in those years. I think it will be a good way to begin discussions about how American life has changed and what brought about the changes.

Nov. 8–12

I think I am going to teach my basic art and crafts classes using the same format—primitive man, Native Americans, colonial—but then I want to bring in crafts from other countries: Batik from Bali, etc. I will probably connect the theme of change the same way I did in pottery—through the evolution of man's knowledge and art. The students seem to like to see the comparisons between each stage, and also to guess why the change happened.

Nov. 15–19

Not much going on. The students continue to learn to master the wheel. We are discussing what they will make for the general store. One student has mastered a basic candle holder. That was one of the clay objects they felt was appropriate for a colonial store. After Thanksgiving, we will take a trip to the library to do some digging in books. If we want to sell items that they make, we have to find things that can be mass produced. The simpler, the better. They came up with the idea that they could each do a part of an object like the Native Americans did. One person could make a cylinder on the wheel, another could trim and foot glaze, and yet another will glaze it. Sounds good to me.

I hate teaching an interdisciplinary course without input from the other disciplines. We need common planning time. And we need to share the same kids.

Martha Thompson,
Mt. Everett Regional High School
Sheffield, MA

Interview with Student in Martha's Class

What changes have you noticed in art class from last semester to this one?

It's more organized. We have an assigned project for each technique. We can be creative after practice. It's really different from last year. Then, you just came in and did your own thing. Themes make it more interesting.

Last time I had this class, I was failing out of it. Because the projects were so individual, I didn't know what to do. Now when I come in I have a direction. It's much better.

Case Study Discussion Questions

1. Martha writes of now feeling that she must explain the changes in her teaching to the students, even though they have not had this art course with her before. Discuss the value of articulating her development as a teacher to her classes.

2. Martha was involved in developing an integrated unit on local history, which is rich in stories from colonial times, and in which pottery plays a prominent role at the time that she was writing this journal. How does her enthusiasm for the unit come out of what she writes in the journal?

3. In the arts, where a teacher is showing students how to make things or perform like expert artists, it is natural for the teacher to relate to the students as a coach. How can this relationship be manifested in other subject areas? How can the student be the primary worker, with the teacher as coach in science, mathematics or language arts?

4. The student spoke about his response to the change in Martha's teaching. Do you think that students should be involved in a teacher's efforts to improve?

► REFERENCES

Aikin, W. M. (1942). *The story of the eight year study.* New York: Harper and Row.

American Association for the Advancement of Science (AAAS). (1989). *Science for all Americans: Project 2061.* Washington, DC: AAAS.

Barell, J.(1991). *Teaching for thoughtfulness: Classroom strategies to enhance intellectual development.* New York: Longman.

Brophy, J. (1992). Probing the subtleties of subject-matter teaching. *Educational Leadership, 49*(7), 4–9.

Caine, R. & Caine, G. (1991). *Making connections: Teaching and the human brain.* Alexandria, VA: ASCD.

Clark, B. (1986). *Optimizing learning.* Columbus, OH: Merrill.

Dewey, J. (1933). *How we think.* New York: D. C. Heath.

Dewey, J. (1938). *Experience and education.* New York: Macmillan.

Dillner, M. (1993). Using hypermedia to enhance content area instruction. *Journal of Reading, 37*(4), 260–272.

Erikson, F. & Schultz, J. (1992). Students' experience of the curriculum. In P. W. Jackson (Ed.), *Handbook of research on curriculum.* New York: Macmillan.

Fogarty, R. (1991). *The mindful school: How to integrate the curricula.* Palatine, IL: Skylight Publishing, Inc.

Freire, P. (1974). *Pedagogy of the oppressed.* New York: Seabury Press.

Goodlad, J. I. (1984). *A place called school.* New York: McGraw-Hill.

Goodlad, J. I. (1990). Connecting the present to the past. In J. I. Goodlad, R. Soder, and K. A. Sirotnik (Eds.), *Places where teachers are taught.* San Francisco: Jossey-Bass.

Jacobs, H. H. (1989). *Interdisciplinary curriculum: Design, development, and implementation.* Alexandria, VA: ASCD.

Jacobs, H.H. & Borland, J. (1979). A model for developing interdisciplinary curriculum. *The Gifted Child Quarterly,* Winter.

National Academy of Sciences (NAS). (1994). *Standards for science.* Washington, DC: NAS.

Lowry, L. (1989). *Number the stars.* Boston: Houghton Mifflin.

National Council of Teachers of Mathematics (NCTM). (1991). *Curriculum standards for school mathematics.* Reston, VA: NCTM.

Ogle, D. (1986). K-W-L: A teaching model that develops active reading of expository text. *The Reading Teacher, 39,* 564–570.

Parker, F.W. (1894) *Talks on pedagogics.* New York: E. L. Kellogg & Co.

Petrie, H. G. (1992). Interdisciplinary education: Are we faced with insurmountable opportunities? In G. Grant (Ed.), *Review of Research in Education,* V. 18. Washington, DC: American Educational Research Association.

Rudnitski, R. (1994). *In the thick of things: Teacher-initiated curriculum reform at a Massachusetts high school.* Paper presented at the Annual Meeting of the American Educational Research Association, New Orleans, April, 1994.

Rumelhart, D. E. (1980). Schemata: The building blocks of cognition. In R. J. Spiro, B. C. Bruce, and W. F. Brewer (Eds.), *Theoretical issues in reading comprehension.* Hillsdale, NJ: Erlbaum.

Samples, B. (1992). Using learning modalities to celebrate intelligence. *Educational Leadership, 50*(2), 62–66.

Sizer, T. (1992). *Horace's school: Redesigning the American high school.* Boston: Houghton Mifflin.

Taba, H. (1962). *Curriculum development: Theory and practice.* New York: Harcourt Brace Jovanovich.

Tanner, D. (1989). *A brief historical perspective on the struggle for an integrated curriculum.* Educational Horizons, Fall, 7–11.

Whitehead, A. N. (1929). *The aims of education and other essays.* New York: Macmillan.

Tanner, D. & Tanner, L. (1980). *Curriculum development: Theory into practice.* New York: Macmillan.

Yolen, J. (1990). *Sky dogs.* San Diego: Harcourt Brace Jovanovich.

SECTION

II

Pedagogical Strategies

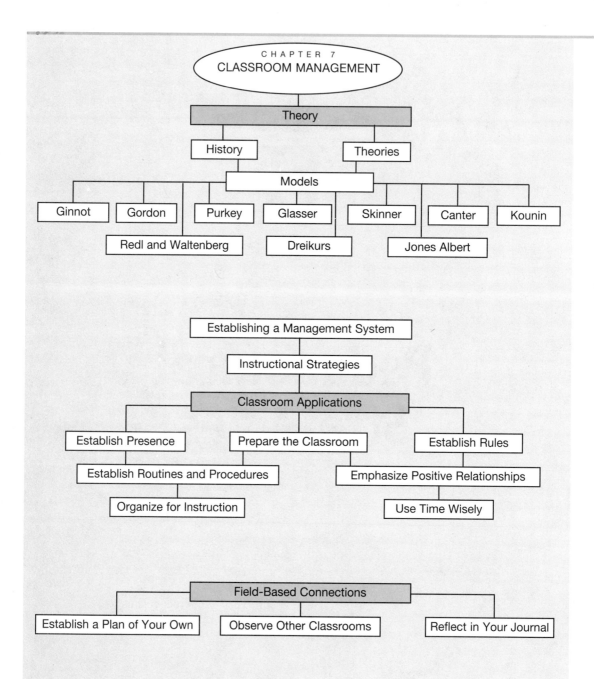

CHAPTER 7
CLASSROOM MANAGEMENT

Theory

History

Theories

Models

Ginnot

Gordon

Purkey

Glasser

Skinner

Canter

Kounin

Redl and Waltenberg

Dreikurs

Jones Albert

Establishing a Management System

Instructional Strategies

Classroom Applications

Establish Presence

Prepare the Classroom

Establish Rules

Establish Routines and Procedures

Emphasize Positive Relationships

Organize for Instruction

Use Time Wisely

Field-Based Connections

Establish a Plan of Your Own

Observe Other Classrooms

Reflect in Your Journal

Classroom Management and Discipline

Introduction

Management of the classroom and a system of disciplining the students must be established in order for instructional delivery to be effective. The first order of business in the classroom is to develop an organized system for routines, behavior, and communicating expectations that enhance successful teaching and learning. Classroom management and discipline are two interrelated practices that are typically categorized together in research studies. These practices are dependent on successful organization of the classroom, positive teacher/student relationships, and the use of appropriate instructional strategies.

The volume of books and articles about classroom management and behavior clearly demonstrate both the importance of and need to develop a personal plan for management. Reading and thinking about classroom management and relating these thoughts in a field-based experience is necessary to comprehend the complexities of teaching. The reasons and styles of classroom management vary, but the importance is clear— classroom management facilitates learning and helps to develop appropriate social behavior.

Traditional classroom management focused primarily on control through teacher intervention when students misbehaved. However, these discipline intervention strategies were ineffective and disrupted instruction. Current theories view classroom management as a proactive approach to prevent inappropriate behavior by involving students in procedures and learning in order to keep them interested in the lesson. Teachers develop these skills through reflection of pedagogy and knowledge that relates to a personal educational belief system.

The diversity of needs in today's schools and students usually means that teachers seldom follow one specific management theory, but create a system that works for the needs and goals of the class. An organized classroom management plan provides structure, while communicating expectations and consequences agreed to and discussed by the students. Understanding the theories for constructing a management system is essential since discipline is a prerequisite for learning. The teacher's theoretical base and pedagogical beliefs form the blueprint for the classroom management plan.

▶ THEORY

Introduction

The research and history of management and discipline is recent and abundant due in part to parent and teacher outcry. The *Phi Delta Kappan* publishes—every year since 1969—the Gallup Poll of public reaction and views towards education. Discipline has been at or near the top as a major problem every year since the poll began. Numerous studies (Abernathy et al., 1985; Farber & Miller, 1981; Gold, 1985; Iwanicki, 1983) attribute discipline as a major factor in teachers' burnout and departure from the classroom. According to Elam (1989), poor management and discipline produce stress so severe that it can lead to exhaustion, tension, and depression. During the first two years of teaching, classroom management and discipline cause the greatest difficulty and feeling of inadequacy (Cangelosi et al., 1988). Recent research shows significant correlations between classroom organization, student relationships, and instruction to good behavior and high achievement. McDaniel (1987) classifies classroom management research into three models: behavioral, human relations, and pedagogical.

Behavioral

Punishment

Prior to 1960 there was little research about classroom management or discipline. Methods

relied on theories like "don't smile till Christmas," and "to the tune of a hickory stick." When students misbehaved they were physically or verbally punished. Corporal punishment, as it is known, is the act of inflicting pain as a penalty. Fathman (1990) points out that corporal punishment is prevalent today and indicates that thirty-one states still consider it legal. James (1991) describes several court cases that teachers should consider when deciding about management and discipline. In the case of *Tinker v. Des Moines,* (1969) high school students won the right to protest the Vietnam War. This landmark case opened the debate over student rights. One such right, due process for students in *Goss v. Lopez* (1975), found that teachers are required by law to inform students of the reasons for suspension. Due process needs to be considered in any disciplinary action. Finally, *Garcia v. Miera* (1978) created the right for students to sue their teachers for punishment that is harmful. Teachers need to think about legal consequences especially when using physical responses to students' actions. Physical punishment can lead to emotional and physical injury, so educators and researchers began to study the psychology of behavior. These behavioral change techniques, however, still deserve ethical and legal considerations (Bentley, 1987).

Human Relations

Behavior Modification Model

Although B. F. Skinner never designed a discipline model, numerous psychologists and educators adapted his work with laboratory animals into a system of controlling student behavior. Axelrod (1977), McIntyre (1989), O'Leary and O'Leary (1977), and Sharpley (1985) are but a few who have promoted and extended Skinner's findings into classroom models to control students behavior in school. Behavior modification, a popular term used to describe Skinnerian techniques, is based on reinforcement through punishment and rewards. The use of positive reinforcement encourages desired behavior in students. When a teacher observes appropriate student behavior, it is reinforced with a reward to maintain that desired behavior. It is critical to make sure that students are rewarded for the desired behavior while ignoring the inappropriate behavior. By ignoring, a teacher extinguishes the undesirable behavior. The difficulty lies in identifying reinforcers that encourage desirable behavior without strengthening undesirable behavior. Positive reinforcement strengthens whatever behavior that follows. There are many reinforcers that teachers can use (Figure 7–1).

Caution is needed, according to several researchers (Deci, 1972; Hill, 1990; O'Leary et al., 1969; Selman, 1980; Wherry, 1983), when using behavior strategies, especially when teachers use praise as a reinforcer. Brophy (1986) believes that teachers are successful when praise is consistent, sincere, and tied to significant behavior with precise language.

Assertive Discipline Model

Canter (1976) developed a widely used form of behavior management called assertive discipline. This behavior control strategy demands respect for the teacher and learning process in the classroom. Canter believes that no one student keeps the teacher from teaching or the students from learning. For this strategy to work, teachers outline clearly stated classroom rules and consequences for behavior, then post these rules in the room for students to see and follow. Constant review and reinforcement of the rules occurs when students are consistently rewarded for on-task behavior and consistently punished for off-task behavior. Assertive discipline pro-

FIGURE 7–1 Common Reinforcers for Good Behavior

Type	Examples
Tangible	Real objects such as: food, pencils, ribbons, sports cards, books, notes, certificates
Graphic	Various markings such as: happy faces, stars, stickers, checks, symbols
Activity	Doing favorite activities such as: singing group work, classroom responsibilities, excused homework, special projects
Social	Verbal and non-verbal expressions such as: kind words, positive gestures, smiles, wink, pat on the back, handshake, high five, thumbs up, "I like" statements

vides strong teacher control to insist on meeting the rights and needs of everyone in the classroom. Students know, in advance, what is expected and have several chances to modify their behavior after several warnings. Figure 7–2 suggests a graduated system of consequences for off-task behavior.

Canter believes that teachers must be assertive to establish and maintain a classroom learning environment. Teachers must follow through with their assertive discipline plans by quick action to insure compliance. Students become conditioned to write their name on the chalkboard or move a clothespin or similar clip on a chart on the cue from the teacher whenever inappropriate off-task behavior happens. Canter states that teachers must be consistent when incorporating and implementing assertive discipline. This

behavior management model is easily adapted and used by many schools as a district or schoolwide plan.

Several researchers argue that there are serious drawbacks to the effectiveness of assertive discipline as behavior modification (Jones & Jones, 1990; Curwin & Mendler, 1988; Render et al., 1989). Hill (1990) questions student dependency on the teacher to consistently reinforce rewards or apply punishment to control and modify behavior.

Counseling Model

Early work by Redl and Wattenberg (1959) describe ways for teachers to influence, rather than punish, students to maintain behavior. They were some of the first

FIGURE 7–2 Typical Consequences for Assertive Discipline

Misbehavior	Elementary Classroom	Secondary Classroom
First Warning	Name on board or move clip	Name on board
Second Warning	One check by name or move clip—time out	One check by name—time out
Third Warning	Two checks by name or move clip—lose recess	Two checks by name—30-minute school detention
Fourth Warning	Three checks by name or move clip—student phones parents and explains behavior	Three checks by name—60-minute school detention
Fifth Warning	Four checks by name or move clip—detention, meet with principal or parent conference	Four checks by name—in-school suspension, conference with parents

researchers to believe that physical punishment of students should only be used when all else fails.

The belief that control and punishment of students should shift to an emphasis of emotional support followed the humanistic psychology movement. Ginnot (1971) and Gordon (1974) believed that positive relationships and improved self-esteem would result in improved student behavior. Dreikurs (1968) and Glasser (1969) developed a counseling model where students learn to control behavior through the help of the teacher who assists students in making good choices. Dreikurs went so far as to question the use of punishment as a logical consequence of behavior. Teachers were expected to be more democratic, while encouraging students to be responsible for their own behavior. Glasser's "time-out strategy," where students are removed from instruction for a brief period of time to allow them to think about what they were doing and should be doing, provides a way for students to correct—in their thoughts—their misbehavior. Jones and Jones (1990) stated that although teachers do not have the time to use in-depth counseling techniques, many of these strategies are helpful for students in learning how to control themselves.

Pedagogical

Instructional Model

Kounin's (1970) initial findings showed that teachers with effective instructional delivery systems prevented misbehavior and created a supportive learning environment. Further study by Brophy and Evertson (1976) confirmed these findings. Kounin believed that by engaging students in the learning process, teachers prevent, rather than control, misbehavior. Kounin, through viewing numerous videotapes of classroom teachers at all levels, discovered several management strategies for the entire class, groups, and individuals. Kounin used specific terms to define classroom observations. The first technique defined was the "ripple effect," which happens when a teacher praises a specific behavior and that behavior then spreads out to other students in the class. Therefore, if a teacher acknowledges a student who is attending to task, others in the group are encouraged to do the same. "Withitness" implies that a teacher knows what is happening in the classroom at all times. Teachers need to position themselves where they can constantly observe students to achieve this goal. Timing is important when attending to students. Time awareness is important to "overlapping," which is the ability of a teacher to manage several tasks at one time: groups and individual students. Overlapping and withitness demonstrate to students that the teacher is monitoring student learning.

Kounin found a relationship between behavior and the teacher's ability to move or pace (Pacing is the ability of the teacher to judge the students' attentiveness and motivation in a lesson.) from one activity to the next. Good pacing involves adapting the sequencing of activities to suit the attention and interest level of the students without "showdowns." Momentum keeps the lesson moving along in an acceptable time frame to avoid satiation and maintain student interest. "Overdwelling" occurs when teachers spend too much time explaining or talking. Transition involves an orderly change between activities or subjects, and "jerkiness" occurs when teachers neglect to prepare students for the next activity. Kounin's techniques and terms focus around the teachers' ability to maintain student attentiveness while challenging the students through a variety of classroom activities.

Preventive Model

Kounin's research sparked numerous studies and models that analyzed the instructional and preventive mode of classroom management (Charles, 1989; Duke & Meckel, 1984; Wolfgang & Glickman, 1986). Results of staff development and training in use of these management models show limited success. Any management model should be used as a supplement to a larger and more comprehensive discipline and management system (Emmer & Aussiker, 1987). Further study by Emmer & Aussiker (1988) found that many of these management models neglect to deal with the everyday skills students need to prevent problems before they occur. Many models for classroom management developed by psychiatrists, psychologists, and theorists depended on previous models for new conceptual frameworks. Review shows many ideas from behavioral and human relations models assist teachers in understanding the complex pedagogical relationship between effective instruction and management (McDaniel, 1987). Teachers need to be researchers who analyze and choose preventive and control strategies to influence decisions about management and instruction (Richardson, 1990).

Achievement and Behavior

Successful teachers implement a systematic approach to management at the beginning of the year (Evertson & Emmer, 1982; Evertson & Harris, 1992). How a teacher organizes for instruction during the first few days and weeks of school has a positive impact on student achievement (Brophy, 1988). Effective teachers know how to manage classroom routines and procedures to maximize on-task behavior (Evertson & Harris, 1992). Research by Soar and Soar (1986) indicates that structure—not necessarily teacher rules—in the classroom is essential for learning to occur. The initial classroom management plan needs to be adapted with student input throughout the school year to meet the constant change in the lives and needs of students and teachers (Figure 7–3)

The quality of teacher-student relationships has an impact on the achievement and behavior of students. Students learn more in classrooms that meet their personal and psychological needs (Albert, 1989; Brophy, 1983). Student needs are varied and change; therefore, teachers must develop practical techniques to prevent and correct disruptive behavior while keeping students and learning on-task. Positive relationships with teachers build student self-esteem and promote a healthy self-concept. The need for fun, freedom, power, and a sense of belonging exists in all students regardless of socio-economic status, culture, gender or special needs.

Many times problems caused in the home environment can transfer to behavior and achievement in school. The home environment offers no excuses for teachers who are in a position to encourage students in the classroom. Teachers who take the time to let students know they care can prevent inappropriate attention-seeking behavior. Glasser (1988) believes that ninety-five percent of student discipline problems stem from the lack of having

FIGURE 7–3   Beginning the Year Management Treatment

1. **Readying the classroom.** Be certain your classroom space and materials are ready for the beginning of the year.

2. **Planning rules and procedures.** Think about what procedure students must follow to function effectively in your classroom and in the school environment: Decide what behaviors are acceptable or unacceptable; develop a list of procedures and rules. Students should discuss and participate in rulemaking as needed.

3. **Consequences.** Decide ahead of time consequences for appropriate and inappropriate behavior in your classroom and communicate them to your students; follow through consistently.

4. **Teaching rules and procedures.** Teach students rules and procedures systematically; include in your lesson plans for the beginning of school sequences for teaching rules and procedures, when and how they will be taught, and when practice and review will occur.

5. **Beginning-of-school activities.** Develop activities for the first few days of school that will involve students readily and maintain a whole-group focus.

6. **Strategies for potential problems.** Plan strategies to deal with potential problems that could upset your classroom organization and management.

7. **Monitoring.** Monitor student behavior closely.

8. **Stopping inappropriate behavior.** Handle inappropriate and disruptive behavior promptly and consistently.

9. **Organizing instruction.** Organize instruction to provide learning activities at suitable levels for all students in your class.

10. **Student accountability.** Develop procedures that keep the children responsible for their work.

11. **Instructional clarity.** Be clear when you present information and give directions to your students.

Reprinted with permission, C. Evertson, E. Emmer, J. Sanford, and B. Clements (1983), "Improving Management: An Experiment in Elementary School Classrooms," *Elementary School Journal, 84*, 173–188.

someone listen to them. Even though it is diffi-cult to analyze the reasons why students mis-behave and disrupt learning, take time to clari-fy and discuss with students reasons for their behavior. Major studies conclude that school environments fail to meet students' needs (Boyer 1983; Glasser, 1988; Goodlad, 1984; Kozol, 1991; Sizer, 1984). Teachers must believe they can make a difference and show it, especially through establishing positive human relationships to meet the personal, psychologi-cal, and academic needs of all students.

Special-Need Students

Some students can be disruptive or difficult to manage. Curwin and Mendler (1988) believe the most chronic behavior problems relate to dignity. Students who constantly disrupt do so because they believe they cannot and will not be a success at school. When students' dignity is at stake they will do anything to protect themselves. Curwin and Mendler offer several suggestions to prevent problems, such as mov-ing disruptive students closer to the teacher, breaking tasks into parts, and setting time lim-its. Keep trying various techniques with dis-ruptive students; but avoid power struggles.

Students with special needs (see Chapter 2) can be difficult for some teachers to manage in the regular classroom. Since Public Law 94-142, students with emotional or learning prob-lems are being mainstreamed into the regular class for part or all of the day, depending on the least restricted educational environment. Special-need students benefit from highly structured and supportive classrooms (Jones, 1987). Gifted students also have special needs to be considered to prevent them from becom-ing bored and disruptive.

Conclusion to Theory

Managing classroom routines and establish-ing a system for discipline is necessary for teaching and learning. Classrooms with good management have higher on-task behavior and achievement. Effective classroom man-agement considers student needs and facili-tates appropriate social behavior.

Traditional classrooms focus on control-ling student behavior. There are several behavior modification models that teachers and researchers use to condition students to behave in an appropriate way. Skinner's research was used by educators in beginning discipline models. Many behavior models exist and today the *Canter Assertive Discipline* model is used in many schools.

Human relations models are also important to assist students in looking at their behavior for improvement. Dreikurs was one of the first researchers to question punishment as a logical consequence of behavior. Glasser has devel-oped a counseling approach to management that helps students to think about choices.

Pedagogical models combine behavior and human relations strategies with a focus on instruction. Kounin discovered that good teaching prevented disruptive behavior and created a supportive learning environment. A good balance between prevention and control leads to higher academic achievement.

Teachers need to change views of how instruction is organized to prevent manage-ment problems. In many instances, teachers need to look at how they teach to prevent man-agement problems. Future research findings are likely to qualify and change the way teach-ers respond to classroom organization, stu-dent relationships, and appropriate pedagogy for developing responsible individuals.

► CLASSROOM APPLICATIONS

Introduction

Research shows many techniques for teachers, to develop a comprehensive personal management system. Selecting theories and ideas from behavioral psychology, human relations counseling, and instructional pedagogy helps teachers organize preventive and control measures that facilitate positive student behavior and increased achievement.

There is no single universal panacea for classroom management as some of the theories seem to suggest. Teachers need to consider the countless variables that influence students outside school and the home. The suggestions following are examples from major research models and theories and from teachers and students working in many schools and classrooms. These suggestions are not intended to be memorized, used as a quick fix or cookbook of strategies or used instead of planning and thoughtful reflection about the needs of students. They are listed for easy referral as you learn in a field-based school.

Seven Major Topics: Personal Management System

Following are seven major topics to help organize the development of a management system:

- Establish a presence in the classroom and school;
- Prepare the classroom;

- Establish classroom rules;
- Establish routines and procedures;
- Emphasize positive relationships with students;
- Organize for instruction; and
- Use time wisely.

Establish a Presence in the Classroom and School

Our experience tells us that most teachers are not risk-takers. We believe that teachers should take charge of their professional responsibility and assume the right to establish a caring positive learning environment in the classroom that meets the needs of the students. Teachers are empowered with responsibility for students and with themselves as agents for learning and personal development. Be a positive person who sees solutions instead of problems. Boost morale and esteem in your classroom and school through example and thoughtful consideration.

Boosting Morale and Esteem

Here are several suggestions to help establish a presence in the classroom and school:

- *Be a responsible role model.* Be on time, practice positive talk, be firm and consistent. Enjoy work, smile, and convey the importance of education and responsibility.
- *Take charge.* Be assertive, but democratic. Speak out and stand up for your educational beliefs.

- *Demand respect and show respect.* School cultures need to show and get more respect. Dignity and respect are important ingredients for students and teachers. Help students learn respect for themselves and each other.

- *Note sensitivities.* Control your pet peeves and show tolerance for others. Understand and show concern for multiculturalism. Appreciate diversity, language, and gender.

- *Support school events.* Enthusiastically attend school, parent, and student events. Take personal pride in your school and students.

- *Know school policy.* Read district personnel policy to know your rights and limits. Find answers to potential problems before you encounter them.

- *Greet others.* Take time to smile and engage in conversation with students, parents, administrators, coaches, colleagues, custodians, secretaries, and other school staff.

- *Establish cohorts and team spirit.* Work with others in your subject or grade level. Share ideas and develop collegiality. Working together saves time and duplication of work.

- *Know your students.* Look at cumulative records, being careful not to form negative opinions. Converse with students regularly to help meet individual needs. Find out their likes and dislikes to develop positive teacher/student relationships.

- *Tour the community.* Drive through the school's attendance zone to familiarize yourself with the environment of the students. Make short home visits or telephone calls to parents when appropriate.

- *Use effective communication skills.* Constantly communicate with parents, teachers, and staff. Speak courteously and directly to others. Avoid negative lounge talk about students, teachers, parents or administrators.

Prepare the Classroom

An organized learning environment saves time for learning, especially if extra time is needed for teachers who share classrooms or teach laboratory courses. Begin to collect and save materials, resources, and ideas for your classroom throughout your field-based experiences. Organizing a classroom the first year of teaching can be difficult, so make it easier by keeping lists and sketches of routines, procedures, lessons, and activities you observe.

Preparing for Instruction and Learning

Here are several suggestions to help prepare the classroom for instruction and learning.

- *Arrange seating.* Decide how you want to prepare seating for instruction and place desks or tables for easy movement around the classroom. You can use rows, tables or group desks together. Try several possible seating arrangements based on different instructional activities.

- *Prepare bulletin boards.* Create a bulletin board that reinforces lessons. Make use of this space for instructional review or to display student accomplishments.

- *Use chalkboard or overhead projector.* The chalkboard is a helpful resource to visually present directions, assignments or information relevant to your lesson. Use the chalk board frequently to visually present important concepts and information.

- *Display student work.* Provide an area in the classroom to display all students' work. This provides an opportunity for you to acknowledge the worth of all students as well as the importance of what you teach.

- *Distribute textbooks.* Have textbooks ready to distribute as well as a form if one is not provided by the school. Account for each textbook matched to each student. Most states provide textbooks and the student is responsible for keeping and maintaining the book. Fines are usually levied for damaged books and replacement costs must be collected.

- *Provide reference materials.* Collect old magazines, books, encyclopedias, atlases, supplies, and dictionaries. Create an area in your room for students to access information to extend learning or create projects.

- *Check and maintain equipment.* Routinely check overhead projectors, computers, VCRs, slide projectors or other equipment before instruction. Make sure the equipment is available, that it works, and you know how to operate it properly.

- *Prepare material for parents.* Develop a communication system for parents. Establish visiting hours, conference times, and a means to send information and work home to parents and non-custodial parents as well.

Establish Classroom Rules

Following rules and demonstrating appropriate social behavior is a major goal of education that helps to prepare students for society.

Clearly articulated rules allow students to meet classroom expectations. Students need to know and participate in designing classroom rules and consequences. Rules are used in conjunction with pedagogy to meet the needs of students. Rules should be developed that encourage self-control and responsibility rather than teacher control. Rules intend to prevent and correct management problems to allow instruction to occur.

Common Routine Suggestions

The following suggestions will help you to devise, maintain, and adapt classroom rules:

- *Set priorities.* Think about what is most important for you to function as a successful teacher and for students to learn. Decide what is necessary to meet your philosophy and vision of a teacher.

- *Involve the students in developing rules.* A sense of ownership and the value of opinion is an important need. Students who have a say in the classroom behave better. Also, it is important to know why and how rules benefit people who work together.

- *Keep rules brief and attainable.* Develop rules and prioritize them according to those that are most important to you and your students.

- *State rules positively.* Avoid negative rule statements. Rather, state terms positively, such as "use good manners." Take time to discuss and give examples of what the rules mean to you and the students.

- *Develop consequences for rules.* Let students help decide and understand the rewards and consequences of their actions. Stress the rewards and consistently reinforce those who follow rules. Follow through quickly when students misbehave and invoke the consequences attached to the rule.

- *Post the rules in the classroom.* Show the importance of rules by posting them in a place for all to see. As students make choices, refer to the rules to encourage good behavior.

- *Periodically review rules.* Constantly—especially at the beginning of school—discuss, review, and revise rules with the students. Positively encourage and show satisfaction for how well students are behaving. This proactive approach is better than referring to rules only when rules are not followed.

- *Model rules of good behavior.* Help students learn the importance of rules through your actions and discussions. Avoid complaining about rules you must follow to the students. Demonstrate constructive ways to disagree and revise rules.

Establish Routines and Procedures

There is a specified amount of time students spend in school. Development of routines and procedures determines how much time students will be on-task learning. The amount of time a teacher has to instruct also depends heavily upon how well classroom routines and procedures are organized. The number of routines and procedures in a school and classroom can be overwhelming; thinking about ways and means you can increase on-task learning time is worth the effort. Saving five minutes on routines a day adds two and one half hours of instruction for each six-week

period. The "engaged" time (amount of time students are involved in learning) can be organized and structured to save time in the "allocated" time (specified limit of time scheduled). Routines and procedures should be organized in a way that increases instructional time while lessening disruption of instruction and learning. Clearly defined procedures should be discussed, explained, and rehearsed to insure understanding and correct implementation. There are many classroom routines to organize.

Common Routine Suggestions

Here are some common routines and suggestions to help organize instructional time:

- *Entering and beginning class.* Post a schedule on the chalkboard that includes an activity for students' arrival to the classroom. Develop specific routines and habits (sitting down, getting material ready) for students to follow when entering the classroom. Communicate and practice these procedures to start promptly in the instructional process.

- *Taking attendance: noting tardiness and absenteeism.* Take role quickly. Use a seating chart and check off students as you are teaching. Set up a file folder or work basket for seatwork, assignments, and projects for absent students. Appoint a peer to assist with missed classroom notes and overview of class activities for those tardy or absent.

- *Providing for students without materials or supplies.* Students will forget books, pencils, papers, and other materials for class. Some teachers have extras available or allow students to share. The responsibility to come to class prepared is a good trait to expect from students. Define your expectations regarding students responsibility for class preparation and consistently deal with this problem quickly to facilitate instruction and learning.

- *Clarify assignments.* Explain the details for each assignment. Provide information about pen/pencil, written/typed, heading, style, format, neatness, evaluation criteria, length, due date, late work, incomplete work, tests, make-up policies, and any other requirements necessary for the nature of the assignment. Clarify the assignment on the front end to save time, confusion, and frustration for you and the student.

- *Completing in-class assignments.* Students work at different levels and speed. Provide for individual and group work needs concerning quantity and quality in the class time period. Guidelines and limits must be placed so students can be engaged and stay on-task. A warning about the time remaining before class is dismissed is useful. Teachers should move about the room to monitor and encourage student progress. Students can be paired or peer tutored to assist in the understanding and completion of in-class assignments.

- *Completing assignments ahead of schedule.* Some students complete assignments more quickly than others. It is smart to plan extra activities, such as challenging worksheets or interesting reading assignments for these students. Many gifted students who complete work early or are not challenged by the assignment can disrupt the classroom. Prepare materials to meet the needs of special education students.

- *Assigning homework.* When assigning homework, use the same procedures that are described in the "clarify assignments" discussion above. Some students will need modification of assignments due to special needs. A teacher can lessen the amount or redesign material for students to gain knowledge and successfully complete the assignment. Give several examples to help students complete homework assignments and spend reasonable time presenting and discussing the homework assignment. Homework is a valuable and effective strategy when used to review, reinforce or extend material taught in class.

- *Distributing and collecting papers.* Develop specific procedures for handing out and collecting papers and assignments. Have built-in procedures to identify those who did not complete the work. Students can help with this routine and their assistance can save instruction time. Some teachers use collection and distribution centers that allow each person to be responsible for obtaining and returning assignments.

- *Define times for classroom movement.* Let students know when they can move to centers, sharpen pencils, get books, and go to the teacher. State specific periods and times in the day when students can move to various areas in the class. It is usually better for the teacher to move about the class when assistance is needed than to have the students come to you.

- *Describe ways for schoolwide movement.* Students need to know appropriate ways and times for moving about the school. Usually, some type of school pass is required and time limits are imposed between class period changes. Younger students will need to be taught where and how to go to the library, restroom, playground, cafeteria, auditorium, and offices. It is best to move students through several short stops instead of the entire distance when moving in the school. This prevents running and disturbing other classes.

- *Define noise levels.* Set times when students can interact with each other and times for attentive listening. Allow various levels of constructive noise. Define noise limits for group activities (whisper) and silence when individuals address the class.

- *Use seatwork productively.* Since students spend a great amount of time at their desks, seatwork should be interesting and related to the lesson. Teachers should also move about the room to assist and adjust students' progress. Provide examples and clear instructions and be sure to have all the students' attention when giving direction; allow students to help one another, because this procedure is one way to help evaluate and diagnose student progress. Keep seatwork short and avoid overuse of this strategy.

- *Teach group expectations.* When students work in cooperative groups they need to be taught rules, responsibilities, and expectations. Decide on rules for group work and set clear expectations as to what each group is to accomplish. Assign each person in the group a particular task to perform in order to share the responsibility and work load. Take time to practice group work until students learn ways to function in the group. Establish noise levels and clear expectations.

- *Inform students and parents of grading system.* Teachers have been known to create some of the most confusing coding systems ever designed for grading students.

Keep your system easy to understand and use. Whatever system you decide upon, explain your grading process to students and parents. Allow opportunity for a variety of grades and record grades quickly and accurately. Grading students causes stress and concern, so record grades frequently instead of at the six-week grading term only.

- *Lessen opportunity for cheating.* Explain your disposition and the school's policy for those who cheat on school assignments, papers, and exams. Initiate procedures in the classroom that deter the opportunity for cheating. Provide a wide variety of ways for students to work together and individually to gain encouragement and confidence. Communicate your lack of tolerance for those who have others do their work. Explain the moral, ethical, and legal issue involved in plagiarism and the need to learn and develop pride in completing their own work.

- *Provide direction for class disruption.* Today's classrooms are constantly bombarded with interruptions from the PA system, principals, university students, evaluators, visitors, and parents. Teach students ways to continue with on-task behavior. Prevent embarrassment and disruption by developing a plan with the students on how they will behave when visitors come to class. Their ideas and involvement in this process will allow for smooth continuation of learning.

- *Dismissing class.* The lesson should not end when the bell rings. At least five minutes before the class ends, provide closure or review of the lesson with an exciting preview for the next class. Establish a lining up technique that works best and is safe for your grade or subject level.

Emphasize Positive Relationships with Students

Research shows that students' behavior and achievement is influenced by teachers. Positive teachers have positive students who achieve higher and demonstrate productive on-task classroom skills. Teachers who create exciting learning environments that involve students input and activity have fewer disruptions. Positive and friendly still means incorporating a classroom environment that is firm, consistent, and challenging. The blend of warmth and care is a difficult balance to achieve, particularly for beginning teachers. Friendly, positive teachers still maintain classroom order and structure. A sense of confidence with command and respect is an important image to convey to students. Teachers are real people and should demonstrate openness and concern for student needs. Empathy and sensitivity, combined with a professional attitude, demonstrate traits needed to promote self-esteem and high self-concepts that promote successful learning. Effective teachers know the importance of classroom management and encourage student dialogue to create interesting classrooms and procedures. Personal attention from a teacher helps students to know that someone cares about them. Teacher acknowledgement gives students a sense of worth, dignity, freedom, and power necessary to experience genuine success.

Building Positive Teacher-Student Relationships

Here are some suggestions for building positive teacher-student relationships:

- *Allow students a voice.* Through communication, the teacher receives valuable feedback from the students. Take time to discuss issues and attentively listen to what students say. Provide numerous and varied opportunities for students to provide you with verbal and written evaluations.

- *Allow students a choice.* Autocratic teaching styles that emphasize control bring about unnecessary power struggles. We live in a democracy and classroom management should reflect democratic principles. Whenever possible, allow students to make thoughtful choices concerning their behavior, consequences, and learning experiences.

- *Assess student interest and needs.* Devise surveys, interviews, interest inventories, and communicate personally to students at their level to discover their needs and interests. Many difficult and disruptive students can be reached by relating classroom experiences and lessons to student interest. Student interest can be used for motivating and rewarding appropriate behavior which can assist in building positive relationships.

- *Be sensitive to the students' lives.* Many students live in hardship or traumatic environments. Open dialogue *and* communication with students, parents, and guardians help you to get to know the problems they encounter away from school. Sometimes you discover abuse. In most states you must, by law, inform school personnel (nurse, principal) of suspected abuse. You need to know the policies and legal responsibilities to report suspected abuse.

- *Individualize when needed.* Students can excel if you relate assignments and school work to their interests. Allow students to develop alternative plans for completing assignments, homework or projects. Break large assignments into smaller sections. Provide options frequently to allow students to gain confidence and success in completing assignments in a self-determined manner. Self-motivation is often overlooked as a strategy for disruptive students.

- *Use a variety of reinforcers.* All students want attention. Therefore, as a teacher, you need to encourage desirable behavior. Otherwise, students will attract your attention through negative off-task behavior. Use positive, tangible, graphic, activity, and social reinforcers when you catch students in the act of being responsible and attending to task.

- *Provide verbal and non-verbal encouragement.* Students (and teachers) need recognition. Positive praise combined with high expectation enhances teacher-student relationships. Give praise for being good as well as praise for accomplishment. Positive talk and non-verbal cues are successful strategies to build cooperative relationships.

- *Use contracts when needed.* Some students have difficulty relating and responding to verbal and non-verbal praise. A written contract between teacher and student that specifies outcomes and behaviors is a valuable strategy for improving student behavior and achievement.

- *Promote good study skills and habits.* Review study techniques to help students achieve. Note taking, outlining, reading for comprehension, using references, and other study skill strategies need to be taught. Students build upon prior knowledge. Provide outlines and study guides to help students gain an overview of what to learn.

- *Model good citizenship.* Respect students and treat them with dignity at all times.

Remain calm in tense and emotional situations. Listen to all points of view and encourage students to solve their problems. Avoid sarcasm, value judgments, negative statements, and critical remarks. These are not only ineffective, but they damage teacher-student relationships. Avoid large group scenes and power struggles in front of others. Discuss differences in a respectful and private manner.

Organize for Instruction

Good teaching is linked to good behavior. Spend most of your time creating, implementing, and maintaining effective teaching practices that support behavior and learning and less time on control of students. Constant monitoring and changes in lessons are necessary to compete with the everyday distractions and high-tech programs facing students. Teachers must solve problems and make quick decisions to alter lessons to keep and maintain classroom management that promotes on-task behavior. Successful teachers engage students in the instructional process to prevent classroom disruption.

A Comprehensive Plan of Instruction

The following suggestions based on Kounin's work and expanded by numerous researchers are not isolated skills, but components to be used in a comprehensive, well-thought-out plan for instruction:

- *Develop a plan.* You certainly wouldn't build a house or go on a long trip without a plan.

"Winging it" (teaching without a plan), leads to behavior problems. Think through what students should accomplish as a result of this lesson. Like a good play or symphony, a lesson has a beginning, middle, and end. Other points in this sectin are part of a good plan prevents management problems and promotes successful learning.

- *Give clear directions.* Disruptive behavior will occur when students do not know what to do or how to do it. Procedural direction tied with quality examples helps students to begin and complete the assignment. Write the directions on the chalkboard and point to them when questions about what to do are asked. Give directions in small parts with examples while being sure that students are attentive and listening.

- *Introduce lessons with a purpose.* Generate excitement and motivation at the beginning as well as throughout the lesson. At the same time, students should be told what they are going to do and learn as a result of the lesson. Knowing the goal or objective of the lesson and sharing it with the students is an effective teaching practice; students who are informed about the learning process become more productive and involved in it.

- *Relate learning to the everyday lives and prior learning of students.* Put the content of the lesson in perspective of how the information can relate to the lives of the students. Build upon student interest and prior learning. Describe ways that the information learned can be used in real life situations to give a purpose and desire for the student to learn the knowledge and skills being taught.

- *Demonstrate enthusiasm and excitement.* Show life and enthusiasm for teaching. In today's world, a leader has to compete with high-tech films and MTV to gain an audience. Sitting at the desk screaming out instructions about seatwork is ineffective. Teachers must create lively lessons that engage students in the learning process. Do the unexpected at the beginning of each lesson to engage and maintain student interest.

- *Observe student reactions.* Be "with it" at all times by constantly watching and reading the student audience. By observing the students, you can monitor on-task behavior and attentiveness to the lesson. Learn to use hand gestures to bring students back to the lesson. Also, walk about the room to observe students' engagement in the assignment, check their understanding, and monitor the degree of progress.

- *Maintain students attention.* Keep the pace of the lesson moving. Remember attention spans and divide lessons into interesting segments. Avoid excessive teacher talk and overdwelling of a particular topic. Stay focused on the lesson's objective and keep the students on task. Impose time limits in your plans to keep the lesson moving with high teacher-student interest. Simply: If you are bored, so are the students.

- *Use a variety of instruction.* Students have different learning styles. Adjust and use a variety of auditory, visual, and tactile learning experiences in your lessons. Students of today are accustomed to visual stimulation. Whenever possible, supplement each lesson with a variety of visual learning. Employ videos, films, overheads, computers, and technology to meet the learning needs of students.

- *Monitor individual and group activities.* Once assignments are made and clear directions are given, a teacher must move about the room to clarify and encourage on-task behavior. Praise and encourage groups for their efforts and quickly help students and groups solve dilemmas they encounter. Seatwork and group work are not times for teachers to do paperwork or grading activities at the desk. Prevent disruption by working with the students during these in-class activities and assignments.

- *Use active instruction.* Students learn when they are actively engaged in doing what has been taught. Learning takes place when students experience and apply content and skills. Students also learn when they demonstrate they can do what they were taught.

- *Remove distractions.* Students can be easily distracted by any number of things available to them. Remove pencils, toys, equipment or personal objects that will compete with your teaching. Scan the room constantly to see what students are observing and remove these distractions quickly and quietly as you proceed with the lesson. Some distractions—world events, death, illness, etc.— need acknowledgement and discussion because of emotional involvement. Deal with these issues as student needs indicate, with agreement to move onto the lesson when a crisis is resolved or becomes repetitive.

- *Set time limits.* When students express a need to deal with an important issue or an anxiety-producing situation, set a limit on the amount of instructional time you will schedule for discussion. Students will frequently get off-task with lengthy teacher talk. Pace the lesson to include student-cen-tered learning experiences. Time limits will keep the lesson moving and increase student attention.

- *Provide smooth transition between activities.* Smooth transition from one activity to the next is a very important classroom management strategy. Students need to be prompted ahead of time to be informed when transition will take place. Giving a warning that five minutes remain to complete group work helps students to maintain work involvement. Abrupt endings without warning and change of activities without warning distract the learning process.

- *Reinforce student accomplishments throughout the lesson.* Teachers who take time to praise students who work on-task have fewer disruptions and higher student achievement. Take the time to acknowledge high expectations and performance.

- *Give immediate, specific, and honest feedback.* Receiving feedback is associated with success. Students frequently feel insecure or uncertain about their performance or success. The quality of feedback is more important than the quantity. The importance of quality feedback helps students to develop healthy academic perceptions of themselves. Give the quality feedback immediately to increase the effect. Praise, if late, underused or overused, is not an effective strategy.

- *Use outlines and advanced organizers.* Identify the main ideas and supporting concepts to help students understand basic content before instruction. Use several examples, situations, and demonstrations to make the content meaningful and possible to learn. Providing examples helps students to organize for learning and reinforces good study habits.

- *Summarize the lesson with frequent review.* Take the time in the instructional process to briefly repeat major points and concepts. Ask students to extend, provide examples, and relate concepts to their lives. This strategy helps to check for understanding throughout the lesson, while reinforcing basic content and skills that students are expected to learn.

- *Provide for evaluation.* Evaluation of instruction exists in two forms: one is to assess the extent of student learning for each lesson; the other is to evaluate your performance as a teacher. Take time to reflect and think about the effectiveness of the lesson. Seek student input and alter instructional procedures accordingly. Constantly evaluate your performance to improve and increase student behavior and achievement. Keep track of your instruction in your journal.

Use Time Wisely

One of the most frequent complaints we hear from teachers is about the demands on teacher time. Using good time management strategies in your classroom, professional, and personal life will lead to productivity and reduced stress. Only so much can be completed in a given amount of time, so *how* teachers use time is an important issue in classroom management. Time for teachers is more than accomplishment of procedural responsibilities. Teachers need time to reflect on their practice and routines in order to change, improve, and be an effective professional.

Time Efficiency

Beginning and experienced teachers need to take time to think about ways to use time efficiently in order to restructure and improve the quality learning process.

- *Schedule time to reflect and organize.* Front-end planning saves time. Schedule time each day to reflect and organize ways to improve your instruction and classroom management. When working in grade levels or subject teams, prepare a brief agenda and follow it. Make lists from reflection time of things you want to accomplish each day and check them off as they are completed.

- *Structure routine paperwork.* Handle each paper once. When you grade papers record the grade at the same time. When you get a memo that needs a response jot down your response at that time. Use a computer to organize your record keeping and planning. Save only important papers and organize a filing system.

- *Delegate when possible.* Seek support from university professors' students. Allow them the opportunity to learn while they assist you in the classroom. Let the students help with bulletin boards, collections, and other routine procedures that develop their responsibility and save you time. Use parents and volunteers to help you in your classroom. Take the time to teach them your expectations and communicate daily with those who assist you to provide direction and save more time. Shed the notion that "if you want it done right, do it yourself." Today's students need as much assistance as you can provide in your classroom.

- *Talk to colleagues.* Talk to grade level and subject level teachers in your school, district, and at professional meetings. Share ideas and plans to save time. Form cooperative planning groups to develop exciting lessons and thematic units, remembering that several great minds are better then one. Support from other teachers provides an outlet to discuss issues and problems that can lead to productive solutions.

- *Communicate to administration and parents.* Many times administration and parents can be extremely helpful in providing support needed for projects or equipment. Discuss and include administration in your plans and share your successes. Seek to get parents involved in their child's education and learn to seek their input and support to assist you.

- *Seek outlets to reduce stress.* Take time to pursue non-teaching interests. Develop a life outside of the classroom to lessen stress. Teaching is very stress-producing, especially when the students or you have a difficult day. Rebound and reflect on prevention strategies to get back on track.

- *Begin and end class on time.* Keep the engaged learning time in the classroom at maximum. Remember, five minutes saved a day is two and one half hours in a six-week grading period. Model the importance of being prompt and avoid slow classroom starts. Keep yourself on-task in the same way you work with students' on-task behavior.

- *Upgrade teacher skills and keep informed about current research.* Teachers, as professionals, need to constantly improve, learn, and upgrade their skills and knowledge. Be

scholarly-like, because teaching and learning does not end with a degree.

▶ FIELD-BASED CONNECTIONS

Introduction

Intern students tell us frequently how difficult it is for them to develop management strategies in a classroom with a pre-established management plan. Often, this established plan does not fit with their expectations, philosophy or vision of how a management system should be organized.

Students who are in an internship have instructional responsibilities and must establish and implement their own classroom management system with the assistance of the mentor teacher. This process is an important step in the growth of the intern. Students respond to adults differently. The students need to know the intern's expectations and the consequences of their classroom management system in order to adapt to their instructional management philosophy. It is almost impossible to experience a quality internship without establishing and implementing a personal classroom management system. Interns must be viewed as teachers, and mentors must promote cooperative respect when working together. We strongly suggest at the beginning of the field-based experience that mentor teachers and intern students take the time to discuss classroom management and decide how the intern/mentor responsibilities will be organized and implemented into the classroom.

Intern students need to organize and implement their personal management plan. Through reflection, guidance, and feedback from the mentor teacher and university professor, the management plan will add necessary pedagogical experience for the intern.

Guidelines for Interns

Pick and choose the activities that best suit you and your needs. Use these suggestions for your unit plans, portfolio collection, and your journal entries where appropriate.

1. Use the interview form (Figure 7–4) to gain insight from the mentor teacher concerning classroom management. Arrange an appointment and read the school's mission statement before you do the observations.

2. Use the observation form (Figure 7–5) to guide you through an analysis of the classroom management systems.

3. Obtain and compare different districts' policies on discipline and management. Discover what guidelines the State Department of Education has toward discipline and classroom management. Compare these to the districts' and school's policies.

4. Interview a student who is consistently disruptive and interview a student who is well behaved. You might consider these students for your child study.

5. Do an observation that involves monitoring students in the numerous routines both in and out of the classroom. Reflect and write in your journal procedures that you would consider to be more effective and time efficient.

6. Observe students throughout the school. Look for behavior in elective classes, hallways, restrooms, cafeteria, etc. How does the behavior you observed relate to the school's vision? Keep track of your observations and thoughts in your journal.

7. Create a model discipline plan that fits with your philosophy and vision of classroom organization, teacher/student relationships, and pedagogical practices.

▶ CHAPTER CLOSURE

Summary

There is no single or easy solution to good classroom management. Managing the expectations of today's students is a challenging and difficult task. Teachers need to implement a variety of techniques that become a part of their personal management system.

Research demonstrates that teachers who establish solid classroom organization, positive relationships with students, and appropriate instructional strategies have higher achieving students who are well behaved.

The emphasis on classroom management is to prevent, support, and correct behavior as opposed to control. Teachers who reflect and respond in firm and consistent ways are able to spend more time teaching students. Students who are involved in the decisions of the classroom process improve in behavior and also learn strategies for self-esteem and problem-solving. Expect in the beginning of school to spend time and energy establishing a classroom management system that complements instruction.

FIGURE 7–4 Mentor Teacher Interview Form

Name: _____

Date of Interview: _____

Teachers: _____

School: _____

Grade of Subject: _____

Length of Interview: _____

Direction: Set an interview appointment with the teacher. Let the teacher know that the interview relates to classroom management. Ask and write the responses to the suggested questions and other questions that you feel are important to you regarding classroom management. The questions that follow focus on the seven major classroom application topics from this chapter.

Establish a Presence in the Classroom and School

(1)   How did you begin and implement your classroom management system?

_____

_____

_____

(2)   How do you work with others in the school with discipline-related matters?

_____

_____

_____

(3)   How do you encourage respect?

_____

_____

_____

4)   What communication style and procedures do you use?

_____

_____

_____

FIGURE 7–4   continued

Prepare the Classroom

(1) How did you decide seating arrangements?

_____

_____

_____

(2) How do you use bulletin boards and chalkboards to promote behavior?

_____

_____

_____

(3) What advice do you have to help me prepare my first classroom?

_____

_____

_____

Establish Classroom Rules

(1) What are your priorities?

_____

_____

_____

(2) How were the students involved in making the rules?

_____

_____

_____

(3) How well do the students follow the rules?

_____

_____

_____

FIGURE 7–4 continued

---

(4) What do you do to students who do not follow the rules?

_____

_____

_____

(5) How do you deal with an impossible, disruptive student?

_____

_____

_____

(6) What are important rules for a first-year teacher?

_____

_____

_____

Establish Routines and Procedures

(1) What are the most important classroom routines and what do you do to see that they are followed?

_____

_____

_____

(2) How do students help with routines?

_____

_____

_____

(3) How do you save time with your routines and procedures?

_____

_____

_____

FIGURE 7–4   continued

---

(4)   What problems do you encounter with students' movement in the school and classroom?

_____

_____

_____

Emphasize Positive Relationships with Students

(1)   What strategies do you use to learn about your students?

_____

_____

_____

2)   What strategies do you use to build self-esteem?

_____

_____

_____

(3)   How do you use reinforcers to modify behavior?

_____

_____

_____

(4)   How do you use praise and how do students receive it?

_____

_____

_____

Organize for Instruction

(1)   How do you see the relationship between instructional pedagogy and classroom management?

_____

_____

_____

(2)   How do you plan lessons to prevent classroom behavior problems?

_____

_____

_____

FIGURE 7–4   continued

(3) How do you grade?

_____

_____

_____

(4) What procedures do you have for incomplete, missing, and late assignments?

_____

_____

_____

(5) How do you organize for the various levels and special needs in your classroom?

_____

_____

_____

(6) How do you keep students on-task?

_____

_____

_____

Use Time Wisely

(1) Teachers frequently complain about teacher time, so how do you adjust to personal demands on your time?

_____

_____

_____

(2) When do you take time to organize and reflect about your classroom?

_____

_____

_____

(3) What do you do to increase students' engaged time in learning?

_____

_____

FIGURE 7–5 Classroom Management Observation Form

Name: _____

Date of Observation: _____

Teacher: _____

School: _____

Grade of Subject: _____

Length of Observation: _____

Direction: Set an appointment with the teacher to observe the classroom management system. Use this form to write down notes and guide your observation. Look for other management points you feel are valuable to you. The questions that follow focus on the seven major classroom application topics from this chapter.

Establish a Presence in the Classroom and School

(1) How does the teacher communicate to the students?

_____

_____

_____

(2) What type of respect has been developed between the teacher/students?

_____

_____

_____

_____

_____

_____

(3) Does the teacher emphasize control or prevention management techniques?

_____

_____

_____

FIGURE 7–5 continued

Prepare the Classroom

(1) How does the seating promote interaction, involvement, and learning?

_____

_____

_____

(2) How does the teacher use the chalkboard and other equipment to manage instruction and behavior?

_____

_____

_____

(3) Does the room display student work and accomplishments? Give examples.

_____

_____

_____

(4) Does the classroom promote and stimulate learning? Give examples.

_____

_____

_____

Establish Classroom Rules

(1) Can you see the classroom rules and, if so, do they seem fair?

_____

_____

_____

(2) Do the students follow the classroom rules? Give examples.

_____

_____

_____

FIGURE 7–5   continued

(3)   What are the consequences for infractions of the rules and does the teacher follow through?

_____

_____

_____

(4)   Do the students seem well behaved and respectful? Give examples.

_____

_____

_____

(5)   Are there any disruptive students and what did they do?

_____

_____

_____

(6)   What rules would you change for this classroom?

_____

_____

_____

Establish Routines and Procedures

(1)   Do the students follow routines and procedures? Give examples.

_____

_____

_____

(2)   Do the students help with routines? Give examples.

_____

_____

_____

(3)   Do you think time is saved or wasted with the classroom routines and procedures?

_____

_____

_____

FIGURE 7–5 continued

Emphasize Positive Relationships with Students

(1) How does the teacher relate to the students?

_____

_____

_____

(2) How do the students relate to the teacher?

_____

_____

_____

(3) Does the teacher praise and reinforce positive behavior? Give examples.

_____

_____

_____

(4) Does the teacher appear to be positive, warm, and friendly? Give examples.

_____

_____

_____

(5) Does the teacher demonstrate a genuine concern for the students? Give examples.

_____

_____

_____

Organize for Instruction

(1) Does the teacher appear to be organized for instruction? Give examples.

_____

_____

_____

(2) How does the teacher give directions and assignments?

_____

_____

_____

FIGURE 7–5   continued

(3) How are the students reacting to the lesson and does the teacher appear to be "with it?"

_____

_____

_____

(4) Do you see any disruptive behavior? Give examples.

_____

_____

_____

(5) How does the lesson provide for individual and special needs of students?

_____

_____

_____

(6) How does the teacher keep the students on-task? Give examples.

_____

_____

_____

Use Time Wisely

(1) Does the teacher monitor and adapt the lesson to the class allocated time? Give examples.

_____

_____

_____

(2) Does the teacher keep the students engaged in the lesson? Give examples.

_____

_____

_____

(3) Does the pace of the lesson hold students interest?

_____

_____

_____

Chapter Discussion Questions

1. How do the individuals listed view discipline and classroom management? What are the key elements in their models? Use cooperative learning groups to prepare a one-page comprehensive summary and a fifteen-minute oral report to the class about one of the following models. References to their classic works can be found in the references. Also, most of these models are available on video or film.

INDIVIDUAL	MODEL
1. Skinner (1971)	Shaping Behavior
2. Redl & Wattenberg (1959)	Group Behavior
3. Kounin (1970)	Group Management
4. Canter (1976)	Taking Charge
5. Ginnot (1971)	Address Students
6. Dreikurs (1968)	Mistaken Behavior
7. Glasser (1969)	Good Decisions/ Basic Needs
8. Gordon (1974)	Open Communication
9. Jones (1987)	Body Language
10. Albert (1989)	Cooperative Discipline

2. What classroom management strategies do you think are most effective? Why would these be effective for you?

3. Why is corporal punishment considered an acceptable and legal form of discipline? Why would or wouldn't you use this technique?

4. What makes your mentor teacher a good classroom manager? Use data collected from interviews and observation forms provided in the Field-Based Connection section of this chapter.

5. Why is it important to establish routines? What routines do you think are most difficult and important? Why is modeling and practicing routines a good strategy?

6. How successful is the school and classroom management model in your school? What would you change?

7. How will you incorporate the elements of: organizing the classroom, developing teacher/student relationships, and instructional pedagogy described in your personal educational belief system?

CASE STUDIES

The following case study examples can be used for analysis in small or large groups. Questions follow each case study as suggestions for discussion.

CASE STUDY 7–1: by Shannon Lamm, Intern Student

Gustavo is my most challenging second-grade student to keep on-task. His disruptive behavior seems to stem from several diagnosed learning and physical problems: He has been assessed (labeled?) as learning disabled, having an attention deficit, and being hyperactive. Furthermore, he is deaf in one ear, and younger and less mature than an average second-grader.

The goals of Gustavo's behavior, then, seem to vary between attention seeking and fear-of-failure. The two situations in which I particularly notice his attention-seeking behaviors are during journal writing and during story reading time. His behaviors during the journal writing hour are:

- sharpening his pencil at least five times;

- flipping through the book shelves three or four times;

- a trip to the bathroom;

- wandering about the classroom five or six times;

- and, in between, fussing with the materials in his desk.

His behaviors during twenty minutes of story reading time include:

- talking to his neighbors fifteen times;

- staring around the room all but three, nonconsecutive minutes;

- rocking back and forth or squirming all but three minutes;

- and, in between, fussing with the paper scraps, pebbles, and anything else on the carpet.

The preventive techniques I have used include proximity, praising any sign of appropriate behavior from him, noting the good behavior of the students around him, asking him a direct question, using his name while reading or teaching, giving eye-contact, and including him in the actual teaching (such as having him hold the book or help call on other students). All of the techniques, with the exception of the last one, only stops his misbehavior for, at best, two minutes. During one of Mrs. Schaughnessy's lessons, I even sat next to him with my arm around him, and he still continued to tap his pencil and fuss loudly in his desk.

His most on-task behavior occurred when I physically involved him in the lesson. He was attentive to his task of calling upon students and holding the book. Unfortunately, he was so involved in his task that he seemed to tune out the lesson itself; at least, though, he was not distracting the others.

His fear-of-failure behavior seems to stem from his low reading and mathematics skills. These behaviors during small group reading time include:

- not following along in the book;

- skipping pages to catch up to the others;

- loudly interrupting the others by asking, "Wait for me!" and "Where are we?;"

- any of the behaviors shown during his search for attention.

I also observed most of these behaviors during any mathematics assignment. Furthermore, during addition or subtraction facts tests, he refuses to attempt any of the problems.

The prevention techniques I have used included praising any effort or improvement, acknowledging the difficulty of reading long or solving subtraction problems, and breaking down the task ("Show me your work after three problems..."). During one test, I called him to the back of the classroom in order to guide him through the subtraction; that somewhat controlled his loud refusal to even try the work. Additionally, Gustavo is receiving tutoring after school in both reading and mathematics. In the short time I have been in the classroom, I have not been able to see a change in his willingness to risk trying any assignments.

Fortunately for Gustavo, he has one tremendous factor helping him succeed in school: His family seems stable and supportive. His parents are married and interested in his progress in school. Consequently, parent-teacher conferences helped change his classroom behavior. His mother has asked to be kept informed about his progress in class and has agreed that if his school behavior is off-task, he will lose privileges at home, such as watching television. If his mother's supportive attitude remains constant, I suspect that as his reading improves and his maturity increases, his disruptive behaviors will lessen.

On a personal note, I have found Gustavo to be the hardest second-grade student with whom to deal. Since much of his behavior is physiological, I do not know how long he is physically capable of sitting and listening. Furthermore, I cannot blame him for losing interest if he is unable to hear what is being read or spoken. Therefore, I never know where to draw the line about his behavior. And yet, his behavior frustrates me tremendously, since it is constantly disruptive and often a catalyst for other students to misbehave; moreover, prevention techniques improved his behavior no more than two out of ten times. In fact, during the days I was alone with the class, his inappropriate behavior was extreme enough to send him to time-out across the hall for two of the three days; this improved the whole nature of the rest of the class. If I were with this class on a long-term basis, I might try a behavioral contract with Gustavo. Perhaps he needs something more positive and more specific than the three-step system of reminder-warning-time-out in order to help guide his behavior.

Case Study Discussion Questions

1. How would you classify Gustavo's behavior?

2. What are the preventive, supportive, and control techniques that Shannon tried to use?

3. Why do you think she was unsuccessful?

4. How do you feel about her conclusion?

CASE STUDY 7–2: by Cyndi Hartman, First-Year Teacher

I did not set up my classroom management system overnight—it was a gradual, cumulative process encompassing all my previous experiences in the classroom. Management is essential because you must have the attention and cooperation of your students before you can teach them anything. So I asked myself, "How am I going to accomplish this?"

First, I sat down and made two lists: one of the behavioral and affective outcomes I desired to attain, and another of those I wanted to avoid. Once I decided what was important to me, I asked myself, "How am I going to communicate this to my students?"

A positive, yet firm, approach with clearly stated expectations works naturally for me. Thus, on the first day of school I talked with the children about me, my expectations, and my classroom rules. Then I asked them about their expectations and included these in our classroom rules. With their input, the children started taking responsibility in *our* classroom. As a class, we agreed to focus on respect and good manners. We role-played inappropriate and appropriate reactions to a wide array of everyday classroom scenarios.

Besides modeling desired behaviors, I also explicitly told the children about my personal "absolutes." For example, yelling is "absolutely not allowed by anyone in my room." I told the children that I would never yell at them, and they were to show the same respect to me as well as each other. During the first weeks especially, I would get frustrated because the children would constantly push my limits. I responded by modeling strategies we discussed for dealing with anger—(such as) writing feelings down, tearing up the paper, and then throwing out the anger along with the torn paper. Every time a classroom rule was broken, we would stop, evaluate, and discuss or role play how the situation should have been handled. I worried at first that this was wasting valuable instructional time; however, it turned out to be extremely worthwhile. Now my classroom runs smoothly, with few management or discipline problems. A large part of this is the accountability I have placed upon the students for their behavior and for our classroom climate.

An effective management system needs a discipline system to complement and support it. Since I made the students responsible for their behavior choices (they *choose* to behave or misbehave), they also choose the accompanying rewards or consequences that follow. In my classroom, I utilize a "clip system" where each child starts each day as a "Super Worker." If I have a problem with a child, I give them a look or a verbal warning. If that doesn't work, I simply state, "Michael, you're making a poor choice. You need to move your clip." And that's it—no more attention or discussion about the matter. It is a concrete visual for the children so they can see where they stand.

Since I prefer a positive environment, I rely more heavily on positive reinforcement. I love to catch children being good. When I see a desired behavior, I'll give out a sticker. I'll say "Analisa, I love how you are showing your best manners—here's a sticker." Instantly other children look at the child to see the desired behavior so they can emulate it. Sticker cards are redeemed for prizes at the end of the six weeks. Discipline and management seem to work in a domino effect style—when I focus on the positive, the children do too.

Although setting up my management system was one of the hardest challenges of my life, my smoothly running classroom has been my greatest reward. Now that routines are established, I feel like I am facilitating the children's movements during the day. My classroom is a reflection of my personality, and that is why it has worked so effectively for me.

I think it is important to be *fair, consistent* and *persistent*. Children are challenging, and the first month of school is overwhelming because they will test you to the best of their ability. If your management system reflects your personality, however, it *will* be successful!

Case Study Discussion Questions

1. What would you do differently?
2. How would you classify Cyndi's classroom?
3. What makes Cyndi's management plan successful?
4. What strategies does Cyndi use?
5. As a first-year teacher, what would you change?

▶ REFERENCES

Abernathy, S., Manera, E., & Wright, R. E. (1985). What stresses student teachers most? *The Clearing House, 58,* 361–362.

Albert, L. (1989). *A teacher's guide to cooperative discipline: How to manage your classroom and promote self-esteem.* Circle Pines, MN: American Guidance Service.

Axelrod, S. (1977). *Behavior modification for the classroom teacher.* New York: McGraw-Hill.

Bentley, K. J. (1987). Major legal and ethical issues in behavioral treatment: Focus on institutionalized mental patients. *Behavioral Sciences and the Law, 5,* 359–372.

Boyer, E. (1983). *High school: A report on secondary education in America.* New York: Harper and Row.

Brophy, J. (1983). Classroom organization and management. *The Elementary School Journal, 83,* 4: 265–285.

Brophy, J. (1986). Classroom organization and management. In D. Smith (Ed.), *Essential knowledge for beginning educators.* Washington, DC: American Association of Colleges for Teacher Education.

Brophy, J. (1988). Educating teachers about managing classrooms and students. *Teaching and Teacher Education, 4,* 1: 1–18.

Brophy, J. & Everston, C. (1976). *Learning from teaching: A developmental perspective.* Boston: Allyn and Bacon.

Cangelosi, J. S., Struyk, L. R., Grimes, M. L., & C. Duke. (1988). *Classroom management needs of beginning teachers.* Paper presented at the Annual Meeting of the American Educational Research Association, New Orleans.

Canter, L. (1976). *Assertive discipline.* Los Angeles: Lee Canter Associates.

Charles, C. (1989). *Building classroom discipline: From models to practice,* 3rd edition. New York: Longman.

Curwin, R. L. & Mendler, A. N. (1988). *Discipline with dignity.* Alexandria, VA: Association for Supervision and Curriculum Development.

Deci, E. (1972). The effects of contingent and noncontingent rewards and controls on intrinsic motivation. *Organizational Behavior and Human Performance, 8,* 217–229.

Dreikurs, R. (1968). *Psychology in the classroom,* 2nd edition. New York: Harper and Row.

Duke, D. & Meckel, A. (1984). *Teacher's guide to classroom management.* New York: Random House.

Elam, S. (1989). The second Gallup/Phi Delta Kappan poll of teachers' attitudes toward the public schools. *Phi Delta Kappan, 70,* 10:785–798.

Emmer, E. & Aussiker, A. (1987, April). *School and classroom discipline programs: How well do they work?* Paper presented at the Annual Meeting of the American Educational Research Association, Washington, DC.

Emmer, E. & Aussiker, A. (1988, June). Assertive discipline ineffective. *Classroom Management SIG Newsletter,* 1–2.

Evertson, C. & Emmer, E. (1982). Effective management at the beginning of the school year in junior high school classes. *Journal of Educational Psychology, 74,* 485–498.

Evertson, C. M. & Harris, A. (1992). What we know about managing classrooms. *Educational Leadership, 49,* 1:74–78.

Farber, B. A. & Miller, J. (1981). Teacher burnout: A psychoeducational perspective. *Teachers College Record, 83*(2), 235–243.

Fathman, R. E. (1990). School corporal punishment: Legalized child abuse. *Holistic Education Review,* 47–52.

Ginnot, H. (1971). *Teacher and child.* New York: Macmillan.

Glasser, W. (1969). *Schools without failure.* New York: Harper and Row.

Glasser, W. (1988). On students' needs and team learning: A conversation with William Glasser. *Educational Leadership, 45,* 38–45.

Gold, Y. (1985). Does teacher burnout begin with student teaching? *Education, 105*(3), 254–257.

Goodlad, J. (1984). *A place called school: Prospects for the future.* New York: McGraw-Hill.

Gordon, T. (1974). *Teacher effectiveness training.* New York: Wyden.

Hill, D. (1990). Order in the classroom. *Teacher, 1*(7), 70–77.

Iwanicki, E. F. (1983). Toward understanding and alleviating teacher burnout. *Theory Into Practice, 22*(1), 27–32.

James, B. (1991). Student misbehavior and the law. *School Safety*, 28–29.

Jones, F. (1987). *Positive classroom discipline.* New York: McGraw-Hill.

Jones, V. F. & Jones, L. S. (1990). *Comprehensive classroom management: Motivating and managing students.* Boston, MA: Allyn and Bacon.

Kounin, J. (1970). *Discipline and group management in classrooms.* New York: Holt, Rinehart and Winston.

Kozol, J. (1991). *Savage inequalities: Children in America's schools.* New York: Crown Publishers, Inc.

McDaniel, T. R. (1987). *Improving student behavior: Essays on classroom management and motivation.* Lanham, MD: University Press of America.

McIntyre, T. (1989). *The behavior management handbook: Setting up effective behavior management systems.* Boston: Allyn and Bacon.

O'Leary, D., Becker, W., Evans, M., & Saudargas, R. (1969). A token reinforcement program in public school: A replication and systematic analysis. *Journal of Applied Behavior Analysis, 2,* 3–13.

O'Leary, D. & O'Leary, S. (Eds.). (1977). *Classroom management: The successful use of behavior modification,* 2nd edition. New York: Pergamon Press.

Redl, F. and Wattenberg, W. (1959). *Mental hygiene in teaching.* New York: Harcourt, Brace and World.

Render, G., Padilla, J., & Krank, H. (1989). What research really shows about assertive discipline. *Educational Leadership, 46,* 72–75.

Richardson, V. (1990). Significant and worthwhile change in teaching practice. *Educational Researcher 19,* 7:10–18.

Selman, R. (1980). *The growth of interpersonal understanding: Developmental and clinical analyses.* New York: Academic Press.

Sharpley, C. (1985). Implicit rewards in the classroom. *Contemporary Educational Psychology, 10,* 349–368.

Sizer, T. (1984). *Horace's compromise: The dilemma of the American high school.* Boston: Houghton Mifflin.

Soar, R. & Soar, R. (1986). Context effects in the teaching-learning process. In D. Smith (Ed.), *Essential knowledge for beginning educators.* Washington, DC.: American Association of Colleges for Teacher Education.

Wherry, J. N. (1983). Some legal considerations and implications for the use of behavior modification in the schools. *Psychology in the Schools, 20,* 46–51.

Wolfgang, C. & Glickman, C. (1986). *Solving discipline problems: Strategies for classroom teachers,* 2nd edition. Boston: Allyn and Bacon.

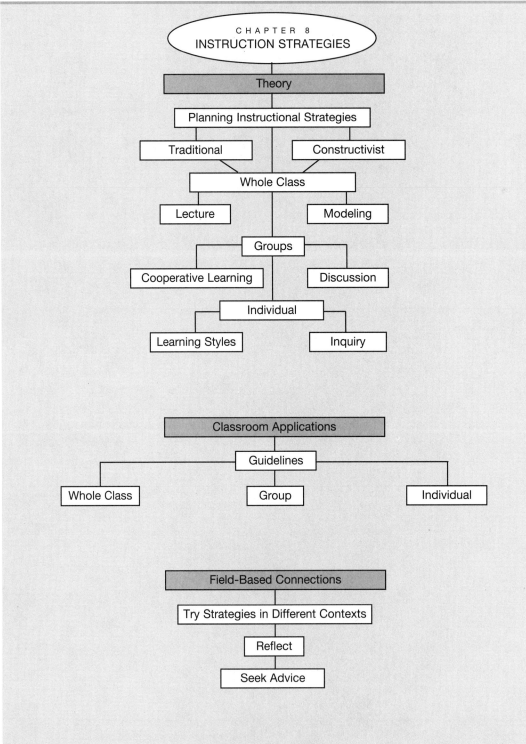

CHAPTER 8
INSTRUCTION STRATEGIES

Theory

Planning Instructional Strategies

Traditional | Constructivist

Whole Class

Lecture | Modeling

Groups

Cooperative Learning | Discussion

Individual

Learning Styles | Inquiry

Classroom Applications

Guidelines

Whole Class | Group | Individual

Field-Based Connections

Try Strategies in Different Contexts

Reflect

Seek Advice

Instructional Strategies

Introduction

Instruction is a personal craft, so teachers must be confident in choosing a variety of strategies to motivate and engage students in learning. Numerous studies conclude that effective instruction increases good behavior and academic achievement. After establishing classroom management and positive student relationships, a solid theoretical and content base is needed in order to plan methods and activities for learning. Teachers should be empowered to select from the variety of methods and materials that meet the wide range of student ability in a classroom. Teachers cannot depend upon one instructional delivery system to be effective.

Good planning that incorporates a solid content and skill base, combined with motivational techniques, is critical to teaching success. Just like a carpenter needs a plan to construct a house, the teacher also needs a plan to formulate a lesson. Teachers must decide the needs, goals, and content first, and then choose appropriate instructional strategies.

Instructional strategies form a continuum (Figure 8–1) from direct to indirect teaching. On one end there is direct instruction, which is teacher centered. Teacher-centered instruction believes that learning is a result of direct transmission of knowledge from teacher to student. On the other end, indirect instruction is student centered. Student-centered instruction believes that learning is a result of a student's ability to understand and process information. The teacher facilitates indirect learning. Combinations of direct/indirect instruction are possible, depending on the nature of the lesson, student needs, and teacher preference. Wherever a teacher is on the continuum, remember that the focus of instructional strategies remains on student achievement.

Lesson organization centers around three fundamental modes of instruction: whole class, small group, and/or individual. Lesson organi-

---

FIGURE 8-1 Developing a Personal Instructional Philosophy

TEACHER-CENTERED   STUDENT-CENTERED

≺≺≺ DIRECT INSTRUCTION ----(continuum)----INDIRECT INSTRUCTION ≻≻≻

AUDIENCE	Whole Class	Group	Individual
METHODS	Lecture Modeling	Cooperative Learning Discussion	Learning styles Inquiry
ACTIVITIES	Seatwork Textbooks	Role-playing Learning centers	Problem-solving Decision-making

≺≺≺ PASSIVE--ACTIVE ≻≻≻

---

zation must also keep in mind variables such as age, learning styles, multicultural, prior learning, language, ability levels, class size, gender, content, and goals before deciding on whole class, group or individual instruction.

There are several basic methods of instruction: lecture, modeling, cooperative learning, discussion, individualized learning style instruction, and inqury. A strong correlation exists between instructional methods and student achievement. Matching student needs with teaching strategies increases the amount of learning and interest. Long-term learning occurs through active involvement in a variety

of instructional strategies that are thoughtfully and purposely planned by the teacher.

▶ THEORY

Planning Instructional Strategies

Effective instruction begins with a plan. Teachers spend ten to twelve percent of their weekly time planning (Clark & Yinger, 1979).

Every plan should have a beginning, a middle, and an end. Begin a lesson by describing *what* (content) the students will learn; progress to the middle of a lesson by describing *how* (procedures) students will learn; end a lesson by describing *how* learning will be assessed (evaluation). According to Moore (1992), the instructional strategy is how teachers present lesson content or how they transmit or facilitate information to students. A successful strategy follows an organized pattern, such as the lesson cycle plan (Figure 8–2). The lesson cycle is one strategy to help teachers organize and plan their instruction, because for each step in the cycle there are several choices of activities that need to be decided.

Instructional strategies organize the content, skills, and outcomes of a lesson (McNair, 19789). Research by curriculum planners and theorists such as Tyler (1950), Hunter (1981), Melton (1978), and Roberts (1982) believe learning and achievement increases when instructional strategies are planned according to student performance outcomes. The lesson cycle (Figure 8–2) exemplifies this traditional and somewhat dominant perspective. Determining goals and outcomes is the first step for planning instruction followed by activities that should help in achieving the desired outcomes. Some research, however, indicates that, in reality, teachers do not adhere to this traditional goal/objectives model. These findings indicate that many teachers rely on activities rather than content objectives for instructional planning decisions (Brown, 1988; Clark & Yinger, 1979; Morine-Dershimer, 1978).

In stark contrast, the constructivist's model views teachers as developers and deliverers of curriculum where students process knowledge. Constructivist teachers believe learners build or connect information to past learning. Students actively experience information by interacting with it. Teachers must spend time reflecting on their role as a facilitator of knowledge in order to guide appropriate learning experiences where students learn to understand their world. Constructivist teachers constantly evaluate and reevaluate their instructional strategies to plan innovative ways of meeting cognitive and developmental student needs (London, 1990).

Making decisions and planning for instructional strategies is a critical step in teaching because planned versus unplanned activities improves student outcomes. Planning instructional strategies involves teachers in complex and personal classroom decisions which constantly require balance between direct and indirect instruction (Zeichner & Liston, 1987). Joyce and Weil (1986, p. 20) summarize by stating, "Since no single teaching strategy can accomplish every purpose, the wise teacher will master a sufficient repertoire of strategies to deal with the specific kinds of learning problems he or she faces."

Whole Class

Whole class instruction is usually direct and the teacher is the provider of information through lectures, recitations, textbooks, seatwork, and discussion. Whole class activities are best when, according to Cuban (1986), the teacher's goals are to disseminate information unavailable through other instructional strategies. Studies (Brophy, 1979; Evertson et al., 1980; Good, 1979; Hunter, 1981; Rosenshine, 1987; Stallings, 1980) found that students learn basic skills faster and score higher on standardized tests when they receive instruction directly from the teacher. Whole class instruc-

FIGURE 8–2 The Lesson Cycle

OPENING	**Beginning of the lesson (STEP ONE)**
FOCUS	An introduction that sets the stage for the lesson.
STATE OBJECTIVE AND PURPOSE	A statement of what the students will do to demonstrate learning and why it is important.
INFORMATION	**Middle of the lesson (STEP TWO)**
EXPLANATION	What the students need to know to be successful in meeting the objective.
MODELING	An illustration of the information in the explanation.
MONITORING KNOWLEDGE AND COMPREHENSION	A request for the students to demonstrate knowledge and/or understanding of the information.
GUIDED PRACTICE	A teacher-directed activity which causes the students to apply the information.
ASSESS MASTERY	An activity used to determine if students need to be retaught or need independent practice.
RETEACH (if necessary)	Provides students who did not master the objective with alternative strategies.
INDEPENDENT PRACTICE	The application of information without the assistance of the teacher.
ENRICHMENT	An activity that expands the information learned.
EVALUATE MASTERY	An activity used to assess the degree of student's learning.
CLOSING	**End of the lesson (STEP THREE)**
SUMMARY/REVIEW	A review of the learning.
LARGER CONTEXT	An activity that relates the learning to real-life experiences.

tion is most successful when teachers follow a sequence similar to the lesson cycle found in Figure 8–2. The lesson cycle provides a foundation for effective direct, yet active, teaching strategies.

Active teaching is a multi-step process of specific teaching techniques directed towards involving the whole class. Ross et al. (1993) stress that the active teacher follows six basic steps:

1. help students see a purpose;
2. present [information] in small easy steps;
3. check student understanding;
4. provide regular and immediate feedback;
5. monitor independent practice; and
6. review.

When you present content that requires thinking or problem-solving, however, Borich (1988) believes whole class instruction is less effective. Many studies conclude that direct teaching methods have a place, particularly when raising low achievers' test scores is the goal. Ross et al. (1993), however, notes,

> If researchers had set out to determine the strategies that would be most effective in reaching other educational goals (e.g., higher-level thinking, creative thinking, mathematical problem-solving, scientific processes and attitudes), [instead of raising test scores,] their findings might have been very different. (p. 108)

Two common direct-teaching strategies are lecture and modeling.

Lecture

A commonly used instructional strategy is the lecture method. There are several studies

(Adams & Biddle, 1970; Goodlad, 1984; Sizer, 1984), that verify teachers' predominant use of a lecture format. Lectures should incorporate a balance of teacher and student dialogue in order for it to be successful and effective in an elementary or high school. Spaulding (1992) states that lecture is an efficient means of communicating only when students listen. Critics of this strategy claim the learner becomes a passive receiver of information and, as a result, may find learning to be boring. When used in isolation, the lecture strategy fails to take into account the specific needs of each learner. When used in conjunction with other strategies, however, the lecture can be extremely effective, "It saves time, communicates to the most students, communicates accurate information, and gives teachers a high degree of control" (Houston, 1988, p. 197). Freiberg and Driscoll (1992) lend the following advice for successful lectures:

1. Present material in small steps.
2. Focus on one thought per lecture.
3. Avoid digressions.
4. Model when possible.
5. Accompany with many examples (visual, auditory).
6. Be creative in your repetition and examples.
7. Check for understanding before moving on.
8. Monitor with questions.
9. Be enthusiastic, give of yourself.

To maintain student attention in lectures requires more than teacher talk to grab and sustain attention. Teachers should not lecture for more than ten minutes before integrating activities which initiate discussion (Cangelosi, 1992).

Modeling

Modeling is another important strategy for whole class direct instruction that allows teaching through example. Through modeling, the teacher demonstrates the content and procedures to be learned. When students relate to the model, the results increase learning (Spaulding, 1992). Modeling actively demonstrates the how and what necessary to complete a given task.

Groups

Group instruction is an indirect approach that requires teacher patience and student involvement. Students need to be taught at all levels how to work together if group instruction is to be successful (Montague et al., 1989). Group strategies center around students' participation with the lesson content. Freiberg and Driscoll (1992) describe time and comfort as two important issues because group strategies require time to plan and implement and some students may be uncomfortable with group work, thus allowing one or two students to dominate. When assessing group work, teachers need to monitor the participation of each student. Sharan (1980) states that group investigations allow students to learn from each other by synthesizing group ideas for solutions to problems. Through working in groups, students realize that there are a number of ways to solve problems to reach a solution.

Several reasons exist to support the use of groups as an instructional strategy. As our society evolves into an information age, students must be able to work together in order to process data for employers. Second, working with others requires each employee to have competent social skills. Students also need experience interacting, since many television and family structures of today create situations that model poor communication. Learning to get along with others in a group is a lifelong skill, so students working in groups learn to integrate interaction between cultures and gender. Finally, group experiences give students the opportunity to collaborate in the development of higher-ordered thinking skills and problem-solving abilities (Kagan, 1990). Group tasks provide students with the necessary experiences for a twenty-first century citizen residing in a democratic society. Two common group strategies are cooperative learning and discussion.

Cooperative Learning

Cooperative learning is a strategy to help organize successful small group instruction. Slavin (1983) defined cooperative learning as a set of alternatives to traditional (direct) instruction. Generally, cooperative learning means students working together in groups to complete academic tasks. Many forms of cooperative learning exist, with each designed to achieve a specific instructional purpose (Graves & Graves, 1990; Joyce, 1991). Substantial research by Kagan, 1990; Johnson and Johnson, 1989; Johnson et al., 1990; Slavin, 1990, and many others show that using cooperative learning activities increases student performance and achievement. Researchers agree on the importance of cooperative learning and also inform that it should not be the only form of instruction. Johnson, Johnson, and Holubec (1990) suggested that, ideally, cooperative learning should be used 60-70 percent of the time. To be most effective, cooperative learning requires clear group goals and student accountability (Slavin & Madden, 1989).

Simply placing students in groups does not constitute cooperative learning and, according to Johnson, Johnson, and Holubec (1990), for a group to be truly cooperative, it must have five components.

First, positive interdependence should exist and students must believe that they "sink or swim together." Students have a dual responsibility: to complete the assignment and to ensure that all others in their group also understood the assignment.

The second component is face-to-face positive interaction, including verbal exchanges among students of a group. Members promote each other's learning through encouragement and assistance and, in order to foster meaningful face-to-face interaction, groups must be small, ranging from two to six students.

Third is individual accountability, where student performance as individuals is assessed within the group. Students must realize that they cannot "ride on the coattails" of others in the group and the group should help those who need more assistance or encouragement to complete an assignment.

Fourth, a cooperative group must learn and use interpersonal skills. Researchers agree that cooperative skills must be *taught*, since we do not have the innate ability to effectively interact with others.

Fifth, cooperative learning needs group processing. Group processing is a reflection time in which group members discuss productive and non-productive actions, deciding which actions should change and which should continue.

Teachers should start cooperative learning groups with pairs or threesomes until students become more skillful and experienced, and then later increase the group size to a maximum of six members. Heterogeneous ability groups are recommended to provide for greater perspective in discussions as well as tolerance and acceptance of various learning styles, opinions, and talents. Teachers organize groups through random selection or a mixture of heterogeneous ability. Groups should work together until they successfully complete the assignment, which means that breaking up troubled groups may be counterproductive since students need to resolve their own conflicts. Students can be assigned to different learning groups throughout the day. Figure 8–3 provides detail about the teacher role for organizing cooperative learning groups.

Another important function of the teacher is to systematically teach cooperative group skills. Johnson, Johnson, and Holubec (1990) describe five major steps in teaching cooperative skills.

- The first step is to help students see the need for the skill, thus providing motivation to learn the skill.

- The next step is to ensure that students understand the skill, how to perform it, and when to use it. To help students, teachers model the skill and then have the students role play it.

- Repetitive practice situations is the third step in teaching cooperative skills. Students need to practice a skill in order to master it.

- The fourth step is for students to process and evaluate their use of the skill through discussion and reflection.

FIGURE 8–3   The Teacher's Role in Cooperative Learning Groups

---

MAKE DECISIONS

Specify Academic Collaborative Objectives. What academic and/or collaborative skills do you want students to learn or practice in their groups? Start with something easy.

Decide on Group Size. Students often lack collaborative skills, so start with groups of two or three students; later advance cautiously to fours.

Assign Students to Groups. Heterogeneous groups are the most powerful, so mix abilities, sexes, cultural backgrounds, and task orientations. Assign students to groups randomly or select groups yourself.

Arrange the Room. The closer the students are to each other, the better they can communicate. Group members should be "knee to knee and eye to eye."

Plan Materials. Materials can send a "sink or swim together" message to students if you give only one paper to the group or give each member part of the material to learn and then teach the group.

Assign Roles. Students are more likely to work together if each has a job which contributes to the task. You can assign work roles such as reader, recorder, calculator, checker, reporter, and materials handler or skill roles such as encourager of participation, praiser, and checker for understanding.

SET THE LESSON

Explain the Academic Task. Prepare students by teaching them any material they need to know, then make certain they clearly understand what they are to do in the groups. This might include explaining lesson objectives, defining concepts, explaining procedures, giving examples, and asking questions.

Structure Positive Interdependence. Students must feel that they need each other to complete the group's task, that they "sink or swim together." Some ways to create this are by establishing mutual goals (students must learn the material and make certain group members learn the material), joint rewards (if all group members achieve above a certain percentage on the test, each will receive bonus points), shared materials and information, and assigned roles.

Structure Individual Accountability. Each student must feel responsible for learning the material and helping the group. Some ways to ensure this feeling include frequent oral quizzing of group members picked at random, giving individual tests, having everyone in the group write (pick one paper at random to grade), or having students do work first to bring to the group.

Structure Intergroup Cooperation. Having groups check with and help other groups and giving rewards or praise when all class members do well can extend the benefits of cooperation to the whole class.

Explain the Criteria for Success. Student work should be evaluated on a criteria-referenced rather than a norm-referenced basis. Make clear your criteria for evaluating the groups' work.

FIGURE 8–3 continued

Specify Expected Behaviors. The more specific you are about the behaviors you want to see in the groups, the more likely students will do them. Make it clear that you expect to see everyone contributing, helping, listening with care to others, encouraging others to participate, and asking for help or clarification. Younger students may need to be told to stay with their group, take turns, share, ask group members questions, and use quiet voices.

Teach Collaborative Skills. After students are used to working in groups, pick one collaborative skill they need to learn, point out the need for it, define it carefully, have students give you phrases they can say when using the skill, post the phrases (praise, bonus points, stars), and observe for and encourage the use of the skill until students are doing it automatically. Then teach a second skill. Consider praising, summarizing, encouraging, checking for understanding, asking for help, or generating further answers.

MONITOR AND INTERVENE

Arrange Face-to-Face Interaction. The beneficial educational outcomes of cooperative learning groups are due to the interaction patterns and verbal exchanges that take place among students. Make certain there is oral summarizing, giving and receiving explanations, and elaborating going on.

Monitor Students' Behavior. This is the fun part! While students are working, you circulate to see whether they understand the assignment and the material, give immediate feedback and reinforcement, and praise good use of group skills.

Provide Task Assistance. If students are having trouble with the task, you can clarify, reteach, or elaborate on what they need to know.

Intervene to Teach Collaborative Skills. If students are having trouble with group interactions, you can suggest more effective procedures for working together or more effective behaviors for them to engage in. You can ask students to figure out how to work more effectively together. If students are learning or practicing a skill, record on an observation sheet how often you hear that skill, then share your observations with the groups.

EVALUATE AND PROCESS

Evaluate Student Learning. Assess how well students completed the task and give them feedback on how well they did.

Process Group Functioning. In order to improve, students need time and procedures for analyzing how well their group is functioning and how well they are using collaborative skills. Processing can be done by individuals, small groups, or the whole class. To start, have groups routinely list three things they did well in working together today and one thing they will do better tomorrow. Then summarize as a whole class.

Provide Closure. To reinforce student learning, you may wish to have groups share answers or papers, summarize major points in the lesson, or review important facts.

Reprinted with permission, D. Johnson, R. Johnson, and E. Johnson-Holubec, (1988), *Cooperation in the Classroom*, Edina, MN: Interaction Book Co., 2–28—2–39.

- The last step in the process of teaching cooperative skills is to ensure that students persevere in practicing the skill until it is integrated into their behavior.

Aronson et al. (1978) believe when students learn both content and a new process, probably neither will be mastered and they suggest that students work through team-building activities before the content is presented.

Although there are many different types of cooperative learning methods, all of them involve groups of students working toward a common goal (Figure 8–4).

The cooperative learning strategies in Figure 8–4 demonstrate positive results in achievement, group relationships, mainstreaming, and self-esteem (Slavin, 1991).

Cooperative learning shows impressive, positive outcomes that afford students the opportunity to practice skills in cooperation, competition, and problem-solving. When thinking and planning for cooperative learning as an instructional strategy, remember what Gamoran (1987) said while critiquing Slavin's research: "Grouping does not produce achievement, instruction does."

Discussion

Discussion promotes comprehension and provides learner feedback and clarification. There are, however, advantages and disadvantages to discussion. Research by Joyce and Weil (1986) concluded that small group discussion increases learning on standardized tests. Discussion can enhance motivation and problem solving for some students, however, it is no more effective than lecturing. When discussion is combined with lecture, the depth of understanding is increased (Olmstead, 1970). Group discussion encourages students to become involved in learning and, therefore, promotes the ability to reason (Gall & Gall, 1976). The discussion strategy relies on questions to the group. A description of questioning techniques for discussion is explained in the next chapter.

Individual

Individualized instruction is a specific strategy that meets the needs, interests, and abilities for each student. Obviously, large classes present obstacles to this strategy, but it can be used effectively with certain lessons and individuals. Teachers must consider a multitude of variables to accommodate the range of individual needs. The school environment makes it difficult to teach each student individually. The individual, however, is crucial to consider when planning all strategies. Teachers must address individual needs and concerns within the larger context of a group.

One way to meet these differences is to select activities and materials that fit an individual's learning modality. There are several basic learning modalities to consider: visual (see), auditory (hear), tactile (touch), and kinesthetic (movement). A lesson that uses several modalities will increase the likelihood of meeting individual needs. For example, if you show (visual) and discuss (auditory), you involve more senses in the learning process. As a result, a teacher reaches a larger percentage of students.

Another variable is the physical condition of the room and various environmental (lighting, temperature, etc.) and social (grouping, seating, personality, etc.) conditions abound.

FIGURE 8–4   Selected Cooperative Learning Strategies

Method/Proponent	Brief Description/Comments
Learning Together (Johnson & Johnson 1987, 1989/90)	Emphasizing cooperative effort, *Learning Together* has five basic elements: positive interdependence (students believe they are responsible for both their learning and the team's); face-to-face interaction (students explain their learning and help others with assignments); social skills (students communicate effectively, build and maintain trust, and resolve conflicts); group processing (groups periodically assess their progress and how to improve effectiveness). Uses four- or five-member heterogeneous teams.
Student Teams-Achievement Division (STAD) (Slavin 1978)	Four student learning teams (mixed in performance levels, sex, and ethnicity); teacher presents lesson, students work in teams, and help others master material. Students then take quizzes; cooperative efforts are not allowed on quizzes; team rewards are earned. Applicable to most grades and subjects.
Teams-Games-Tournament (TGT) (DeVries & Slavin 1978)	Using the same teacher presentation and teamwork as *STAD*, *TGT* replaces the quizzes with weekly tournaments in which students compete with members of other teams to contribute points to team scores. Competition occurs at "tournament tables" against others with similar academic records. The winner of each tournament brings six points to her or his team. Low achievers compete with low achievers (a similar arrangement exists for high achievers), which provides all students with equal opportunity for success. As with *STAD*, team rewards are earned. Applicable to most grades and subjects.
Jigsaw (Aronson, Blaney, Stephan, Sikes, & Snapp 1978)	Students are assigned to six-member teams to work on academic material that has been divided into sections. Each member reads a section; then members of different teams meet to become experts. Students return to groups and teach other members about their sections. Students must listen to their teammates to learn other sections.
Jigsaw 2 (Slavin 1987)	Students work in four- or five-member teams as in *TGT* or *STAD*. Rather than being assigned specific parts, students read a common narrative (e.g., a chapter). Students also receive a topic on which to become an expert. Learners with the same topics meet together as in Jigsaw, and then they teach the material to their original group. Students take individual quizzes.

FIGURE 8–4 continued

Method/Proponent	Brief Description/Comments
Team Assisted Individualization (TAI) (Slavin, Leavey & Madden 1986)	Uses four-member mixed-ability groups (as with *STAD* and *TGT*); differs from *STAD* and *TGT* in that it combines cooperative learning and individualized instruction and is applicable only to mathematics in grades three through six. Learners take a placement test, then proceed at their own pace. Team members check one another's work and help with problems. Without help, students take unit tests that are scored by student monitors. Each week the teacher evaluates and gives team rewards.
Cooperative Integrated Reading and Composition (CIRC) (Madden, Slavin & Stevens 1986)	Designed to teach reading and writing in upper elementary grades, *CIRC* assigns students to different reading teams. Teacher works with one team, while other teams engage in cognitive activities: reading, predicting story endings, summarizing stories, writing responses, practicing decoding, and learning vocabulary. Teams follow sequence of teacher instruction, team practice, team assessments, and quizzes. Quizzes may not be taken until the team feels each student is ready. Team rewards are given.
Group Investigation (Sharan & Sharan 1989/1990)	Groups are formed according to common interest in a topic. Students plan research, divide learning assignments among members, synthesize/summarize findings, and present the findings to the entire class.

Courtesy of M. Manning and R. Lucking, (1991), "The What, Why, and How of Cooperative Learning," *The Social Studies,* 122.

These factors can greatly impact an individual's ability to learn.

Intelligence is another individual variable often overlooked and viewed in traditional ways. Gardner (1983) believes there are seven different intelligences. Traditional classrooms stress verbal/linguistic and logical/mathematical intelligence and, therefore, do not meet the individual student needs. Teachers must provide opportunities and instructional strategies for engaging students in the other five intelligences: spatial, musical, kinesthetic, personal, and interpersonal abilities.

Teachers who individualize lessons must consider each student in terms of interests and capabilities. The task of the teacher is to discover what variables will increase each student's ability to learn. Try to accommodate in an instructional strategy as many student needs as possible. Two common strategies that provide for individual differences are learning styles and inquiry.

Learning Styles

The concept that people learn in different ways or have various learning styles, is not new. As early as 1921, Carl Jung proposed that people take in information differently, resulting in four types of learners: feelers, thinkers, sensors, and intuitors. In 1950, the term "learning styles" first appeared in research literature; however, it was not until 1970 that the concept of learning styles moved into the classroom.

One of the most popular learning style programs is the Learning Style Inventory (Dunn, Dunn, & Price 1989). The inventory assesses five areas to identify individual learning styles: environmental (sound, light, temperature, and design); emotional (motivation, persistence, responsibility, and structure); sociological (peers, self, pairs, team, authority, and varied); physical (perceptual, intake, time, and mobility); and psychological (analytical/ global, cerebral preference, and reflective/impulsive). Learning style research identified conditions that support individual learning and achievement. Learners need to go beyond seeing and hearing to include hands-on experience and performance. McCarthy (1987) suggests that teachers do not need to individualize lessons, but rather use a diversity of strategies that incorporate a variety of learning styles. When teachers adjust plans to meet students' individual learning styles, student achievement increases (Dunn, 1983, McCarthy, 1987; Joyce & Weil, 1986).

Research on brain hemisphericity is closely tied to learning styles. Kolb (1984) developed a model with roots in the perception and processing of the learner. Left- or right-brained dominance determines the way a person perceives information. Concrete experiences in perception reflect a left-brained modality, while abstract conceptualization refers to a right-brained modality.

Kolb's research later became the basis for the 4MAT system. The 4MAT system (Figure 8–5) is an eight-step cycle of instruction capitalizing on individual learning styles and brain dominance processing preferences (McCarthy, 1990). Because teaching should engage the whole brain, rather than the traditional left brain, the 4MAT forces acknowledgement of right-brain experiences (O'Brien, 1989).

To an educator, the 4MAT system allows implementation of many aspects of learning styles, from Dunn and Dunn to Gardner. 4MAT translates learning styles theory into practical application, providing for Gardener's multiple intelligences as well as Dunn and Dunn's influential stimuli. Educators, therefore, are able to create lessons that meet students' needs and their preferred learning styles. At the same time, the 4MAT curriculum challenges other modes of learning where the student is less comfortable (McCarthy, 1990).

Inquiry

Inquiry teaching is a student-centered strategy where teachers view their role as a guide and not as a transmitter of knowledge. Inquiry is discovery-oriented or discovery-guided. Discovery inquiry is based on two fundamental beliefs: students collecting information to solve a problem enhances critical thinking; and seeking knowledge increases student motivation (Joyce & Weil, 1986). In discovery-oriented inquiry, individuals or small groups uncover answers to questions formulated by the students. In guided discovery, the teacher sets the topic or the question and guides the students through to the conclusion. In both

FIGURE 8–5 The 4MAT System

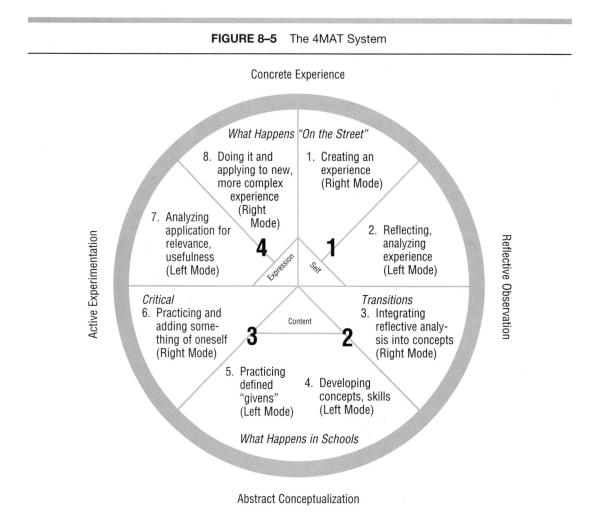

Reprinted with permission, B. McCarthy, (1990), "Using the 4MAT System to Bring Learning Styles to Schools, " *Educational Leadership*, 33.

types of inquiry, however, students work independent of the teacher to seek answers to the questions.

Inquiry lessons involve several steps. First, students or the teacher formulate a question around a puzzling or discrepant event. Then, students collect information about the question, formulate, test, and verify their hypothesis. Finally, students examine and communicate the results. Inquiry lessons lend themselves to several types of activities, especially researching areas of student interest.

Conclusion to Theory

No one teaching strategy is better than another, can accomplish every goal, or satisfy every purpose. Therefore, teachers need to choose instructional strategies related to student needs, content, and lesson objectives. There are many variables to consider when meeting individual needs. Strategies range from direct teacher-centered to indirect student-centered instruction. In each instance, active and engaging lessons increase achievement. Teachers need to develop and use a variety of instructional strategies to accomplish whole class, group, and individual learning experiences.

▶ # CLASSROOM
▶ # APPLICATIONS

Introduction

Instructional strategies form the heart and soul of teaching, empowering teachers to make professional decisions about issues concerning the achievement and climate of the classroom. Sadly, research shows that most teachers select methods of instruction that rely heavily upon teacher-centered talk and student memorization. Teachers must identify a purpose and establish clear goals in order to select appropriate instructional strategies. Reliance upon any one instructional technique will not accomplish every goal and satisfy every student's need in the classroom. Teachers must be empowered to select, reflect, and choose from a wide body of strategies and techniques that will meet the needs of their students.

A teacher needs to use a combination of whole group, small groups, and individual work on the lesson during the class period. An important point to remember is to take time to analyze and reflect on the *purpose* of the lesson when choosing the most appropriate instructional strategies for the lesson.

Developing Instructional Strategies

Following are specific suggestions for choosing and developing instructional strategies for your lesson or unit. These suggestions provide you with a quick reference to analyze your lesson before and after you teach.

- *Use active learning.* Plan to actively involve students in the learning process. Students' learning increases when they are able to do something with the information.

- *Set a purpose.* Relate new information to previous learning or prior knowledge. Let students know what it is they are going to learn and why it is important.

- *Make connections.* Help students to see relationships between information and skills taught in other subjects and to important issues in students' lives. Integrate learning as much as possible.

- *Incorporate student interests.* Allow students to become involved in planning and participating in lessons. Let them create, choose, share, and develop ideas and activities to help make learning meaningful.

- *Use a variety of materials and activities.* Use a variety of materials to meet the various learning styles and individual differences in the classroom. Vary activities to keep a high interest throughout the year.

- *State concise instructions for activities.* Describe the rules, behaviors, outcomes, and times for the learning activities. Write directions and discuss these with the students prior to beginning any activity. Write a schedule for the activity on the chalkboard.

- *Take risks.* Be unconventional; use creativity, information, and student curiosity to plan and teach your lessons. Devise and try personal activities and methods that you feel best reach your students.

- *Be prepared.* Have materials ready to maximize engaged time in learning. Check materials and equipment prior to beginning the lesson. Keep students attentive and on-task while you move from one activity to another during your lesson.

- *Provide multicultural components.* Structure lessons to include information appropriate for various cultures and genders. Avoid stereotype images and allow for equal representation in content and strategy.

- *Show enthusiasm.* Put emotion into your lessons; laugh, raise and lower your voice, and demonstrate your genuine interest in your lesson.

- *Know your students.* Take time to listen to students for confusion, interests, motivation, or boredom. Know students' strengths, weaknesses, and interests. Find methods and activities students enjoy. Communicate and interact frequently with students so you can adjust your lesson.

- *Provide feedback.* Select positive reinforcement for students' learning. Maximize the involvement and participation of all students and check for understanding. This process helps you assess the degree of student learning.

- *Create outlines, definitions, agendas, and study guides.* Modify material to help students follow the lesson and focus their learning. The use of these can provide students with a broader picture while breaking down information into smaller and easier to handle components.

- *Monitor seatwork.* Move around the room while students are working on group activities, worksheets, or assignments to encourage and check progress. Use this time to extend and reinforce student learning.

- *Pace the lesson.* Learn to look at and read your students' actions. Look for nonverbal cues to assess students' attentiveness. Provide changes in activities to keep the pace and interest moving along.

- *Summarize and review learning.* Take time to review frequently and constantly connect information to past lessons.

Whole Class

Whole-class instruction is useful when it is active instead of passive. Whole-class activities are best if they are student-centered rather than teacher-centered. Variety in whole-class instruction is necessary in order to maintain student interest. Some popular whole class strategies that teachers can select for successful learning are: lecture, modeling, textbooks, and seatwork. The suggestions that follow are provided as a quick reference to assist you in planning and evaluating each instructional strategy.

Lecture

Lecturing is frequently overused, so teachers need to be enthusiastic and provide students with visual aids and a variety of materials to keep their interest. Constantly monitor the audience and sequence activities to keep students on task.

- *Organize the lesson.* Create a brief outline so students will know the purpose and content of your lesson. Stress the important parts of the lesson to connect prior, current, and future learning.

- *Allow students to assimilate information.* Observe the students to see how they are reacting to your lecture. Allow students to discuss and ask questions about information or material in the lesson. Use visuals to highlight important concepts that students should know.

- *Present information in small parts.* Organize and sequence the information to facilitate learning. Break down large bodies of knowledge and new information into smaller parts so students can make connections between concepts.

- *Alter lesson pace.* Consider the difficulty of the information and slow down when content is confusing. Use visuals and teaching aids to adjust for the range of abilities, learning styles, and learning disabilities.

- *Present information actively.* Use self-expression to build drama into your teaching styles. Use humor, sensitivity, and sharing of interesting personal details. Involve students with pictures and objects in your lecture.

- *Use questions.* Approach teaching and learning with questions to help students use indirect problem-solving and higher-order thinking. Use small group discussions and questions to review fundamental concepts after brief lectures.

- *Use non-verbal cues to keep the lecture moving.* Develop body language, facial expressions, and hand motions to stress points and keep students' attention during the lecture.

Modeling

Students learn a great deal through observing and modeling others. Modeling is a showing technique where you present or demonstrate information. Your students can help, too, since many times peers can be very effective in helping other students to learn. In modeling, you don't just tell students information, as in a lecture, you also show them.

- *Use posters, transparencies, chalkboard, illustrations, and real objects.* These objects will help make the information visual and tactile to appeal to a variety of senses and learning modalities.

- *Provide several examples and tell how to arrive at the solutions.* Point out the important steps and elements necessary to complete an assignment. Label and describe each aspect of an assignment and what components make an exceptional example.

- *Show expectations by doing them.* Model group projects and individual tasks with some of your students. Let the class observe while you and selected students show what is expected and what is needed to complete instructional tasks.

Textbooks

Textbooks are a resource and should be used in the classroom as a means to *support* instruction. They are organized so that teachers can follow precise steps in providing learning experiences to students. However, textbook teaching is frequently criticized such as when there is total dependency on textbook instruction as the primary instructional strategy. Beginning teachers often become dependent upon the textbook because they lack security in using a variety of instructional strategies that address the diverse needs of their students. Explore and vary textbook strategies to include and integrate teaching and learning. The textbook can be a powerful tool to help you organize lessons.

- *Explain to students how the textbook is organized.* Point out the features of the book, the front matter, pictures, questions, study guides, answer keys, graphs, glossary, and especially the index so students can locate specific information in the text.
- *Study the ancillary materials.* Check to see if the teacher workbooks, filmstrips, tests, and student worksheets provide the kind of reinforcement and instruction that meet your goals. Be sure to align the textbook and ancillary materials with your beliefs and goals to be certain the textbook meets your needs and the needs of the students.
- *Encourage the use of the textbook as a resource.* Use the textbook as one source to obtain information about specific topics you are studying. Make sure assignments in the textbook match the mode of learning and interest of the students.
- *Avoid page by page reading.* Determine what is an acceptable sequence. Select and choose the concepts, materials, and problems you believe meet the goals of your lesson. Do not feel you have to teach the entire textbook in sequence. Be selective in the kinds of information you use for the students.

- *Enrich the textbook information with your own ideas.* Plan and think of ways you could use activities that would enhance and motivate students when using the textbook. Think about exact ways you could supplement the lessons in the text.

Seatwork

Students often spend up to half their time doing seatwork assignments. Use this strategy in moderation as one way to provide practice and indicate the level of understanding.

- *Assign seatwork that is related to the information being taught.* Relate seatwork to the interest and maturity level of the students. Allow for differences and special needs of students by assigning more time when needed. Modify the amount of information to meet needs.
- *Give clear instructions.* Tell students and write on the chalkboard exactly what they need to do. Provide examples and work several problems together. Establish a procedure for students to ask questions while they are completing seatwork.
- *Check difficulty level of seatwork.* Gauge the reading level and difficulty level of the material used for seatwork. Be sure materials selected create an opportunity for success. Change and alter content to match students' level.

Groups

Groups must know the expectations, goals, and behaviors involved in the activity. Students must be taught how to work in a group. Frequently, teachers assume students already know how to work and behave in group settings. Take the time to develop and model the responsibilities, rules, and roles for increased success and participation in group activities. Establish with the students rules for group behavior and post these rules so students can follow them when learning in group activities. Also, define the roles and responsibilities for each member in relationship to completing group tasks. Some possible roles are: leader (the person in charge of the group), recorder (the person who keeps track of the information), reporter (the person who reports back the group's results), sheriff (the person who helps maintain group order), and gopher (the person allowed to move about the room to get materials and supplies to complete the group's task). Grouping strategies usually require more preplanning and preparation, but students are highly motivated when working together and sharing learning experiences. Some common group strategies and activities are: cooperative learning, discussion, role playing, and learning centers. The suggestions that follow are provided as a quick reference to assist you in planning and evaluating each instructional strategy.

Cooperative Learning

Students in cooperative learning groups work together to perform tasks, learn information, or solve problems. Research indicates that cooperative learning promotes higher achievement compared to competitive individual learning. Cooperative learning provides teachers and students with a strategy to learn information in a collaborative and interesting way. This strategy, however, involves more than simply assigning students to a group. The fol-

lowing information suggests ways to establish and implement cooperative learning in your classroom.

- *Decide if cooperative learning groups are appropriate.* Cooperative learning should be used regularly, but not necessarily every day. Sometimes a team or partner approach would be more appropriate for review, laboratory projects, or skill practice. When deciding to use cooperative learning, think about students: learning content from each other, working with social and academic outcomes, verbalizing and discussing problems and solutions. Be certain this strategy is best suited for the content and information to be learned.

- *Teach students how to function in a group.* Make sure students understand the expectations, roles, and responsibilities involved in order to complete the group's goals. Take time to model group behavior and expectations by having one group in front of the class demonstrate how to maximize learning, on-task behavior, and group dynamics.

- *Assign students with varying abilities to groups.* The size and makeup of the learning group will vary according to the activity. A common arrangement is to use five students (tie breaker in case of a vote) in a group. Usually the group consists of a high achiever, a low achiever, and three middle achievers. Seek a balance between gender, ethnicity, and economic background.

- *Provide necessary materials.* It is important to make sure each group has the references and resources necessary to complete the assignment. Gather the materials and collect the resources necessary, prior to beginning the group activity. Think through the procedure as to how you want students to obtain materials and resources, particularly if you are using an abundance of these resources.

- *Summarize and evaluate students' progress.* Sometimes cooperative learning groups can deal with activities that take place over a day or week. Make sure you provide short term summarization to check each group's progress and understanding. Also indicate a level of evaluation and be sure students understand the criteria to be used in evaluating the group's performance.

Discussion

The purpose of discussion is to examine information in order to develop a deeper and broader understanding of a topic. Students should have some prior knowledge and experience with a current topic for discussion to be successful, however. Through discussion, there is the opportunity for higher order thinking and increased interaction among all students. The larger the group, the more difficult it will be to carry on interpersonal discussion. Consider the following when organizing a discussion.

- *Identify an interesting topic.* Introduce ideas and encourage the exchange and interaction of information and ideas related to the topic. Focus the discussion on one topic, but do not dominate the discussion by too much "telling" or "talking."
- *Use brainstorming.* This discussion strategy allows students to state their opinions and ideas about a topic without making any initial evaluations. There is no opportunity to criticize or evaluate discussion until all

ideas are exchanged. Summarize and synthesize ideas so they are rank-ordered, which will help establish a consensus among the group's ideas shared during the discussion.

- *Be tolerant.* Students need opportunities to discover and state opinions. Students should be encouraged to express their ideas freely. Teachers, at times, can play "devil's advocate," which is to take an opposite point of view to stimulate discussion.
- *Review and summarize the discussion.* After the topic and ideas are discussed, summarize the ideas that fit the goals and topic of the lesson. Promote compromise at the end of the discussion to combine ideas in order to reach a final consensus.

Role-Playing

Role-playing fosters small group interactions. It allows students the opportunity to act out selected text. Role-playing is useful and enjoyable for learning about people, places, events, and times. During role-playing, a small group of students presents the content while others in the class observe. Students have the opportunity to experience and analyze the specific situation being studied. There are several steps that are involved in organizing role-playing as a teaching strategy.

- *Identify goals and a situation students are to role-play.* Select students to participate in role-playing and prepare the audience to observe.
- *Give students preparation time.* Students need to think about the situation, practice, and organize their role-playing enactment before they present it.

- *Discuss and evaluate the role-playing.* Discuss the accuracy, content, application, and students' perceptions about the role-playing activity. Let students share the content and experience to identify understandings and generalizations that evolved from the role-playing.

Learning Centers

A learning center is an area in the classroom where students can go for reinforcement or practice of specific content taught. The center should contain numerous sources that could be used to provide extra drill and experiences to extend students' understanding. The center also provides an opportunity for students to select and practice from a variety of activities. This strategy is student-centered and allows students to work independently. There are several considerations when organizing a learning center as an instructional strategy.

- *Establish and post rules.* Select an area in the classroom where you can set up the center. Post the rules for the students' behavior when they are working in the center. Include such things as what to do, how to do it, and how long students are permitted to be there. Provide examples and models of the activities and ways in which these activities can be completed.

- *Organize the center.* Obtain materials and code these either by number or by color. Explain where students go to get materials necessary to complete activities in the center. Provide a means for students to sign in and out of the center, which would keep track of when and how long the students were at the center. Also establish a place

where students can place their completed work when they finish.

- *Allow students to self-check their work.* Provide checklists and answers so students can receive immediate feedback and reinforcement of their learning.

- *Prepare a variety of activities.* Use the various senses in activities and manipulatives when preparing the center. Use a variety of writing, reading, and listening activities. Develop materials students can complete in a short period of time that relate to the goals of the lessons presented in class. These materials and activities should be self-checking and answers should be provided in the center.

Individuals

It is extremely difficult, if not impossible, to totally "individualize" a classroom. There are times in the classroom, however, where it is absolutely necessary for a teacher to provide individual attention and instruction for students who need extra assistance or for special populations: gifted, at risk, disadvantaged, handicapped, bilingual, or those who have a diagnosed learning or emotional disability. As more students are being mainstreamed into the regular classrooms, it is important to understand basic methods and activities used to promote individualized learning. When planning any strategy, the teacher must consider ways to meet the varying needs of the students. Learning styles, inquiry, problem-solving, and decision-making are strategies that provide for individual needs. The suggestions that follow are provided as a quick reference to assist you in planning and evaluating each instructional strategy.

Learning Styles

The most common variation in learning styles is defined by the senses. Most students are visual learners, so planning should incorporate techniques that help students view content they are learning. Learning styles have also been categorized according to ways individuals organize and process information. Learning styles identify the best way a student learns and since individuals do not learn in the same way, what may be a useful approach for one individual may not be successful or helpful to another. One particular learning style is no better or worse than others, but simply different. Teachers must recognize that students do learn in different ways and must be able to provide multisensory activities and materials to effectively reach all students.

- *Provide an abundance of visuals.* Link visual objects with classroom narrative. Frequently use the chalkboard and overhead so students can visualize key points and information of the lesson. Use listening centers, bulletin boards, and so forth to display and use a variety of learning modalities for the content taught.

- *Increase student participation.* Use active instruction involving games and activities that engage students visually, auditorily, and kinesthetically. Students should provide input in the planning process to relate their needs and interests to activities and lessons.

- *Be sensitive to students' needs.* Listen to their needs. Survey students to find out room environment preferences: lighting, seating, movement, and so forth.

Inquiry

Inquiry relies on activities and resources to encourage finding solutions to questions investigated by students. The teacher provides structure, questions, and problems to stimulate student thinking and interests. Students should formulate their own questions for investigation. Initially, teachers should guide students through the inquiry process rather than allowing pure discovery.

- *Probe students' thinking.* Use thought-provoking questions to encourage students to hypothesize, reflect, and inquire. Pose initial questions to organize students' interests and investigation into a topic or question.

- *Define the inquiry task.* Explain to students that inquiry is a way they can independently seek information to identify solutions to their problems.

- *Begin with a question.* Initiate inquiry with a question to help students focus on the topic. The question helps students seek solutions and formulate plans for seeking answers to the question (see Figure 9–3).

- *Assist students in gathering information.* Students must have sufficient materials to select, analyze, and evaluate. Help individual students gather, organize, and analyze the information needed for their inquiry.

- *Set time limits.* Plan and communicate the approximate amount of time needed to complete an inquiry. Allow time for students to share their findings with others. The inquiry process involves time to form, infer, generalize, and conclude results.

Problem-Solving

Problem-solving strategies use a systematic, sequenced method to seek solutions. Teachers and students must clearly define and clarify the problem to be solved. Because problem-solving is an important life skill that students will use throughout their life, take time to develop the thought-processes necessary to carry over into everyday real-life problem-solving. Allow students to explore creative ways and structured ways to solve problems.

- *Follow specific steps when teaching problem solving:* (a) identify a problem; (b) collect reference material and information related to the problem; (c) hypothesize solutions while analyzing the tasks necessary to solve the problem; (d) evaluate, synthesize, and/or experiment to check the hypothesis; (e) conclude by offering an answer, generalizations or alternatives to the problem; and (f) communicate the findings of the investigation.

- *Monitor students' progress.* Keep students on task while they are working on a problem. Be sure students follow the problem solving steps to insure higher-order thinking skills and learning achievement. Later, encourage students to use creative problem solving by modeling steps and procedures.

- *Arrange time.* Problem-solving requires time for investigation, reflection, and evaluation. Schedule time in a lesson for students to solve problems and communicate results.

- *Prepare the necessary materials.* Compile references, laboratory equipment, and other supplies. Provide journals to help students record their findings.

Decision-Making

Decision-making, like problem-solving, is a real-life skill and students must be taught the techniques involved in the decision-making process. Students in the learning process need to have the opportunity to make good choices from several alternatives. Approaches should incorporate strategies for students to make decisions related to their learning. Whenever possible, teachers should allow students to be involved in making decisions. Students must be taught how to make a decision before we expect them to become proficient in this particular skill.

- *Define the decision-making process.* In order for students to make a decision, they must: identify the choices, identify the alternatives, think about the consequences, and make a decision based on reason.

- *Identify possible alternatives.* Without alternatives, there is no need for a decision. Help students think of possible alternatives involved in decisions.

- *Identify possible outcomes for each alternative.* When analyzing and thinking about the alternatives, students need to think about the possible outcome of each particular alternative.

- *Make the decision.* After alternatives and thoughtful analysis of outcomes has been discussed, students should make decisions. These decisions are based on the likelihood of outcomes of the choice that meets their needs and desires.

- *Implement a plan of action.* Allow students the opportunity to organize ways to develop an action plan that will support their decision.

Special-Needs Students

Thought for instructional strategies must also be given to the various populations in the classroom. Teachers must strive to use methods and techniques that reach students with special needs students, bilingual students, and at-risk students. The following suggestions provide an easy reference for you to review when planning instructional strategies that meet the needs of all students.

Special Needs Students. Teaching strategies must be developed to meet the needs of all students with the least restrictive environment possible. Public Law 94-142 mandates that public schools must provide all students with the opportunity to participate in regular education experiences. Moving special education students into the regular classroom is referred to as inclusion. Mainstreaming will affect you by placing students with special needs in your classroom for all or part of the school day. There are several important strategies to consider:

1. *Do not make assumptions.* Treat all students as individuals. Avoid generalizations or stereotypes about students with special needs. All students have the same basic classroom needs for belonging and attention.

2. *Seek assistance.* Learn as much as you can from the student's special education teachers and the counselor. Ask for assistance as needed with activities and assignments.

3. *Be yourself.* Continue with classroom routines in a positive and enthusiastic way. Provide extra support and structure when needed, but do not accept inappropriate behavior.

4. *Organize lessons and activities with special needs in mind.* Plan specific goals and objectives for special needs students with the special education teacher. Challenge students to their highest level without frustrating them.

Bilingual Students. Bilingual students and Limited English Proficiency (LEP) students come from homes where standard English is not the primary language. Often bilingual students are perceived as low achievers. Teachers need to provide enriched language experiences to help these students overcome language barriers. Helping them gain security and acceptance requires understanding and acceptance of cultural differences. There are important considerations to keep in mind when working with bilingual students:

1. *Use visual aides.* Show pictures and words together. Reinforce the sounds of the letters and basic sight words to assist with language development.

2. *Learn about the culture.* Take time to learn and understand about the culture of the students. Learn several basic words in the students' first language to develop sensitivity and trust. Talk to parents with an interpreter if possible and where necessary.

3. *Use bilingual material.* Locate and use material available to help students keep learning as they grow in their English proficiency. Use the district bilingual specialist if available and seek support and materials.

4. *Provide extra support.* Think about activities to facilitate language growth. Use peer

tutoring and cooperative learning. Use a multisensory approach to meet needs of bilingual students. Provide a classmate to reinforce language and frequently write words on the chalkboard.

At-Risk Students. Students at risk are defined as individuals who, at an early age, are failing to complete their education at minimum skill levels. Teachers should to focus on students' strengths and abilities rather than weaknesses. Instructional strategies need to provide experiences that will remediate the learning deficits of these students. There are several important considerations for teaching these students:

1. *Develop lessons that focus on the students self-esteem.* Show positive talk and encouragement throughout the day. Use congruent verbal and non-verbal communication.

2. *Check your perceptions.* Analyze how you feel about each student. Think about what you say and do to check any discriminating behavior. Let students know you value and believe in them.

3. *Provide extended experiences.* At-risk students frequently lack basic life experiences. Provide videos, field trips, pictures, and so forth to enhance their background knowledge.

4. *Emphasize high expectations.* Know students' background, knowledge, needs, and interests. Provide tasks that are challenging and related to their needs.

5. *Select appropriate activities.* Use language and visually rich materials. Provide group activities to help them learn social as well as academic skills. Be patient and encouraging.

FIELD-BASED CONNECTIONS

Introduction

Many excuses can be used for being dependent on one instructional strategy. Yet, there is a need for beginning classroom and intern students to experience and integrate most, if not all, of the major instructional strategies (Figure 8–6). Interns need to make decisions about goals and content before deciding which instructional strategies will satisfy the needs of the teacher, student, and lesson objectives.

Numerous books and articles contain activities that can be used to integrate various instructional strategies at the elementary and secondary level. These professional magazines and methods textbooks can be extremely useful when planning lessons and choosing activities.

Initially, intern students should spend time planning a direct instruction lesson, (Figure 8–7). The lesson plan should be checked and approved by the mentor teacher. As the experience and success grow, university students need exposure to group lessons cooperative learning, inquiry, and individual teaching strategies. Invaluable is the monitoring, reflection, communication, and evaluation between mentor teacher and intern student for lessons planned and taught (Figure 8–8). Written feedback and videotaping will assist interns in reflecting upon and appraising their instructional competencies. We strongly encourage written, direct, and open dialogue between the mentor and intern. The focus is not to clone the intern into the mentor but to allow the intern to discover and build a personal educational belief system that is unique and successful.

FIGURE 8–6 Instructional Strategies Observation Form

Directions: Observe your mentor teacher or other teachers in the school using various instructional strategies. Analyze these activities in terms of how you see them working and how they would fit into your personal instructional philosophy.

Activity	What I Like	What I Dislike	Appropriateness for Your Philosophy
DIRECT 1. Lecture	_____ _____ _____	_____ _____ _____	_____ _____ _____
2. Modeling	_____ _____ _____	_____ _____ _____	_____ _____ _____
3. Textbook	_____ _____ _____	_____ _____ _____	_____ _____ _____
4. Seatwork	_____ _____ _____	_____ _____ _____	_____ _____ _____
GROUP 1. Discussion	_____ _____ _____	_____ _____ _____	_____ _____ _____
2. Cooperative Learning	_____ _____ _____	_____ _____ _____	_____ _____ _____

FIGURE 8–6 continued

Activity	What I Like	What I Dislike	Appropriateness for Your Philosophy
3. Role Playing			
4. Learning Centers			
5. Projects			
INDIVIDUAL 1. Inquiry			
2. Learning Styles			
3. Decision-Making			
4. Problem-Solving			
Other			

FIGURE 8–7   Lesson Plan Framework

BEGINNING: What is the guiding question to help you and students focus?

    1.   Objectives: What do you want students to learn?

    2.   Content: What knowledge will be taught?

    3.   Introduction: How will you motivate students?

MIDDLE: How will you organize instruction and activities?

    1.   Procedures: How will you sequence the lesson?

    2.   Time: How will you pace the lesson?

    3.   Checking for Understanding: How will you check progress throughout the lesson?

END: Did students learn?

    1.   Closure: How will you deliberately end the lesson and apply it to students' lives?

    2.   Reinforcement: What projects, tests or homework will you select to apply lesson?

    3.   Evaluate: How will you account for student progress?

Guidelines for Interns

Pick and choose the activities that best suit you and your needs. Use these suggestions for your unit plans, portfolio collection, and your journal entries where appropriate.

1. Use the form in Figure 8–6 to observe a wide variety of instructional strategies. Make appointments to visit other teachers to observe a range of delivery styles and instructional strategies.

2. Observe your mentor teaching a direct lesson. Use the lesson cycle form (Figure 8–2) to help you analyze the lesson. Discuss your impression and questions with the mentor teacher. Have the mentor explain how certain parts of the lesson were planned, such as focus, closure, and others.

3. Plan and teach whole class, small group, and individual lessons using the form in Figure 8–7. Meet with the mentor teacher before and after to receive feedback about your plan and your teaching. Specifically talk about what you can do to increase achievement and on-task learning.

FIGURE 8–8   Lesson Observation Form

Name: _____

Date of Lesson: _____

Mentor Observing Lesson: _____

School: _____

Grade or Subject: _____

Instruction Strategy: _____

Directions: Use this form to keep notes while the intern teaches a lesson. Have the intern complete the reaction and then schedule a time to discuss the lesson with the intern.

Beginning:

_____

_____

_____

Middle:

_____

_____

_____

End:

_____

_____

_____

Suggestions:

_____

_____

_____

Reaction:

_____

_____

_____

4. Seek out teachers in the school who are known for being masters at certain strategies, such as lecture, inquiry, and cooperative learning. Ask these teachers how they organize for instruction and why they are successful in their teaching.

5. Obtain copies of learning style inventories from your professors or professional journals. Use these instruments to help analyze the various learning styles of students in your class.

► CHAPTER
► CLOSURE

Summary

There is a continuum of methods a teacher can select, from direct to indirect and passive to active, when planning whole-class, small group, and individual instructional strategies. Teachers must be knowledgeable about and able to select appropriate methods and material for implementing lessons that meet the needs of students. Smart choices are needed from the multitude of strategies and activities available to teachers.

Instruction is a personal craft and teachers must be empowered to use a variety of strategies that excite and engage students in learning. Teachers and students must be active participants in the classroom. A balance is needed between direct, indirect, passive, and active instructional strategies. Active, direct teaching follows specific teacher and learner behaviors. This teaching style follows sequential steps that generate higher achievement outcomes on standardized tests. Constructivist teaching follows active learning behaviors related to building connections between knowledge and the world. Learning, say constructivists, is discovered through interaction with the environment. Both active teaching and constructivism have something to assist student learning.

Selecting strategies that promote group interaction with knowledge is also useful to many students. Students need opportunities to apply information in cooperative settings that enhance socialization, higher-order thinking, decision-making, and problem-solving. Analyzing and applying content to real world situations is beneficial to the learning process. The key ingredients to instructional strategies are integration, variety and planning. Decide during planning what your students need to know, which integrated teaching techniques you will use, and what activities will meet the goals of your lesson and the needs of the students. Through variety and planning, the likelihood of increasing learning takes place. Variety allows the teacher to meet more of the learner's needs and planning allows thoughtful delivery of instruction. As concerns arise in the classroom, smart teachers are quick to analyze their personal educational belief system, think on their feet, and adjust strategies to maintain optimum learning and high student interest.

Chapter Discussion Questions

1. In groups, discuss the advantages and disadvantages of lecture, modeling, discussion, cooperative learning, learning styles, and inquiry. Prepare a one-page comprehensive report and a fifteen minute oral

report for the class. Describe other strategies and activities that were not discussed in this text.

2. Is there a danger in using prescribed activities in trade journals, magazines, and textbooks?

3. What characteristics make your mentor teacher a good instructional leader? Use data collected from the forms from the Field-Based Connections section in this chapter.

4. Why is it essential to use a variety of instructional strategies? When is it best to use whole-class, group, and individual instructions?

5. Describe the advantages/disadvantages of active, direct teaching. Why are the basic sequential steps needed?

6. Describe the advantages/disadvantages of constructivism. Why is constructivism an important aspect of teaching?

CASE STUDIES

The case study examples can be used for analysis in small or large groups. Questions follow each case study as suggestions for discussion.

CASE STUDY 8–1: by Alison Witte, Practicum Student

When I began my practicum experience, I thought I already knew what teaching was all about. But as I worked with my students, it was easy to see that, in the teaching profession, learning and adapting is essential. No matter how much experience or talent a teacher might possess, learning and adaptability is the key to being an excellent teacher.

Because I was with a first-time master teacher, she really had no idea what to do. As we became familiar with one another, I saw that she and I possess very different teaching skills. I believe that learning should be fun and entertaining, making use of creative talents and ideas. My master teacher, however, works a majority of the time with worksheets and textbooks.

When my master teacher and I discuss teaching techniques, she is open to my ideas on teaching a certain idea. She is genuinely interested in my input on lesson plans because, as she admits, she does not possess the ability to think of fun and creative techniques for teaching. A good example of this is our recent lesson on long division. Long division has consistently been a difficult concept to master, and we decided that a good understanding was essential for the students to go on in school. When we looked at the material, I immediately thought of a "rap" that I had heard that explained the concept of long division. It was very exciting for me to teach the children this song and hear their comprehension as they sang.

I see each student as a challenge. Each of my students has different needs and learns in different ways. Every one of my students can and will learn long division. That must be the ultimate goal. It is so neat, though, to watch the students as they take a test on the concept and whisper the long division rap to themselves. In that sense, sneaky techniques for learning do work.

The other day, one of my students caught on to the idea of fun learning. He asked me if what we were doing was important to know. I told him that everything we learn in the classroom is important to know. They constantly catch themselves having fun in math, and step back and look at what they were doing. One boy told me that I tricked him into learning his multiplication tables. I responded by reminding him that at least now he knows them.

When I heard my students telling me the other day that they did not want me to leave, because we were just starting to learn, I almost cried. I was not sure that I wanted to work with fifth-graders, but my experience has given me a good perspective to judge what I really want to do.

Case Study Discussion Questions

1. How does Alison adapt a math lesson to meet the needs of the students?

2. Does Alison have a good communication system established with her mentor teacher?

3. How do you relate to Alison's instructional experience?

CASE STUDY 8–2: by Diane Blake, Middle School Reading Specialist

It is interesting to watch teaching techniques get "re-labeled," heartily endorsed, and thoroughly promoted every so many years. These shifts, coincidentally, are generated by the lofty and learned educational authors and championed by promoters of basal readers. What I learned as language experience was renamed whole language and suddenly it became not only the catch phrase of the times, but a mandate from wherever these trends originate. At least in the last few years we've been asked to jump on the bandwagon of familiar territory with adequate materials to foster the technique. I would like to think we'd never rename and bring back the unstructured, packet-based, do-your-own-thing, emphasis on electives that took precedence over basics a few years back. I wouldn't bet on it though.

I remember our local experiment with ITA (initial teaching alphabet), where all the pre-primers, primers, and readers were written phonetically. The results were as predicted—the good readers sped along, the slow readers struggled, and almost everyone struggled with correct spelling in later grades.

I had a conversation with an elementary teacher in a nearby district that wants its teachers to use small group learning as the primary teaching technique. Both of us have, of course, already used this technique as one of our learning tools. Good teachers know you need an eclectic approach.

I happen to believe it's very important for students to hear what each other has to say, to respect another's point of view, and to be able to discern what is applicable to the task at hand. I am comfortable with a reasonable amount of noise generated by such group activities as long as it is productive. When I began teaching fifteen years ago, I quickly discovered two things: The teacher needs to carefully orchestrate, define, and supervise the activity; and each student must make a meaningful contribution. This requires a lot of preparation by the teacher and I had to severely curtail this activity for several reasons. My district schedules students according to band/music, and meets state requirements for the "gifted" and below-grade-level readers by grouping them homogeneously in reading and math. Group activities for 170+ students, thus grouped, produced a special challenge. The "top" class handled group activities beautifully; self-motivated, enthusiastic, and efficient. The "low" class could not—would not—stay on-task and those few students who wanted to do the assignment would end up doing the work, getting a mediocre grade on the evaluation, and the others were indifferent to any consequence.

The only group activities I could use with all my classes were ones that involved physical movement, some form of media (tapes, video, music, art material, etc.) minimal interaction with the teacher, and something they perceived as containing some element of "fun." Thinking of activities that met the criteria and selling them to 170 suspicious eighth-graders, tied in with getting them to see a link between prose, poetry, and art form. Living near Lake Erie, the students were familiar with lake freighters. I distributed the newspaper account of the sinking of the Edmund Fitzgerald, examining the article and discussing prose. Next, we shared a poem by Gordon Lightfoot and, finally, they listened to his recording. Following directions, students were divided into groups, given newspapers, located an article that interested them, summarized it, converted it to poetry, and then to music. Groups were videotaped and shown to the other classes. Some group members provided backup vocals, brought in instruments to play, opted to "rap," sign with interpretation, etc. I have tried similar activities for book reports and library orientation, but each year discipline became more difficult. Some students would refuse to be involved in any manner of group activity and it became impossible to continue these activities with all but the top group. I wish the elementary teachers who will be asked to use the group method much success. I hope they are adequately inserviced and personally motivated. Maybe it's easier at the elementary level to get the children involved and they'll continue to enjoy working in groups when they get to junior high. I'll ask my friend to let me know—I left teaching last year.

Case Study Discussion Questions

1. What part of Diane's instructional strategy do you find most interesting?

2. What seasoned discoveries does Diane point out?

3. What problems did Diane encounter?

4. Why do you think Diane recently left the teaching profession?

▶ REFERENCES

Adams, R. & Biddle, B. (1970). *Realities of teaching: Explorations with videotape.* New York: Holt, Rinehart and Winston.

Aronson, E., Blaney, N., Stephan, C., Sikes, J., & Snapp, M. (1978). *The jigsaw classroom.* Beverly Hills, CA: Sage.

Borich, G. D. (1988). *Effective teaching methods.* Ohio: Merrill Publishing Company.

Brophy, J. (1979). Teacher behavior and its effects. *Journal of Educational Psychology, 71,* 733–750.

Brown, D. S. (1988). Twelve middle-school teachers' planning. *The Elementary School Journal, 89*(1), 69–87.

Cangelosi, J. S. (1992). *Systematic teaching strategies.* New York: Longman.

Clark, C. M. & Yinger, R. J. (1979). *Three studies of teacher planning.* (Research Series No. 55). East Lansing, MI: Michigan State University. ERIC Document Reproduction Service No. ED 175-855.

Cuban, L. (1986). Persistent instruction: Another look at constancy in the classroom. *Phi Delta Kappan, 68,* 7–11.

Dunn, R. (1983). Learning style and its relation to exceptionality at both ends of the spectrum. *Exceptional Children, 49,* 496–506.

Evertson, C., Emmer, E., & Brophy, J. (1980). Predictors of effective teaching in junior high mathematics classrooms. *Journal of Research in Mathematics Education, 11,* 167–178.

Freiberg, J. H. & Driscoll, A. (1992). *Universal teaching strategies.* Boston: Allyn and Bacon.

Gall, M. & Gall, J. (1976). The discussion method. In N.L. Gage (Ed.), *The psychology of teaching methods: The seventy-fifth yearbook of the national society for the study of education, part I.* Chicago: University of Chicago Press.

Gamoran, A. (1987). Organization, instruction, and the effects of ability grouping: Comment on Slavin's 'Best-Evidence Synthesis.' *Review of Educational Research, 57*(3), 341–345.

Gardner, H. (1983). *Frames of mind: The theory of multiple intelligences.* New York: Basic Books.

Good, T. (1979). Teacher effectiveness in the elementary school. *Journal of Teacher Education, 30,* 52–64.

Goodlad, J. (1984). *A place called school: Prospects for the future.* New York: McGraw-Hill.

Graves, N. & Graves, T. (1990). *Cooperative learning: A resource guide.* Santa Cruz, CA: The International Association for the Study of Cooperation in Education.

Houston, R. W. (1988). *Touch the future, teach.* New York: West Publishing Company.

Hunter, M. (1981) *Increasing your teaching effectiveness.* Palo Alto, CA: Learning Institute.

Johnson, D. W. & Johnson, R., T. (1989). *Cooperation and competition: theory and research.* Edina, MI: Interaction Book Company.

Johnson, D., Johnson, R,. & Holubec, E. (1990). *Circles of learning: Cooperation in the classroom.* Edina, MI.: Interaction Book Company.

Joyce, B. & Weil, M. (1986). *Models of teaching,* 3rd edition. Englewood Cliffs, N.J.: Prentice Hall.

Joyce, B. R. (1991). Common misconceptions about cooperative learning and gifted students. *Educational Leadership, 48*(6), 72–74.

Kagan, S. (1990). *Cooperative learning: Resources for teachers.* San Juan: Resources for Teachers.

Kolb, D. R. (1984). *Experiential learning: Experience as the source of learning and development.* Englewood Cliffs, NJ: Prentice-Hall, Inc.

London, C. B. G. (1990). A Piagetian constructivist perspective on curriculum development. *Reading Improvement, 27*(2), 82–95.

McCarthy, B. (1987). *The 4MAT system: Teaching to learning styles with right/left mode techniques.* Barrington, IL: Excel.

McCarthy, B. (1990). Using the 4MAT system to bring learning styles to schools. *Educational Leadership, 48,* 31–36.

McNair, K. (1978-79). Capturing inflight decisions. *Educational Leadership Quarterly, 3*(4), 26–42.

Melton, R. (1978). Resolution of conflicting claims concerning the effect of behavioral objectives on student learning. *Review of Educational Research, 48,* 291–302.

Montague, E. J., Huntsberger, J., & Hoffman, J. (1989). *Fundamentals of elementary and middle school classroom instruction.* Columbus, OH: Merrill.

Moore, K. D. (1992). *Classroom teaching skills,* 2nd edition. New York: McGraw-Hill.

Morine-Dershimer, G. (1978). Planning and classroom reality: An in-depth look. *Educational Research Quarterly, 3,* 83–89.

O'Brien, L. (1989). Learning styles: Make the student aware. *NASSP Bulletin,* 85–89.

Olmstead, J. A. (1970). *Theory and state of the art of small group methods of instruction.* Alexandria, VA: Human Resources Research Organization.

Roberts, W. K. (1982). Preparing instructional objectives: Usefulness revisited. *Educational Technology, 22*(7), 15–19.

Rosenshine, B. (1987). Explicit teaching and teacher training. *Journal of Teacher Education, 38*(3), 34–36.

Ross, D. D., Bondy, E., & Kyle, D. W. (1993). *Reflective teaching for student empowerment: Elementary curriculum and methods.* New York: Macmillan.

Sharan, S. (1980). Cooperative learning in small groups: Recent methods and effects on achievement, attitudes, and ethnic relations. *Review of Educational Research, 50,* 2–21.

Sizer, T. (1984). *Horace's compromise: The dilemma of the American high school.* Boston: Houghton Mifflin.

Slavin, R. (1990). Achievement effects of ability grouping in secondary schools: A best-evidence synthesis. *Review of Educational Research, 60,* 471–499.

Slavin, R. (1991). Synthesis of research on cooperative learning. *Educational Leadership, 48*(5), 71–82.

Slavin, R. & Madden, N. (1989). What works for students at risk: A research synthesis. *Educational Leadership, 46*(5), 4–13.

Spaulding, C. L. (1992). *Motivation in the classroom.* New York: McGraw-Hill, Inc.

Stallings, J. (1980). Allocated academic learning time revisited, or beyond time on task. *Educational Researcher, 9,* 11–16.

Tyler, R. W. (1950). *Basic principles of curriculum and instruction.* Chicago: University of Chicago Press.

Zeichner, K. M. & Liston, D. P. (1987). Teaching student teachers to reflect. *Harvard Educational Review, 57,* 23–48.

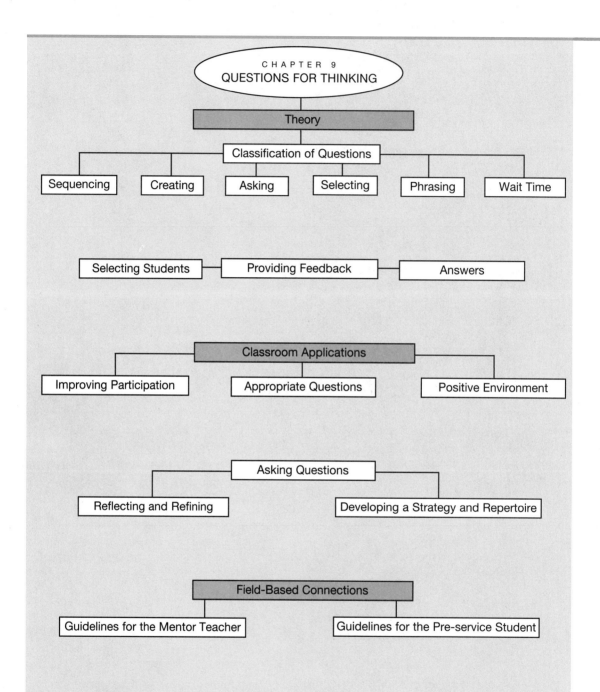

Questions for Thinking

Introduction

Questioning is the oldest and most common teaching technique and it is fundamental to outstanding teaching. Questions are the spark that ignite students' thought processes. To improve student thinking, teachers must learn how to be skillful questioners. Knowing how and when to use appropriate questions is an important ingredient for all instructional strategies (Figure 9–1).

Questioning and thinking are crucial components in all subjects and classrooms. Teachers select questions and respond to student answers according to specific goals or purposes. There are a variety of reasons why teachers use questions: increase involvement, pre-assess knowledge, check for understanding, determine if directions are followed, assess knowledge, and encourage student thinking. One of the most important uses of questions is to promote higher-oriented thinking skills. Teachers must know and use good questioning strategies to develop thinking students.

Today's student in tomorrow's world will need to question and seek solutions to the growing problems in our society and the world. Thinking is a skill that requires knowledge and daily practice on the part of teachers and students. Thinking is difficult to define because of the individual creative and critical qualities involved in processing information. The teaching of thinking is a deliberate and planned effort that must be constantly incorporated into and across the curriculum. Planning and reflecting about questions before, during, and after a lesson helps to improve teacher effectiveness. Good thinkers are good questioners and good questioners are good thinkers. Questioning and thinking are not taught in isolation, but taught in the context of a lesson.

Thinking is central to challenging individual and group problem-solving, decision-making, and logic activities. There are many resources and activities to assist teachers in developing students' creative and critical thinking. Rather than establish separate pro-

FIGURE 9–1 Good questions elicit good responses.

grams and activities for questioning and thinking, it is best to integrate them into all lessons and learning activities. Teachers must consider the purpose of their questions in order to integrate questioning into lessons and activities that challenge students to think.

Teachers need to know and identify the types of questions they ask in order to achieve variety and balance in classroom communication and interaction. Students need to be taught how to appropriately respond to questions, while teachers must know how to respond appropriately to the students' correct or incorrect answers. Careful listening and thoughtful feedback are important behaviors that should be modeled and encouraged during questioning for maximum learning and thinking in the classroom. Teachers need to be sensitive to students' needs in order to create a safe classroom atmosphere for successful discussion of the various types of questions.

► THEORY

Types of Questions

During the course of any school day, teachers ask their students hundreds of questions serving a variety of purposes. Pasch et al. (1991) state that questioning can facilitate classroom management (e.g., Robert, How can you help your group?) or focus students' attention and help them understand the content of a lesson (e.g., What changes occurred because of the War of 1812?). Questions can also encourage students to express values and opinions (Wassermann, 1991) (e.g., How can we help the homeless?).

Good questions invite student response, focus on important issues, and generate thinking. Sullivan and Clarke (1991) believe that teachers must select types of questions where: (1) students do more than recall information in order to answer; (2) students learn during the process of answering; (3) questions have a variety of paths leading to several acceptable answers.

There are two broad types of questions. The first is convergent. Convergent questions are content specific and seek direct, right/wrong answers with little interaction or interpretation. These questions usually have only one answer and create closed communication where no alternative answer or discussion is possible. Classroom interaction is at a low-level because it is based only on factual recall. Direct, right/wrong, low-level, and closed response questions are called convergent because different information converges or leads to the one and only answer. Teachers typically ask only convergent questions (Brophy & Good, 1974; Centra & Potter, 1980; Gall, 1970; Hare & Pulliam, 1980). Most objective test items also emphasize the convergent level of fact and recall (Melton, 1978). Often, standardized test items drive the curriculum and level of instruction in many schools. Content questions are important to understanding and achievement, however, questions should also seek to go beyond the level of recall (Gall, 1984). Those questions that do are called divergent.

Divergent questions are process-oriented questions that encourage independent, creative, and critical thinking. Divergent questions are open-ended and promote reflective thought, generalizations, and inferences. Classroom interaction is at a high level because the students use of many mental thought processes. Indirect, multiple answers, high level and open responses are called divergent because different information diverges or leads to a variety of correct answers.

Dillon (1982) found that 86.6 percent of the time, students respond to questions at a similar or higher level and concluded that divergent questions at higher levels encourage students to think critically. In a follow-up study, Harms et al. (1989) stated that asking divergent questions gives students the opportunity to practice using their critical-thinking skills. Redfield and Rousseau (1981) and Berliner (1987) found that when teachers use mostly higher level questions, gains in standardized achievement increase.

One of the goals of questioning is to encourage students to think critically and answer questions beyond the level of recalling facts. Unfortunately, many teachers continue to ask only lower-order, fact-recall questions since teachers tend to question students in the manner they themselves were once questioned (Wassermann, 1991; Wilson, 1973). Practicing and using divergent questions can break this cycle.

This is not to suggest that fact-recall questions are without instructional purposes or controversy. Ryder (1991) found in his study of questioning strategies that specific teacher-directed questions presented prior to the reading of material served to increase students' overall comprehension. Ryder determined that if the material contained especially difficult concepts, giving the students guiding questions helped them to identify the key issues. Good questioning involves a thoughtful balance between fact-recall questions that guide comprehension and higher-order questions that challenge students to think critically while searching for several solutions (Jarolimek & Foster, 1993).

Teachers most often use recall questions since they are easier to evaluate and because answers are either right or wrong. Teachers, therefore, can quickly assess students' learning. The predominance of recall questions occurs despite research consensus that such assessments actually tell teachers very little about students' understanding of material or ability to apply it to other situations (Montague et al., 1989). The use of divergent questions during instruction links thinking to knowledge.

Classification of Questions

Questioning strategies are central to interactive teaching. Skilled teachers use questions to set the stage for discussion, draw students into dialogue and evoke higher thought processes (Strother, 1989). Divergent questions initiate the process for developing thinking skills. There are many classification systems for describing levels of questioning and thinking (Doyle, 1986; Ennis, 1985; Paul, 1988). Bloom's *Taxonomy of Objectives* (1956) is still the most prominent and widely used system for question classification even though this was not the original intent. Bloom's Taxonomy consists of a hierarchy of six levels (Figure 9–2). Example questions are suggested for each level. Glatthorn (1993) believes that all teachers should know and be able to use Bloom's Taxonomy as a means for classifying their lesson questions.

The taxonomy shows the lower to higher levels of students' thinking skills. Questions must be adjusted to suit the need of the student (Duffy et al., 1985). Gall (1984) found that different levels of questions are effective, depending on the learner and the content of the lesson. Certain lessons require more recall, whereas other lessons require more thought. The key to effective questioning, according to this research, is to be certain that a knowledge base is established before moving into the levels of higher-oriented thinking skills.

The classification of questions to a higher-level hierarchy is useful for promoting var-

FIGURE 9–2   Questioning and Levels of Thinking

	QUESTION TYPE	STUDENT BEHAVIOR	EXAMPLE QUESTIONS
LOWER-LEVEL THINKING	KNOWLEDGE	RECALL RECITE	What (Who, When, Where, Why) are the thirteen colonies? Define photosynthesis.
	COMPREHENSION	DESCRIBE SUMMARIZE	What is the main idea? How is the major character portrayed?
	APPLICATION	SOLVE SHOW	What is the latitude of NY? Joe has 58 cents; how many 9 cent stamps can he buy?
HIGHER-LEVEL THINKING	ANALYSIS	INFER COMPARE	What does this paragraph tell us about the author's life? How are plants and animals alike/different?
	SYNTHESIS	CREATE PREDICT	What is a good title for this painting? How can we help the homeless?
	EVALUATION	JUDGE CHOOSE	Do you believe in capital punishment? Which soft drink is best?

ious kinds of thinking. Questions, however, do not always fit easily into these designated levels. Planning for the level of questions is, therefore, necessary and should be based on the purpose of the lesson and need of the students. Within each lesson, teachers need to plan a sequence for the types of questions they ask. This sequence illuminates questions that are used to initiate, extend, and close interaction.

Sequencing Questions

Beginning-lesson questions are extremely important because during these initial minutes the teacher gains the interest, attention, and cooperation of the students. The beginning of the lesson sets the tone and is known as establishing set (Louisell & Descamps, 1992). A useful strategy is to begin a lesson with a question to guide the learning, (Figure 9–3).

Initial questions are used to elicit a response, extend a response idea, or to redirect a response. Eliciting questions are directed to the entire class and should involve most students (Sciortino, 1988; Orlich et al., 1990).

Once students respond to eliciting questions, the teacher should encourage further discussion through extending responses. One way of extending responses is to use questions that focus on the main idea. Redirection questions help to involve more students in responding and discussing at higher levels. Eliciting, extending, and redirecting strategies (Figure 9–4) lessen teacher domination and increase student participation, which in turn increases student achievement (Brophy & Evertson, 1976; Denham & Lieberman, 1980; Soar & Soar, 1973).

FIGURE 9–3 Why Begin a Lesson with a Question?

1. Promotes Thinking

2. Creates Focus

3. Initiates Discussion

4. Appraises Experiences

5. Organizes Concepts

6. Aids Evaluation

7. Reinforces Reading

8. Motivation

Probing is another questioning technique to encourage discussion. While eliciting questions are concerned with the quantity of student responses Sciortino (1988) states that probing questions are concerned with the quality of responses. A probing question (Figure 9–5) requires students to expand a response, clarify what has been said, or justify a response (Montague et al., 1989).

The last step in the sequence is to end or conclude questioning. Concluding questions are termed closure and help students form conclusions, generalizations or solutions generated by the questioning sequence. The questioning sequence would be incomplete if some form of summary did not occur. A student summary of the discussion should provide corrected and additional information. Teachers should be sure students under-

---

FIGURE 9–4   Samples of Initial Questions

Eliciting Questions

1. Who are community workers?

2. How do we solve problems?

3. What are the effects of pollution?

4. What is inflation?

Extending Questions

1. What does the mail carrier do?

2. Are there other ways to solve problems?

3. Can anyone else describe experiences with pollution?

4. How does inflation affect your life?

Redirection Questions

1. Who else knows another community worker?

2. How does the answer relate to problem-solving?

3. What information do we need about pollution?

4. That is interesting, but what do you think about inflation?

---

stand (Figure 9–6) at the end of the lesson and correct any misconceptions that exist (Montague et al., 1989).

Creating a Questioning Environment

Successful use of the various types of questions involves creating a safe environment where students feel secure when thinking and responding. For good thinking to occur, students must also be given the opportunity to question and seek responses. Teachers must select, sequence, and deliver questions that promote freedom of thought and respect. When students are valued they are more likely to feel free to question and respond (Siegel, 1988). When creating a positive environment, a teacher must know the purpose and perception of group and individual questioning techniques.

FIGURE 9–5 Samples of Probing Questions

Expanding Questions

1. How do community workers help us?

2. When do you use problem-solving?

3. What are some other points of view about pollution?

4. Does anyone have another idea about inflation?

Clarifying Questions

1. Can you describe your community worker?

2. Could you give an example of a problem?

3. Would you repeat your view about pollution?

4. Why do you think inflation will increase?

Justifying Questions

1. Explain why you like community workers.

2. How did you solve the problem?

3. Where did you see the pollution?

4. How does your example show inflation?

The intent of a question should be academic unless it is procedural. Questions to punish or intimidate students should never be used. Borich (1988) believes that questions are academic tools which should be prized for their chosen purpose. To misuse questions for any other purpose may affect how students will react in the classroom. For example, the student might think "Did I get the hard question because the teacher thinks I'm smart or because I'm being punished?"

The *tone* of the question is also important because the same question might either be perceived by the students as hostile and

---

FIGURE 9–6   Samples of Closure Questions

---

1.   Name a community worker.

2.   How can problem-solving help us every day?

3.   What steps will you take to end pollution?

4.   What does the information about inflation show us about our economy?

---

intimidating or encouraging and friendly. When tone is combined with non-verbal language (eyes rolled, sneering, or smiling) a student might feel differently about the content of the question (Meyers, 1986). When inappropriate tone or incongruent non-verbal language is used on a student it could create a negative classroom environment. An appropriate tone encourages participation, whereas an intimidating tone during questioning decreases student participation (Frieberg & Driscoll, 1992).

A major factor to a positive environment is freedom. Students should be allowed to express themselves and have the right to raise questions. The teacher and students should nonjudgmentally listen to each other's concerns and ideas. Mutual respect encourages a diversity of questions and responses (Hunkins, 1976). Teachers, according to Siegel (1988), are obligated to respect students while recognizing their right to question, challenge, and demand reasons for what is taught. Creating a safe psychological climate is important to the questioning process. Eby (1992) points out that the physical environment is important as well. The students must be able to see and hear

one another to facilitate thinking and discussion. Arranging seating to accommodate good communication encourages students to contribute to the discussion.

Asking Questions

Good questions begin with a purpose and depend on thoughtful delivery. Student preparation should include prior knowledge and experience before beginning questioning. When questioning there are five basic steps:

1.   Selecting the type and level of question

2.   Phrasing the question

3.   Allowing wait time for thinking

4.   Selecting students

5.   Providing feedback

Throughout these steps, the teacher and students model appropriate communication skills in a safe environment. Careful planning and practice is important to the process.

Selecting the Type of Question

Choosing the type of question depends upon the learning task and the needs and abilities of the student. Brown and Edmondson (1984) suggest that questions can be directed to individuals, the entire class or students of varying degrees of ability. Therefore, selection of questions requires careful thought to meet the variety of student needs and abilities. Glatthorn (1993) advocates that appropriate levels of questions are a function of the type of discussion and the sequence of the learning. If a teacher wants an answer to a given level of thinking or type of response, then a question must be selected that will elicit that response from the student.

Phrasing Questions

Clarity in phrasing questions is crucial for effective questioning (Land, 1980; Gall & Gillett, 1980). The phrasing of the question affects the quality of student responses and class discussion. Pasch et al. (1991) suggest that class interaction is improved by phrasing questions so all students know they are responsible for considering a response. A question started with a student's name, for example, allows the other students to ignore both the question and the answer. A question beginning with "Who can tell me..." invites students to call out responses, thereby depriving other students of sufficient time to think. Teachers should phrase questions clearly and ask one question at a time. The wording of questions should be modified to the language ability of the class.

Allowing Wait Time for Thinking

One of the most important factors in pacing questions according to Pasch et al. (1991) is wait time; that is, time allowed between the asking and answering of the question. Pacing is the pausing or waiting that allows time for students to think. Rowe (1974) discovered that teachers, on the average, ask about two to three questions a minute. In addition, teachers waited less than one second for student answers before rephrasing the question or calling on another student. This short wait time does not allow students sufficient time to think or consider answers. Many students learn that if they out-wait teachers, another student will be called on or the teacher will answer the question. Generally, teachers should wait approximately three to five seconds before rephrasing or asking another question.

Research by Rowe (1980), Tobin (1986), Tobin and Capie (1982), and White and Tisher (1986) suggest that the following occurs when wait time is three seconds or longer after a question is asked and when wait time is allowed after the response:

- Length of responses increases
- Number of responses increases
- Failure to respond decreases
- Complexity of response increases
- Speculative thinking increases
- Interaction between students increases
- Students ask more questions
- Student confidence increases

- Disciplinary problems decrease

- Low-achieving student responses increases

These findings indicate the necessity of wait time both before and after students' responses.

Selecting Students

Teachers should ask questions to all students in the class so no one is ignored. Cooper and Good (1983) reported that teachers are often biased in their questioning patterns. They might for example, call on high-achieving students more than low-achieving students. They might choose boys more than girls, higher-economic students more than lower-economic students, or students seated near the front of the room more than those seated in the back of the room. All of these patterns send non-verbal messages to students that some are capable and important, while others are not.

Generally, teachers ask the question and then ask a student for a response. When individuals are selected before the question, the high achievers are called on more often than the low achievers (Good & Brophy, 1977). When a student is identified before the question, other students usually cease to think about the question. Frequently selecting students first is misused as an attempt to control behavior.

Allowing any student in the class to respond to a question without indicating which student is to respond, creates confusion and encourages shouting out answers that can disrupt the lesson. Allowing students to shout out answers makes it impossible to conduct questioning in ways that will pro-

mote thinking and good group interaction (Montague et al., 1989). Teachers need to develop a system to limit calling out of answers so eager students do not limit the involvement of classmates. However, in classes where students are reluctant to respond, the teacher might allow some spontaneous answers to stimulate student involvement (Ross et al., 1993). All students should have an equal opportunity to participate and interact with classroom questions.

Providing Feedback

The way teachers respond to student questions affects the student's perception of discussions. Generally, Brophy and Good (1986) state that the most common teacher response is praise. Although praise sometimes creates a positive classroom atmosphere, it is frequently misused. The response of "good," for example, can be overused and becomes the equivalent of no response. Praise can also be too general (e.g., You are a good student.), and therefore lacks acknowledgement of the student's specific contribution. Praise can stifle interaction since students often perceive it as a terminal message, believing that the correct answer was accepted and no further interaction is desired. Ultimately, early feedback might have a detrimental effect on problem-solving and higher-level thinking (Brophy & Good, 1986).

Costa (1985) recommends that more effective responses might be acknowledging ("That's one possibility . . ."), which allows for continued student efforts, or redirecting ("What do you think, Joe?") to another student. Probing ("Why do you say that?") leads to clarification and to gathering further information. Prompting can be used to cue students toward a more complete and higher-order thinking response.

Student Answers

Answering questions involves interpreting the question and formulating an appropriate response. Convergent questions are evaluated as correct or incorrect. Divergent questions that involve thinking are evaluated by the depth and quality of the response. Insist on an answer to each question and avoid repeating students' answers (Glatthorn, 1993). Student answers can be categorized in four major ways: correct, incomplete, incorrect, or no response (Louisell & Descamps, 1992).

When students give correct answers, the teacher must consider feedback. Generally, a teacher indicates that the response was correct or asks another question if students understand that no response from the teacher indicates a correct answer. Affirm correct responses, but avoid the misuse of praising students (Brophy, 1981). Avoid overuse of global praise such as: good, very good, and I like that answer. Rowe (1974) and Brophy (1981) emphasize that students with teachers who use select amounts of praise demonstrate higher task involvement, self-confidence, and problem-solving ability than students with teachers who use praise frequently for correct answers.

When an answer is incomplete, the teacher needs to help the student achieve an acceptable response rather than ask another student to answer. Affirm the correct part of the answer and assist the student in completing the response. Brophy (1979) suggests

that incomplete answers are opportunities to help students improve by asking or probing with additional questions. Incomplete answers create an opportunity for teachers to use probing and extending questions.

Students who answer incorrectly need to be corrected and helped. Students have to know when answers are incorrect. Correcting student responses is more helpful than praise (Anderson & Faust, 1973; Good & Brophy, 1977; Soar & Soar, 1979). Avoid repeating the question because this does nothing to correct the student's answer (Dunkin & Biddle, 1974). Teachers must communicate when the answer is wrong and attempt to help the student. When correction is necessary, teachers should be direct, but not critical. Provide the student with additional information or rephrase the question. If this is unsuccessful, then provide the correct answer, especially for knowledge level questions.

Teachers ask questions to involve students in the learning process and it is a responsibility shared by all students (Dillon, 1986). When students do not respond, the teacher should reflect on the appropriateness of the question and the wait time allocated for the answer. Sometimes the reason for lack of student response is due simply to poor questioning strategies.

Many students learn early in the classroom experience that if they do not answer, the teacher will move on to another student. It is easier for these students to say nothing than to risk failure or embarrassment. Encourage a response even if the response is, "I don't know." Ross et al. (1993) says that you might think that it is cruel to require a student response, but it is more cruel to allow the student to progress through school without learning.

Conclusion to Theory

Research on questioning provides practical solutions for improving classroom interaction and points out ways that questioning hinders interaction. Questioning is one of the oldest and most widely used practices in teaching. Findings indicate that planning questioning strategies based on teacher and students goals helps facilitate learning in an effective classroom. Through questions, teachers promote involvement and thinking while providing opportunity for all students to enhance communication and expression.

Questions comprise a large percentage of what teachers and students do in the classroom. The selection of appropriate questioning strategies from theory initiate an important component in the development of your personal educational belief system.

► CLASSROOM APPLICATIONS

Introduction

The need for studying and improving questioning skills is evidenced in research. Studies indicate a startling percentage of classroom time is devoted to questions and teacher-talk. Several studies indicate that over 50 percent of classroom communication is teacher-talk, and some studies indicate that hundreds of questions are asked during a lesson. Clearly, the need for good questioning strategies in today's classroom is underestimated. Students need to become involved in the classroom instead of passively sitting and listening to teacher-talk.

Improve Students' Verbal Participation

One of the most important and most used skills for the teacher is questioning. Good questions will improve student responses, participation, and learning. In order to make these improvements, there are several steps a teacher can follow to improve students' verbal participation and skills in the classroom.

1. Select the appropriate type of question based upon the goals and purposes of the class, lesson, and individual needs of the students.

2. Create an environment conducive to open dialogue and discussion to encourage student participation and reflective thinking.

3. Ask questions to ensure student participation within the established classroom environment.

4. Be equipped with appropriate responses to the students' answers in order to encourage and develop thinking and communication among students.

Selecting the Appropriate Question

Teachers must be aware of the types of questions they ask. The key to good questioning is selecting the right question that meets your plan and purpose. Remember that convergent questions are one-response answers that require only recall; they are useful in *certain* lessons. The quality of a question is related to its purpose, how it is stated, and its compatibility to the students. The convergent, or lower-level, questions are not only good to use, but helpful in assessing content learning.

For example, if you need to check comprehension, understanding, or accuracy of knowledge, these questions are appropriate. However, a teacher should not overuse, or totally rely on, convergent questions without linking it to a specific learning purpose.

Divergent questions encourage and enhance the thinking ability of students. This ability is critical in an information-based society where students need to infer, conclude, and connect pieces of information. Divergent questions allow for more imaginative, critical, and creative responses that logically and thoughtfully connect information. Higher-level questions broaden the learning base and better prepare students for an information society where facts can be recalled from a variety of technological and non-technological sources. Providing practice in the classroom for students to interact with higher-level questions builds the skills of thinking and problem-solving; seeking solutions to situations and problems that will be encountered throughout life. Even though higher-level questions require thoughtful planning and more classroom time, it is time that is valuable in developing real life skills and problem-solving abilities.

Thinking and planning for initial questions is an important beginning. Initial questions are directed to the entire class to elicit responses. Students can help to choose initial questions for study and learning. They should be divergent and meet the various levels and abilities of all students. Once classroom discussion is initiated, it is important for the teacher to redirect responses to involve students. Redirection is a useful questioning strategy that extends and engages more students in the initial questioning stage. Probing questions extend the discussion and student responses. Probing helps students to think through, summarize, clarify, or justify a response. Prompting questions also help to improve student responses. Prompting can be difficult to plan or think of in advance, since the need for it occurs during the lesson and requires quick thinking in order to prompt students to extend and clarify a response. This is, therefore, difficult and requires some practice. Prompting uses information from the response to aid students in extending their response. Prompting questions often allow students to answer a question successfully. The following is an example of how a teacher can use prompting:

Teacher: What happens when a river becomes polluted?

Student: Well, the water will be ugly.

Teacher: What do you mean by ugly?

Student: Dirty and stinky.

Teacher: That is one possible answer. What do you think will happen to the fish?

Notice in the example that the teacher is prompting the student to give additional information to general answers. Always prompt in a positive manner and give recognition to the correct part of the answer. Prompting is a technique a teacher will use many times during questioning to amplify and correct responses. When you hear a partial response, begin to prompt the student rather than passing it over or passing the question on to another student. Facilitate student learning and thinking and also allow students to generate questions.

Selecting and Matching Questions

Think about the following suggestions, particularly when you are working with students to increase your learning and understanding, when selecting and matching questions to specific purposes and goals of instruction.

- *Ask questions that are in line with your purpose.* When knowledge or facts are required, ask convergent questions. When you want to stimulate thinking and enhance problem-solving, use divergent questions.

- *Design questions for higher level thinking.* Before the lesson, take time to write out, plan, and sequence questions that are appropriate to a specific higher order thinking category. Write questions for analysis, synthesis, and evaluation. Putting these on notecards helps you recall key questions as you are proceeding through the lesson.

- *Use convergent questions to occasionally check for understanding, knowledge, and comprehension throughout the lesson.* Questions help to assess students' learning throughout the lesson. This process helps you make decisions about when and who can move on to independent practice.

- *Prompt, redirect, and probe student responses.* Use these types of questions to extend, clarify, or amplify the students' answers. This helps students use their thinking skills. Use these techniques throughout the questioning process to ensure active participation by all students. Take time to identify and practice eliciting, redirecting, prompting, and probing during the teaching of a lesson.

- *Vary the type of questions used to stimulate verbal interaction.* Let students think aloud and describe their reasoning to you and their classmates when using higher-order thinking skills and divergent questions. This "think aloud" process enhances the verbal reflection and problem-solving ability of both the teacher and the student, while encouraging a broader discussion. Ask students to provide a reason for reaching a particular conclusion.

- *Begin your lessons with a question.* Write the question on the chalkboard, computer, or overhead. The reasons for doing this are outlined in Figure 9–3. The chalkboard question creates the focus for your lesson to ensure that the discussion does not become, or drift to, unrelated dialogue between students and teachers.

Creating a Positive Questioning Environment

The teacher always encourages the need for good questioning and thinking in order to create an environment for success. A questioning environment is organized and maintained through the principle that good thinking and questioning occurs in all subjects at all times. The teacher and students are constantly reflecting and discussing examples of good thinking and thinkers. Good questions are used in a variety of settings and instructional strategies. The classroom has a variety of experiences and a variety of questions for the teacher, the whole class, and individual students. This variety allows students to think and apply their reasoning skills to various activities that build communication and interpersonal relationship skills.

Establishing a Favorable Environment

The classroom and teacher must promote an atmosphere of openness and safety. Good questions and thinking and appropriate communication skills are constantly taught and reinforced across the curriculum. Students in a successful environment are able to produce and justify aloud their reasons and conclusions. Students should never feel threatened or embarrassed to ask questions of the teacher or classmates. A high quality classroom environment is sensitive to the individual needs and abilities of all students and the teacher. The teacher is constantly encouraging questioning and thinking as opposed to telling. The questioning environment is created where all participate in problem-solving and thinking with an emphasis on the development of interpersonal communication skills. Following are suggestions to think about as you are establishing a favorable environment for questioning.

- *Establish rules and procedures.* Define, seek student input, and post your expectations with the class. If you require students to raise their hands, you need to tell them to do so and reinforce this behavior. Students should follow good listening, speaking, and interpersonal communication skills. Encourage students to speak clearly and with appropriate volume and listen to one another, as well as responding to each other in an appropriate manner. The rules and procedures should be developed around student input and will vary according to students' needs, your goals, and the purposes of a particular questioning or instructional strategy.

- *Avoid using questioning as a form of punishment.* Do not ask a student a harder question after a student gives an incorrect response. Trying to probe and redirect questions to control disruptive students is a senseless technique. Attempt to be encouraging, sensitive, and thoughtful when asking students questions. Verbal abuse or sarcasm is never appropriate or professional. When questions are used unwisely, student participation will diminish.

- *Use a variety of instructional strategies in order to keep student interest.* Research suggests that too many teachers rely on the question, recite, question strategy. Do not overuse questioning as a teaching technique. Allow students to work in both small and large group settings with thought-provoking activities and questions.

- *Encourage student-to-student interaction.* Provide opportunities for students to interact with classmates as well as the teacher in order to clarify and reveal their thinking. Students should be given the opportunity to apply their knowledge and thinking skills through projects, writing, drawing, and group work. Encourage peer interaction to show students' thinking that reveals how new knowledge is connected or constructed to previous knowledge. Give students the opportunity to question each other and explain their conclusions.

- *Encourage and promote thinking through modeling.* Lifelong learning involves acquiring and processing information. Teachers should think aloud and show examples of how they arrive at particular conclusions. Use self-questioning to demonstrate the process and the steps involved in arriving at logical conclusions.

- *Use small groups for questioning.* All too often settings for questioning involve only large group instruction. Plan on activities where you will work with smaller groups to encourage and help develop students' abilities in questioning and thinking. Set aside time to reflect on ways to integrate and incorporate thinking into lessons and activities. Create an environment where thinking is an integral part of your classroom and personal educational belief system.

Asking Questions

When teaching a lesson, it seems natural to ask questions. Usually teachers improvise questions as they are going through the lesson. Seldom do teachers have much training or give much thought to the questioning process; rather, they generally model the kinds of experiences they've observed from their teachers. Perhaps this is why research indicates that so many teachers dominate discussions and rely heavily upon convergent questions during a lesson.

Asking good and appropriate questions takes some pre-planning. The purpose of the lesson is crucial in determining what type of questions you are going to ask. Through planning and knowing what you want to do within your lesson, you will be able to ask questions to suit your goals and objectives. When reviewing or checking for knowledge, you would be asking many convergent questions. However, to facilitate thinking, you would ask more divergent-type questions classified to the various levels in Bloom's Taxonomy.

When asking divergent questions, also redirect through prompting and probing questions. Redirecting questions through prompting and probing requires active teaching. You have to listen and think about the students'

responses in order to ask questions that will encourage extension and clarification. Asking redirecting questions requires quick thinking and an awareness of the process that amplifies student learning and participation.

Reflect and Refine Your Questioning Technique

Following are guidelines to think about as you explore and develop your skills in asking questions. Use these suggestions to assist you in reflecting and refining your questioning techniques.

- *State questions in a brief and clear manner.* Think about the wording and phrasing of your questions. Avoid questions that are long and ambiguous. State your questions in a grammatically correct form.

- *Ask one question at a time.* Be careful not to ask for several pieces of information at the same time. Avoid multiple questions when you are planning or asking questions.

- *Ask the question before calling on a student.* Research reveals that students will be much more attentive and hear the questions if you do not state the student's name prior to asking a question. Good listening skills and speaking skills are important. Take the time to encourage and acknowledge appropriate communication and interpersonal skills.

- *Pause or wait approximately three seconds after asking a question.* As stated in research, this wait time is absolutely crucial to the success of your questioning strategies. This "think time" will produce better responses on the part of the students. Mentally count to be sure you have waited an adequate amount of time.

- *Use a variety of questions.* All classrooms have a range of interests and abilities. By using a variety of questions, you will increase the opportunity to engage participation from all students. Through the use of prompting and probing questions, you will be able to increase student participation.

- *Know why you are asking a particular question.* Relate the main or guiding questions to your goals and objectives. Sometimes by having a variety of questions, it is easy to forget the reason you are asking questions. Stop to think about the reasons as you prepare for your questions.

- *Sequence questions.* The order of questions should lead students somewhere. Sequence questions so that ideas build upon each other from the simple to the complex and follow a logical direction that relates to your purpose. Each proceeding question builds upon the last one in order to provide a logical order.

- *Use appropriate feedback.* As indicated in research, listen for overused praise. Be specifically aware of the overuse of terms, such as "good," when responding to questions. However, in dealing with students with special needs, it is important that they receive frequent feedback. Take the time to find out what type of feedback will work best for your students.

- *Encourage students to ask questions.* Questioning is an important skill. Students should have opportunities to practice asking good questions of classmates, teachers, and others when seeking and researching information. Teach students the different types of questions and how to use divergent questions. Allow students the opportunity to ask and pursue their questions and answers to guide data gathering.

Students' Answers to Questions

The way a teacher responds to a student's answer is just as important as asking the question. Responding to answers requires good listening. Listening helps you to know how to respond, clarify, or redirect in order to extend student thinking. Student answers can tell you whether or not students are comprehending what has been taught. Model good listening skills with eye contact and acknowledgement.

The way teachers respond to students' answers influences the students' thinking and classroom interaction. Usually when a teacher agrees or disagrees or offers feedback, classroom discussion stops. The teacher role is to facilitate the students' responses by helping them analyze their answers and encouraging others to respond. When teachers ask convergent questions, there usually is only one, correct answer; therefore, classroom discussion will be at a minimum. Teachers must affirm or correct a student's answer. When an answer is incomplete, the teacher can probe or prompt the student for a more indepth response. Whenever students give an incorrect responses to convergent questions, the teacher should give the correct response.

When teachers ask divergent questions, there are a variety of responses. The openness of divergent questions seeks to increase student participation. When students fail to respond, it might be due to several factors. Students might feel insecure, unsafe, or lack knowledge or experience to respond to questions because of previous experiences. They might not understand the question and the teacher may need to rephrase the question or probe the student. It is important to encourage students to participate because responding to questions should be expected for all students.

Develop Strategy and Repertoire of Questions

Dealing with students' responses takes practice because it is a skill that can be developed. The following are guidelines and suggestions to consider as you develop a strategy and repertoire of questions that successfully promote good questioning and thinking.

- *Require a response.* All students need to answer questions. Rather than ignoring student apathy, teachers should model students on how to answer questions. Help students respond by identifying prior knowledge. Also model answering a question by thinking out loud, to show your thought processes in thinking through a question and formulating an answer. Underachievers or students who lack experience or confidence need assistance instead of having their answers passed over. For these students, it is beneficial to paraphrase the question using known terms. Students can also write down some answers to allow them to think and be prepared to respond. It is an injustice to allow students to sit in a classroom without

encouragement to respond, participate, and learn.

- *Allow opportunity for all students to participate.* Develop an accounting system, where you can identify students who respond and students who do not respond, to ensure that all students have participated. Call on students in random sequence to increase the opportunity to involve all students. Typically, less effective teachers do not call on slower or low-achieving students. Perhaps this is due to a sensitivity of not wanting to embarrass the student. It is best, of course, not to embarrass students because this would lessen the learning of those students. In cases where students are hesitant to respond or are non-volunteers, encouragement, prompting, and probing are good strategies to use. Be sure to call on students of various backgrounds and abilities. All too often, teachers tend to rely and only call on high-achieving volunteers with raised hands.

- *Allow students to complete their response.* Frequently, teachers interrupt students when they answer. Teachers, in this instance, quickly cut off the student and supply the remainder of the answer. The teacher can also interrupt and cut off an incorrect answer. Both of these situations deprive the student of a complete response and deprive the teacher of the opportunity to redirect, prompt or probe the student's response. It is important to allow students to complete their responses whether they are right or wrong. Model good communication skills and listening skills by not interrupting students.

- *Affirm correct responses.* It is best to acknowledge a student's correct response. This acknowledgement does not have to be praise. A simple statement or non-verbal head nod indicating whether a response is correct will suffice. Let students know that you will only correct inaccurate responses during rapid, convergent questioning. When praising, the praise should be specific and focused on the content and quality of the answer, not the individual. Praising the correct response for a low-achieving student can be beneficial if the accomplishment is significant for that student.

- *Correct wrong answers.* Effective teachers clearly communicate when responses are wrong and take the time to lead students in developing correct responses before calling on other students. The teacher must avoid negative statements, such as "No," "You are way off," or "That is wrong." Instead, create a non-threatening environment where both teacher and student analyze the answer to help think through a response. Probing and prompting strategies can help lead to the correct answer. Avoid being sarcastic, putting down students, or punishing them for a wrong answer.

- *Praise is useful; however, it should be used cautiously.* Prior to current research, teachers were told, "The more praise the better!" Too much praise has potentially negative effects upon students because it does away with intrinsic or self-motivation. There is a lessening of desire to respond unless students gain their own sense of self-worth from participating. Teachers should avoid praising too often or too enthusiastically because overreacting with praise creates dependency on the teacher. Some students do not want public praise

and sometimes it is useful to praise in private. Teachers who praise answers indiscriminately undermine the value of praise. Praise can be valuable initially, however, to students who are low-achievers, have anxiety about responding, or need encouragement to answer questions.

- *Control your responses.* Teachers often overreact when students give the answers to questions they are expecting or respond with ridiculous statements, such as "superfantastic," "stupendous," and so forth. This overreaction for some questions could make some students feel their answers are less favorable, less valued by the teacher, or embarrassing. Your questioning intent is to engage the students; therefore, do not answer the question yourself.

- *Avoid repeating student responses.* The teacher should only repeat an answer when it is crucial to continue the discussion, it is a complex idea, or there is a need to restate or reinforce the correct answer. Constantly repeating student responses creates teacher-centered dialogue. Students must learn to listen to one another and to respond to each other. The habit of always repeating answers distracts and wastes time.

- *Use wait time after students respond.* Teachers need to use wait time, approximately three to five seconds, after students respond to your question to allow others to think about the response. After-response wait time encourages and allows thinking time for dialogue between students. This strategy lessens the dominance of the teacher acting as the clearing house or censor for all interaction. Allowing wait time after student responses greatly increases the interpersonal and interactive skills of the students. You should encourage students to debate and resolve issues by listening and responding to each other, not just you.

FIELD-BASED CONNECTIONS

Introduction

Questioning is a strategy that needs to be thought out and practiced in a field-based setting in order to enhance the development of this necessary teaching skill. Mentor teachers and intern students should both take the time to analyze the types of questions and the interaction that occurs in the classroom when they teach.

Reflect About Your Questions

Teachers need to evaluate and analyze questions to insure that the goals and objectives of instruction are meeting the needs of students. Through reflective thought, mentor teachers and intern students can determine the effectiveness and the level of thinking skills in the classroom.

- Analyze the types of questions and the level of questions you are asking in your classroom (Figure 9–7) by keeping information about questioning in your journal and videotaping or audiotaping a brief lesson. Then, when watching or listening to the tape, use Figure 9–7 to reflect on the

quantity and quality of questions asked during the lesson. The purpose for analyzing and evaluating your questions is to help you determine the variety of questions and the level of thinking during lesson.

- Analyze your responses and the student's responses to your questions (Figure 9–8). by videotaping or audiotaping a brief lesson. Then, when watching or listening to the tape, use Figure 9–8 to reflect on the responses that take place between you and the students, and between students. The purpose for analyzing and evaluating the types of interactions and responses that occur is to help you determine patterns of teacher and student responses. Also, it will help you see whether the students are being held accountable for participating, thinking, and using good communication and interpersonal skills.

- Think through initial questions and begin lessons with a question for teacher and student focus. Plan an initial question that will elicit a range of divergent responses. This will allow you to gain confidence and experience while dealing with the varied responses of the students. Alsp plan a lesson where you could also work with convergent questions. After the lesson, take the time to reflect on the concerns, successes, and issues you had using these questioning strategies. List concerns about students who are non-participatory or who give incorrect responses.

- Interns should reflect on their personal educational belief system regarding questioning skills. Take the time to analyze and observe how students are responding to your questions. Be certain that all students are participating in discussions and

FIGURE 9–7 Analyzing Types of Questions

Directions: Plan a 15- to 20-minute lesson where you ask a variety of questions. Audiotape or videotape the lesson while you are teaching. Listen to or view the tape and use the form below to evaluate your questions. Reflect on ways that you can improve your questioning skill. Put a mark next to the question type each time you hear it.

Types of Questions	Frequency	Personal Comments
Convergent		
Knowledge		
Comprehension		
Application		
Yes/No		
Divergent		
Analysis		
Synthesis		
Evaluation		
Probing		
Prompting		
Wait time of three seconds or more		

_____ Total number of convergent questions.

_____ Total number of divergent questions.

Reflections for Improvement: For example, think about the variety, balance, and purpose of your questions. (Use the space for self-analysis):

_____

_____

_____

_____

FIGURE 9–8   Analyzing Responses

Directions: Plan a 15- to 20-minute lesson where you ask a variety of questions. Audiotape or videotape the lesson while you are teaching. (Note: You could use the same lesson that you taped for Figure 9–7.) View the tape and use the form below to evaluate the students' and your responses to the questions. Reflect on ways that you can improve your questioning skill. Put a mark next to the response each time you hear it.

Response	Frequency	Personal Comments
Praise		
Calling out		
Correct		
Incorrect		
Redirected		
Extended		
Interrupted		
Girls		
Boys		
Teacher to student		
Student to student		
Wait time of three seconds or more after response		

_____ Total number of teacher responses.

_____ Total number of student responses.

Reflection for Improvement: For example, think about the frequency of low and high achievers responding and enthusiasm of students. (Use this space for self-analysis):

_____

_____

_____

_____

evaluate your ability to prompt and probe student responses. Assess how students are engaged in analyzing, synthesizing, and evaluating questions. Promote more student interpersonal skills, social behavior, and interaction with each other. Good group and peer social interaction is an important lifelong skill for students to develop.

Guidelines for Interns

Pick and choose the activities that best suit you and your needs. Use these suggestions for your unit plans, portfolio collections, and your journal entries where appropriate.

1. Write a lesson plan for your unit where you include major questions at the various levels of Bloom's Taxonomy that you want to ask during the lesson. Take time after your lesson to reflect on how the students responded to the different types of questions you asked.

2. Study Figure 9–7, which provides you with a form to assess the types of questions that are asked during a lesson. Schedule a time with your mentor teacher to observe a lesson that includes questioning strategies. Familiarizing yourself with the form, observe the scheduled lesson. Then audiotape one of your lessons to evaluate the types of questions you ask during your lessons. Figure 9–7 will guide you through your reflection and analysis to improve your skills.

3. Study Figure 9–8, which provides you with a form to assess the students' responses with classroom interaction

during questioning. Familiarize yourself with this form and schedule a time to observe your mentor teacher during a lesson that includes questioning strategies. Use the form to analyze the interaction and responses in the classroom. Then audiotape one of your own lessons to evaluate the interaction and responses that occurred during the lesson. Figure 9–8 will guide you through the reflection and analysis to improve your ability to respond to questions.

4. Good questioning does not always take place in front of the whole class. Plan for small group work and write a variety of questions for the group to answer. Allow students to discuss and share their thoughts about your questions. Observe how the students work with the convergent and divergent questions on your list. Reflect on student participation in small groups and large groups. Move around the class: Encourage active participation and guide discussion within each of the groups.

▶ CHAPTER CLOSURE

Summary

Questions are the centerpiece for instructional strategies. Teachers must be knowledgeable and have experience drawing from the types of questions in order to promote classroom discussion. Good questions do not happen by accident. They are planned and have a purpose. Teachers can use questions as a useful tool that will check understanding, promote thinking, and create practice for interpersonal communication skills. There are four important steps in the questioning and responding pattern: (1) selecting the appropriate type of question, (2) creating an environment for questions, (3) asking questions, and (4) responding to student answers.

There are basically two types of questions: convergent, which is closed and has only one correct response; and divergent, which is open and has a multitude of responses. Questions can also be classified to Bloom's Taxonomy according to a level of thinking. When selecting the appropriate level of questions, use a variety of questions at that level.

Creating an environment is also important to facilitate questioning. The teacher needs to be sensitive, positive, and open to encourage good communication and interpersonal skills. The classroom environment should encourage and value student to student questions and responses.

Asking the right question takes knowledge and practice. Sometimes it can be very difficult to insert a question in a fast-paced discussion. Knowing how and when to ask the right type of question depends upon your objective as well as the students' needs. Good grammar and phrasing of the questions will help students to understand and respond.

Just as important as asking questions is the ability to respond. Responding takes quick thinking on the part of the teacher. Knowing and practicing when to redirect, rephrase, prompt, and probe requires careful listening and the ability to decipher the responses quickly and accurately. Knowing when to cor-

rect and praise is dependent upon the unique ability of each child, the type of question you are asking, and the purpose of the question. Questioning is a skill that teachers can use to enhance the learning and achievement of their students. Clearly, the skill of questioning should be practiced and analyzed in order to improve your questioning ability.

Chapter Discussion Questions

1. What is the purpose of Bloom's Taxonomy and how does it benefit planning questioning strategies? Choose a topic and compare the questions you would use for that topic at each level of the taxonomy.

2. Why is it important to encourage and model thinking in the classroom?

3. When is it best to use convergent questions?

4. When is it best to use divergent questions?

5. Describe your mentor teacher's questioning skills. What made these techniques effective/ineffective? Evaluate the situation and the kinds of questions that your teachers asked in terms of their effectiveness.

6. What will you do to develop good questioning skills?

7. Why is prompting and probing helpful to teachers and students?

8. How will you react to: (a) non-participating students; (b) wrong answers; (c) correct answers; (d) calling out answers; and (e) poor mentor questioning skills?

CASE STUDIES

The case study example can be used for analysis in small or large groups. Questions follow the case study as suggestions for discussion.

CASE STUDY 9-1: by Debra Ann Alaniz, First-Year Special Education Teacher

Questioning my students did not seem like a big deal. Ask a question and receive a response. However, in the real world, this is not always the case.

Questioning is a very important part of my everyday routine. It helps me understand where my students are in relationship to the skill being taught. It also helps me determine how my students are thinking. I teach students who are learning disabled and it was difficult at first to help them understand that there wasn't necessarily a right or wrong answer. I just wanted them to try. I repeated this over and over again: "Just try." Many of my students have had a multitude of failures in their regular classroom experiences and were just plain afraid to answer questions, whether they be yes or no questions or more extensive, thought-provoking questions. They were not willing to take the chance that their answer might be wrong.

In order to help overcome some of these fears, I started by asking simple, comprehension questions following a short lesson. This would help my students review and find success in answering questions. The answers were written on the board during the lesson (and left there purposefully), found on a sheet or project given to them, or based on prior knowledge (i.e., life experiences). This strategy provided my students with answers found right in front of them. This technique built a foundation of comfort for several of my students. It later helped them overcome their fears about offering answers to more divergent questions.

Still, I had several students who were not comfortable with answering questions or participating orally in any way. At this point, I would sometimes ask a question and everyone had to contribute an answer, even if someone else gave the same answer. This technique helped my students find small successes answering questions even though they weren't offering their own personal thoughts. As their confidence increased, these students began to open up a little more in front of their peers. Soon they started answering questions using their own thoughts.

I feel there are two key elements needed to help students respond to questions: knowing when to ask the right type of question, and building student confidence in responding to those questions. If it is the beginning of the year, you are new, or you know your students have had difficulties in the past, go easy on them. Build their confidence. Help them understand that you are not going to badger them to the ground if they do not have the right answer to a direct question or a different answer than their peers to open-ended questions. Once your students are comfortable with your questioning style and more confident in themselves, it paves the way for asking greater, more in-depth, questions that help students problem-solve and discover their world.

Questioning is a big deal and helping your students respond to questions is important every day.

Case Study Discussion Questions

1. What do you think about Debra's techniques for dealing with non-participating students? How do you think she handled her dilemma?

2. What other alternatives would you suggest to help Debra's increase student responses?

▶ REFERENCES

Anderson, R. C. & Faust, G. W. (1973). *Educational psychology: The science of instruction and learning.* New York: Dodd, Mead.

Berliner, D. C. (1987). But do they understand? In V. Richardson-Kowhler (Ed.), *Educators' handbook: A research perspective.* New York: Longman.

Bloom, B. S. (1956). *Taxonomy of educational objectives, handbook I: Cognitive domain.* New York: David McKay.

Borich, G. D. (1988). *Effective teaching methods.* Columbus, OH.: Merrill Publishing Company.

Brophy, J. (1979). Teacher behavior and student learning. *Educational Leadership 37*(1), 33–38.

Brophy, J. (1981). Teacher praise: A functional analysis. *Review of Educational Research, 51,* 5–32.

Brophy, J. & Everston, C. (1976). *Learning from teaching: A developmental perspective.* Boston: Allyn and Bacon.

Brophy, J. & Good, T. (1974). *Teacher-student relationships: Causes and consequences.* New York: Holt, Rinehart and Winston.

Brophy, J. & Good, T. (1986). Teacher behavior and student achievement. In M.C. Wittrock (Ed.), *Handbook of research one teaching,* 3rd edition. New York: Macmillan.

Brown, G. & Edmondson, R. (1984). Asking questions. In E. Wragg (Ed.), *Classroom teaching skills* (97–119). New York: Nichols.

Centra, J. A. & Potter, D. A. (1980). School and teacher effects: An interrelational model. *Review of Educational Research, 50*(2), 273–291.

Cooper, H. & Good, T. (1983). *Pygmalion grows up: Studies in the expectation communication process.* New York: Longman.

Costa, A. L. (1985). Teacher behaviors that enable student thinking. In Arthur L. Costa (Ed.), *Developing minds: A resource book for teaching thinking.* Alexandria, VA: Association for Supervision and Curriculum Developmental.

Denham, C. & Lieberman, A. (1980). *Time to learn.* Washington, DC: National Institute of Education.

Dillon, J. T. (1982). Cognitive correspondence between question/statement and response. *American Educational Research Journal, 19*(4), 540–551.

Dillon, J. T. (1986). Student questions and individual learning. *Educational Theory, 36,* 333–341.

Doyle, W. (1986). Classroom organization and management. In M. C. Wittrock (Ed.), *Handbook of research on teaching,* 3rd edition. New York: Macmillan.

Duffy, G., Roehler, L., Meloth, M. , & Vavrus, L. (1985). *Conceptualizing instructional explanation.* Washington, DC: American Educational Research Association.

Dunkin, M. & Biddle, B. (1974). *The study of teaching.* New York: Holt, Rinehart and Winston.

Eby, J. W. (1992). *Reflective planning, teaching, and evaluation for the elementary school.* New York: Macmillan.

Ennis, R. (1985). A logical basis for measuring critical thinking skills. *Educational Leadership, 43*(2), 44–48.

Frieberg, J. H. & Driscoll, A. (1992). *Universal teaching strategies.* Boston, MA: Allyn and Bacon.

Gall, M. D. (1970). The use of questions in teaching. *Review of Educational Research, 40,* 707–721.

Gall, M. D. (1984). Synthesis of research on teachers' questioning. *Educational Leadership, 41,* 40–47.

Gall, M. D. & Gillett, M. (1980). The discussion method in classroom teaching. *Theory into Practice, 19*(2), 98–102.

Glatthorn, A. A. (1993). *Learning twice: An introduction to the methods of teaching.* New York: Harper Collins.

Good, T. L. & Brophy, J. E. (1977). *Educational psychology: A realistic approach.* New York: Holt, Rinehart and Winston.

Hare, V. C. & Pulliam, C. A. (1980). Teacher questioning: A verification and an extension. *Journal of Reading Behavior, 12,* 69–72.

Harms, T., Woolever, R. , & Brice, R. (1989). A questioning strategies training sequence: Documenting the effect of a new approach to an old practice. *Journal of Teacher Education, 40,* 40–45.

Hunkins, F. P. (1976). *Involving students in questioning.* Boston: Allyn and Bacon.

Jarolimek, J., & Foster, C. D., Sr. (1993). *Teaching and learning in the elementary school,* 3rd edition. New York: Macmillan.

Land, M. L. (1980). Teacher clarity and cognitive level of questions: Effects on learning. *Journal of Experimental Education, 49,* 48–51.

Louisell, R. D. & Descamps, J. (1992). *Developing a teaching style.* New York: Harper Collins.

Melton, R. (1978). Resolution of conflicting claims concerning the effect of behavioral objectives on student learning. *Review of Educational Research, 48,* 291–302.

Meyers, C. (1986). *Teaching students to think critically.* San Francisco: Jossey-Bass.

Montague, E. J., Huntsberger, J., & Hoffman, J. (1989). *Fundamentals of elementary and middle school classroom instruction.* Columbus, OH: Merrill.

Orlich, D. C., Harder, R. J., Callahan, R. C., Kauchak, D. P., Pendergrass, R. A., Keogh, A. J., & Gibson, H. (1990). *Teaching Strategies,* 3rd edition. Massachusetts: D. C. Heath & Company.

Pasch, M., Sparks-Langer, G., Garner, T. J., Starko, A. J., & Moody, C. D. (1991). *Teaching as decision making.* New York: Longman.

Paul, R. (1988). *31 principles of critical thinking.* Rohnert Park, CA: Center for Critical Thinking and Moral Critique.

Redfield, D. & Rousseau, E. (1981). A meta-analysis of experimental research on teacher questioning behavior. *Review of Educational Research, 51,* 237–245.

Ross, D. D., Bondy, E., & Kyle, D. W. (1993). *Reflective teaching for student empowerment: Elementary curriculum and methods.* New York: Macmillan.

Rowe, M. B. (1974). Pausing phenomena: Influence on the quality of instruction. *Journal of Psycholinguistics Research, 3,* 203–233.

Rowe, M. B. (1980). Wait-time and rewards as instructional variables, their influence on language, logic, and fate control: Part one—wait-time. *Journal of Research in Science Teaching, 11,* 81–94.

Ryder, R. J. (1991). The directed questioning activity for subject matter text. *Journal of Reading, 34,* 606–612.

Sciortino, E. (1988). *Strategies for teaching.* Raleigh, NC: Contemporary Publishing Company.

Siegel, H. (1988). *Educating reason.* New York: Routledge.

Soar, R. & Soar, C. (1973). *Follow through classroom process measurement and pupil growth (1970-1971, final report).* Gainesville, FL: University of Florida, Institute for Development of Human Resources.

Soar, R. S. & Soar, R. M. (1979). Emotional climate and management. In P. L. Peterson and H. J. Walberg (Eds.), *Research on teaching: Concepts, findings, and implications.* Berkeley, CA: McCutchan.

Strother, D. (1989). Developing thinking skills through questioning. *Phi Delta Kappan*, 324–327.

Sullivan, P. & Clarke, D. (1991). Catering to all abilities through 'good' questions. *Arithmetic Teacher*, October, 14–18.

Tobin, K. (1986). Effects of teacher wait time on discourse characteristics in mathematics and language arts classes. *American Educational Research Journal, 23*(2), 191–201.

Tobin, K. & Capie, W. (1982). Relationships between classroom process variables and middle-school science achievement. *Journal of Educational Psychology, 74*, 441–454.

Wassermann, S. (1991). The art of the question. *Childhood Education, 67*, 257–259.

White, R. T. & Tisher, R. P. (1986). Research on natural sciences. In M.C. Wittrock (Ed.), *Handbook of research on teaching*, 3rd edition. New York: Macmillan.

Wilson, I. A. (1973). Changes in the mean levels of thinking in grades 1–8 through use of an interaction analysis system based on Bloom's taxonomy. *Journal of Educational Research, 66*, 423–429.

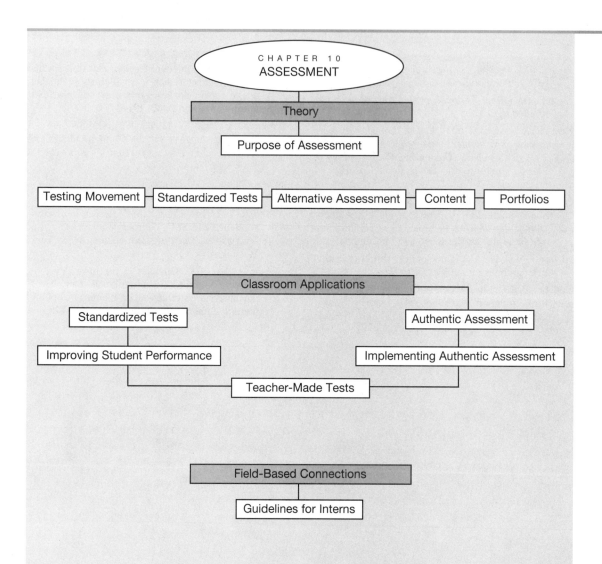

CHAPTER 10
ASSESSMENT

Theory

Purpose of Assessment

Testing Movement — Standardized Tests — Alternative Assessment — Content — Portfolios

Classroom Applications

Standardized Tests

Authentic Assessment

Improving Student Performance

Implementing Authentic Assessment

Teacher-Made Tests

Field-Based Connections

Guidelines for Interns

10

Summative Assessment and Testing

Introduction

Assessment of student learning has evolved into a central position in the teaching and learning process. Its current use is growing, as many states are passing laws to use outcome-based evaluation (OBE) as a means of linking evaluation to an instructional goal or outcome. Legislative mandates for assessment are typically met with criticism and resistance. Most educators and students abhor taking tests. Nothing in education seems to stir up as much controversy and opinion as assessment. Assessment, however, is useful when used in the proper context and for the appropriate purpose.

The big measuring stick in assessment is the standardized test. These achievement-type tests seek to evaluate the amount of learning after a certain time period of instruction. Standardized tests are fairly easy to administer, but costly in terms of taking time from instruction and reporting/interpreting the scores. There are major problems with standardized tests, but the most profound and misunderstood is the interpretation of the test results. All too often, school districts' decisions are based solely on the results of standardized tests. This limiting and narrow perspective of standardized tests breeds anguish, pressure, and test-driven instruction and curriculum in many schools. Often, test data are not shared with teachers, parents, and students. Because of misuse and narrow interpretation, many educators advocate alternate forms of assessment.

Alternative assessment strategies evolved from the frustration and controversy surrounding standardized tests. Proponents of alternative assessments decry the many weaknesses and abuses of standardized tests. Although proponents note some value of standardized tests, many are quick to point out that when used alone, testing usually creates more problems in education than solutions. Alternative assessments offer a balance to the test-only mentality and when used with standardized tests can offer a more complete picture of student learning. Because alternative assessments are not universally accepted, are time consuming, and lack standardization, implementation has been slow or nonexistent in many schools and state assessment plans.

Some of the more common forms of alternative evaluation are closely related authentic and performance-based assessment. Authentic assessment requires students to apply knowledge in real-life situations. Students must demonstrate their *ability to use* knowledge. Performance assessment, on the other hand, is one way students can use knowledge in an authentic way to *demonstrate* what they have learned. Performance is easy to observe and to evaluate whether the student is able to accomplish a learned task. A major concern of performance assessment is agreeing on the criteria and the difficulty in the degree or level of performance standards. For performance to be authentic, it must be done in a real-life setting or context, since there is undoubtedly a need for students in the twenty-first century to demonstrate or perform their learning in an authentic context. As time goes by, and teachers are trained and standards are developed, more authentic types of assessment are likely to be used to give a more accurate and total perspective of student learning. One way to use authentic assessment is through a portfolio to demonstrate student learning and work.

The teacher's role, responsibility, and accountability towards student achievement is growing as states continue to pass laws for testing. Teachers should accept and understand the role and importance of testing to improve the students' performance on standardized tests. Test scores in today's society can either open or close doors to the future. Accepting responsibility for test performance is a growing area of concern in the expectations for teachers and schools. Research suggests that teachers can improve a student's test-taking skill. To understand how much of education has evolved to test dependency, it is helpful to know the terminology, history, types of tests, teacher's role, and the impact of assessment on the teaching and learning process.

Terminology

There is a need to understand and define educational testing terminology. At times the interchangeability of terms can be confusing or misleading. Popham (1993) states that there is no one best definition and, therefore, educators must exchange terminology before study or discussion. Glance through the terms and refer to them when needed as you read this chapter. Terms in this book are defined as follows:

Evaluation and Assessment: *Evaluation* is a single occasion, specifically timed, one-dimensional activity that determines success or failure. *Assessment* is an activity that can take many forms, extend over a period of time, and seek to determine the quality of a program or student's work. These two terms for practical purposes are generally interchangeable. Both seek to determine how well a program or student is doing.

Formal and Informal: *Formal* assessment is standardized in terms of designing, administering, scoring, and interpreting. Standardized tests are formal means of evaluation. *Informal* assessment is teacher- designed, administered, scored, and interpreted. Teacher-made tests, questionnaires, rating forms, and surveys are informal means of evaluation.

Formative and Summative: *Formative* assessment (see Chapter 4) is used to determine how well a student is progressing before and during instruction. It measures the degree of learning (mastery) of the lesson objectives or educational goals. *Summative* assessment is used to determine the extent of program or student learning after instruction. It is a final measure of learning that reveals the level of success of teaching and learning.

Criterion-Referenced and Norm-Referenced Tests: Both of these tests are usually used for summative assessment. *Criterion-referenced* tests evaluate a student's performance to a standard or criteria, which is usually the number correct or incorrect. A passing score is generally all that matters. Criterion-references tests are usually the type used to measure the success of a district's and school's teaching of the state's minimum curriculum. The reporting of these scores shows the percentage of students who passed according to the skill areas and established criteria. *Norm-referenced* tests compare the student's score to a predetermined standard or norm. This standard is obtained by giving the test to a representative sample of students. Then the score is compared to other students who take the test. An example is the SAT.

Performance and Authentic Assessment: Both of these closely related terms are forms of alternative assessment strategies. *Performance* assessment is used to determine if a student has the ability to complete or demonstrate what has been learned. For example, if the behavior taught is singing, then a student sings. If it is to write, a student writes.

Performance in the general sense is not new; John Dewey (1897) promoted evaluation based upon student performance many years ago. What is unique about this term in today's assessment literature is that performance is attached to authentic assessment. *Authentic* assessment requires that a student not only complete or demonstrate learning, but to apply it to a real-life setting. Therefore, the "context" of learning is the major difference between these two terms. To improve performance assessment a teacher should use, whenever possible, an authentic environment.

Validity and Reliability: *Validity* simply refers to the degree that a test measures what it intends to measure. *Reliability* simply refers to the consistency of the test to repeatedly measure what it is suppose to measure.

▶ THEORY

Purpose of Assessment

Assessment can provide important information for improving every aspect of education. It is indispensable for both practical and sound pedagogical reasons. Mitchell (1992) recognizes four main purposes of assessment:

- For information about the student's learning to both the teacher and the student.

- For the purposes and improvement of instruction.

- For decisions affecting the student's future, whether about appropriate placement or postsecondary paths.

- For accountability to political authorities.

Proper assessment means that educators and legislators must look beyond the scores and try to interpret what the results mean for students, programs, parents or community measures (Madaus & Stufflebeam, 1989).

Testing Movement

Testing as a means of assessment has a long and varied history. Examples are found in the Roman schools for orators, in the Inns of Court during Shakespeare's childhood, and in the late medieval Spanish schools of science, where various rulers sought to determine standards of competence for public life through tests (Davies, 1984). The early beginnings of assessment consisted of informal and often crude forms of measurement that relied on subjective judgment (Gerberich et al., 1962).

Through history, people believed they were capable of evaluation by relying on their own sense of knowledge and common sense. Ancient civilizations were possibly much more confident in their intuition than we are about ours today (Bergman, 1981). As our society developed and more children began attending school, individual differences became more outstanding. Teachers desired more than intuition as a way to evaluate students.

Alfred Binet developed a widely used test that measured a student's intelligence quotient (I.Q.). This test determined if students would benefit from regular school instruction. The I.Q. test was revised after Binet's death and became known as the Stanford-Binet. Some researchers believe that the I.Q. test is one of the most successful, most valid, and most reliable psychological tests ever developed (Bergman, 1981).

The success of Binet's I.Q. test created an interest in developing a variety of tests. These tests focused on achievement, aptitude, and personal, and social development. Standardized tests, as Perrone (1991a) points out, are a relatively new phenomena in the history of education. One of the first standardized tests was the Throndike Handwriting Scale, developed in 1909, less than a century ago.

At the beginning of the cold war, testing increased to an annual rate of ten to twenty percent every year since 1950 (Haney & Madaus, 1989). Perrone (1991b) notes that testing exploded in the period after 1965 because of the increase in special programs that allocated specific funds. The funding increased dramatically when the federal government funded the Title I Program (now Chapter I). Senator Robert Kennedy and others pushed for legislation entitled The Elementary and Secondary Education Act (ESEA) of 1965, which was the first legislation to require formal systematic program evaluation in order to receive government funds. The congressional requirement of program evaluation promoted the development and expansion of the testing movement and industry. ESEA legislation initiated accountability at the local level and an obligation to provide Congress with an evaluation report of how these funds were used and the effectiveness of a program (Popham, 1993). From this legislation, the use of standardized tests has increased steadily through calls for programs of educational reform. In return, standardized tests were increasingly challenged because of the impact on students and teachers. Many educators and researchers have criticized testing as reducing or narrowing education to learning bits of information (Bracey, 1987; Jaeger, 1991; Shepard, 1991; Worthen, 1993).

Currently, educators are suggesting that performance assessment be used in addition to standardized tests. Feuer and Fulton (1993) have placed performance assessments into seven categories: constructed-response items, essays, writing, oral discourse, experiments, exhibitions, and portfolios. These assessment categories have been used extensively in the classroom in summative ways for generations. Today, the importance is to use these categories as strategies to evaluate a student's ability to perform a given task in an authentic environment. The trend does not call for abolishment of standardized tests completely, but to implement testing programs that include alternatives of authentic and performance-based assessment (Figure 10–1) (Shepard, 1991).

The testing movement continues to evolve, with many educators recognizing the need to go beyond the standardized test to include authentic and/or performance assessment. The future of testing remains controversial. There is a need for teachers to know and understand standardized tests as well as the implications and possibilities for alternative

FIGURE 10–1   Comparison Between Traditional and Authentic Assessment

TRADITIONAL	AUTHENTIC
Specific time period	Time established by teacher and students
Lower-level skills	Higher-level skills
Drill and practice	Critical and creative strategies
Narrow perspective	Wholistic perspective
Facts	Concepts
Group standards	Individual standards
Memorization	Internalization
One correct solution	Multiple solutions
Skills	Processes
Teach to test	Teach to needs

assessments because both forms of assessment combined can more accurately evaluate student learning.

Standardized Tests

When standardized tests are used properly, they hold appeal for many Americans. According to the 1992 Gallup Poll, 71 percent of Americans favor "requiring the public schools in this community to use standardized national tests to measure the academic achievement of the student" (Elam, Rose, & Gallup, 1992). President Bush's *America 2000* (1991) calls for national testing that would, for the most part, use a traditional standardized testing format (Doyle, 1991). Cizek (1990) asserts that standardized tests are one of the few ways to obtain objective data about performance. Standardized tests are frequently used because they are a quick and relatively inexpensive method of assessment (Maeroff, 1991; Willis, 1990).

Controversy

Despite the relative ease of administration and the public support given to standardized testing, a substantial number of educators find several faults with this type of assessment. Perrone (1991a) believes that standardized tests are in direct conflict with current trends in education, such as cooperative learning and problem-solving. Instead of cooperating to find many possible answers, students must work alone to find the one right answer. Another criticism of standardized tests is that they are biased against minority racial, cultural, and social groups (Worthen & Spandel, 1991). A chief concern among many educators is that standardized tests are being allowed to drive the curriculum. Ashworth (1990) finds this influence potentially positive; Worthen and Spandel (1991) write that many teachers indicate that they can make more informed decisions about the educational needs of their group of students based on these tests. Teachers should be especially alert to and disturbed by standardized tests that only measure lower-level skills and avoid analysis, synthesis or evaluation questions.

One of the biggest and often most overlooked problem is the misuse of standardized tests and the interpretation of the results. Worthen and Spandel (1991) believe that it is not the tests that cause controversy, but the way the test results are interpreted and misused. They list several standardized test pitfalls to avoid (Figure 10–2). Even though there are problems and controversy over standardized tests, there is a distinct influence that these tests have on curriculum and instruction.

Instructional Influence

Pressure to raise scores on standardized tests and an effort to meet the demand for accountability has allowed pedagogy to remain more in touch with the 1920s than the 1990s (Simmons & Resnick, 1993). Assessment, curriculum, and instruction should be integrated. Successful teachers are masters of informally assessing students abilities and finding ways to move ahead or reteach. Recently, teachers in many states have been stymied by the pressure to raise standardized test scores. The influence of the standardized test and the importance placed upon it by administrators, parents, and the general public have caused a narrowing of the curriculum, sometimes to the level of only teaching the basic skills found

---

FIGURE 10–2   Pitfalls to Avoid When Using Standardized Test Results

---

1. **Using the wrong tests.** Schools often devise new goals and curriculum plans only to find their success being judged by tests that are not relevant to those goals or plans, yet are imposed by those at higher administrative levels.

2. **Assuming test scores are infallible.** Every test score contains possible error; a student's observed score is rarely identical to that student's true score (the score s/he would have obtained had there been no distractions during testing, no fatigue or illness, no lucky guesses, and no other factors that either helped or hindered that score.)

3. **Using a single test score to make an important decision.** Given the possibility of error that exists for every test score, a single test score is too suspect to serve as the sole criterion for any crucial decision.

4. **Failing to supplement test scores with other information.** Private observations and practical awareness of students' abilities can and should supplement more objective test scores.

5. **Setting arbitrary minimums for performance on tests.** When minimum test scores are established as critical hurdles for selection and admissions, as dividing lines for placing students or as the determining factor in awarding certificates, several issues become acute, such as test validity and whether the minimum standard is set correctly.

6. **Assuming tests measure all the content, skills or behaviors of interest.** Every test is limited in what it covers.

7. **Accepting uncritically all claims made by test authors and publishers.** Most authors or publishers are enthusiastic about their products, and excessive zeal can lead to risky and misleading promises.

8. **Interpreting test scores inappropriately.** The test score per se tells us nothing about why an individual obtained that score. A student's test score is not a qualitative evaluation of performance, but a mere numeric indicator that lacks meaning in the absence of some criteria defining what constitutes good or bad performance.

FIGURE 10–2   continued

---

9. **Using test scores to draw inappropriate comparisons.** Unprofessional or careless comparisons of achievement test results can foster unhealthy competition among classmates, siblings or even schools because of ready-made bases for comparisons, such as grade-level achievement.

10. **Allowing tests to drive the curriculum.** Remember that some individual or group has selected those tests, for whatever reason. If a test unduly influences what goes on in a school's curriculum, then someone has allowed it to override priorities that educators, parents, and the school board have established.

11. **Using poor tests.** Tests can be flawed in a multitude of ways, from measuring the wrong content or skills to measuring the correct content or skills.

12. **Using tests unprofessionally.** When educational tests are used in misleading or harmful ways, inadequate training of educators is often at fault.

Reprinted with permission, B. R. Worthen and V. Spandel, (1991). "Putting the Standardized Test Debate in Perspective." *Educational Leadership, 48*(5), 65-69.

on the standardized test. Dorr-Bremme and Herman (1983), Herman and Golan (1991), Kellaghan and Madaus (1991), Shepard (1991), Smith and Rottenberg (1991), and Hutchings and Reuben (1988) believe that standardized tests reduce teaching when compared to the content and skills that teachers want students to learn. This reduction clouds the focus of expansive, higher-level thinking skills that students need for the next decade. Students' and teachers' creativity and natural thirst for exploring is essentially squelched (Worthen, 1993; Shepard, 1991).

Due to the problems and concerns about standardized testing, legislators and influential decision makers are beginning to recognize inadequacies in these tests (Brandt, 1992). Legislation is moving towards including performance assessments with standardized testing in many states, such as Texas and New York. The emerging trend to alternative assessment improves many areas of concern to teachers. Alternative assessment helps students accelerate beyond the narrow scope of basic skills and recall of content in standardized tests. This would be far more consistent with the current research on teaching and learning while providing a clearer connection between what is taught, what is learned, and what is assessed (Lieberman, 1991).

Alternative Assessment

There are forty-seven states that have standardized testing programs and almost half of these have performance assessments in place (many of these are essay writing) or are exploring the possibility (O'Neil, 1992). Meyer (1992) points out that authentic assessment and performance assessment differ because of context. Student performance cannot be authentic in contrived situations. Authentic assessment, as an alternative, uses strategies that test connections students make with real-life situations and conditions (Worthen, 1993). Figure 10–3 describes criteria for authentic assessment tasks. The growth of alternative assessment means that teachers must be knowledgeable to support and develop new forms of evaluation.

Alternative forms of assessment are one component in our nation's educational reform. Assessments that set performance standards, as opposed to evaluation of minimum skills, encourages an educational system to rethink its objectives and goals to match what teachers and students do in a quality classroom. Alternative assessment methods include open-ended questions, exhibits, demonstrations, hands-on experiments, creating new products, performance, computer simulations, and portfolios. Alternative assessment techniques encourage students to master more than basic skills. Performance, as an alternative assessment, tests a student's ability to use skills to solve problems, integrate disciplines, use higher-order thinking skills, perform experiments, write the stages of how a problem was solved or offer evaluation of problem outcomes. Richard Stiggins (in O'Neil, 1992) writes:

The achievement targets we have are more complex than ever before. We now realize that without performance assessment methodology, it's not possible to create a complete portrait of student achievement. You can't evaluate writing without asking students to write, and you can't evaluate whether a student has learned a foreign language without asking that student to speak [that language].

Authentic assessment, as an alternative assessment strategy, encourages teachers to implement a curriculum that goes beyond coverage of skills and recall of information. The added depth in the curriculum is another positive consequence associated with authentic assessment. Depth, instead of coverage of skills only, allows teachers increased opportunities to teach what they know is important, such as enriched content, problem-solving, analysis, and higher-order thinking skills. Teachers using authentic assessment show more adeptness at teaching and becoming coaches of learning instead of information givers (Wiggins, 1989). According to Worthen (1993), classrooms have been dependent on traditional assessment for decades and the present push for authentic performance assessment serves the need for broader application in evaluation. Authentic assessment legitimizes and refines many informal teacher assessment processes.

As more states and school districts experiment with alternative assessment, many find it difficult to reach a consensus. Maeroff (1991) states that alternative assessment strategies lack the speed and low cost of norm-referenced tests, and is time consuming, labor intensive, expensive, and often

---

FIGURE 10–3 Criteria to Judge the Authenticity of an Assessment

---

Authentic Assessments Involve:

1. *engaging and worthy problems or questions of importance,* in which students must use knowledge to fashion performances effectively and creatively. The tasks are either replicas of or analogous to the kinds of problems faced by professionals in the field, or adult citizens and consumers.

2. *faithful representation of the contexts* facing workers in a field of study, or the real-life 'tests' of adult life. The formal <u>options, constraints, and access to resources</u> are apt as opposed to arbitrary. In particular, the use of excessive secrecy, limits on texts and methods, the imposition of arbitrary deadlines or restraints on the use of resources to rethink, consult, and revise, etc.—all with the aim of making testing more efficient— should be minimized and carefully evaluated for inappropriate impact.

3. *non-routine and multi-stage tasks—<u>real</u> problems.* Recall or 'plugging in' is insufficient or irrelevant. Problems posed require a repertoire of knowledge, hence, good judgment in determining which knowledge is apt when and where; and skill in prioritizing and organizing the phases of problem clarification and solution.

4. *tasks that require the student to produce a quality product* and/or performance.

5. *transparent or de-mystified criteria and standards.* The test allows for thorough preparation, as well as accurate self-assessment and self-adjustment by the student; questions and tasks may be discussed, clarified, and even appropriately modified, etc. through discussion with the assessor and /or one's colleagues.

6. *interactions between assessor and assessee.* Tests ask the student to justify answers or choices, and often respond to follow-up or probing questions.

7. *involve response-contingent challenges* where the effect of both process and product/performance (sensitivity to audience, situation, and context) determine the quality of the result. Thus, there is concurrent feedback and the possibility of self-adjustment during the test.

8. *<u>trained</u> assessor judgment,* in reference to clear and appropriate criteria. An oversight or audit function exists: there is always the possibility of questioning and perhaps altering a result, given the open and fallible nature of the formal judgment.

9. *the search for <u>patterns</u> of response,* in diverse settings, under differing constraints. Emphasis is on the consistency of student work—the assessment of habits of mind in performance.

Reprinted with permission, G. Wiggins, (1991), Director of Research and Programs for the Center on Learning, Assessment, and School Structure (CLASS).

imprecise. Still, many teachers believe that the benefits of alternative assessment, for the teacher and students, are worth the time and inconvenience (Wolf et al., 1992). Teachers must show parents, administrators, and legislators the importance of student products in evaluating learning to overcome the obstacles and shortcomings of standardized tests only policy.

Obstacles

O'Neil (1992) believes one of the biggest obstacles in creating statewide alternative forms of assessment is money, because estimates are two to three times more expensive per child than norm-referenced tests. In addition, time is needed to establish validity and reliability standards and teachers need staff development to be trained in creating, administering, and scoring the assessments (Maeroff, 1991; Popham, 1993).

Those involved in creating alternative assessments must also realize the importance and difficulty in selecting assessment criteria. A benefit of performance assessment is that "assessment drives instruction, and instruction drives assessment . . . the assessment task is part of the instruction" (Maeroff, 1991). If Maeroff is correct, then the criteria incorporated in the assessment will be what the teachers use in their instruction. Great care and forethought is needed when selecting formative criteria for authentic assessment.

Standardization and subjectivity is a concern in scoring alternative assessments. Standardization is necessary to put the results of alternative assessments in context and to be able to compare students within a state and

with students in other states (Maeroff, 1991). Standardization can be difficult in alternative assessment because of the subjective nature involved. For example, teachers can score students' reading, writing, and oral responses according to a list of criteria, but then use their own interpretation (subjectivity) of "what meets" the criteria. When teachers differ on these, reliability becomes a concern (Willis, 1990). However, reliabilities, costs, training, and other obstacles can be overcome when educators use and show the benefits of authentic assessment.

Content

Authentic assessment is best when based on authentic content and learning. Valencia (1991) suggests the following guidelines for determining or deciding authentic content:

- Materials should reflect important themes and ideas of the lesson or curriculum.

- Materials should be consistent with the goals of the subject area curriculum in your district.

- Materials should be rooted in real-world experiences and have application to the world both inside and outside school.

- Materials should be sensitive to the developmental progression of students.

- Materials should allow students to engage in higher-order thinking.

In addition, materials should allow students to offer tentative solutions to problems to be solved and allow for many possible responses and solutions. Assessment must match the content. Teachers should understand the content and context of authenticity in order for assessment to be effective.

There are many student products that can be used for authentic performance-based assessment. Teacher-made tests, essays, writing, experiments, exhibitions, and speaking are all used routinely in most classrooms; but they are seldom used effectively as an assessment tool. Computer programs have been developed to help teachers with the time consuming record-keeping tasks. Portfolios as discussed in Chapter 1 are a useful and practical form of assessment.

Portfolios

As research suggests, traditional assessment methods can narrow curriculum, leave students ill-prepared for future assessment, and lack continuity to current learning theories (Herman, 1992). Good assessment should be reflective, constructive, related to individual goals, and provide for self-evaluation (Bransford & Vye, 1989). Good evaluation incorporates affective and metacognitive skills (McCombs, 1991) and encourages the use of real-life problems, which require people to work collaboratively (Herman, 1992). One growing trend is the use of a portfolio for alternative assessment.

The term *portfolio* in the educational setting must be distinguished from a work folder or stock market investments. Paulson et al., (1991) does so by defining a portfolio as:

> . . . a purposeful collection of student work that exhibits the student's efforts, progress, and achievements in one or more areas. The collection must include student participation in select-

ing contents, criteria for selection, criteria for judging merit, and evidence of student self-reflection. (p. 60)

Key to the process of portfolio success is student input and reflection. Students choose a learning product to include, write a rationale for choosing that piece, write or describe their evaluation of their level of achievement, and decide on the areas that need improvement (Frazier & Paulson, 1992; Hansen, 1992; Knight, 1992; Paulson et al., 1991; Valencia, 1990; Wolf, 1989).

Crucial to portfolio assessment is the demonstration of progress with an emphasis on process instead of product. The portfolio must reveal what the student can accomplish (Wolf et al., 1992; Hebert, 1992). The student shows the value of learning by choosing the items in the portfolio and explaining these choices. The student participates in the process as opposed to being the object of assessment. Above all, a portfolio provides a forum that encourages students to use and develop independent, self-directed learning (Paulson et al., 1991).

Teachers must view portfolios, as well as other forms of authentic assessment, as a vital part of the learning experience. As adults, students will be assessed by authentic means in their work and everyday lives. This type of assessment prepares students for future success.

Conclusion to Theory

The standardized testing movement is relatively new to education. The use of standardized tests resulted in many changes in instruction and curriculum. Research suggests that standardized tests narrow the curriculum and cause "teaching to the test."

Society on the whole accepts standardized tests and results. Legislators keep passing mandates to include testing of student learning, despite the controversies surrounding state and national standardized tests. When used properly, tests can yield beneficial information. The test results and decisions based on those results are often misused, however, which, in turn, has a negative impact on the teaching and learning process.

Alternative assessment is a current movement to add balance to standardized tests. Authentic assessment is a strategy that puts the students' learning in a real-life context. Students get to perform their knowledge in their work and everyday lives. Authentic assessment can add to the total evaluation of the student. However, authentic assessment is not yet accepted or understood by society, and many teachers need staff development to practice and learn appropriate techniques. In the meantime, teachers must continue to teach students how to take tests while seeking more experience in using and interpreting authentic student performances.

CLASSROOM APPLICATIONS

Introduction

The thought of tests makes most people cringe. Yet, with all that we know about the problems of standardized testing, it still dominates most school cultures and curriculum. Testing prevails because it is the fundamental way to evaluate student learning and provides for teacher accountability, even though that

may not be the major goal or purpose of the assessment. Although limitations and imperfections exist in assessment, it continues to be a major component in developing a personal educational belief system.

Teachers need to understand the controversies and uses of standardized tests and authentic performance to improve student test performance. Standardized tests, whether you are for or against them, still play a vital role in decisions about you and your students. Understanding the impact of how tests are viewed in the schools is critical in the development of the teacher. Also, teachers need to be knowledgeable and adept at constructing informal teacher-made tests and other assessment instruments. Above all, students must be taught how to transfer knowledge to a standardized testing format in order to be successful test takers.

Standardized Tests

Standardized tests are one type of formal, summative assessment devised to measure aptitude or student achievement. The results of these tests are compared in two ways, either by specific criteria that is tested or by established norms to which students are compared. Each has advantages and disadvantages (Figure 10–4).

A criterion-referenced test measures a student's level of success in skills or content by comparing the student's performance to a specified criterion. A criterion test determines if a student needs further instruction in a particular skill. The items on this test should be of roughly the same difficulty.

Norm-referenced tests are different because they attempt to compare the performance of a particular student to a norm or

FIGURE 10–4 Comparison of Criterion-Referenced Tests (CRT) and Norm-Referenced Tests (NRT)

CRT	NRT
Focus is limited.	Focus is broad.
Many items per task.	Few items per task.
Individual scores.	Wide range of scores.
Tests for mastery.	Surveys knowledge.
Compares mastery.	Compares scores.
No attempt at difficulty.	Builds in difficulty.
Performance determined by times correct.	Performance determined by position in a group.

average established by other students. Such tests generally cover a broad range of skills, as opposed to specific skills on the criterion-referenced tests. Norm-referenced tests draw comparisons between students and include some questions that everyone is expected to answer and some questions that are difficult to answer. An important distinction is to note that the percentile scores reported for these tests do not indicate a percentage of questions answered correctly. They report the percentage of students who scored higher or lower than the student taking the test. The student is compared to all students taking the test.

Another way of interpreting norm-referenced tests is the grade equivalent score. For instance, if an exceptional third-grade student received a grade equivalent score in mathematics of 6.2, the score refers to sixth-grade, second month. Such a score does not indicate that the student should be transferred to the middle school, but indicates that the student performed as well as the average sixth-grade student. The information these tests yield can be helpful or harmful depending on the decisions made because of the test scores.

Standardized achievement tests are used to make all kinds of school decisions. These tests only provide one piece of information and that information can either be very helpful or harmful in the teaching/learning process. If used properly, tests are a valuable resource. Understanding the limitations and interpreting the results in terms of the purpose can make standardized tests very useful for the teacher.

Improving Student Test Performance

Many students cannot transfer knowledge to the standardized test. Because the community relies on and has faith in the test results, teachers must work towards helping students perform well, even though there are many concerns regarding standardized testing. The students and you will be judged by school officials, parents, etc., accordingly, regardless of your testing philosophy.

Teachers should construct standardized test examples according to the test format to practice with and show how knowledge is applied to tests. Here is one classroom example of how and why you must transfer knowledge to the standardized testing format. When you are teaching the skill of alphabetizing, you might authentically assess students by asking them to use the phone book to find the phone number, and address of a restaurant, such as Spaghetti Warehouse. The student goes to the phone book, looks at the restaurant section, finds Spaghetti Warehouse, and provides you with the phone number and address. In this instance, the student was able to perform an "authentic" task. On a test day, the same student is asked to alphabetize four restaurants and is incapable of successfully completing this "test" task. Even though the student was able to use the real-life skills of locating a restaurant, phone number, and address, the student was unable to *transfer* this information onto a printed format where alphabetization is tested in a multiple-choice format. It is necessary, when teaching students, to provide them with an experience of transferring knowledge from lessons, activities or authentic performances to paper-and-pencil test-taking tasks. Here, the teacher can demonstrate examples

of ways to alphabetize and provide examples to help students gain skill and practice in transferring the skill of alphabetizing test-like questions. This step of transferring knowledge to a testing format helps students become familiar with—and hopefully more successful at—taking standardized tests. However, at no time is it appropriate to teach the test. The goal for the student is to transfer knowledge and increase test-taking skills.

Below are some suggestions and examples for improving students' test-taking abilities:

- *Let students and parents know about the test,* why it is important, and how the test scores will be used.

- *Be positive about the standardized test;* give the students positive and realistic expectations for their performance. A teacher's attitude will greatly influence student attitudes.

- *Ask students about their thought processes* in answering questions and solving problems. This can uncover areas needing more direct instruction or review.

- *Teach problem-solving skills;* help students explore various ways to solve a problem so they can transfer these skills to a variety of situations.

- *Review throughout the year;* familiarize students with different question formats may appear on standardized tests and with proper procedures for taking a test, whether standardized or teacher-made.

- *Point out time limitations and teach students to think about and follow the directions.* Teach students to underline important words.

- *Show students how to move through a test* so they do not dwell on one question. Let them know they can answer the easier questions first, then go back to the difficult ones. Unless there is a penalty for wrong answers, answer all questions.

- *Give children opportunities to practice test-taking skills through experiences,* such as writing assignment answers on their own paper so the transferring of answers in the test will seem natural. Teach students to read headings, subheadings, chart titles, etc., since many answers are found using these clues.

- *Provide pacing and relaxing strategies* because stamina is a big problem in long testing situations, just as it is when we have a big, time-consuming task at hand. Students need to learn to work/rest/ work/rest and adopt a process of pacing themselves: work three problems, then stretch your arms forward, work three more, then stretch your arms up in the air, work three more, roll your head, etc.

- *Use mnemonics or key word associations to help students recall important information.* Mnemonics is associating something new to something already known. Show examples of how to use mnemonics, such as learning the names of the Great Lakes: HOMES = Huron, Ontario, Michigan, Erie, and Superior.

Authentic Assessment

Another type of formal evaluation is authentic assessment. Authentic assessment is a strategy where teachers employ real-life context to evaluate specific learning tasks or behaviors.

The previous example of locating a restaurant in the phone book is one way to test authentic performance of the students' ability to alphabetize. Authentic strategies provide a broader and more realistic assessment of student learning.

The theory regarding standardized tests and authentic assessment recommends a balance and combination of both types. Using both assessment strategies provides the teacher with a better understanding of the degree and quality of learning, and provides a comprehensive evaluation of student learning. Because society has placed so much pressure and accountability on the teacher, authentic assessment should be used as a technique to supplement standardized testing. Teachers should avoid being dependent upon one testing strategy, because assessment strategies should be selected according to instructional goals.

Authentic performance strategies provide variety and are more in line with current instructional strategies. Authentic assessment demands that students be active, reflective, and independent learners who evaluate and connect knowledge. In order to assess the depth and quality of the students' work, authentic performances are beneficial.

Implement Authentic Assessment

Following are some examples to initiate and implement authentic performance assessment.

- *Writing Samples*: Writing is a common activity that is already used in many states for performance assessment. This strategy is useful to demonstrate the students' ability to use language and composition skills. Through writing samples, a teacher can evaluate the students' understanding of structure, spelling, grammar, and purpose. More information about a student's writing ability can be determined through writing rather than testing. Examples of writing samples include journals, book reviews, and poetry.

- *Speaking*: Speaking is also a way to demonstrate understanding of language. This activity is essential for younger students who have not yet mastered writing. A teacher can evaluate students' fluency, style, grammar, and content organization through speech. Speaking ability is difficult to assess with paper and pencil; however, video cameras and tape recorders can be valuable tools for evaluating oral information.

- *Essays*: Essays can demonstrate a student's ability to analyze, synthesize, and summarize information. A teacher can evaluate essays by producing a scoring rubric to compare essay responses. More information about what a student knows can be extracted from essays than multiple-choice tests.

- *Research Projects*: Research can be used to demonstrate the students' ability to locate and document, through different sources, information to answer a student or teacher question. A teacher can evaluate the students' work through written, visual or oral presentations. Through original research, students can explore topics with variety and detail.

- *Experiments*: Experiments can be used to demonstrate the students' understanding of scientific processes. The hands-on of sci-ence helps students to discover meaning and connections as opposed to memorization of scientific fact. Several states' tests are using or plan to use standardized experiments as part of performance assessment. A teacher can evaluate experiments by observing and discussing with students the way that they solved problems as well as the use of results obtained during the experiment. Many science process skills (hypothesizing, measuring, weighing, estimating, concluding, and others) can be observed during one experiment.

- *Exhibitions*: Exhibitions require students to produce a demonstration of learning to show others. Exhibitions integrate tasks and subjects in a creative way. Exhibitions can be displays or live performances to an audience. A teacher can evaluate exhibitions by identifying criteria to use in scoring. Frequently judges are used to evaluate exhibits. However, criteria are still needed to direct the students as well as the judges. Exhibitions can show a broad range of learning that relates to individual or group interest.

- *Portfolios*: Portfolios are a collection of students' work over a period of time. Portfolios are usually used for language arts, but can also be helpful as a collection for artifacts that represent specific work or jobs. A teacher can evaluate portfolios through student reflection and selection of outlines, drafts, revisions, and final compositions as well as the quality of the student product. Portfolios can contain many items such as student journals, learning logs, books read, creative work, music, dance, video, poems, and so on. The teacher and student should decide and select a variety of products to put in the portfolio.

Teacher-Made Tests

Informally, teachers are assessing all the time in the classroom; however, summative assessment can be developed by constructing teacher-made tests. Teacher-made tests are important because they can be used frequently to provide feedback for the teacher in adapting and modifying curriculum to meet the needs of the students. Informal teacher-made tests are used frequently to add to summative evaluation that judges or grades the degree of successful student performance. Teacher-made tests are another tool that is helpful in providing assessment information.

Many times the textbook, author-prepared tests do not measure or match intended instructional outcomes for your lesson or class. Therefore, teachers need to construct test items that measure their desired outcome, objective or purpose for learning.

Develop Teacher-Made Tests

A teacher-made test must be valid (measures the intent), reliable (measures the same each time), and appropriate (matches ability). Good test questions provide a good indication of the students' learning. There are several types of teacher-made tests: completion, true/false, multiple choice, matching, and essay. Teachers should develop a test of questions. A more in-depth look at the types of tests teachers can develop with sugges-

tions on how to write each type of test follows. Remember that quality questions take time to prepare.

Completion: Completion involves filling in the blanks. It relies on recall of knowledge. In most instances, it is better to ask a direct question rather than leaving blanks in a sentence for the student to fill.

- Avoid taking sentences directly from the textbook and replacing certain words with blanks.
- Blanks should be of equal length (larger words don't need longer blanks).
- Each word omitted should have its own blank.
- Only omit one or two key words in each sentence.
- Desired responses should avoid trivia and seek important content.
- Explicitly state and qualify the item so that only one response is correct.
- Make the sentence structure as simple as possible so the question is clear to all students.

True/False: True or false test questions are easy to use and score. What true and false questions measure is questionable, however. Students have a fifty/fifty chance of "guessing" the correct answer. There is no diagnostic value in this test. It is best used for review and discussion. Be sure to require that students put a (+) for true and a (-) for false, preventing capital Ts and Fs from looking alike.

- Avoid value judgments and negative statements.

- Absolute terms such as all, none, always, and never are associated with (-) false.

- Indefinite terms such as sometimes, usually, and occasionally are associated with partly (+) true and partly (-) false.

- When possible, have student supply the correct response for a (-) false question and a reason why a true response is correct.

- Write statements that can be unquestionably judged as (+) true or (-) false.

- Use short, concise statements.

Multiple Choice: This item is useful for measuring learner outcomes at the knowledge, understanding, and application levels. Because of its versatility, it is the most widely used of the objective-type items.

- Keep the reading level appropriate for the grade level and content (avoid wordiness and complex sentence structure).

- Write concise, unambiguous, and grammatically correct items.

- Use alternative responses that are consistent and similar in form.

- Avoid clues to the correct answer.

- Review each completed item for clarity and for relevance to the specific learning outcome to be measured.

- Provide the same number of responses for each question.

Matching: The matching item may be used to measure the lower levels of knowledge. They are easy to score. The response items are interdependent in that one response can influence all other responses being matched. Vocabulary, dates, events, and simple relationships can be efficiently and effectively measured.

- Establish a frame of reference for answering the test items.

- Write clear directions indicating the basis for matching and indicating if the responses may be used more than once.

- Be clear, concise, and use correct grammar.

- Keep the content in the columns the same.

- Avoid technical terminology.

Essay: The essay examination can be used in assessing the student's higher-order mental processes: application, analysis, synthesis, and evaluation. The essay item can also measure the student's ability to select and organize ideas in writing. The essay is difficult to correct and lends itself to subjectivity. The teacher should develop a desired response to have a key for grading.

- Major attention should be given to the reasons for the test.

- The background and ability of the group to be tested must be considered.

- The content of the question should be related to an important objective of instruction that can be defined in terms of expected student behavior.

- The students should know the ground rules so they have the same opportunity to plan and organize their time. Allow time to review and revise answers.

- The question can require the student to make comparisons, supply definitions, make interpretations, make evaluations or explain relationships.

There are many ways to evaluate student learning. Use the Field-Based Connections to identify, develop, and refine various testing strategies to help in developing your beliefs about assessment.

▶ FIELD-BASED CONNECTIONS

Introduction

Teachers, on the whole, dislike tests. Testing can create stress, confusion, insecurity, and a sense of dissatisfaction. Tests require time to construct, administer, grade, and interpret. Few teachers have the time, expertise or training to implement a comprehensive authentic performance-based assessment program in the classroom. Teachers need to reflect on instructional strategies and then determine the types of assessment needed. A balanced assessment plan is beneficial to the class and the field-based experience.

Work thoughtfully with the mentor teacher to initiate your assessment strategies. Collaborate with the mentor to devise ways to increase the transfer of knowledge to test-type formats. Through collaboration, growth in assessment practices can be explored. Standards and criteria can be developed to initiate demonstrations of student performance learning. Communicate to the mentor to share ideas about criteria and standards that are crucial to proper assessment of alternative assessment strategies. Explore ideas and any current initiatives for working with student portfolios.

Initially, intern students should observe both formal and informal testing whenever possible. A review of student files to see test score results tied to student observations will provide insight and questions about individual, remedial, and diagnostic needs. Discuss these findings in a confidential way with the mentor and in the university class.

Intern students should prepare instructional activities and assessment strategies to explore authentic performance. Develop, with your lessons, informal criteria and formats for assessing student learning. Take time to construct and experience the use of a variety of teacher-made tests. Discover ways to enhance student test-taking skills and create effective alternative assessment techniques that show problem-solving and other forms of creative critical thinking.

Guidelines for Interns

Pick and choose the activities that best suit you and your needs. Use these suggestions for your unit plans, portfolio collection, and your journal entries where appropriate.

1. Study forms of standardized tests to familiarize yourself with the questioning format and the scoring of the tests. Think of ways you could transfer knowledge that you can use to teach this format.

2. Read the district's and your school's test results. Discover the impact these scores have on curriculum instruction.

3. Interview the district research and evaluation consultant if there is one. Find out what plans exist for alternative assessment. Try to define the level of district commitment and staff development in alternative strategies.

4. Develop a variety of teacher-made tests during your field experience. Describe in your journal the students' reactions and results with each type of test you use.

5. Identify specific learner activities and match a performance-based assessment to student learning in your unit and lessons.

6. Initiate, if not in use, journal writing and student logs in the classroom. The practice of student writing into a journal every day is a good way to informally evaluate and get to know the students.

7. Work with the teacher to initiate or explore portfolio assessment. Discuss types of entries for portfolios and the various criteria needed to evaluate classroom student products.

8. Compare and visit other schools who have like- populations, but different test scores. Analyze why you think the differences exist. Visit schools with successful implementation of alternative assessments and analyze why it is working.

▶ CHAPTER CLOSURE

Summary

Constant conflict, controversy, and debate will more than likely continue as assessment practices evolve. Assessment is a test of a student's ability to perform a given task. Some view this task as an ability to pass a standardized test. Others view the task as an ability to demonstrate learning through an authentic

performance. A combination of standardized and alternative assessment strategies is needed because each one has the potential to contribute to student growth, but each one also presents problems for teachers.

Standardized tests have historically been used for comparative purposes. These score comparisons are frequently abused with unfair or inaccurate test result interpretation. These interpretations are often used for high-stake decisions, such as school funding, student placements, and graduation requirements, which cause alarm in the reform of curriculum and instruction in the schools.

Assessment changes are only part of the answer to quality instruction and learning. A holistic approach is needed to allow all students access to needed skills and knowledge that alternative assessment strategies represent. To date, there is little research evidence to show that students who perform poorly on standardized tests will perform any better with alternative assessment; however, more research and evidence is needed.

Teachers can work to improve student assessment and test result interpretation. First, teachers need to communicate the narrow perspective of standardized tests and the impact the results have on teaching, learning, and the decision-making process. One test should not determine major changes in curriculum or instruction. Stress and use a balance of assessment strategies and promote inclusion of alternative strategies in student assessment. Show how student exhibits and performances are valid measures of assessment to parents and administrators.

Second, teachers should provide test-taking skills for students, but should not teach the test because this is unethical. Provide examples and in-class experiences using sample questions to show students how to transfer knowledge to a testing format.

Attempt to balance standardized tests and alternative assessment. Discover ways of assessment that work for you and the students when developing your personal educational belief system.

Chapter Discussion Questions

1. Identify the benefits of standardized and alternative assessments. Defend each one in your personal instructional philosophy.

2. Why do most teachers fear assessment? How can teachers overcome these fears?

3. Discuss your findings about district test results. How do the scores portray the students in your field-based experience?

4. What are some of the problems you see with standardized tests, authentic assessment, and performance assessment?

5. What occurs for successful implementation of alternative assessment? Use information learned from school visits where you analyzed these schools.

6. What criteria would you use to make learning and assessment authentic?

7. Describe activities you used to show how students successfully transferred knowledge to the abstract paper-and-pencil test format. Evaluate why/why not these activities were beneficial to students.

CASE STUDIES

The case study examples can be used for analysis in small or large groups. Questions follow each case study as suggestions for discussion.

CASE STUDY 10–1: by Laura Duff, Early Childhood Teacher

There was a time six years ago, about midway in my teaching career, that the mention of standardized testing made the hair on the back of my neck stand straight up. I was having a real struggle with the ends justifying the means. Was a set of scores compiled mainly for comparison purposes really worth the stress it was placing on my twenty-two first grade students? Did the state's mandated need for this data justify placing so much pressure on a six-year-old that he cut the ends off of his socks so he could use his fingers and toes to deal with the "big numbers" he heard would be on the test? Working hard is only as admirable as the purpose of that work. Was this test truly worth the effort put forth? These are the questions that plagued my mind that year, and for some time after.

One difficulty was that I didn't think the test was truly assessing the things that I deemed important for my students to know. However, I found myself spending less time on those important areas in order to devote more effort to teaching the isolated skills assessed on the test. This was due, in part, to my own desire to see my students perform well, but mostly it stemmed from the pressure placed upon me in regular doses by my principal to raise those scores! I longed for the days prior, when I taught kindergarten and didn't have to deal directly with standardized assessment.

This, coupled with several other factors, led me to change my teaching assignment to fourth grade four years ago. The pressure to perform was relieved somewhat. I was still expected to cover the tested skills, but was spared any direct connection with the assessment. I enjoyed the respite briefly. Then the state made some alterations and I found myself facing "The Test" once again. This time, however, I felt much less trepidation. The combination of maturity, experience, and a less imposing administrator—among other things—made this situation more palatable. Since ten-year-olds are more able to cope with testing stress, that was not the problem it had been. Working collaboratively with grade-level teachers, reading specialists, counselors, and other interested staff, we were able to develop strategies that would help the students pass the writing portion, and could be applied to areas beyond the test. This task was eased by the fact that this section of the test leans more toward authentic assessment. It was quite gratifying to see that transfer of knowledge by the students. They performed better in the classroom and on the test.

This small success, coupled with the current push for more authentic assessments, gives me hope. Perhaps someday I will feel truly comfortable "teaching to the test," because the test will fit a more in-depth curriculum. It will have moved beyond the basics, and actually assess the higher-order skills and connections between these skills students need for life in the year 2000.

Case Study Discussion Questions

1. Describe Laura's feelings toward standardized tests.

2. Explain how Laura overcame "The Test."

3. How did collaboration help to implement authentic assessment for Laura?

4. How did Laura link assessment to instruction?

CASE STUDY 10–2: by Tim Miller, Intern Student

My first day at school started out well enough. My teacher and I had already moved the desks, set up the learning centers, and had begun to put burlap on the bulletin boards when our principal announced over the intercom that all teachers were to meet in the cafeteria for a staff meeting. This was just what some teachers needed, another meeting away from their disorganized classrooms, but we were compelled to attend. Probably just a pep talk to get the school year off to a good start, my teacher and I said to ourselves. What we encountered in the cafeteria, however, was something far from the traditional "have a good year and a smile."

Two of the top administrators from the school district were waiting for us when we took our seats in the cafeteria. Our principal introduced one of the administrators and, as he stood in front of the staff with a tight face, we could see a seriousness in his eyes. He said he was there to bring to our attention the fact that there was a new method of evaluating the performance of schools and districts in the state as a result of an amendment to the school finance bill that had just passed the Senate. The amendment described how elementary schools and their districts would now be required to evaluate their performance according to the attendance rates and the scores on the assessment of academic skills tests. Schools and districts that did not raise their rates and scores to meet certain standards, or did not raise their rates and scores from the previous year, were in danger of losing their accreditation or being annexed to another district.

The reaction from the teachers was immediate and intense. The questions and concerns they voiced mirrored the thoughts in my own head. Why had the state chosen to use attendance to evaluate the effectiveness of the schools and districts? Attendance at this school had been near perfect last year and it seemed that time and energy could be spent on more worthwhile things than trying to move the attendance rate from the previous year's 97 percent to a rate of 98 percent or higher. More importantly, why had the state chosen to use the state assessment of academic skills to evaluate the effectiveness of the schools and districts?

The district my school was in has consistently scored low on the test. This shows, I think, that there is something wrong with the test itself, rather than the effectiveness of the teachers. The test has been criticized by many to be discriminatory and vague, a poor assessment tool for students from different backgrounds. Why should the state use an assessment device that fails to accurately evaluate the performance level of the students? While the argument can be made that there has to be some standard way of assessing the wide variety of schools in the state, there should be a more flexible alternative to the use of a controversial assessment method.

The administrator concluded his "good tidings of great joy" by saying that the teachers should make every effort to raise the test scores. The teachers left the cafeteria, worried not only about whether they will still have enough time to set up their classrooms and prepare for the arrival of the students, but with the new threat of low test scores hanging over them. Instead of spending their time and energy pursuing new and innovative ways to teach their students, the teachers now had to think about ways to teach to the standardized test that would be one of the deciding factors for the future of the school and district.

Case Study Discussion Questions

1. How would you feel if you were in Tim's shoes?

2. In Tim's school, how was assessment used to make high-stake decisions? What other criteria could be used in making such decisions?

3. What would you predict about the morale of the teachers in Tim's school? What are your reasons?

▶ REFERENCES

Ashworth, K. (1990). Standardized testing: A defense. *The Education Digest, 56,* 40–42.

Bergman, J. (1981). *Understanding educational measurement and evaluation.* Boston: Houghton Mifflin.

Bracey, G. W. (1987). Measurement—driven instruction: Catchy phrase, dangerous practice. *Phi Delta Kappan, 68,* 683–686.

Brandt, R. (1992). Overview: A fresh focus for curriculum. *Educational Leadership, 49,* 7.

Bransford, J. D. & Vye, N. (1989). A perspective on cognitive research and its implications in instruction. In L. B. Resnick and L. E. Klopfer (Eds.), *Toward the thinking curriculum: Current cognitive research.* Alexandria, VA: ASCD.

Cizek, G. (1990). Reasoning about testing. *Education Week, 9,* 64.

Davies, C. W. (Ed.), (1984). *The uses and misuses of tests.* San Francisco: Jossey-Bass.

Dewey, J. (1897). My pedagogic creed. In Martin S. Dworkin (Ed.),. *Dewey on education* (1959). New York: Teachers College Press.

Dorr-Bremme, D. & Herman, J. (1983). *Assessing student achievement: A profile of classroom practices.* Los Angeles: UCLA, Center for the Study of Evaluation.

Doyle, D. P. (1991). America 2000. In J. W. Noll (Ed.), *Taking sides: Clashing views on controversial educational issues* (7th ed.). Guildford, CT: The Dushkin Publishing Group, Inc.

Elam, S., Rose, L., & Gallup, A. (1992). The 24th annual Gallup/*Phi Delta Kappan* poll of the public's attitudes toward the public schools. *Phi Delta Kappan, 74,* 41–53.

Feuer, M. J. & Fulton, K. (1993). The many faces of performance assessment. *Phi Delta Kappan, 74,* 478.

Frazier, D. M. & Paulson, F. L. (1992). How portfolios motivate reluctant writers. *Educational Leadership, 49,* 62–65.

Gerberich, J. R., Greene, H. A., & Jorgensen, A. N. (1962). *Measurement and evaluation in the modern school.* New York: David McKay.

Hansen, J. (1992). Literacy portfolios: Helping students know themselves. *Educational Leadership, 49,* 66–68.

Haney, W. & Madaus, G. (1989). Searching for alternatives to standardized tests: Whys, whats, and whithers. *Phi Delta Kappan, 70,* 383–387.

Hebert, E. (1992). Portfolios invite reflection—from students and staff. *Educational Leadership, 49,* 58–61.

Herman, J. L. (1992). What research tells us about good assessment. *Educational Leadership, 49,* 74–78.

Herman, J. L. & Golan, S. (1991). *Effects of standardized testing on teachers and learning- another look. CSE Technical Report #334.* Los Angeles: UCLA, Center for the Study of Evaluation.

Hutchings, P. & Reuben, E. (1988). Faculty voices on assessment. *Changes, 20,* 48–55.

Jaeger, R. M. (1991). Legislative perspectives on statewide testing goals, hopes, desires. *Phi Delta Kappan, 73,* 239–242.

Kellaghan, T. & Madaus, G. (1991). National testing: Lessons for America from Europe. *Educational Leadership, 49,* 87–93.

Knight, P. (1992). How I use portfolios in mathematics. *Educational Leadership, 49,* 71–72.

Lieberman, A. (1991). Accountability as a reform strategy. *Phi Delta Kappan, 73,* 219–220.

Madaus, G. F. & Stufflebeam, D. (Eds.). (1989). *Educational evaluation: Classic works of Ralph W. Tyler.* Boston: Kluwer Academic Publishers.

Maeroff, G. I. (1991). Assessing alternative assessment. *Phi Delta Kappan, 73,* 272–281.

McCombs, B. L. (1991). The definition and measurement of primary motivational processes. In M. C. Wittrock and E. L. Baker (Eds.), *Testing and cognition.* Englewood Cliffs, NJ: Prentice Hall.

Meyer, C. A. (1992). What's the difference between authentic and performance assessment? *Educational Leadership, 49,* 39–40.

Mitchell, R. (1992). *Testing for learning: How new approaches to evaluation can improve schools.* New York: The Free Press.

O'Neil, J. (1992). Putting performance assessment to the test. *Educational Leadership, 49,* 14–19.

Paulson, F. L., Paulson, P. R. & Meyer, C. A. (1991b). What makes a portfolio a portfolio. *Educational Leadership, 48,* 60–63.

Perrone, V. (1991a). On standardized testing. *Childhood Education, 67,* 132–142.

Perrone, V. (Ed.). (1991). Expanding student assessment. *ASCD, 33,* 9–12.

Popham, W. J. (1993). *Educational evaluation,* 3rd edition. Boston: Allyn and Bacon.

Shepard, L. A. (1991). Will national tests improve student learning? *Phi Delta Kappan, 73,* 232–238.

Simmons, W. & Resnick, L. (1993). Assessment as the catalyst of school reform. *Educational Leadership, 50,* 11–15.

Smith, M. L. & Rottenberg, C. (1991). Unintended consequences of external testing in elementary schools. *Educational measurement: Issue and practice, 10,* 7–11.

Valencia, S. W. (1990). A portfolio approach to classroom reading assessment: The whys, whats, and hows. *The Reading Teacher, 43,* 338–340.

Valencia, S. W. (1991). You can't have authentic assessment without authentic content. *The Reading Teacher, 44,* 703–713.

Wiggins, G. (1989). Teaching to the (authentic) test. *Educational Leadership, 46,* 41–46.

Willis, S. (1990). Transforming the test. *ASCD UPDATE, 32,* 3–6.

Wolf, D. P. (1989). Portfolio assessment: Sampling student work. *Educational Leadership, 46,* 35–39.

Wolf, D. P., LeMahieu, P. G., & Eresh, J. (1992). Good measure: Assessment as a tool for educational reform. *Educational Leadership, 49,* 8–13.

Worthen, B. R. (1993). Critical issues that will determine the future of alternative assessment. *Phi Delta Kappan, 74,* 444–457.

Worthen, B. R. & Spandel, V. (1991). Putting the standardized test debate in perspective. *Educational Leadership, 48,* 65–69.

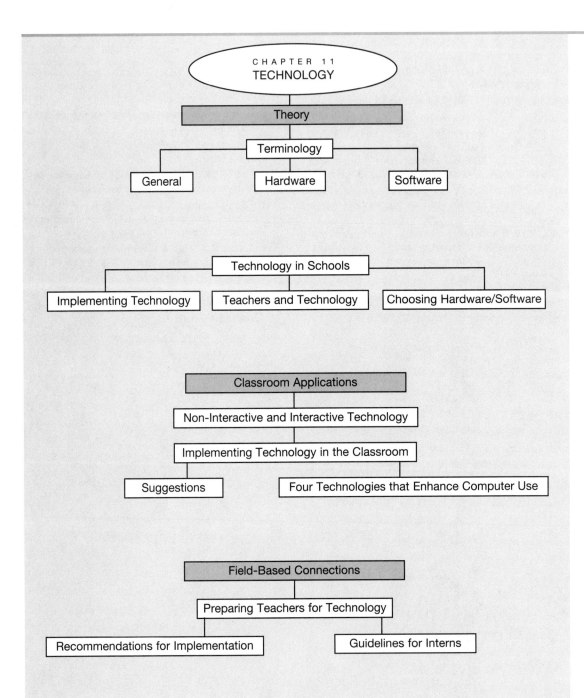

CHAPTER 11
TECHNOLOGY

Theory

Terminology

General Hardware Software

Technology in Schools

Implementing Technology Teachers and Technology Choosing Hardware/Software

Classroom Applications

Non-Interactive and Interactive Technology

Implementing Technology in the Classroom

Suggestions Four Technologies that Enhance Computer Use

Field-Based Connections

Preparing Teachers for Technology

Recommendations for Implementation Guidelines for Interns

11

Computers and Technology

Introduction

Technology has the potential to revolutionize American schools. Current reports on educational reform dedicate portions of their research to educational technology. Since the goal of education is to create lifelong learners who will be productive members of society, students must be given tools to manage the ever-increasing presence of information and technology in schools and our society. The most dramatic change in the last decade is the increasing presence of the computer in classrooms. Even technology like the telephone, which remained out of classrooms for years, is now beginning to be used in the school through modems connected to computers.

Technology plays an increasingly large role in today's society, but faces skepticism and fear in today's schools. Initially, mentioning technology instills thoughts of improving the effectiveness of education; however, most teachers are overwhelmed and need staff development to learn and implement technology. Keeping up to date with technology is a challenging and difficult task for the busy teacher. Numerous reports applaud the inclusion of technology in the classroom, but often blame teachers for failures or problems that might occur. The lack of training, coupled with the lack of time to learn or experiment with new programs, results in frustration and often opposition to technology.

The major obstacle technology presents to teachers is that it changes and improves at a dramatic rate. Also, schools lack funds for appropriate hardware, software, and staff development to keep up with these changes. These obstacles make it extremely difficult to learn and access the best technology for the classroom. The small amount of technology that might be available in schools becomes quickly outmoded.

Definition of Educational Technology

Students, however, must be technologically literate for life in the twenty-first century. Success for tomorrow requires technological knowledge and skill. The term *technology* has a catch-all definition. In Fitzgerald (1992), the Association for Educational Communications and Technology in the United States defines educational technology as:

> . . . a complex, integrated process involving people, procedures, ideas, devices, and organization for analyzing problems and devising, implementing, evaluating, and managing solutions to those problems, involved in all aspects of learning... (p. 57)

Technology includes interactive and non-interactive machines (hardware). Some non-interactive technology machines include: tape recorders, film projectors, video cassette recorders (VCRs), and television (TV). These machines are difficult for the user to alter. Cassette tapes, filmstrips, and video cassettes contain the content for non-interactive machines. Interactive technology can be altered by the user. Some interactive technology machines include: computers, laser discs, compact disc (CD) players, modems, and videodiscs. Software programs and discs contain the content for interactive machines.

Technology means different things to different people and your use of technology in the classroom needs to begin where you are comfortable. Technology is another strategy and a tool a teacher can use to increase achievement and learning. Technology has key terms and definitions that are basic to comprehending and understanding related information. To pre-pare for study and be informed, it is helpful to know the key terms. Knowing the terminology is also necessary to enable you to develop your personal educational belief system about technology. As you read and prepare for the study of technology, refer when needed to these helpful definitions. Following the terminology is a brief history of computers and a review of technology in schools.

Technological Terminology

The following terms are not intended to be an exhaustive list; they are provided to help familiarize you with key terms that will enable you to learn about educational technology. To keep up with rapid changes and new technology, it is recommended that you go beyond this list to study and read, on a regular basis, technological journals such as: *Technology and Learning, Electronic Learning* or *Educational Technology*. Learning computer language is desirable, but not necessary to use technology. It is best to use these words with the appropriate hardware and software in this field-based experience.

General

Hardware: The visible, physical information processing and transferring machines. Hardware refers to technical equipment, such as the computer CD player, LCD panel, scanner, modem, keyboard, printer, disc drive, Video-Spigot, Xapshot, and any other physical machine.

Software: These are the programs (word processors, drawing programs, computer discs, games, etc.) that run the hardware. Software is stored on floppy discs, hard drives, CD-ROMs, videodiscs, videotape, audiotape, and other learning resources. Software makes the hardware function.

Interface: A device that connects various hardware to allow them to work together, such as a computer and printer.

Interactive Technology: Technology that enables teachers and students to interact with the technology by stopping and starting, viewing select pieces of video or answering questions, thus effecting the output of the technology. For example, when viewing an interactive video about the American Revolution, a student can view the battle of Valley Forge, jump to a document written about the battle, then view select biographies of people involved.

Non-Interactive Technology: Technology that a person cannot actively interact with other than viewing. For example, watching a documentary video or a movie about the American Revolution is considered non-interactive technology.

Multimedia: The term for using many different types of technology. Multimedia uses a variety of hardware and software, usually including a combination of computer data, graphics, audio, and video.

Hypermedia: A combination of buttons, fields, and text. It escapes the linear, sequential presentation of material because a student can explore a subject in any order and to whatever depth desired. By pointing and clicking a mouse to a word or image on the screen, the student opens windows where more information is displayed about the word or image. "Hypertext/hypermedia material provides a view of information that better reflects the interconnectedness of knowledge for a richer, interactive, learning experience" (Campoy, 1992). Multimedia is an important supplement to hypermedia.

Distance Learning: These are information television programs that link students with teachers via satellite or fiber-optic services. Utilizing a compilation of multimedia equipment, this eliminates the need for long-distance travel, especially in rural areas where certain subjects have few students (e.g., calculus, foreign languages, economics, etc.). Distance learning allows schools to share courses where too few students exist to justify an on-site instructor. Distance learning is also useful in staff development, parent courses, etc. Some programs require membership fees or individual payment.

Network: Any system of linking schools, districts, states, and people across the nation together. Data are transmitted through cable, telephone lines, and modems, allowing students to retrieve and download articles, newsclips, slides, videos, and programs from computers. The National Science Foundation hopes to establish a high-speed fiber-optic network that will interconnect American universities and public schools by the year 2000 (Lewis, 1991). Networking is also known as telecommunications and requires a modem. Networks enable students to do extensive research because they can access, via the computer, libraries, and other resources across the country and world without leaving the classroom. INTERNET is one example of a network.

Internet: An international electronic mail (e-mail) network connecting schools and universities, military, government, and commercial computer users through thousands of computer networks. The name, INTERNET, is used because it is the main connector of all sub-networks. Some examples of sub-networks include: BITNET (Because It's Time NETwork), EARN (European Academic Research Network), USENET, APRANET, CSNET, and many others. A recent network to connect universities and schools is NREN (National Research and Education Network). Networking allows for inexpensive and rapid sharing of information and ideas throughout the world.

Electronic Mail (e-mail): Electronic messages are sent as files via the telephone lines by modem or via networks from one computer to another, and are directed through a computer address. Each member in the network receives the e-mail. It is faster than the post office, doesn't waste paper, and messages are retrieved and stored at the user's convenience. Users need an e-mail address, for example, my e-mail address is BFRAZEE@ Trinity.Educ.

Upload/Download: Upload refers to sending information over the network; download refers to receiving information from the network.

Computer Simulation: Students are put in real-life situations, where they must make decisions that directly affect the outcome. An example is a flight simulation.

Virtual Reality (VR): A computer-generated, three-dimensional, multisensory, interactive environment through which students move by "wearing a specially wired helmet or goggles, by gesturing with a special glove, and by moving their eyes" (Lewis, 1991). It seems as though you are virtually there and utilizes sophisticated hardware and software. Education is beginning to use through virtual books available on CD-ROMs and hypermedia.

Artificial Intelligence (AI): AI is "the branch of computer science devoted to the study of how computers can be used to simulate or duplicate functions of the human brain [making] it appear as though the computer is thinking, reasoning, making decisions, storing or retrieving knowledge, solving problems, and learning" (Freznel, 1987).

Hardware (Figure 11–1)

Computer: The brains of a technology program. It consists of a central processing unit, memory storage, and ports where other hardware can be connected.

Modem: The machine that enables the computer to communicate with other computers or a network over the telephone lines.

Scanner: This machine photocopies images and translates them into images your computer reads. These images can then be stored in memory or directly transferred from the computer to other pieces of hardware, such as a printer.

Liquid Crystal Display (LCD) Panel: When this is connected to your computer and placed on an overhead projector, it projects the images from the computer onto a screen. This process enables the whole class to view and work together on a computer program.

CD Player: This machine allows you to play and retrieve information from a CD-ROM disc. You can then interact with it through the computer. There is computer software to facilitate the use of the CD-ROM.

Xapshot: This camera enables you to take still pictures, store the information on a floppy disk, and transfer it directly into your computer.

VideoSpigot: This camera, like the Xapshot, enables you to take moving pictures and incorporate the images into your computer for use.

Mouse: An input device that interfaces with the computer to access data by clicking a button on the mouse to a prompt or picture on the monitor. Other input devices include keyboard, keypad, light pens, joysticks and monitor touch.

FIGURE 11–1   Hardware Considerations

	ADVANTAGES	DISADVANTAGES
Computer:	Needed for information-age and job skills. Can save time and organize work.	Knowing capabilities. Need several in classroom. Keeping up with innovations.
Modem:	Can network and communicate worldwide.	Needs a dedicated telephone line. Cost for time and user service.
Scanner:	Anything can be scanned and transferred onto documents.	Color scanners are expensive. Learning proper use. Complex pictures do not scan well.
LCD Panel:	Whole class instruction. More interaction.	Clarity on some models is poor.
CD Player:	Children can interact with software. Great sights and sounds plus memory capabilities.	Expensive software programs needed. Keeping up with new releases.
Xapshot/VideoSpigot:	Brings picture media into computers to enhance information.	Expense of hardware. Finding time to transfer and edit pictures.
Mouse:	Input device that interfaces with the computer.	Requires time to become accustomed to its use.

Software (Figure 11–2)

Laser Discs: Laser discs, also known as video discs, are capable of storing 54,000 pages of information on a twelve-inch disc similar to a record. The difference is that laser discs also have information, graphics, and sound that is displayed and heard on the computer monitor. These are updated easily, and soon may be replacing textbooks as a primary teaching tool (Lewis, 1991).

Compact-Disc, Read-Only-Memory (CD-ROM): These smaller discs incorporate high-quality sound, pictures, and full-motion video. *Compton's Multimedia Encyclopedia,* from Encyclopedia Britannica's Educational Corporation, holds an entire encyclopedia of nine million words, 5,000 articles, 63,000 entries, 15,000 photographs and charts, sixty minutes of sound, and forty-five animation sequences —plus the entire Merriam-Webster Intermediate Dictionary—on a single compact disc (Brooks & Perl, 1991).

Digital Video-Interactive (DVI): Similar to the CD-ROM and visual discs, this is another interactive video system.

Computer-Assisted Instruction (CAI) or Integrated Learning System (ILS): These are software programs that include tests and practice problems that are used and stored in the computer. This integrated system allows students to access programs under the teacher's direction, while the system tracks their progress and scores. Learning is interactive and individualized. "Children don't learn at the same rate and are not interested in the same subjects at the same time" (Brooks & Perl, 1991). These instructional programs provide basic skill development, drill, and review.

Word Processing: These programs let students publish projects and papers. Numerous programs are available. Examples include Bank Street Writer and Microsoft, which are common for everyday publishing of student and teacher work.

FIGURE 11–2 Software Considerations

There are different types of software:

1. Tutorial for individualized instruction
2. Whole class instruction
3. Games and simulations
4. Drill and practice

There are different levels of sophistication:

1. Text only
2. Still graphics/still video
3. Animated graphics/motion video
4. Sound
5. Combination of any or all of the above

The scope and sequence of learning will vary:

1. Review of specific problems
2. Teach a single concept
3. Present an entire unit
4. Replace a book(s)
5. Extend classroom learning

Adapted from D. M. Adams and M. Fuchs, (1986). *Educational Computing.* Chicago: Charles C. Thomas.

Art Processing: These are art and drawing programs. Examples include Kid Pix, Splash, and MacPaint. These programs let students draw with the mouse, choose from templates or color pre-programmed patterns.

Hypercard: A specific hypertext program that allows non-programmers to custom-make instructional material for students. Experienced students can use hypercard to create reports or projects. It combines buttons, fields, scripting, sound, and clip art. Education hypercard allows teachers to format grade reports, attendance, and other routines.

Technology Modifications for Special Needs Students

Muppet Board: A muppet board is put over the keyboard to show pictures instead of letters. This lets very young students interact with the computer. Keyboard simplifications can also be used with slow learners and students with limited fine and gross motor skills.

Touch Window: Students are able to respond to the computer by touching a transparent panel that covers the screen, making it touch-sensitive. Touching various areas on the computer screen allows students to access information in an easy-to-use way.

Screen Magnification: Magnifies the screen to enable visually impaired students to interact with the computer.

Voice Recording and Playback: This orally records student responses, and can be used with young children or those without fine motor skills.

Voice Output: This modification reads the computer directions, so visually impaired students, or non-readers, can interact with the computer.

▶ THEORY

History of Computers

There was a time when only highly trained specialists worked with computers in enclosed rooms that were carefully monitored for temperature, humidity, and dust; these specialists would converse in cryptic languages with machines that filled the room. Time has passed and the technology has matured to where teachers can use desktop computers to accomplish what use to require huge machines. "The heart of education s technological transformation is the computer, an information processing and transferring engine comprising several components . . . " (Lewis, 1991). Technological transformation began in the Orient thousands of years ago. Shopkeepers used the abacus—a set of counting beads in a wooden frame—to calculate their sales. Many centuries later, in seventeenth-century France, Blaise Pascal (1623–1662, French mathematician and philosopher) invented a device which enabled him to add and subtract numbers up to eight digits. Years later, G.W. Leibniz, a German mathematician (1646–1716), improved upon Pascal's machine, incorporating the abilities to multiply, divide, and find the square roots of numbers. All these machines, however, rested upon untrustworthy mechanics, so they remained unpopular (Thomas & Kobayashi, 1987).

Charles Babbage proposed his "analytic engine" in the 1830s, which would include a punched-card for data input and output, a memory unit to store numbers, a unit to do arithmetic computations, and a unit to tell the engine the order of operations to be performed. Again, the mechanical industry was unable to produce a trustworthy machine, so the analytic engine was never completed and produced (Thomas & Kobayashi, 1987).

Various developments continued for one hundred years. Herman Hollerith invented a punch-card system for accurately tabulating the United States Census in the 1880s. These and other advancements in science, mathematics, and engineering eventually made possible the first trustworthy computer-like machines. Computer development, therefore, was an accumulation of years of discoveries and advancements (Thomas & Kobayashi, 1987). Though the educational circles of the early twentieth century were already beginning to ponder the consequences of technology in their fields, it was not until after World War II that the explosion in teaching-machine development was truly implemented. Two years after conclusion of World War II, the first computer became operational. This new age was spurred on with the launching of Sputnik by the Soviet Union and "triggered unprecedented national interest in education in the United States, first as a means of regaining technological superiority and later as an instrument of social policy" (Pajak, 1993).

Computers are generally classified into four generations. First-generation computers, such as Harvard University's Mark I completed in 1944, used electrical switching elements for data entry instead of the punch cards initiated by Hollerith. This machinery, however, was too large for any sort of mass production; the Mark

I was fifty feet long and eight feet high. Second-generation computers emerged around 1959, when the transistor replaced the vacuum tube. This replacement made the computers smaller, faster, more energy-efficient, and more dependable. Third-generation computers evolved out of the United States government's research in space exploration. Astronauts required a miniaturization and increased efficiency of all necessary hardware components. This occurred in the late sixties and early seventies (Thomas & Kobayashi, 1987).

In the early and mid-1980s, the fourth-generation, the development of microcomputers known as personal computers, changed the utility of technology. Computers were small, efficient (in speed and memory capacity), reliable, and inexpensive enough for everyone to own one and have it to work on at home (Thomas & Kobayashi, 1987).

When fourth-generation computers first appeared, predictions were made that they would revolutionize education, home life, and society. Suddenly, computer literacy became the next great crisis in American education. Educators believed that every student needed some sort of computer competency to be employable, and various computer courses in schools quickly became accepted as desirable and necessary. The application of computer technology for school purposes has been available since the 1950s, but widespread use in the classroom did not occur until very recently (Ornstein, 1992). The earlier expectation for its use never materialized, because the machines were introduced with the notion that they would lighten the teachers' load and, in some cases, replace them. Additionally, availability was limited, teachers were never adequately trained to use computers or computer language; it was felt that they were more trouble and expense than they were worth, and consequently many of these earlier computers were not used.

Today's computers, however, are stronger and more diversified; they are easier to use and software programs do not require extensive use of computer language. These computers can correct errors in spelling and grammar as well as read aloud to you. They can be used to play games or translate data from one foreign language to another. Computer networking has increased tremendously, controlling and monitoring everything from airline reservations and library-information services to the growth of research on artificial intelligence and robotics. These easy-to-use computers are indispensable to society and education (Thomas & Kobayashi, 1987).

Currently, computer use and education is being supported more than in the past. On December 9, 1991, President Bush signed the "High Performance Computing Act" into law. It stipulates that technology "offers the potential to transform radically the way in which all Americans will work, learn, and communicate in the future" (Bush, 1991). Included in this act was federal funding for a National Research and Education Network (NREN). Through electronic mail, communication, and networking, K-12 teachers, professors, and administrators are now able to access resources available by libraries, publishers, and anyone else connected to the network. Networking improves communication and cooperation among government, business, industrial, and educational communities. NREN promises to be twenty-five times faster than its predecessor, INTERNET. Networking is the communication mode of the future. Kinnaman (1993) reports that President Clinton has urged Congress to appropriate funds for research and develop-

ment of a "superhighway" telecommunication network. The superhighway is expected to provide a digital network connecting all homes and businesses within five years. The White House receives approximately 700 e-mail messages a day.

Kinnaman (1990) believes computer power and use will continue to increase at outstanding rates. This belief is verified by the increased number of computers in schools (Figure 11–3). Computers have the potential to be a key ingredient for reform and success, depending on the context for which they will be used. The teacher's role does not change by simply putting a computer in the classroom. "The change occurs only to the extent to which a shift of responsibility to the learners occurs" (Hannafin & Savenye, 1993). Technology has been slow to reform education or teachers. Perhaps this is due to fear of change, rather than endorsement of the numerous possibilities of multimedia technology. There is, however, research that demonstrates that technology will impact and reform schools in the future.

Technology in Schools

School change and reform embraces technology. *A Nation At Risk* (1983) espoused a belief in improving the current educational system, making people more accountable for their work. Technology was seen as a way to monitor and standardize procedures already in place. Another school reform sprouted from *A Nation Prepared* (1986), which called for the restructuring of the schools. It called for student-centered learning, with technology at the root of change. These and numerous other reports include technology as a cat-

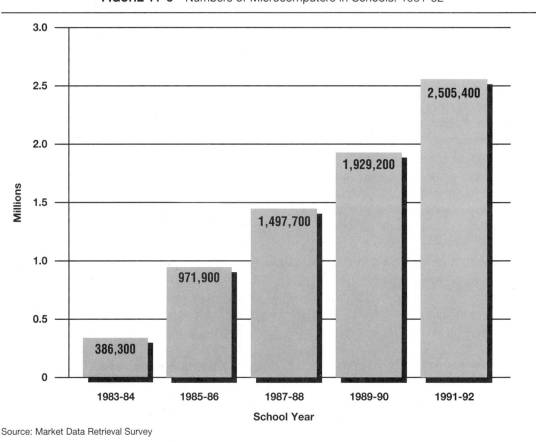

FIGURE 11–3 Numbers of Microcomputers in Schools: 1991-92

Source: Market Data Retrieval Survey

Reprinted with permission from *Education Week*, September 9, 1992.

alyst for change (Bruder, 1990; Collins, 1991; Sheingold, 1991).

Educating Americans for the Twenty-First Century, a National Science Board Report (1983), reports that basic education must include technology and an understanding of technological advances and applications. Technology helps provide students with skills they need for today's workplace, and kindergarten is not too early to begin. Even different social skills will be needed in the twenty-first

century. New types of interpersonal skills will be needed for occupational roles in which computer-mediated communications is important. The workplace will require getting along in computer-supported managing of collaborative learning and reflection (Kiesler et al., 1984; Wilson, 1991).

Schools can no longer remain isolated from the rest of society with respect to educational technology. The information age involves a change in thinking, management, instructional strategies, problem-solving strategies, and communication skills (Wilson, 1991). "Doing more of the same will only produce more of the same. Automating current educational practices will not affect the quality of learning" (Campoy, 1992). Technology infusion involves more than a beep indicating a correct or incorrect answer on a history fact-recall test, or a try-and-check center for arithmetic computations. Technology and the programs tied to these technological advances are only tools. Even though teachers do not have to know how to "program" computers, strategies for their "use" *must* come from teachers. The process of devising those strategies must begin by asking what a teacher wants in a program, rather than how to use what currently exists. It requires teachers to consider the important curricular questions of what is worth knowing, why and what learning is appropriate, and for whom. Above all, it avoids letting the technological tail wag the pedagogical dog (Callister, 1992). Teachers, whose first commitment is to pedagogical considerations, will be able to use technology to enhance their teaching and their students' learning. Technology can help change the nature of teaching and learning, but only if teachers understand it, accept it, and use it well. Pedagogy itself must change in order to encourage the creative problem-solving and higher-order thinking required for producing computer-literate students.

There is little research evidence in the past to support the assertion that technology has improved education (Schramm, 1977). What current evidence there is, however, is weak in supporting the value of technology as a learning tool (Hannafin & Savenye, 1993). In fact, while technology becomes more readily available, it does not mean that technologies will be effective in the complicated culture of schools. There is abundant evidence of powerful technologies being used quite poorly (Hawkins & Collins, 1992).

Extensive problems exist with the research on technology in the schools, not necessarily with the technology itself. First, technology is not a quick-fix or a cure-all for educational problems. Second, there is inadequate evidence regarding the use of computers because experiments about how technology improves education simply have not been completed (Bork, 1991). Human beings cannot be identically matched and the variables in learning situations cannot be isolated or controlled. Traditional research is inappropriate for much of the agenda about technology's role in the reform of learning (Hawkins & Collins, 1992).

Most studies about technology in schools fail to take into account the following considerations:

1. Implementation takes years to bring about changes and show results;

2. Standardized test scores do not directly correlate to technology infusion;

3. Too often, school district objectives are too vague to measure concretely;

4. Technology implementation is not standard and cannot be reduced to standard measures (Wilder & Fowles, 1992);

5. A distinction must first be made between the effectiveness of the computer (or hardware) itself and the applications (or software) being used (Bork, 1991), because many researchers find that problems with technology do not result from the computers, but rather from the instructional software that students use (Clark, 1991);

6. Schools and teachers within those schools implement technology in different ways because teachers have various levels of training;

7. Researchers also underestimated the importance of the role of the teacher when implementing technology in the classroom (Hannafin & Savenye, 1993).

Implementing Technology

For teachers, the largest obstacle to technology implementation is fear of change and the unknown, especially when there is a lack of support, equipment, and funds. Whenever a new type of technology is introduced, teachers may be concerned over how it will affect the daily routine, the amount of time consumed, how they will learn about the technology, and if it is right for their students and curriculum. Proper training and continuing support must be part of each new technological advancement. The success of implementing technology depends on establishing an environment of acceptance and the use of technology at a personal level (Poirot, 1992). Technology is an instructional strategy; in order for it to be effective, you must internalize its potential, gain the necessary knowledge, have all the components, and receive the support necessary to be successful.

The successful implementation of technology requires a change in traditional thinking. Technology is a great strategy because it has the potential to organize problems for students to study, discuss, and solve. Multimedia environments help students construct personal knowledge and makes learning meaningful to them (Wilson, 1991). Student motivation, attention, and enthusiasm increases with technology in the classroom. Through technology, students become active participants, who are encouraged to creatively problem-solve, explore, and expand their horizons beyond the classroom.

Students' interests need to be considered when selecting technology. Students need to make connections between the technology and the lesson's objectives, which should improve their learning and problem-solving skills (Self, 1985). Technology must be integrated into the day, and is not accomplished by a separate technology class time. Technology in isolation or lack of student control rarely adds meaning to the lesson (Zimmerman, 1990). Students need to have personal meaning and make connections for learning to occur (Hawkins & Collins, 1992).

Teachers and Technology

Perhaps the most critical issue in dealing with technology is that of training. Implementation of anything cannot be expected to be long-lasting without a thorough and ongoing staff development program, and this is especially true with complex technology (Zappone, 1991). Inclusion of teachers in the planning and implementation process and decision-making process is vital, and ongoing training is critical to success. Teaching with technology is a skill itself, and careful planning and commitment to training are necessary because teachers are at the heart of instructional technology (Langhorne et al., 1989). Research indicates educators need a strong knowledge base, an opportunity to communicate, access to help, and supportive administrators (Zorfass, 1993). Technology works when the users are comfortable with it and have the necessary support from the educational community.

Technology is such a rapidly changing field that it is virtually impossible for anyone to teach it as they were taught. The past fifteen years have seen a remarkable growth in the range and power of technology available to teachers. In the past, teachers had chalkboards, slides, audio cassettes, overhead projectors, and films. Current technology includes videotapes, personal computers, interactive video, networks, distance learning, and CD-ROM (Falk & Carlson, 1992). Effective change in education often results from an altered attitude of learning and teaching. It is also important to keep in mind that students learn differently today, differently from the learning modes familiar to us. In the twentieth century, students and teachers used discussion, chalkboards, worksheets, and paper-and-pencil drills. Students of the twenty-first century are multisensory stimulated and need multimedia material to maintain interest (Reif & Morse, 1992).

Teacher training is crucial to the success of technology. Researchers are conclusive about the importance of teacher training, including frequent updates, easily accessible support, and trouble-shooting (Bork, 1991; Campoy, 1992; Falk & Carlson, 1992; Furst, 1992; Green, 1993; Lewis, 1991; Massey, 1993; Poirot, 1992; Reck, 1991; Reif & Morse, 1992). A well trained and confident teacher is needed to facilitate and plan the content and skills necessary for successful integration of computer and technological instruction. According to Cuban (1986; 1989), when technology fails, teachers are the focus of the blame. Therefore, if society wants schools to produce computer and technologically liter-

ate students, the place to begin is with the computer and technologically literate teachers. Unfortunately, this training is rarely done (Manuel & Norman, 1992).

Technology restructuring and improvement of schools complement each other (Bagley & Hunter, 1992; Campoy, 1992). Teachers in the twenty-first century must go beyond turning on a computer. Learning how to use the latest technology is a necessary requirement for effective and successful teaching and learning.

Choosing Hardware/Software

The hardware and software choices require asking many important questions. Does this hardware/software meet a specific curricular need? Is there a congruence and compatibility among the hardware, software, curriculum goals, and school priorities? What is the cost of the hardware/software? Is it technically sound? What about later upgrades and interfaces? With these issues in mind, a teacher must examine hardware and software based on program requirements and student needs (Langhorne et al., 1989).

Hunter et al. (1984) identified the process of selecting computer hardware and software as being confusing and difficult. Many guidelines have been published, but are rarely helpful due to the lack of demonstrations of hardware capabilities and preview copies of software. Judging the quality and usability of hardware and software becomes almost impossible before purchase and teachers must rely on the producers to adequately represent their products.

Teachers also have little control over prices, site licenses, demonstrations, and support services (Strickland, 1990). Bork (1992) states that "market forces alone will not result in production of suitable hardware and software by industry." This means that no matter how good the decision-making process is, optimal choices may not exist. The implications of these issues are that teachers need to be aggressive to shape the industry, invest in personal expertise, become involved in current technology, and follow future technologies.

Lockard et al. (1987) found that appropriate software is exceedingly scarce. The quantity of available educational software has increased dramatically in the last few years, and experts estimate that nearly 20,000 educational computer programs are available today (Geisert & Futrell, 1990). Although there has been significant improvement in the quantity of software, there is widespread agreement and substantial evidence that quality problems remain. Neill and Neill (1990) reviewed over 11,000 pieces of software, reported finding a large number of poor programs, and identified only 7 percent of the programs, as excellent. Currently, a variety of software reviews are available in every issue of many journals.

The most frequent criticism of hardware/software is the predominance of traditional drill and tutorial programs. The use of the technology for only skill and drill is a waste of time, money, and potential. New hardware and software permits a variety of student-appropriate levels that provide instant feedback of instruction based on the student's responses. If the student fails to learn a task or concept, the technology breaks the concepts down even further, giving additional examples and suggestions (Lauda, 1989). The advent of multimedia and multisensory interfaces creates new frontiers and challenges for classroom and teachers of the future.

Conclusion to Theory

Just a few years ago, technology was synonymous with computers. Schools initiated efforts to put computers into classrooms in the hope of improving education and exposing students to the tools of the future. Unfortunately, the introduction of computers and other technology has not brought forth the expected results. Despite these findings, there appear to be indications that new and future technologies will reform education. Faster and easy to use notebook computers, CD-ROM, satellite delivery systems, virtual reality, and videodiscs present dramatic new educational possibilities and opportunities.

Electronic-mail and computer network technologies create an instant community of support and information. A network system enables teachers to share information with educators across the nation and throughout the world. This educational resource makes information easily available from conferences, universities, libraries, and government documents. Students and teachers in classrooms across the country can now communicate with one another through a computer modem connected to a network.

Interactive computer technology, multisensory media, and telecommunications have greater potential for enhancing the instructional and learning process today than did the computer of the past. Technology has great potential for the present and future, but to be successful, teachers must adapt and learn how to implement technology into their instructional strategies. Teachers also need to break away from their traditional roles and shift to interactive technology that emphasizes multimedia. Students in technology classrooms are actively involved, with a high degree of control over unlimited resources that meet a variety of needs and individual differences. Many schools are beginning to initiate and provide numerous technological opportunities. Teachers need to study, prepare, and use technology with the students in order to be prepared for the classroom of the future.

CLASSROOM APPLICATIONS

Non-Interactive and Interactive Technology

Technology is classified by two distinct categories: non-interactive and interactive. While both have unique qualities and specific purposes (Figure 11–4), interactive technology is the best way to involve the children in a hands-on, learn-by-doing (interactive) approach.

Non-Interactive Technology

Non-interactive technology follows a traditional approach. This technology cannot be changed or altered, but it can be used in positive ways that enhance instruction. Non-interactive technology is useful when linked to teacher purpose and student need. Some guidelines for non-interactive technology are:

- Introduce a concept or skill.
- Set the mood for instruction.

- Increase motivation during the lesson.
- Reinforce concepts and skills (strengthen understanding through various learning styles).
- Promote discussion to check for understanding.
- Provide in-depth information on a specific person, event or subject.
- Conclude and review learning.

Before using any type of interactive or non-interactive technology, it is important to preview what you selected before showing it to the class. As you preview, ask yourself the following questions:

- *Does the technology match the maturity levels of students?* Young children have short attention spans, especially if the language is too complex or the selection does not involve movement and action. On the other hand, older students will quickly become restless if the language is too simple for them.
- *Does this meet lesson goals and purpose?* Does this media focus upon the objective and purpose of the lesson? Take notes and formulate the questions you will want to ask your students.
- *What are the copyright laws?* Materials rented or borrowed from your school library are fine to use for non-profit educational purposes. Using copyrighted materials is illegal and these materials should not be used in the classroom. This includes videos, computer software, and most technology. It is highly recommended that the media or technology specialist be contacted to be certain that the most recent laws are followed. When in doubt, seek permission in writing from the company for classroom use of copyrighted materials.

FIGURE 11–4 Comparison of Interactive and Non-Interactive Technology

INTERACTIVE (Contemporary)	NON-INTERACTIVE (Traditional)
Videodisc	Film and Filmstrip, Television/VCR
Computer and LCD	Chalkboard, Overhead, Typewriter
Scanner	Cut and Paste, Tracing Paper, Photocopies, Draw Freehand
Computer Discs	Audio Cassette
Telecommunications	Encyclopedia (24 volumes)
VideoSpigot Xapshot	Camera (cut and paste)
Electronic Mail	Memos and Letters

When using non-interactive technology, make sure the children are involved and thinking. You can involve students by giving them specific tasks while watching or listening to non-interactive media. Relate how the media reinforced or presented alternative perspectives for what was learned in class. While non-interactive technology offers students more information than reading or discussion, it creates passive visual learners.

Interactive Technology

Interactive technology involves students beyond watching, listening, and answering questions. Students become actively involved in the ownership of learning.

Stopping and starting and getting feedback are two of the most distinguishing characteristics of interactive technology. Teachers or students can stop interactive technology, such as an optical disc or CD-ROM, in one place and jump ahead to another based upon teacher discretion or student interest. This allows for expansion or clarification of student or teacher goals or questions. Software programs on the computer give students immediate feedback on correct answers or the consequences of choices made. CAI and ILS assist teachers in developing literacy, computer programming, and problem-solving depending on the software and hardware selected. Interaction enhances the usability and potential because of the shift of responsibility to the learner through technology. Interactive technology does not necessarily imply whole class instruction, it can also be used by small groups or individual students.

Teachers who use interactive technology become managers of information by determining the needs of the class, selecting technology that meets the lesson objectives, and then allowing students to explore the interactive technology possibilities. The importance, as with any instructional strategy, is to use it to achieve a planned purpose that meets students' needs and interests.

Implementing Technology in the Classroom

Become Acquainted with Technology

Providing students with real-life connections is essential for long-term learning. Technology should help students in their everyday lives both in and out of school to make important real-life connections and decisions. Technology's omnipresence in society helps to simulate the actual contexts in which these skills will be needed.

Four Technologies: Computer Use in the Classroom

Following are four technologies that enhance computer use and multimedia instruction in the classroom. Familiarize yourself with these basic technologies, because they are or will be found in most schools.

1. *Videodiscs.* The rationale behind videodiscs is the same as a filmstrip or videotape. Information is transmitted through auditory and visual media. Unlike filmstrips or videotape, teachers can program the videodiscs to view only the sections pertinent to the objectives you are teaching. For example, if you are studying tornadoes in science, a videodisc can be used to visually experience and hear a tornado. The teacher could also move quickly to show another section that demonstrates whirlpools. The class can experience the similarities and differences between these two natural occurrences while wasting less time switching or fast-forwarding tapes. Information on a videodisc is accessible from the push of a button. There is a tremendous amount of information available on videodiscs, and they are simple to use. Often, videodiscs accompany textbooks.

2. *LCD Panel.* An LCD panel interfaces a computer and an overhead projector to combine multimedia techniques. Instead of reinforcing a concept on the chalkboard, the teacher can use the computer with videodiscs, CD-ROMs or VCRs to captivate the attention of the students. The teacher can also use the LCD panel to model—for example—how to turn on the computer and access the files. This sure

beats having an entire class crammed around a twelve-inch computer screen. That approach could cause problems, making individual instruction too time consuming. The panel makes it easy to view and teach computers and other technology in whole class settings.

3. *CD-ROM.* CD-ROMs need to be connected to a computer and are easy to use. A computer disc (CD) is put into the CD player and then played. Many CDs are available in English or Spanish, for Limited English Proficiency (LEP) or bilingual students or for other instructional purposes. Students interact with the computer to highlight words or pictures as it reads, in the language of choice. Click a word or picture with the mouse and the computer supplements students' learning with pronunciations or definitions of unfamiliar words. Broderbund's *Living Books* are useful CDs that allow reading in English or Spanish, along with an array of interactions to encourage and motivate learning. Several CDs allow people and objects on the screen to move. The CDs are powerful motivators for reading and reference. Entire encyclopedias can be stored on one CD. There are many possibilities for instruction and reinforcement of content and skills when students know how to access the CD information.

4. *Modem.* Modems allow teachers and students the potential for accessing telecommunications. Telecommunications requires a telephone line, communication software, and usually an online service provider (Figure 11–5). These national services offer special features for their users.

Networking can also be used to send messages and seek information. A modem opens the door to the information world.

Technological multimedia enhances life-long and future learning. In the future, virtual reality will be developed that will simulate and allow students to take rides in a covered wagon or build pyramids along the Nile River. Keeping up to date with technology's innovations and improvements requires time, dedication, and enthusiasm that will in turn establish a technologically literate partnership with students.

FIELD-BASED CONNECTIONS

Introduction

Technology, with the advent of multimedia, is not a passing fad, but is here to stay. The future for technology in the classroom improves daily as new software programs and enhancements to existing hardware are developed. In a fast-paced world where information comes in combinations of digital text, video, audio, and computer-generated graphics in seconds from satellites, it becomes evident that teachers must become involved and prepared to meet the students of the technological information age in their world. The potential of technology for teaching and learning is mind-boggling. Mentor teachers and interns should be partners in learning to keep informed about emerging technology, and to implement technology in the classroom.

FIGURE 11–5   Companies Providing Online Services

America Online
8619 Westwood Center Dr.
Vienna, VA 22182
(800) 827-6364

AT&T Learning Network
AT&T
P.O. Box 6391
Parsippany, NJ 07054
(800) 367-7225 ext. 4158

CompuServe
P.O. Box 202112
Columbus, OH 43220
(800) 848-8199

Global Lab
LabNet
Terc
2067 Massachusetts Ave.
Cambridge, MA 02140
(617) 547-0430

GTE Education Services Inc.
GTE Place, West Airfield Dr.
P.O. Box 619810
DFW Airport, TX 75261-9810
(800) 927-3000

New Access
Teachable Tech
2179 Hannah Lane9
Tucker, GA 30084
(404) 939-4596

National Geographic Kids Network
17th and M Streets, NW
Washington, DC 20036
(800) 638-4077

Implementing Technology in the Classroom

Regardless of your level or position, think about and explore the following recommendations:

- Realize that technology is more than a computer. Explore as much as you can about the technologies in your school, district, regional education service centers, and state education agencies.

- Visit schools who are using multimedia technology as part of their teaching strategies. Observe how the students and teachers plan and integrate technology.

- Recognize the future of technology. Attend workshops and seminars that will enhance your knowledge and change your attitudes about the role of the teacher and learner in a technological information age.

- Visit with hardware and software sales representatives. Let them show you current and future technologies.

- Read current educational technology journals. The predictions and developments covered in these journals are informative and supportive of emerging technological trends.

- Connect to an electronic network (for example, INTERNET). Users can send electronic mail, access electronic bulletin boards, and access information and resources from numerous institutions across the country and world.

- Analyze a variety of software programs. Use the evaluation guide in Figure 11–6 to assist in the analysis. Use computer software, videodiscs, CD-ROMs, or other multimedia products.

Guidelines for Interns

Introducing Technology to the Classroom

This can be a great educational experience for students and teacher alike. If there is technology available in the school, the following suggestions will help in analyzing and integrating technology in the classroom. If there is no technology in the school, seek a site at a service center or university where the following suggestions will help in analyzing and integrating technology. Do the following suggested activities in a hands-on situation where understanding and use will increase learning.

Pick and choose the activities that best suit you and your needs. Use these suggestions for your unit plans, portfolio collection, and your journal entries where appropriate.

1. Explore the types of technology hardware and software applications available. There are a variety of ways for you to learn about the hardware and software. Read the manuals that come with the machines and software. Collaborate with other interns, teachers or specialists and ask them to show and allow you to practice with various technologies. Look for and attend workshops or demonstrations in or outside of school, and view what is available.

2. Try out the technology and see what you like. Just like your students, you will learn by doing, discovering, and learning. Take some time to experiment, play, and explore. Once you are familiar with the technology in your school, ask yourself the following questions:

   (a) *Which elements of the hardware and software are most familiar to me?* Start where you are comfortable. Start with the word processing program and learn everything there is to know about it. A computer's possibilities through word processing make the multimedia potential endless.

   (b) *Does the technology have capabilities that allow for a variety of teaching and learning?* Experiment with the software available in your school or regional service center. Use Figure 11–6 to evaluate the software. Look for procedures that make it easy or hard to use. Be sure you can modify programs to meet the varying ability levels and need of students.

FIGURE 11–6   Software Evaluation Guide

Program Name: _____

Date Published: _____

Publisher: _____

Reviewer's Name: _____

Type of Software: _____

Cost (if known): _____

Hardware Needed: _____

Audience: _____

Format of Program (Check all that apply):

_____ individual   _____ instructional game

_____ cooperative groups   _____ literature

_____ whole class   _____ problem-solving

_____ drill   _____ informational

_____ competitive   _____ multimedia

_____ practice   _____ hypermedia

_____ tutorial   _____ virtual reality

_____ simulation

Skill Level (Check all that apply):

_____ low   _____ sequential

_____ medium   _____ non-sequential

_____ high   _____ self-instructional

_____ flexible   _____ assistance needed

_____ active involvement   _____ student controlled

FIGURE 11–6 continued

Content (Determine if indicator is well stated and/or understood (high rating) or is not well stated and/or understood (low rating)):

HIGH..LOW	INDICATORS
High ....Low	Goals
High ....Low	Focus
High ....Low	Expectations
High ....Low	Purpose
High ....Low	Needs
High ....Low	Directions
High ....Low	Format
High ....Low	Interaction
High ....Low	Challenge
High ....Low	Motivates
High ....Low	Ease of Use
High ....Low	Pace
High ....Low	Consistency
High ....Low	Compatibility
High ....Low	Success Rate
High ....Low	Quality
High ....Low	Accuracy
High ....Low	Self-correcting
High ....Low	Feedback

Style (Determine if the style of the program has a high quality or low quality according to the indicators):

HIGH..LOW	INDICATORS
High ....Low	Active
High ....Low	Color

FIGURE 11-6 continued

High ....Low	Sound
High ....Low	Movement
High ....Low	Text
High ....Low	Graphics
High ....Low	Voice
High ....Low	Control
High ....Low	Interest
High ....Low	Multicultural
High ....Low	Sexism
High ....Low	Social/Moral

Overall Rating (Describe likes/dislikes from teachers' and students' point of view):

_____

_____

_____

_____

_____

_____

_____

_____

_____

_____

_____

_____

_____

Once you have a chance to experiment and learn about technology, you can begin using it with the students.

3. Show the class how to use technology. Show the class software programs by interfacing a computer to an LCD panel or work with small groups on the computer. Teach the whole class how to use the technology. Set aside a special time during the day for individuals or cooperative groups to show you that they understand how to use the technology. Assign projects, group work, or problem-solving strategies that match the technology to your personal educational belief system. Remember that the technology is a *tool* to support your instruction and the students' learning. Once you and the students become familiar with some technology, as well as managing its use during the school day, start to include more technology in your lessons and units.

4. Integrate step-by-step. Add more and more technology and software programs to your lessons. Find out the students' interests and which programs meet those needs. Then continue to introduce students to other types of technology. Gradually work your way up to multimedia technology. Multimedia has many benefits for teachers and students because it uses multisensory, integrated technologies (Figure 11–7).

5. Take time to learn and explore. Keep expectations high and encourage learning about technology. Set reasonable goals for yourself and your class. Your personal instructional strategy will need time to develop and grow. Technology changes rapidly; therefore, read, share, and collaborate with others to keep you up to date and motivated. Work with technology daily. Encourage and provide students programs and technology that involves higher-level thinking and creativity.

6. Experiment and take risks. Today's technology has endless possibilities and potential. Explore the many uses and use the ones that work best for you and your students.

▶ CHAPTER CLOSURE

Summary

Many new forms of technology are here and others are on the horizon. These technologies require a different view of learning and teaching. The learner becomes active and engages with interactive media and programs. The teacher becomes a guide to enhance and support a multimedia learning environment. Teachers and students who do not learn about and work with technology today will be disadvantaged in the future.

School districts and teachers must keep up to date with technology. Schools must have a technological vision and seek funds to support the purchase of hardware and software, while also providing funds for training in technology. The computer and all the related peripherals form the central unit for implementing and creating interactive technology.

Computer literacy is as basic to education today as reading, writing, and arithmetic. It is a powerful strategy to motivate most students to excel in all subjects. Computers with ports and interfaces create the hub to manage technology. Schools must overcome the obstacles of expensive hardware and software to make technology available. States must look at the inequalities that exist between schools that have technology and those that do not. Plans must be addressed to incorporate technology into all schools in America.

Technology beyond the computer is necessary, since multimedia captivates students because its multisensory approach reaches all students in one way or another. Technology gives students the tools and skills needed to succeed in the future. Through interactive technology, students can see and make connections to real life, learn more, and become lifelong learners, who are equipped with the high-tech, interpersonal experiences necessary to compete in the twenty-first century workplace.

FIGURE 11-7   Benefits of Multimedia

- Reaches all the senses, which enhances learning. Multimedia can be tailored to the learning styles of individuals, whether they are visual, auditory, kinesthetic or tactile learners.

- Encourages and validates self-expression. By allowing students to decide how they want to create a project (through words, images, sound, etc.), teachers are saying it's OK that students have more control and more of a voice in their own learning process.

- Gives a sense of ownership to the user. Students actually create what they learn, and there is often physical evidence, such as a portfolio of work, of that learning.

- Creates an active, rather than passive, atmosphere because it forces the student to participate and think about they are learning.

- Fosters communication. The use of multimedia starts conversations between the students and teachers and allows ideas to flow in ways that may not always be possible through words alone. When students create what their learning, they will probably feel more comfortable with it and want to discuss what they've done with those around them.

- Makes sense. Technology is already built into the lives of today's students (television, radio, phones, computers), so it is something they feel comfortable with.

Reprinted with permission, I. Bruder, (1991), "Guide to Multimedia: How it Changes the Way We Teach and Learn," *Electronic Learning, 11*(1), 22–26.

Keep informed of emerging technologies and include in your personal educational belief system a place for new technological discoveries, such as virtual reality and computer-aided language translators. The possibilities for technology are endless; therefore, share and collaborate with others to promote technology to create a technological environment in the classroom and school for creative problem-solvers.

Chapter Discussion Questions

1. How will technology impact future education?

2. What are your goals for a technology education program? What if your school lacks vision, support, and equipment needed to implement technology?

3. How would you organize computer time in your classroom, especially with only one computer?

4. How would you integrate technology as a normal part of your day?

5. Why is instruction beyond the computer to multimedia important to student learning?

6. Why is interactive technology better for instruction?

7. What is your assessment of your school's and education's response to technology?

CASE STUDIES

The case study example can be used for analysis in small or large groups. Questions follow the case study as suggestions for discussion.

CASE STUDY 11–1: by Sandra Ann Guevara-Zapata, First-Year Teacher

Last year I worked as an intern in a fifth-grade classroom. The school at which I was assigned was a high minority, inner-city school. However, one great advantage for the school was that through recent grants it was able to purchase computers for all classrooms and an expansive software library. Working side-by-side with my mentor teacher, a veteran of thirteen years, I was able to experience the excitement and fears of having technology in the classroom.

I was familiar with the type of computers that were purchased for the school and was very excited about being able to work with students in a "computer-type" setting.

However, my mentor saw the computer as more trouble than what it was worth. Together we pioneered ourselves through the school year.

When the computers and software were first introduced, it was evident that many of the "veteran" teachers were intimidated and very skeptical about the use of computers in the classroom. I believe it is fair to say that many teachers feared the computer because they knew nothing about it. Consequently, a very intense series of inservices were given throughout the year on the computer and with the available software. However, these inservices still scared off a few and left others somewhat confused. The partnerships (mentor/intern) or teams of teachers (grade-levels) began helping each other with their computer skills. This helped give the teachers common ground to bond and work together. For example, at the inservices, my mentor would jokingly tell me to learn all I could, then reteach her in the classroom at her own pace. This retraining on the computer, for the most part, worked wonderfully for us and our class.

I see the computer as a very necessary and helpful tool in the classroom. Perhaps the easiest thing to understand about computers is to realize that they can assist teachers in organizing and better managing the classroom. From seating charts to parent letters, from grades to special awards, the computer does wonders to facilitate the never-ending cycle of "paperwork." And one can personalize everything to his or her own style.

The fun part about computer use in the classroom is that the computer can be used as a great motivator to get the students actively involved in what they are learning. There is a great deal of software on the market that directly related to the curriculum we were teaching. Through the use of time lines, charts, graphs, and simulations, we not only were able to excite the students to explore on their own, but inspired them to work together in cooperative learning groups, and even prompted them to debate the reasons for their decision-making. Students that were not usually actively involved became more engaged in classroom discussions that were centered around their computer work. In fact, the computer plays a very important role in our "young author's conference," as many of the students wrote their stories on the computer and illustrated them.

I feel that, in our classroom, the computer was a very valuable asset. It helped us "spice up" our teaching. Unfortunately, many of the classrooms had teachers who either rarely used the computer or had the computer set up in the back of the room with one student set apart from the group and not engaged in anything related to the curriculum. There were still teachers who said that computers were intimidating or did not understand the full range of uses or capabilities of computers.

This year I have begun working at the same school in what I feel is a very exciting role. My work is not only with the curriculum, but also with the computers and school technology. I have relied heavily on my intern experiences using the computer in the classroom, how we were or were not able to use the computer. I now understand that the inservices need to be helpful and not intimidating for the teachers. And, since many teachers need constant reassurance about their teaching roles with computers, they can be shown ways computers can help them. I also feel that there are many valuable types of software that can fit directly into the curriculum, while others can act as reinforcers. I would like to set a goal for my first "official" year in the school setting by making myself and the other teachers use the computer to the best of our abilities with the students. Technology is definitely a way of the future; I would like to insure its success at our school.

Case Study Discussion Questions

1. How did Sandra's mentor feel about computers (relate to your mentor)?

2. How can interns help mentor teachers implement technology?

3. What did the students in Sandy's class and school do with the computer?

4. What major obstacles to technology do you see from this case study?

► REFERENCES

Bagley, C. & Hunter, B. (1992). Restructuring, constructivism, and technology: Forging a new relationship. *Educational Technology, 32*(7), 22–27.

Bork, A. (1991). Is technology-based learning effective? *Contemporary Education, 63*(1), 6–14.

Bork, A. (1992). Editorial. *Technological Horizons in Education Journal, 20*(2), 6.

Brooks, R. & Perl, B. (1991). Interactive technology for education. *Principal, 71*(2), 20–21.

Bruder, I. (1990). Restructuring: The central kitsap example. *Electronic Learning, 10*(2), 16–19.

Bush, George. (July 11, 1991). Unpublished speech presented at the White House Conference on Library and Information Services.

Callister, T. (1992). The computer as a doorstep: Technology as disempowerment. *Phi Delta Kappan, 74*(4), 324–327.

Campoy, R. (1992). The role of technology in the school reform movement. *Educational Technology, 32*(8), 17–22.

Carnegie Forum on Education and the Economy. (1986). *A nation prepared: Teachers for the 21st century.* Washington, DC: Carnegie Forum on Education and the Economy.

Clark, R. E. (1991). When researchers swim upstream: Reflections on an unpopular argument about learning from media. *Educational Technology, 31*(2), 34–40.

Collins, A. (1991). The role of computer technology in restructuring schools. *Phi Delta Kappan, 73*(1), 27–40, 78–82.

Cuban, L. (1986). *Teachers and machines: Use of technology since 1920.* New York: Teachers College Press.

Cuban, L. (1989). Neoprogressive visions and organizational realities. *Harvard Educational Review, 59*(2), 217–222.

Falk, D. R. & Carlson, H. L. (1992). Learning to teach with multimedia. *Technological Horizons in Education Journal, 20*(2), 96–101.

Fitzgerald, B. E. (1992). Changing the industrial technology curriculum to meet today's needs. *Technological Horizons in Education Journal, 19*(8), 57–59.

Freznel, L. E. (1987). *Crash course in artificial intelligence and expert systems.* Indianapolis: Howard W. Sams and Company.

Furst, M. (1992). New K-2 'system' from Apple. *Electronic Learning, 11*(8), 20.

Green, A. (1993). Staff development: Key to successful technology implementation in public schools. *Technological Horizons in Education Journal, 20*(11), 65–66.

Hannafin, R. D. & Savenye, W. C. (1993). Technology in the classroom: The teacher's new role and resistance to it. *Educational Technology, 33*(6), 26–31.

Hawkins, J. & Collins, A. (1992). Design-experiments for infusing technology into learning. *Educational Technology, 32*(9), 63–67.

Hunter, B., Dearborn, D., & Snyder, B. (1984). Computer literacy in the K-8 curriculum. In J. H. Tashner, (Ed.), *Computer Literacy for Teachers.* Phoenix, AZ: Oryx Press.

Keisler, S., Siegel, J., & McGuire, T. W. (1984). Social psychological aspects of computer–mediated communication. *American Psychologist, 39*(10), 1123–1134.

Kinnaman, D. E. (1990). What the future holds. *Technology and Learning, 11*(1), 43–49.

Kinnaman, D. E. (1993). Push for data superhighway moves into fast lane. *Technology and Learning, 13*(7), 53.

Langhorne, M.J., Donham, J. O., Gross, J. F., & Rehmke, D. (1989). *Teaching with computers.* Phoenix, AZ: Oryx Press.

Lauda, D. (1989). Technology education: Its place in the secondary school. *The Journal of Middle Level and High School Administrators, 19*, 20–28.

Lewis, P. H. (1991). The technology of tomorrow. *Principal, 71*(2), 6–7.

Lockard, J., Abrams, P. D., & Many, W. A. (1987). *Microcomputers for educators.* Boston: Little, Brown & Company.

Manuel, J. & Norman, G. (1992). Three steps to technology immersion. *Technological Horizons in Education Journal, 20*(3), 82–84.

Massey, W. E. (1993). The U.S. challenge to be #1: Opportunity amidst perils. *Technological Horizons in Education Journal, 20*(6), 69–71.

National Commission on Excellence in Education. (1983). *A nation at risk: The imperative for educational reform.* Washington, DC: National Commission on Excellence in Education.

National Science Board. (1983). *Educating Americans for the 21st century.* Washington, DC: National Science Board.

Neill, S. B. & Neill, G. W. (1990). *Only the best: The annual guide to highest-rated educational software for pre-school–grade 12.* New York: R. R. Bowker.

Ornstein, A. (1992). Making effective use of technology. *NASSP Bulletin, 76*(542), 27–34.

Pajak, E. (1993). Change and community in supervision and leadership. In G. Cawelti (Ed.), *Challenges and achievements of American education: The 1993 ASCD yearbook.* Alexandria, VA: Edwards Brothers.

Poirot, J. L. (1992). The teacher as researcher. *The Computing Teacher, 20*(1), 9–10.

Reck, L. (1991). Technology: What and when? *Contemporary Education, 63*(1), 42–46.

Reif, R. & Morse. (1992), G. M. Restructuring the science classroom. *Technological Horizons in Education Journal, 19*(9), 69–72.

Schramm, W. (1977). *Big media, little media.* Beverly Hills, CA: Sage.

Self, J. (1985). *Microcomputers in education: A critical appraisal of educational software.* Brighton, MA: Harvester Press.

Sheingold, K. (1991). Restructuring for learning with technology: The potential for synergy. *Phi Delta Kappan, 73*(1), 17–27.

Strickland, J. (1990). *Making informed decisions: Management issue influencing computers in the classroom.* ERIC Document Reproduction Service, No. ED 316, 866.

Thomas, R. M. & Kobayashi, V. N. (Eds.). (1987). *Educational Technology.* New York: Pergamon Press.

Wilder, G. Z. & Fowles, M. (1992). Assessing the outcomes of computer-based instruction: The experience of Maryland. *Technological Horizons in Education Journal, 20*(2), 82–84.

Wilson, K. (1991). New tools for new learning opportunities. *Technology and Learning, 11*(7), 12–13.

Zappone, F. (1991). Using technology in education: Steps to the future. *Computers in the Schools, 8,* 83–87.

Zimmerman, B. J. (1990). Self-regulated learning and academic achievement: An overview. *Educational Psychologist, 25,* 3–17.

Zorfass, J. (1993). Curriculum: A critical factor in technology integration. *The Computing Teacher, 20*(5), 14–15.

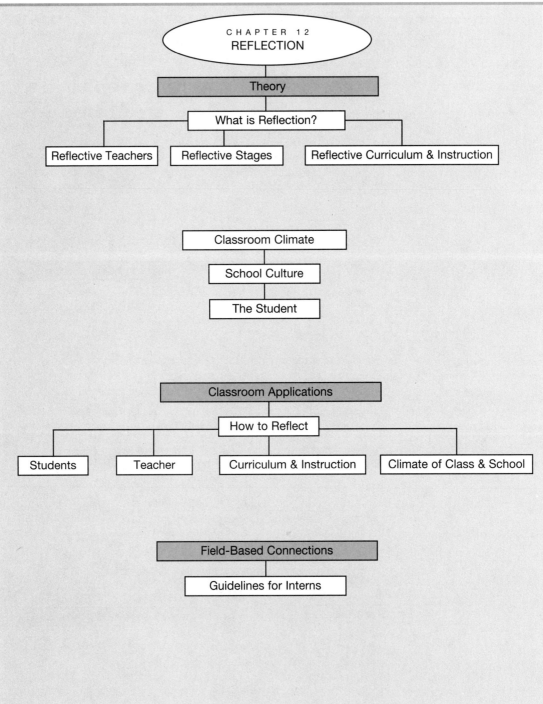

CHAPTER 12
REFLECTION

Theory

What is Reflection?

Reflective Teachers   Reflective Stages   Reflective Curriculum & Instruction

Classroom Climate

School Culture

The Student

Classroom Applications

How to Reflect

Students   Teacher   Curriculum & Instruction   Climate of Class & School

Field-Based Connections

Guidelines for Interns

12

Reflection

Introduction

Experience, knowledge, theory, and practice frame meaning and purpose for reflection. Reflection helps create better teachers, who can articulate their purpose and vision for all facets of education. To improve as a teacher, you must internalize the teaching and learning process. Reflection is a meaningful and useful activity that keeps your beliefs and the needs of the students in balance. The inquiring teacher seeks solutions to educational problems through the process of reflection.

No longer should teachers remain in isolation, depending only upon technical or external advice to solve their classroom problems. Most teachers want to become better and improve. For lasting improvement, teachers must internalize technical advice and reflect on personal beliefs to improve their instruction and student learning. When reflecting, teachers need to identify, plan, and take action to seek their own solutions to everyday problems and dilemmas.

Reflection is more than thinking; it is a much deeper process. Knowledge is needed in the theories and practices of teaching before reflection can fine tune and develop your personal educational belief system. To understand and organize reflective teaching practices, these categories are discussed: the teacher, the nature of curriculum and instruction, the climate of the classroom, the culture of the school, and the student. Following is a detailed example of how a first-year teacher used reflection to improve instruction and student learning.

Reflection Example

It was my first year as an elementary school teacher, and we were about six months into the school year. My students and I had gone through many exciting units of study. Each unit was multi-disciplinary with many active lessons designed around the various learning styles. At the end of each lesson, activity, and unit, I would summarize. I quite cleverly (I thought) added a twist to my closures. I would ask the students to summarize the finer points! Yes, I was quite pleased with the progress we were making.

Then came the fateful night. I was sitting at home leafing through a journal when an article on reflection caught my eye. When I finished reading, I was content that I had been reflecting. Of course, since my students could summarize the salient facts, they too must have been reflecting. During the week, however, I began to experience nagging doubts. I decided that I would design an activity for my students that would put my mind to rest. I spent several hours that weekend writing open-ended questions that would require students to reflect on our units of study to answer. I would allow the students to choose one. I was so excited on Monday as I watched the students take pen to paper, and write several pages in response. I could hardly wait to read them. I hurried home that night. Cradling the papers, I curled up on the couch to savor the fruits of my labor. I was not prepared for the responses I was about to read. The first paper I picked up was a student's reflections on George Washington. She had been asked to choose a great American we had studied, reflect on all she now knew, then write why she felt this person was important to American history. She had introduced her paper by detailing the close friendship between George and Abraham Lincoln. She had cleverly woven facts she knew about each man throughout her accounts of their many escapades together. Not only had Lincoln been Washington's closest military advisor in his campaign against the British, but Lincoln's death had caused Washington to die from a bro-

ken heart. I read each word torn, not knowing whether to laugh or cry. We had made time lines, drawn maps, and reenacted scenes from history. For goodness sake—the students had even summarized! What had gone wrong?

Thankfully, not all of the students had arrived at such drastic understandings. Still, there was enough confusion to warrant a serious contemplative period on my part. Talking with my students the next week gave us all new perspectives. From that time on, reflection has been a part of all classroom activity. Students spend time reflecting, both verbally and in writing, as we learn new concepts. Guidance is given at the first of the year to help students reap the greatest benefits from the process. I too spend time reflecting on all elements of the learning experiences I provide, and the interactions they create.

The difference has been phenomenal. By reflecting on their learning, students develop metacognitive skills, and often pinpoint their own confusions. They glean new conceptual insights and formulate questions for further exploration. By monitoring the journals where students record their thoughts, teachers can look for misconceptions. They can also better understand the thinking strategies employed by their students. Teachers will find that reflection helps them continually refine the entire learning environment. Reflection encourages teachers to travel beyond lesson plans and grades to focus on student learning. It is a journey that benefits all stake-holders and fosters lifelong learning.

Nancy Robinson
First-Year Teacher

Use this example as a model to refer to as you read through and think about this chapter.

▶ THEORY

What is Reflection?

Reflection is not a new idea. Socrates said, "The unexamined life is not worth living." In *How We Think: A Restatement of the Relation of Reflective Thinking to the Educative Process* (1933), John Dewey referred to reflective thinking as the "active, persistent, and careful consideration of any belief or supposed form of knowledge in light of the grounds that support it."

There is a knowledge base for teaching that provides information, not answers. Knowledge alone is not enough for good teaching and it cannot prescribe decisions teachers need to make in their classroom (Lampart & Clark, 1990). In the past, many researchers tried to provide only technical answers to teacher dilemmas. This advise was external; passed on to classroom teachers from educators outside the school culture. Because of the complexity of teaching, many studies today are beginning to examine teachers for solutions to common problems. This current research evolves from the teacher's internal experiences and interpretation of the process of teaching and learning. This process, which is difficult to define, is termed "reflection" (Sparks-Langer & Colton, 1991).

Definitions of reflection vary. One is the practice or act of analyzing actions, decisions or products by focusing on the process of achieving them (Killion & Todnem, 1991). Ross (1987) defines reflection as a way to think about education that involves the ability to make rational choices while assuming the responsibility for those choices. Sparks-Langer and Colton (1991) define the lack or opposite

of reflection as the mindless following of unexamined practice or principles. Although there is disagreement in defining reflection, researchers do agree that reflection is necessary. Reflection is defined in this text as a strategy to help make thoughtful decisions about the theory and practice of teaching.

Reflection relies heavily on the use of questions. Some initial questions are: What do I do in the classroom? What does this mean? How did I come to be this way? How might I do things differently? These questions posed by Smythe (1989) are intended to identify a problem or dilemma and then initiate problem-solving action. According to Schon (1987), when you start questioning actions and results, they begin to solve problems immediately. Self-directed questions encourage teachers to identify what needs to be changed, test understandings, and try out new ideas and actions. This reflective process is cyclical, as shown in Figure 12–1.

This cycle of reflection involves several steps that are not distinct, but overlap. Planning initiates the process and provides a way to identify a problem or dilemma that teachers need to resolve. The next step in the cycle is to act and observe what happens. Throughout the entire cycle, teachers continue to use questions and assess the results of the plan based on the collection of student and teaching evidence. Eventually, this process and cycle becomes internalized (Ross et al., 1993).

Schon (1983) refers to problem-solving as a natural part of reflection. In this process, teachers name the problem and then frame the context for examination. Once a teacher identifies the problem and framework, a basis is established for solving other problems. Taking action is a must, to solve problems in education; simply thinking about problems

FIGURE 12–1   The Reflective Process

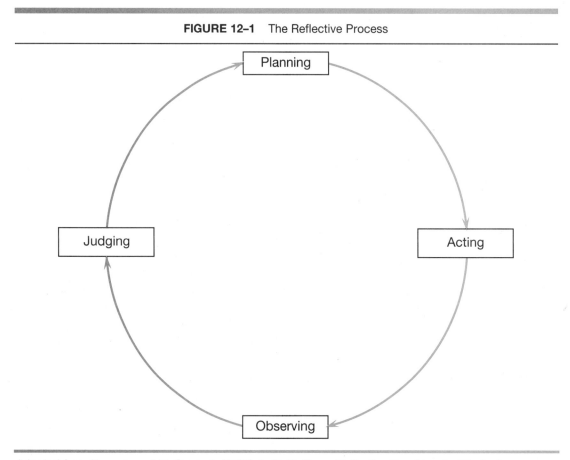

Adapted from Kemmis and McTaggart, (1982), in D. D. Ross, *Reflective Teaching for Student Empowerment: Elementary Curriculum and Methods*, New York: Macmillan, 19.

means little until something is done to change them.

Evaluating the results of reflection helps teachers to observe the effect of reflection. Numerous studies, Carnegie Forum (1986), the Holmes Group (1986), Schon (1987), and Peterson (1988), encourage reflection as an essential element of educational improvement. Even though reflection is a difficult practice to measure, studies show that its use results in improvement in teacher thinking, planning, and decision-making (Clark & Peterson, 1986).

Reflective Teachers

Before reflective teachers are discussed, a better understanding can be developed by examining the typical behavior of a non-reflective teacher. These teachers rely on routine behavior and are guided by impulse, tradition, and authority to simplify their professional lives while uncritically accepting everyday reality in schools (Posner, 1993). Every school, class, and student is different, yet non-reflective teachers seldom change goals to meet varying needs. They establish dull routines and become defensive to promote the status quo (Burbules, 1988). Reflective teachers, on the other hand, constantly question, experiment, re-examine, and improve their teaching practices (Grant & Zeichner, 1984).

Teachers have the ultimate responsibility to help students become functional and empowered citizens of a democratic society (Moore et al., 1987; Tom, 1984; Webb & Sherman, 1989 Zeichner & Liston, 1987;). In a democratic classroom, students need to become responsible for their choices and actions. Similarly, reflective teachers need to take responsibility for their ethical, moral, and rational choices about what and how to teach (Goodman, 1984; Ross, 1987; Zeichner & Liston, 1987). In order to produce democratic citizens, a reflective teacher constantly re-examines answers to the following questions: What do children within a democratic society need to know and be able to do? Which teaching strategies promote this learning? Are my teaching practices based on ethical commitments to children such as caring and/or equity? (Ross et al., 1993). Reflective teachers are responsible for their choices and expect the same from their students.

Reflective Stages

Although different definitions of reflection exist, most researchers agree that all professionals go through developmental stages. Sparks-Langer and Colton (1991) define three stages of reflection. The first, or cognitive stage, relates to how the teacher uses knowledge of content matter, pedagogical methods, curriculum, learning styles, educational pur-

poses, ends, and aims. These are organized through the formation of a schemata, or network of related facts, constructed through the experience of the teacher. Basically, the schemata is what works or does not work. A teacher's schemata is constructed through experiences in the classroom and meaning is created out of what is perceived to be true (Greeno et al., 1979). Since assimilation and accommodation of experiences is personal and difficult to articulate, the schemata of experienced teachers is not easily transferred to beginning teachers. Experienced teachers, however, can help develop an awareness of pedagogy, but teachers need to reflect and decide what works best for them.

The second stage is critical reflection. This requires action to choose the best means to an end. For example, the teacher who chooses cooperative groups encourages a more equitable, accepting society within the classroom. Critical reflection considers the explicit, as well as the implicit, implications of choices. At this stage, teachers examine issues of ethics, morals, and justice by thinking about the role of the school in a democratic society. Critical reflection not only looks at the pedagogical decisions of such strategies as ability grouping, tracking, competitive grading, and management, but also looks at the implied message these choices give to the students (Sparks-Langer & Colton, 1991).

The third and final stage of reflection is narrative writing. Writing helps experienced as well as novice teachers verbalize their thought processes to reach a decision or another set of questions. Through journal writing, it is easier to document and understand the thought processes and developmental

---

FIGURE 12–2 Highlights of Research on Teachers' Reflective Thinking

---

Several implications can be derived from the review of research on teachers' reflective thinking:

- Teacher educators can foster growth in cognitive reflection through micro-teaching with post-teaching reflection journals, teaching with self-analysis of video/audiotapes, action research observation and analysis of selected teaching episodes, coaching, and assessment and discussion of student learning.

- Critical reflection may be promoted through close examination of cases that illustrate particular aspects of context, pedagogy, content, ethical/moral dilemmas, and other elements of teaching and learning that will help teachers develop a rich, flexible repertoire of ideas, attitudes, and skills.

- Teachers need opportunities to construct their own narrative context-based meaning from information provided by research, theoretical frameworks or outside experts.

- A person's preconceptions of teaching, learning, and the purposes of schooling will influence greatly how he or she interprets courses, workshops, and personal teaching experiences. These beliefs must be examined critically from various perspectives to allow for a flexible and thoughtful approach to teaching.

- Future research needs to explore how teachers interpret, give meaning to, and make decisions about their experiences in schools. Teachers themselves will need to be included as co-investigators in such research.

Reprinted with permission, G. M. Sparks-Lander and A. B. Colton, (1991), "Synthesis of Research on Teacher's Reflective Thinking," *Educational Leadership, 48*(6), 37-44.

---

stages of reflection. Writing clarifies and communicates to others the results of teacher action. Figure 12–2 shows various implications of reflective thinking related to these three stages (Sparks-Langer & Colton, 1991).

Posner (1993) suggests six basic reflection questions that affect the stages and development of reflection.

1. *Control.* Who should control what goes on in teaching, and what should be the range of their control?

2. *Diversity.* How unique are learners and how should one treat learners on the basis of their differences?

3. *Learning.* How do people learn in terms of both the process of learning and the motivation for it?

4. *Role.* How formal (versus personal) should teachers be in their relations with the learners?

5. *School and Society.* To what extent do the sources of and solutions to teachers'

problems require structural changes in schools or society?

6. *Knowledge.* What is knowledge? Is knowledge a given set of facts, concepts, and generalizations to be transmitted, or is it more a personal or social construction developed by processes of reasoning and negotiation?

Differences in students, attitudes, experience, and beliefs result in different decisions for action. Talking and sharing with other teachers (collaboration) helps beginning teachers with the reflective process. Henderson (1992) supports collaborative inquiry to support shared community reflection. Canning (1991) also encourages collaborative and collegial reflection and offers some guiding questions to ask each other in professional dialogue:

1. Can you talk more about that?

2. Why do you think that happens?

3. What evidence do you have about that?

4. What does this remind you of?

5. What if it happened this way?

6. Do you see a connection between this and that?

7. How else could you approach that?

8. What do you want to happen?

9. How could you do that?

Reflective questioning through various stages with self and others can develop beliefs and actions to improve curriculum and instruction.

Reflective Curriculum and Instruction

A major goal of reflection in curriculum and instruction is for the teacher to take charge of the curriculum to give the teacher ownership and empowerment. While teachers do not often get to choose what to teach, they are able to choose how to teach it. Teachers inevitably encounter constraints by state and school district policies, administrator styles, and educational philosophy. Through reflection, teachers can find ways to enhance and enrich the classroom. Reflection helps teachers analyze and choose instructional strategies that increase student learning. No matter what constraints, reflection increases teachers' growth in curriculum and instruction (Ariav, 1991).

Onosko (1992) gives the following characteristics to outstanding teachers when they plan their curriculum and instruction. Outstanding teachers engage in sustained examination of a few topics, rather than a superficial coverage of many. Their lessons display coherence and continuity. They ask challenging questions or tasks of the students, and the students offer explanations and reasons for their conclusions. Finally, the teacher models thoughtfulness and has a longer wait time to encourage student thinking.

If students are to become productive members of a democratic society, curriculum and instruction must provide opportunities to use analytical and critical thinking. Learning only facts will not ensure student success in our ever-changing society. Students need to access and analyze information. Mumford (1991) wrote that analytical or critical thinking is an approach, process, and response to problems or issues that call for intensive scrutiny of the evidence and arguments. Curriculum and instruction must challenge teachers and students to think and make decisions.

When reflecting about instructional methods, Surbeck et al. (1991) ask their student teachers to write about:

1. their beliefs and background knowledge about teaching;

2. how such information applied to field experience and/or other classrooms;

3. how children responded, or might respond, to classroom practices; and

4. their personal reflections and feelings about the teaching/learning process.

Once you have an idea about how you desire to teach, you can then begin making decisions about what to teach. Questions, such as "What should we teach?" "How should we teach it? How can we organize it?" "How can we evaluate it?" are ways to reflect about curriculum and instruction.

One way to institute change and improvement is to develop action plans. Figure 12–3 shows a model to help teachers develop and use a reflective action plan. Use this action model as a framework to solve problems or improve teaching and learning (Levesque & Prosser, 1993).

The first step in an action plan is to ask yourself, What will I change? Next, How will I do it? Third is, What will I need? The last step in this plan is to assess how it worked. Taking action upon your reflection is the key to effective and meaningful reflection. Onosko (1992) states, "thoughtful classroom practice requires thoughtful reflection on practice."

Classroom Climate

What happens in teachers' classrooms is influenced by what they think. Teachers act differently because of various belief systems (Clark & Yinger, 1977; Sykes, 1986; Zeichner & Liston, 1987). Unexamined beliefs about teaching and learning can hamper the climate of a classroom. Beliefs should be reflected and deliberate actions taken to achieve a positive climate.

Meyers (1986) believes that the tone and climate teachers establish in their classrooms determines the success or failure of critical thinking. Students must be coached into the roles of discussing, inquiring, and problem-solving. Teaching students critical and creative thinking requires teachers to reflect themselves and then teach their students these strategies (Eby, 1992). A reflective teacher asks, "How will I provide safe physical and psychological environments for thinking and learning?"

A shared sense of purpose by the teacher and students begins with, and is fostered by, the teacher. Students should enter the classroom every day with expectations of success and leave with feelings of achievement (Henderson, 1992). Cooperation and negotiation are key elements of a reflective classroom climate. The reflective teacher constantly re-examines these ideals to insure a success climate in the classroom.

Achieving a success climate involves a re-evaluation of traditional roles in the classroom, since the teacher becomes a coach who encourages student reflection and responsibility. Along with this responsibility comes a degree of freedom for students to make choices to prepare them for responsible and active

FIGURE 12–3   Developing an Action Plan for Reflective Change

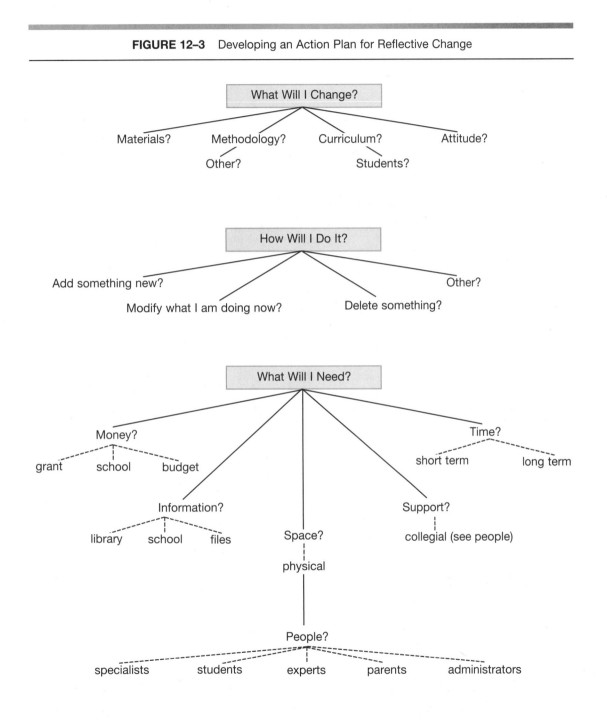

FIGURE 12–3   continued

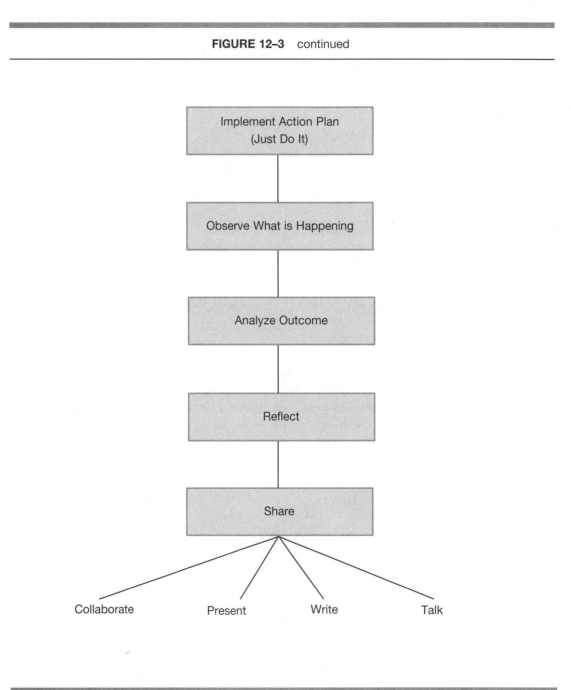

Reprinted with permission, J. A. Levesque and T. M. Prosser, (1993), paper presented at the Association for Supervision and Curriculum Conference, Washington DC.

citizenship roles outside of the classroom (Henderson, 1992). Reflection and responsibility take time, but must be nurtured so students become aware of their schoolwide importance.

School Culture

School cultures that encourage reflective teachers are characterized as a place where principals support the educational decisions and judgments made by teachers (Eby, 1992). Just as students are more committed to classroom rules and procedures they have taken part in developing, so are teachers more committed to schoolwide decisions when they have been involved in the decision-making.

Sergiovanni (1984), in describing school culture, asserts that a sense of purpose rallies people to a common cause, where work has meaning and life is significant. Teachers and students work together and with spirit, where accomplishments are readily recognized. Principals must support the vision and purpose of a school's culture. A school's vision and purpose is revised and updated through continual reflection and re-examination. The school's culture needs to create an atmosphere where teachers can openly question their thinking through collegial disagreement without personalizing the differences (Patterson, 1993).

The responsibility of the principal is to reassure teachers that the school culture is one of collaboration and shared responsibility for achievement of the school's mission. In many schools, however, teachers are left alone to work out their own problems. Many studies show that this isolation is counterproductive to reflection (Florio-Ruane, 1986; Greene, 1978, 1988; Grimmet & Erickson, 1988; Kennedy,

1989; Schon, 1983; Zeichner, 1981). Reflection is more meaningful when collaboration and teacher dialogue (oral or written) is involved. Schon (1983) asserts that teachers need time and encouragement to communicate insights and share them.

The Student

As previously mentioned, a goal of teaching is to help children become democratic citizens. Students need to also become reflective thinkers (Killion & Todnem, 1991). Therefore, teaching requires an ethical and moral commitment to student empowerment. Student empowerment is defined as students who are eager, engaged, successful learners, able to determine their own futures, and to actively participate in making society a better place. To become empowered, students need a wealth of knowledge complimented by a positive and inquiring attitude (Ross et al., 1993).

A teacher must understand the student's point of view, since knowledge is constructed, not transmitted (Ross et al., 1993). Developing another dimension of achieving student empowerment through reflection is through literacy. Ross et al. (1993) define literacy as the knowledgeable use of systems of communicating. Students have the tools to enable them to question, wonder, and evaluate.

Four elements of good thinking, according to Ross et al. (1993), include: disposition, knowledge, critical and creative capacity, and meta-cognition. In today's democratic society, teachers need to emphasize lifelong learning and thinking skills that help students acquire and process information within an ever-changing and growing field of knowledge (McTight & Schollenberger, 1985). Good thinkers will reflect, take control of their lives, and shape their futures.

Students, like teachers, should experience narrative reflection by writing or dialoguing about experiences. Teachers are a role models for students and reflection helps students learn. Reflective teachers committed to professional growth have the background to provide the best instruction for their students (Bagenstos, 1975; Copeland, 1986; Korthagen, 1985; Zeichner & Liston, 1987).

Conclusion to Theory

The process of reflection involves identifying the problem, acting on the problem, and evaluating the results. Reflection is more than thinking and requires rationale and deliberate thought to produce change and improvement.

Teacher reflection initiates action research. Collaboration and professional dialogue helps teachers share and narrate concerns and issues. Teachers must sort through pedagogy (cognitive element) to examine their beliefs (critical element) and communicate their results and experiences (narrative element).

Reflection helps to improve curriculum and instruction. The complex interrelatedness of teaching and learning must be examined. Teachers' decisions about curriculum and instruction are necessary to meet the needs of students and the purposes of teaching and learning.

The environment of the classroom and the culture of the school is impacted by reflective teachers. Identifying goals and visions sets a tone for success and positive experiences. Ways to make the classroom and school meaningful are achieved through reflective examination.

Students shape reasons for reflection. Through thoughtful analysis, a better understanding of students' needs can be achieved. Through reflection, students can learn an important problem-solving, lifelong skill.

▶ CLASSROOM APPLICATIONS

Introduction

Most teachers desire improvement and there are two major ways that this can be done. One is technical and the other is reflective. These two categories have both strengths and weaknesses; when used together, they create a powerful potential for professional growth.

The first means of improvement involves technical advice, which depends upon an individual from outside the school coming to your class to suggest ways to improve curriculum, instruction, classroom management or even educational beliefs. Technical advice can be extremely valuable if you internalize and think about its value and way you can incorporate the advice involved. In the beginning teaching experiences, the university professor, mentor teacher, and peers can offer valuable insight to educational concerns and problems. Technical guidance, on the other hand, provides a beneficial perspective to help evaluate your performance. Technical information can be useful because knowledge is needed to make rational decisions. Keep an open mind about the advise, because the way you receive information is certainly important; what you do with it is even more important.

A second way to improve is through reflection. Reflection is an internal process where you develop skills to make decisions about what is best for your classroom and students. This process requires time and can be difficult, but for lasting improvement and change, it has to happen within the context of your personal educational belief system. Two important support elements will help you become and continue to be a reflective teacher.

These aspects involve collaboration and dialogue. To collaborate, you need to find and value teacher friends within the school or district. By collaborating, you have an audience with which to share situations or dilemmas that you want to change in your school or classroom. Collaboration develops collegiality and shared vision to promote thoughtful educational reform.

Dialogue is an important part of collaboration, where you must constantly discuss feelings, attitudes, and situations that you encounter in your day to day teaching tasks. Most professionals take time to dialogue and think through the kinds of issues and problems that face them in their careers. Teachers are no exception. Collaborating and professional dialogue are two very essential ingredients to help you solve problems, make decisions, and reflect about teaching and learning.

How to Reflect

Throughout research, there are various models and definitions of reflection. Reflection for the practitioner does not require a complex series of steps. In fact, most reflective practices do not have clear lines of distinction; they overlap in many of the stages. Basically, there are three major steps of reflection.

The first is to *identify* a problem to be solved. Once a problem or dilemma is identified, then you develop a plan to solve the problem. Once the plan is thought out, the second major step would be *implementation*. A plan has to be used to determine effects and results. Through action, many process skills are used: collecting evidence, observing, analyzing, evaluating, and so forth. The process of taking action on your problem leads you to pass judgment about your evidence, so the third stage is *evaluation*. When passing judgment, the evaluation of results enables you to modify or enact change and improvement.

Benefits of Reflection

There are many benefits of reflection and the most important ones will be identified by you. Reflection is a satisfying experience because teachers assume the responsibility for their own classroom problems. Reflection does not solve every problem because teaching is a complex activity and occasionally some situations cannot be changed or improved for reasons beyond your control. What reflection does, in many instances, is help you find "better" ways of doing things you identified as problematic. Reflection is not a panacea, but a means to analyze educational problems to fine tune your personal educational belief system. Following are reflective questions that relate to the previous chapter in this book. These questions are organized into the following broad categories: students, teacher, curriculum and instruction, and climate and culture of the school. While it is virtually impossible to identify all reflective questions, the questions presented in this section were written by practicing first-year and veteran classroom teachers. They believed these questions were most important in their first year of teaching.

Students

Teacher reflection should improve student achievement. The teacher's role is to empower students and teach them strategies to become critical thinkers. One way to accomplish this task is to ask students the what, how, and why of their thoughts. For example, when you encounter behavior problems, ask students about the behavior and what could be done to change their actions. In the content areas, ask students about their learning. Ask the what, how, and why concerning their perspectives of learning.

Reflective Questions: Students

These teacher-developed questions intend to guide your reflection about student learning.

- What does the learner already know?
- What learning styles/talents do my students have?
- How will I modify assignments for students?
- How can I teach students to think through their own problems?
- How can I get the students to apply what they know?
- What ways are students verbalizing their thinking? Do I encourage this process by modeling consideration of their thoughts and actions?
- What techniques, such as journal writing, encourage thinking?
- How will I question students about concepts?

- How can I entice the students' interest through question-driven curriculum and encourage them to ask meaningful and productive questions, rather than questions like, "Will this be on the test?" "What is the correct answer?"
- How can I encourage analytical and reflective thinking?

Teacher

As a reflective teacher, you must avoid falling into a rut. To avoid this, you must read current educational research, collaborate, and experiment with strategies that maximize student potential. Begin reflecting about your teaching beliefs by identifying concerns, formulating questions, applying knowledge, talking with others, and acting on your choices.

Reflective Questions: Teacher

Think about your experiences, beliefs, and knowledge gained as you reflect on the following questions written by a second-year teacher.

- What can I do to improve my current teaching practices?
- How will I keep up-to-date with educational research?
- How can I avoid falling into a routine?
- Am I keeping my strengths and weaknesses in mind as I plan classroom methodologies and management systems?
- Are my teaching practices based upon democratic ideals of fairness, justice, and equity?

- What ways can I empower my students to be functional members of the twenty-first century?
- What do children in a democratic society need to be able to do?
- How can I collaborate with other teachers most effectively?
- Can I verbalize why I teach the way I do?
- Do I enjoy teaching and love students?

Curriculum and Instruction

A main goal of reflection in curriculum and instruction is to meet students' needs. Selecting instructional strategies that meet the needs and goals of the lesson requires thoughtful planning. As you become familiar with a variety of teaching strategies, reflection will help you analyze the effective ways that you use to successfully engage students in learning.

Assessment of curriculum and instruction is crucial to improvement and growth. Decide on ways to assess traditionally, as well as authentically. Use performance-based standards in a variety of situations.

Because of rapidly changing technology, students will need experience in how to access data instead of just lower-level skills instruction. The technological implications to the classroom, teacher, and students deserve reflection.

When deciding what to teach, selecting the content can be difficult; it can be helpful to analyze textbooks and state guidelines for a content and skill framework. Carefully reflect on and study the skills and content to align the curriculum to your instructional beliefs. You can maximize student achievement by complementing your curricular expectations

with your pedagogical choices. Keep modifications in mind for individual student interests and abilities.

Reflective Questions: Curriculum and Instruction

These questions intend to initiate reflection about the many issues of curriculum and instruction.

- What is the relevance of my curriculum to the students' lives?
- What instructional strategies are best for student learning and enjoyment?
- How does management relate to instruction?
- Where in the curriculum can parents help the students and the teacher?
- How accountable should the teacher be to the standardized test scores?
- How will reflection and higher-order thinking skills be incorporated into curriculum and instruction?
- When would constructivism and active learning be appropriate?
- How can student discussion be improved during questioning?
- What role will technology have in curriculum and instruction?
- Who will understand and listen to curriculum and instruction concerns and problems?
- How will multicultural and special needs students be addressed in curriculum and instruction?
- How will organization and planning save time?

Climate of the Classroom and Culture of the School

The total school environment will be directly affected by the importance you place on reflection. As you reflect about the classroom and school, you should share your positive thoughts with students because it shows the students what you believe. The school vision and mission is directly related to the attitudes of the community, staff, teachers, students, and parents. Working deliberately to keep positive attitudes in the school culture is an ongoing activity for the reflective teacher. Teacher talk is upbeat and professional dialogue is common in a reflective environment.

Each classroom and teacher sets the tone for the school culture. High expectations, success, and a prevailing mood that every student can learn starts in the classroom. Establish a democratic climate, where students are encouraged to inquire, cooperate, make decisions, and strive for self-directed learning. Keep in mind, also, that the school where you teach will encourage or limit your professional growth and beliefs. Creating and monitoring a positive school environment is challenging work.

Reflective Questions: Climate and Culture

The following questions are meant to direct your reflection for creating a positive classroom climate and school culture.

- What role should students play in developing rules and consequences?
- How can a democratic environment be organized and initiated in the classroom and school?
- How do school discussions focus on positive attributes of community, parents, teachers, and students?
- What are the levels of support for collaboration and a shared vision of success?
- What factors contribute to stress, burn out or low morale?
- How compassionate and caring is the school culture?
- What kind of teacher/student dialogue occurs in the school?
- Who has the authority for decision-making?
- What are the criteria for good school culture and climate?

▶ FIELD-BASED CONNECTIONS

Introduction

Reflection links knowledge to practice. The field-based connection is absolutely necessary to apply and evaluate reflective thought. The reflective cycle requires an authentic context to apply the theory to practice. By now, interns and practicum students should realize that there is no simple answer to everyday teaching dilemmas in the school.

Guidelines for Interns

The field-based experience provided an opportunity for you to discover and learn how theory and application shaped your personal educational belief system. Now is a good time to collaborate, look back, dialogue, and share your pedagogical beliefs. The following activities refer to previous field-based suggestions of portfolio, integrated unit, and journal. These activities were integrated throughout the book and were selected because they provide a platform for you to demonstrate and articulate your accomplishments. Choose one or two suggested activities that you believe best synthesizes and evaluates your experience and performance as an intern. Use the suggested questions in this chapter to help you reflect.

1. *Portfolio:* Think of a theme for your portfolio. Relate your pedagogical beliefs about students, curricula, instruction, teachers, culture, and other chapter topics you decide best reflect your experiences. Think of strategies you could use to present, in no more than fifteen minutes, your portfolio to the class, a peer or a district personnel officer when you interview for a teaching position.

   Select and collect students' work that demonstrates your growth and the results of your teaching. The evidence in your portfolio should exemplify or mirror your beliefs. Check the student artifacts to see if your beliefs are in line with your actions. For example, you would have a difficult time building a portfolio case for a constructivist theme if the bulk of the students' products consists of worksheets.

2. *Integrated Unit:* Copy and share your unit with a peer student or teams of students. Together, develop an assessment questionnaire you can use to reflect over each other's as well as your own units. Use some of the questions from the Classroom Applications section of this chapter to help guide your oral review. Compare classroom management, instructional strate-

gies, questions, assessment, and technology when you reflect. Dialogue and share your experience teaching the unit, and describe successes and concerns when you taught the unit during the internship.

3. *Journal:* Review the four guiding questions outlined in Chapter 1. Closely examine your responses in the journal at the beginning of the experience and the end of the experience. Summarize your growth by writing a pedagogical creed that reflects and articulates the beliefs and actions you stand for as a teacher. Share your pedagogical creed with your mentor teacher, peers, university professor or district personnel officer when interviewing for a teaching position. Refer back to your creed periodically to adjust and focus throughout your teaching career.

▶ CHAPTER CLOSURE

Summary

Reflection is an age-old strategy. Confusion exists over the definition, but experts agree on its need and utility for improving teaching and learning. Teachers change and improve by developing action plans based on reflection. There are different, but basic, stages to promote inquiring reflective teachers. The reflective process involves identifying the problem, planning, taking action, observing, collecting evidence, and evaluating results.

The entire schooling process benefits from reflection. Reflective teachers become empowered and gain autonomy in resolving classroom concerns. Decisions and inquiry into curriculum and instruction result in classroom strategies that maximize students' involvement and learning. School culture and classroom climates become positive, with higher expectations that focus on student achievement. Students gain problem-solving abilities when they, like teachers, begin to reflect on their life and learning.

Reflection is not a panacea, but offers insights and solutions to make schools and classrooms better. Reflective teachers constantly question and inquire, to make decisions that will make classrooms and schools a quality place for teachers, students, and parents.

Chapter Discussion Questions

1. What are the important elements of reflection? Why is it important?

2. How are planning, acting, observing, and judging interrelated?

3. What role do collaboration and teacher dialogue have to reflective teachers?

4. What is the value of questions in the reflective process?

5. How do you see your beliefs contributing to success in the classroom and school?

6. Why should you compare your beliefs to the philosophy of the school and grade-level teachers?

7. What questions are important for you to ask when you interview for your first teaching position?

8. Evaluate your ability and desire to be an inquiring and reflective teacher.

CASE STUDIES

The case study example can be used for analysis in small or large groups. Questions follow the case study as suggestions for discussion.

CASE STUDY 12–1: by Sara Sauer, Practicum Student

Looking back, I cannot remember a time when I did not want to be a teacher. As a little girl, I used to make up tests and give them to my stuffed animals. I knew that what I wanted to do when I grew up would involve children, so I started working with them at an early age. In the fifth grade, I began to baby sit because I loved being around children so much. Before participating in my practicum, I truly believed my love of children would be enough to make me a good teacher. However, after participating in the practicum this past semester, I realize that, while a love for children is important in becoming a good teacher, it is not enough. Working with students can be a lot harder than liking them. I found out the latter when I presented my first lesson to my third-grade practicum class.

The lesson I taught was a reading comprehension lesson. The book used in the lesson involved Indians, which was the subject the class was studying that week. The lesson plan involved reading the book to the students. Then after reading the book, I gave the students a ditto which would reinforce their understanding of the book, would review the different parts of speech, and would also show how a person can make his language more colorful by using different words to say the same thing (i.e., synonyms). It took a few hours to prepare the lesson. The lesson included creating and making a ditto for the students, making a large version of the ditto as an example for the students to model from, and making a couple of overheads to supplement the lesson. I felt that I was extremely prepared for this lesson. I had read the book for the lesson three times, had planned out how the lesson would run, and had gone over the dittos and visuals and how I would present them during the lesson. My feeling of preparedness ended as soon as I entered the classroom.

The first thing that occurred on arriving in the classroom was my teacher informing me I wouldn't be able to complete all of my lesson because the students had an assembly that day. I was surprised by this news, to say the least. I knew I would have to change the lesson I had so "skillfully" planned. I decided to calm down and attempt to do the best I could with the limited amount of time I had. I truly believed I would be able to utilize my time well. Unfortunately, the students had other plans.

First, the children were hyper and unfocused. This was due, in part, to the fact that they were excited about the assembly, but also because they were unable to go outside for recess that day. So sitting on the floor listening to someone reading a story was not a good way for them to utilize their excess energy. In fact, it was probably one of the worst activities they could have been involved in. Second, they wanted to ask a lot of questions. I believe question asking is good and important in the learning process; however, the students not only wanted to ask questions about the book, they also wanted to tell stories and ask questions about totally irrelevant items. Finally, to top everything off, they did not really understand the lesson I was trying to teach. In fact, I do not remember ever seeing so many blank faces in my entire life. Fortunately, through the grace of God, I had to stop because the students had to go to the assembly. Never have I been so happy for something to be over.

After that lesson, sitting in the cafeteria waiting for the assembly to begin, I felt like an utter failure. All the work I had put into the lesson seemed to be for nothing. I thought that my goal of becoming a teacher was nothing but a dream and that I had wasted the past year and a half trying to prepare for that field. My mentor teacher could see that I was distressed and had me write down what I thought was "good" about the lesson and what I thought was "bad." She told me the "good" side should be longer than the "bad" side. As I wrote the list, I had an easy time coming up with problems in the lesson and a difficult time coming up with positive items. However, after thinking for a while, I was able to come up with some positive aspects to the lesson. The latter helped rebuild my confidence and, by the time I returned to the classroom a few days later to present the rest of my lesson, I was mentally prepared to teach again. In fact, the second part of the lesson went relatively well and it helped me to see I might actually make a good teacher someday.

I learned a lot from presenting this lesson. First, I found out the lesson planned may not always work out the way it is supposed to. But part of being a teacher is being flexible and learning how to deal with this type of situation. Second, students are not always going to understand the lesson the first time it is presented to them. It may be necessary to stop and start over again. Third, students are not adults. A third-grader is not going to be able to control his behavior the same way a junior in college would. It may be necessary to change your plans to fit the children's mood. I do not mean stop teaching until the children calm down. Rather, have the students do an activity in which the students' attitudes can help and not be a hindrance to them. For example, on a day when the students are really hyper, it may be a good idea to do a math floor game or an art activity first. That way, the students can release some of their energy and later on they would be more prepared for a "focused" activity. Finally, I learned that working with students is hard work and it takes a lot of energy and patience.

I said at the start of this paper that loving children is an important part of being a good teacher. I still believe that is true. However, working with students involves much more than that. A teacher must be patient, caring, well-spoken, and understanding. A teacher must be willing to put heart-and-soul into the job. A teacher must not get too "down" when a lesson flops. Finally, a teacher has to realize that there are many "bad" parts to teaching, but that a lot of "good things" about teaching do exist. These "good things" outweigh the "bad things" a million to one, and the "good things" can give a teacher the strength to keep on going.

Case Study Discussion Questions

1. How does Sara connect the cognitive, critical, and narrative element of reflection?

2. What reflective evidence supports Sara's judgments?

3. In what ways can you relate to Sara's experience?

▶ REFERENCES

Ariav, T. (1991). Growth in teachers' curriculum knowledge through the process of curriculum analysis. *Journal of Curriculum and Supervision, 6*(3), 183–200.

Bagenstos, N. T. (1975). The teacher as inquirer. *The Educational Forum, 39,* 231–237.

Burbules, N. C. (1988). A theory of power in education. *Educational Theory, 36*(2), 95–114.

Canning, C. (1991). What teachers say about reflection. *Educational Leadership, 48*(6), 18–21.

Carnegie Forum on Education and the Economy. (1986). *A nation prepared: Teachers for the 21st century: A report of the task force on teaching as a profession.* Washington, DC: Carnegie Forum on Education and the Economy.

Clark, C. & Peterson. P. (1986). Teacher's thought processes. In M. Wittrock (Ed.), *Handbook of Research on Teaching.* New York: Macmillan.

Clark, C. M. & Yinger, R. J. (1977). Research on teacher thinking. *Curriculum Inquiry, 7*(4), 279–304.

Copeland, W. D. (1986). The RITE framework for teacher education: Preservice applications. In J. V. Hoffman and S. A. Edwards (Eds.), *Reality and reform in clinical teacher education.* New York: Random House.

Dewey, J. (1933). *How we think: A restatement of the relation of reflective thinking to the educative process.* Boston: D. C. Heath.

Eby, J. W. (1992). *Reflective planning, teaching, and evaluation for the elementary school.* New York: Macmillan.

Florio-Ruane, S. (1986) *Conversation and narrative in collaborative research.* (Occasional Paper Number 102). East Lansing, MI: Michigan State University, Institute for Research on Teaching.

Goodman, J. (1984). Reflection and teacher education: A case study and theoretical analysis. *Interchange, 15*(3), 9–26.

Grant, C. & Zeichner, K. (1984). On becoming a reflective teacher. In C. A. Grant (Ed.), *Preparing for reflective teaching.* Boston: Allyn and Bacon.

Greene, M. (1978). The dialectic of freedom. New York: Teachers College Press.

Greene, M. (1988). The matter of mystification: Teacher education in unquiet times. *Landscapes of Learning, 6*(2), 25-44.

Greeno, J. G., Magone, M., & Chaiklin, D. (1979). Theory of constructions and set in problem-solving. *Memory and Cognition, 7*(6), 445–461.

Grimmet, P. P. & Erickson, G. L. (Eds.). (1988). *Reflection in teacher education.* New York: Teachers College Press.

Henderson, J. G. (1992). *Reflective teaching: Becoming an inquiring educator.* New York: Macmillan.

Holmes Group, The. (1986). *Tomorrow's teachers: A report of the Holmes Group.* East Lansing, MI: The Holmes Group.

Kennedy, M. M. (1989). Reflection and the problem of national standards. *National Center for Research on Teacher Education Colloquy, 2*(2), 1–6.

Killion, J. P. and Todnem, G. R. (1991). A process of personal theory building. *Educational Leadership, 40*(6), 14–16.

Korthagen, F. A. (1985). Reflective teaching and the preservice teacher education in the Netherlands. *Journal of Teacher Education, 36*(5), 11–15.

Lampart, M. & Clark, C. M. (1990). Expert knowledge and expert thinking in teaching: A Response to Floden and Klinzing. *Educational Researcher, 19*(4), 21–23.

Levesque, J. A. & Prosser, T. M. (1993). Paper prepared for the Association for Supervision and Curriculum Development Conference, Washington, D. C.

McTight, J. & Schollenberger, J. (1985). Why teach thinking: A statement of rationale. In A. L. Costa (Ed.) *Developing Minds.* Alexandria, VA: Association for Supervision and Curriculum Development.

Meyers, C. (1986). *Teaching students to think critically.* San Francisco: Jossey-Bass.

Moore, J. R., Mintz, S. L., & Bierman, M. (1987). *Reflective inquiry: Teaching and thinking.* Paper prepared for the Reflective Inquiry Conference, Houston, TX.

Mumford, R. L. (1991). Teaching history through analytical and reflective thinking skills. *The Social Studies, 82*(5), 191–194.

Onosko, J. (1992). Exploring the thinking of thoughtful teachers. *Educational Leadership, 47*(7), 40–43.

Patterson, J. L. (1993). *Leadership for tomorrow's schools.* Alexandria, VA: Association for Supervision and Curriculum Development.

Peterson, P. (1988). Teachers and student's cognitional knowledge for classroom teaching and learning. *Educational Researcher, 17,* 9–18.

Posner, G. J. (1993). *Field experience: A guide to reflective teaching.* New York: Longman.

Ross, D. D. (1987). Reflective teaching: Meaning and implications for preservice teacher educators. Paper presented at the Reflective Inquiry Conference, Houston, TX.

Ross, D. D., Bondy, E., & Kyle, D. W. (1993). *Reflective teaching for student empowerment.* New York: Macmillan.

Schon, D. A. (1983). *The reflective practitioner: How professionals think in action.* New York: Basic Books.

Schon, D. A. (1987). *Educating the reflective practitioners: Towards a new design for teaching and learning in the professions.* San Francisco: Jossey-Bass.

Sergiovanni, T. (1984). Leadership and excellence in schooling. *Educational Leadership, 41(5),* 4–13.

Smythe, J. (1989). Developing and sustaining critical reflection in teacher education. *Journal of Teacher Education, 40*(2), 2–9.

Sparks-Langer, G. M., & Colton, A. B. (1991). Synthesis of research on teacher's reflective thinking. *Educational Leadership, 48*(6), 37–44.

Surbeck, E., Han, E. P., & Moyer, J. E. (1991). Assessing reflective responses in journals. *Educational Leadership, 48*(6), 25–27.

Sykes, G. (1986). Teaching as reflective practice. In K. A. Sirotnik and J. Oakes (Eds.), *Critical perspectives on the organization and improvement of schooling.* Boston: Kluwer Nijhoff Publishing.

Tom, A. (1984). *Teaching as a moral craft.* New York: Longman.

Zeichner, K. (1981). Reflective teaching and field-based experience in teacher education. *Interchange, 12,* 1–22.

Zeichner, K. M. & Liston, D. P. (1987). Teaching student teacher to reflect. *Harvard Educational Review, 57,* 23–48.

Sample
Curriculum Units

The Holocaust: Forget Them Not

by Victoria Desmond and Cara Weiss
Preservice Teachers and Master Degree Candidates, State University of New York,
 College at New Paltz

Philosophy

The Topic and its Importance

Only five decades ago, some of the most senseless crimes in history were committed in the name of creating a perfect "race" of people. After Germany's defeat in World War I, the country was divided. The economy was shattered and there was massive unemployment. Hitler rose to power with promises to alleviate the societal problems and began a massive propaganda campaign against the Jews, who were easy targets of scapegoating. The horrors of World War II, genocide, concentration camps, destroyed cities, starvation . . . could have all been avoided (Taylor, 1974). Because these horrors were carried out, it is our job as educators to teach our youth in order to ensure that they do not happen again.

Developmental Appropriateness

According to Piaget's cognitive developmental stages, children between the ages of eleven and twelve are in a transition from the concrete operational stage of development to the formal operational stage. Their reliance on the physical must develop into an understanding of the abstract. This transition is best fostered through exploration and problem-solving activities. Such exploration should develop critical thinking skills as well as socialized thought (Rielly & Lewis, 1983). A study of the Holocaust would meet the developmental needs of the learner who is forming the ability to think critically and has the skills to understand concepts.

The lessons of the Holocaust would develop the child's current level of morality, which is focused on law and order. Through problem posing and exploring their own contradictions, children are determined to advance their stage of moral development (Hass & Parkay, 1993, Chap. 3). The Holocaust raises many moral issues and dilemmas that will facilitate the process of moral development and have students reach higher levels of moral reasoning.

Societal Importance

According to John Dewey, school has an intimate relationship with the society it serves (Ornstein & Levine, 1989). If this is so, the critical thinking and questioning that emerge from this unit will lead to desirable social actions that change the restrictions society implies. Currently, "our society is tied up in a battle of survival that depends on acceptance of ones' own kind and rejection of the stranger" (Hass & Parkay, 1993, Chap. 2). This xenophobia, the fear and hatred of strangers, is harmful to our society. We need to educate our children to accept and respect others as different, not inferior. By teaching the Holocaust, we can combat this by raising social consciousness and awareness to levels of tolerance for all people.

It is important to remember that education is an institution of society. It is used to create productive individuals who will serve and support the larger community. It not only has the purpose of contributing to personal and societal growth of individuals, but also to use its socializing processes to lead to participation in society (Ornstein & Levine, 1989). This participation must lead to growth and expansion of students' intellect. The understanding of the principal elements of the Holocaust will implement this expansion of the mind. These elements include human rights issues, reactions to positions of authority, and moral development. They are current issues that need to be addressed while educating our youth.

A pertinent point to remember is that "values are created through community deliberation in light of problems experienced and shared. They are refined and made sophisticated by the informing power of the disciplines of knowledge" (Hass & Parkay, 1993, Chap. 1). As educators we must use these community regulated values to heighten awareness of individuals. If this heightened awareness leads to more critical values of society, then we have done our best of implement change. As previously mentioned, education is responsible for refining these goals; change is a natural outcome of this.

The Classroom and the Curriculum

This curriculum is designed to be taught in a sixth-grade, urban community for a period of four weeks. Ideally, the class would be racially and ethnically diverse. The classroom itself will have desks set up in clusters of five in order to promote active participation in discussions and group activities. In the back of the classroom, there will be a Children's Museum displaying the projects and artwork of the students. There will also be learning centers so the children can move about the classroom freely and work on a variety of activities.

The classroom will be a caring and trusting environment where students will have opportunities to engage in cooperative learning along with other traditional methods of instruction. This will promote learning and benefit social relationships in the classroom (Mussen, Conger, Kagan, & Huston, 1990). By encouraging collaboration among peers, students' achievement can be consistently increased due to rewards on the basis of the learning of all group members (Hass & Parkay, 1993, Chap. 4). It is designed to increase cooperation and decrease competition among students, thus diminishing patterns of success and failure in the same individuals. Also, this will be instrumental in positive self-esteem development at a critical adolescent period (Ornstein & Levine, 1989). The curriculum will be a part of a yearlong study of the struggles of many groups of people. Students will critically examine the social, political, economic, and historical factors that influence different cultures. Learning about the struggles of people holds important universal lessons. These lessons would ideally prevent future Holocausts.

► References

Hass, G. & Parkay, F. W. (1993). *Curriculum planning: A new approach.* Boston: Allyn and Bacon.

Mussen, P. H., Conger, J. J., Kagan, J., and Huston, A. (1990). *Child development and personality.* New York: Harper and Row.

Ornstein, A. C. & Levine, D. U. (1989). *Foundations of education.* Boston: Houghton Mifflin.

Rielly, R. R. & Lewis, E. L. (1983). *Educational psychology: Applications for classroom learning and instruction.* New York: Macmillan.

Taylor, A. J. P. (Ed). (1974). *History of World War II.* London: Phoebus Publishing.

Goals and Purposes

Content:

1. The students will develop deep understanding of how and why the Holocaust happened.

2. The students will become acquainted with the Holocaust through literature.

3. The students will develop an understanding of the use and abuse of power and its consequences.

4. The students will develop a deep understanding of the importance of social responsibility.

Skills:

1. The students will be able to think critically.

2. The students will develop reading and writing skills.

3. The students will be able to analyze and synthesize information.

4. The students will be able to use mathematical concepts pertinent to their grade level.

5. The students will increase their level of effective communication.

Affect:

1. The students will develop their values throughout the unit.

2. The students will develop empathy and compassion.

3. The students will develop tolerance of differences.

Description of Activities

1. **Introduction—Historical Background:**
   The teacher will be posting guiding questions in order to introduce the Holocaust.
   A. What was the state of Germany after World War I?
   B. How did Adolf Hitler come to power?
   C. What events led to World War II?
   D. How did Hitler convince Germany that the only answer was the "final solution?"

2. **Read Aloud:**
   The teacher will be reading aloud a variety of literature, non-fiction, and research materials. The students will listen, engage in discussion, and respond in journals. Questions will be provided at times to guide the discussion and journal entries. This will be an ongoing activity.

3. **Map Skills:**
   The students will become familiarized with the locations of the countries involved in the Holocaust. We will show the class a map of the world and have the students describe the location in geographical terms such as hemisphere, continent, longitude, latitude, etc.

4. **Mini Lesson on Friendly Letter Format:**
   The class will be shown a model of a friendly letter. Together they will write a friendly letter inviting a Holocaust survivor to the classroom. See "Activity #4, More Learning Experiences."

5. **Select a Novel:**
   The teacher will briefly introduce five novels and each student will choose one to read and respond to throughout the unit. See "Activity #5, More Learning Experiences."

6. **Literature Circles:**
   The students will meet daily in literature circles and discuss, analyze, and question the actions of characters in their novel. The discussions will at times be guided by the teacher. They will respond in their journal to these meetings.

7. **Response Journals:**
   Throughout the unit, the students will keep response journals and write daily about readings, discussions, movies, ideas, etc. At times the activity will be teacher directed.

8. **Diary:**
   Each student will keep a diary separate from the response journal based on the novel they have chosen. The diary will be written from the point of view of any character in their novel. They may use art, poetry, music, passages from the novel, symbols, and class-guided research to make their diary authentic.

9. **"Triumph of the Will":**

   The teacher and students will together formulate the definition of propaganda. Parts of the movie will be shown to the class. A discussion will then take place and lead into the concept of scapegoating, which will also be defined.

10. **Heil Hitler**

    Adapted from Strom, M. & Parsons, W. (1982), *Facing History and Ourselves: Holocaust and Human Behavior*. Watertown, MA: International Educations, Inc.

    The passage will be read aloud to the class. This is about how children and adults were indoctrinated with Nazi ideology. Germans were required by law to say "Heil Hitler" in all instances of human interaction. This type of propaganda will be explored through discussion. See "Activity #10, More Learning Experiences."

11. **"Daniel's Story":**

    The class will be shown this film to illustrate the effects that the Holocaust had on children. It is told from a child's perspective and therefore relevant to the students. Students will react in their journals to the film.

12. **Resistance:**

    The teacher will explain the Warsaw Ghetto Uprising and other forms of resistance that took place during the Holocaust. Students will then react in their journals to these events.

13. **Food Rationing:**

    The teacher will introduce food rationing to the students and discuss its role in the Holocaust. The students will then be taught mathematical concepts of fractions, decimals, and percentages through manipulation of food. For example, students will be given a week's worth of food and asked, What percentage will each member of the family be allotted each day? What fraction of the food will be used each day? Change these values into decimals. This activity will take place during the three-day experiment.

14. **Experiment:**

    The class will be participating in an exercise to explore the consequences of use and abuse of power which includes the following concepts: propaganda, stereotyping, scapegoating, prejudice, persecution, bigotry, racism, bias, exploitation, and oppression. See "Activity #14, Learning Experiences."

15. **"The Wave":**

    This movie will be shown after the experiment and it will reinforce the ideas that come out of the classroom experiment. The movie is about a teacher who does a similar experiment in his classroom and the effects it had on the students.

16. **Shel Silverstein's "No Difference":**

    After the experiment we will develop a lesson based on this poem to promote unity in classroom and to explore concepts. See "Activity #16, Learning Experiences."

17. **Six-Pointed Star**
    This activity is designed to introduce the students to the shame and humiliation victims felt during the Holocaust. See "Activity #17, Learning Experiences."

18. **The Number on my Grandfather's Arm:**
    This book will be read aloud to the class. The class will discuss the lasting effects of shame and humiliation. See "Activity #18, Learning Experiences."

19. **Formulating Questions:**
    The students will create questions to interview the survivor. See "Activity #20, Learning Experiences."

20. **Survivor:**
    A Holocaust survivor will visit the classroom. Students will use their questions to guide his or her presentation. This interview will be videotaped by the students. See "Activity #19, Learning Experiences."

21. **Thank You Note:**
    Students will use prior knowledge of the friendly letter format to write individual thank you notes to the Holocaust survivor.

22. **U.S. Holocaust Memorial Museum:**
    The class will take a trip to the museum in Washington, D.C., where they will be provided with an identity card bearing the name and picture of a Holocaust victim, matched by gender and similar age to the students. The museum presents a comprehensive history of the Holocaust through artifacts, photographs, films, and eyewitness testimonies. See "Activity #21, Learning Experiences."

23. **Mini Lesson on Haiku:**
    The teacher will present to the students examples of haiku, give them an opportunity to practice the format in groups, and then have them write a haiku about their trip to the museum. The students will also illustrate their poems. See "Activity #23, More Learning Experiences."

24. **"Susan":**
    Children will be shown this video to introduce the medical experiments of Dr. Mengele and others. This subject is to be explored graphically, but the children should be make aware of this occurrence. The children will be able to discuss or write about what they are feeling after this activity.

25. **Children's Quilt:**
    Each child will create a square of the quilt by decorating a piece of fabric. Students will sew the pieces together to form a quilt. Their piece will directly reflect what they have learned throughout the unit.

26. **Extend the Novel:**
   At the completion of the novel, the students will write an extension of the story or have characters meet again in the future.

27. **Pastor Niemoller Quote:**
   The quote will be read aloud to the class and we will discuss the consequences of apathy. This exercise will lead to lessons on the importance of action, activism, and resistance. See "Activity #27, More Learning Experiences."

28. **Kitty Genovese story:**
   This will be used in conjunction with the Pastor Niemoller quote and have similar objectives. It is a more recent example for the children to examine. See "Activity #28, More Learning Experiences."

29. **Mini Lesson on Business Letter Format:**
   The children will be taught this format in a similar way to the friendly letter format. Modifications will be made where necessary.

30. **Letters of Action:**
   The children will choose an issue or a cause that they feel needs to be changed. They will write business letters to corporations, politicians, etc., stating their argument and the need for change.

31. **Talk Show:**
   The students will decide on a moderator, a panel of guests, "experts" pertinent to the topic, and an active audience to participate in a talk show about concerning the Holocaust. This is designed to be impromptu and will be used to assess what the children have retained throughout the unit.

32. **Write a Song:**
   In groups, children will write and perform a song based on any concept explored thus far. They will choose the type of music, for example, rap, pop, reggae, etc.

33. **Extra! Extra!:**
   The students will create an authentic newspaper based on all they have learned throughout this unit. This is one of the culminating projects for the unit designed to take one week. See "Activity #33, More Learning Experiences."

34. **Reenactments:**
   The students will use their literature circle groups to create a reenactment of some aspect of the Holocaust. They may pick a portion of their book, an event such as Kristallnacht, a Nazi rally, the Warsaw Ghetto Uprising, a Nazi War Crimes Tribunal, etc. They will be presented to the class and videotaped for Holocaust Remembrance Day.

35. **A Taste of Eastern Europe:**
   Children make food and refreshments for Holocaust Remembrance Day. This will reinforce the mathematical concepts previously taught.

36. **Children's Museum:**
   Throughout the unit, children will be adding their completed projects to the museum set up in the back of the classroom. These include, but are not limited to, their diaries, their songs, their videos of the reenactments, their haiku with illustrations, the newspaper, photographs of the trip to the museum, etc.

37. **Holocaust Remembrance Day:**
   The children will be sending invitations to parents, family members, community members, faculty, and staff of the school, etc., requesting their presence at this event. There will be food, refreshments, the video of the survivor, and the completed Children's Museum. At the close of the day, the students will conduct a candlelighting ceremony for the victims and survivors, to remember the past in the hopes this will never happen again.

Key Concepts and Terms

action/nonaction
anti-Semitism
apathy
Aryan
Auschwitz
bias
bigotry
boycott
bystanders
censorship
concentration camps
crematoriums
Dachau
democracy *
deportation
dictator
"ethnic cleansing"
ethnocentric *
exploitation *
fascism *
"The Final Solution"
gas chamber
genocide
ghetto
Gypsies
Hitler, Adolf
Holocaust
homosexuals
human rights

Jehovah Witnesses
Jews
Kristallnacht
Nazi
obedience
oppression
peace
persecution
power—use and abuse
prejudice
propaganda
resistance
racism
scapegoating
stereotype
struggle
survival
survivors
swastika
Terezin
Treaty of Versailles
tolerance
totalitarianism *
victims
victimizers
war
Warsaw Ghetto
World War II

* gifted students

Learning Experiences

Activity #14: Experiment

Setting: After learning about the concept of resistance.

Grade Level: Sixth

Goals:

- The students will develop an understanding of the use and abuse of power and its consequences.
- The students will think critically.
- The students will develop reading and writing skills.
- The students will increase their level of effective communication.
- The students will develop empathy and compassion.

Objectives:

- To have students learn a scientific process of reporting data.
- To have students effectively implement the experiment.

Grouping: The entire class divided into two groups.

Materials:

Examples of experiments
Journals
Writing instruments

Focus or Motivation: The students participation in the experiment.

Procedure:

1. The teacher will activate the students' prior knowledge by asking the class "What is an experiment?"

2. Examples of experiments will be shown to the students and, with the help of the teacher, the class will identify the key elements of the process.

3. The teacher will then list the scientific processes on the board so the students can refer to it. This includes gathering and observing information, making a hypothesis, testing the hypothesis, and reporting the results.

4. The students will then be randomly assigned to each of two conditions of the experiment. The groups will be modeled after "Nazis" and "Others" during World War II. These names will not be used, but rather, "Superior" and "Inferior." The identification of each group will also be assigned randomly.

5. The superior group will set up rules of classroom order for the next three days. For example, inferiors must wear badges; inferiors can only write in pencil; inferiors must sit in the back of the room, etc. Each rule must meet the teacher's approval.

6. All students will write in their journals mornings and afternoons daily. The entries should address feelings, thoughts, problems, etc.

7. At the completion of the experiment, each student will submit a lab report using the scientific process and a final reaction journal entry.

Closure: The "superiors" and "inferiors" will role play one another in order to foster understanding of both conditions of the experiment. This is designed to make the group cohesive again.

Evaluation:

- The individual lab reports will allow the teacher to assess comprehension and application of the scientific method.

- The students' journals will be read, looking for elements to show that the experiment was successful in developing empathy.

Extension Activities: The class will be shown "The Wave," which examines a similar experiment and the results of it.

Activity #16: Shel Silverstein's "No Difference"

Setting: After completion of the classroom experiment.

Grade Level: Sixth

Goals:

- The students will develop tolerance of differences.
- The students will develop the understanding of the use and abuse of power.

Objective: The students will gain an understanding of tolerance, bigotry, and persecution.

Grouping: The entire class

Materials:

A pre-constructed questionnaire (see the last page of this activity)
A copy of Shel Silverstein's poem
Writing instruments

Focus or Motivation: The poem

Procedure:

1. A questionnaire will be distributed to each student who will then take approximately ten minutes to complete it. This will involve interaction with peers and movement around the classroom.

2. The students will attempt to form groups according to their answers on the questionnaire. Eventually, with guidance from the teacher, the students will realize that everyone has something in common with everyone else and, therefore, they form one large group.

3. Discussion will take place, stressing the idea that although we are different, we are all the same because we are human. The teacher and students will make a chart on the board comparing their similarities to their differences.

4. The teacher will then turn off the lights, close the shades, and read "No Difference" by Shel Silverstein.

5. The class will engage in a discussion on how the poem makes them feel. They will address their thoughts and ideas that have come out of the poem.

Closure: The following will be written on the board:

> Lack of Tolerance
> Bigotry
> Persecution

> The teacher and class will generate definitions of these and discuss how lack of tolerance leads to bigotry and persecution.

Evaluation: The teacher will know the students have grasped the concepts by looking for an understanding of the terms in the discussion that takes place.

Adapted from United States Holocaust Memorial Council and Committee to Remember the Children *Wall of remembrance teaching guide,* Washington, DC: United States Holocaust Memorial Council, 2234 Rayburn Building, Washington, DC 20515, (202) 225-2111.

Questionnaire for Activity #16

1. How many students in the class have curly hair?

   _____

   _____

2. How many students wear glasses or contacts?

   _____

   _____

3. How many students write with the same hand as you?

   _____

   _____

4. How many students were born between July and November?

   _____

   _____

5. Who loves movies?

   _____

   _____

6. Who loves ice cream?

   _____

   _____

Activity #17: Six-Pointed Star

Setting: Following the Shel Silverstein activity.

Grade Level: Sixth

Goal: The students will develop an understanding of the use and abuse of power and its consequences.

Objective: To have the students realize and empathize with the shame and humiliation of victims of the Holocaust.

Grouping: The entire class which will eventually break into smaller groups.

Materials:

Copies of the passage
Response journals
Writing instruments

Focus or Motivation: The passage written by a twelve-year-old girl

Procedure:

1. The teacher will activate prior knowledge of the six-pointed Jewish star and explain the stigma that the Nazi's attached to it.

2. Copies of the passage will be distributed to each student. One child will read it aloud while the others follow along.

3. The following questions will guide the discussion:
   A. Why does the girl feel humiliated by wearing the six-pointed stars?
   B. What does she mean by saying she is no longer a human being?
   C. Have you even been made to feel bad or humiliated about something you took pride in?

4. The class will break into groups and share the answer to question C.

Closure: The teacher and students will explore the following concepts:

> Bigotry
> Persecution
> Shame
> Humiliation

> The relationship between the concepts will be composed by the class.

Evaluation: The students will respond in their journals to the exercise and the meaning of the concepts. The teacher will look for the following in the journal:

1. Empathy and compassion shown toward the girl in the passage.

2. Personal accounts of embarrassment.

3. Correct use of the terms bigotry, persecution, shame, and humiliation.

Passage for Activity #17

"I refuse to leave the house. I am not going to wear the yellow star! I am not going to appear in public with a Jew badge. I can't be seen wearing that horrible, horrible thing. I will die if any of my schoolmates see me. . . . I know I was hurt and outraged at being made a glaring mark, a thing intended to set me apart and humiliate me. Jew or criminal, what is the difference in their intent? What is the difference in my shame or helplessness? I was no longer a human being, I was singled out at will, an object."

Livia, Hungary, age 12

Adapted from United States Holocaust Memorial Council and Committee to Remember the Children, *Wall of remembrance teaching guide,* Washington, DC: United States Holocaust Memorial Council, 2234 Rayburn Building, Washington, DC 20515, (202) 225-2111.

Activity #18: The Number on my Grandfather's Arm

Setting: The class will be sitting in a circle on the rug.

Grade Level: Sixth

Goals:

- The students will become acquainted with the Holocaust through literature.

- The students will develop empathy and compassion.

Objective: To help students become more aware of the lasting scars of shame and humiliation.

Grouping: The entire class

Materials:

The book
Chart paper
Writing instruments

Focus or Motivation: The book

Procedure:

1. The teacher will activate the students' prior knowledge of the Holocaust by using the K-W-L process. A chart will be constructed answering the following questions:
    A. What do the students know?
    B. What do the students want to learn?
    C. What have the students learned and want to learn?

2. The teacher will read the book aloud to the class.

3. A discussion will proceed based on the following guiding questions:
    A. Why is the topic so painful for the grandfather to talk about?
    B. What do you think he is feeling before, during, and after he tells his story?
    C. What significance did the number have?
    D. What significance does the number have now?

Closure: The discussion will end by relating this activity to the previous one and drawing a conclusion about the effects of shame and humiliation on people.

Evaluation: The K-W-L chart will assess prior knowledge and retention of information. The closing activity will provide insight into the students' realization of the lasting effects of shame and humiliation.

Activity #19: Formulating Questions for the Survivor

Setting: Prior to the survivor's visit.

Grade Level: Sixth

Goal: The children will be able to think critically through an examination of the Holocaust.

Objective: To have the students formulate effective questions for the survivor and use them to guide the visit and gather information.

Grouping: Groups of five students each.

Materials:
Journals
Paper
Writing instruments
K-W-L chart
A video camera
A videotape

Focus or Motivation: The survivor

Procedure:

1. The K-W-L chart will be posted for easy reference.

2. The students will get into groups, and by using the chart and their personal interests will make up at least five questions to ask the survivor.

3. The groups will share their questions with the class as the teacher writes them on the board.

4. The students will check them against the K-W-L chart to be sure all areas are addressed. If there are any duplicate questions or areas not addressed, the class as a whole will generate more questions.

5. Each student will then choose a question that they will ask the survivor.

6. When the survivor arrives, the class will sit in a circle as students are videotaping the survivor's presentation.

Closure: The students will respond in their journals to the survivor's visit and the class will discuss any unfamiliar concepts or ideas that might come out of the visit.

Evaluation: The questions will be assessed based on the relevance they have to the K-W-L chart. The journals will assess the information they have gathered from the survivor. We will look for understanding of empathy and compassion in writing.

Extension Activities:

- The students will write a thank you note to the survivor.

- The students will transcribe the presentation for the class newspaper.

- The students will show the video on Holocaust Remembrance Day.

Activity #21: U.S. Holocaust Memorial Museum

Setting: Washington, D.C.

Grade Level: Sixth

Goals:

- To develop deep understanding of how and why the Holocaust happened.

- The students will develop an understanding of the use and abuse of power and its consequences.

- The students will develop empathy and compassion.

Objective: To have students become an identity and participate in an authentic experience.

Grouping: The entire class; all parents will be invited to attend.

Materials:
Permission slips
Journals
Writing instruments
Cameras and film
Tickets to museum

Focus or Motivation: The museum

Procedure:

1. Students will enter the permanent exhibition and receive the identity of a victim of the Holocaust matched to the student's gender and similar age.

2. The students will tour the permanent exhibition and periodically update their identity card to reveal the fate of this person.

3. After the tour, the class will enter the Hall of Remembrance, which is a place to contemplate what they have just experienced.

4. We proceed to "Daniel's Story: Remember the Children" exhibition which is specifically designed for younger visitors and told from a child's perspective.

5. The class will go to Wexner Learning Center and use the touch-screen computers to access articles, photographs, film footage, maps, videotaped eyewitness testimony, and music of the period.

6. The class will proceed to the basement to view the Children's Wall.

7. The class will go to the Gonda Educational Center where there are classrooms.

8. The class will fill in the K-W-L chart. The students will brainstrom ideas for their quilt.

Closure: The class will discuss its thoughts and feelings from the experience.

Evaluation: Assessment will be based on additions to the K-W-L chart.

Extension Activities: The students will write a haiku and make a children's quilt.

More Learning Experiences

Activity #4: Friendly Letter Format

Grade Level: Sixth

Goals:

- The students will develop writing skills.
- The students will increase their level of effective communication.

Objective: To have students learn the friendly letter format.

Grouping: The entire class.

Materials Needed:
Lined paper
Writing instruments
Sample friendly letter

Focus or Motivation: The anticipation of the survivor's visit

Procedure:

1. The students will be shown an example of the friendly letter format.
2. The students will write a letter to the person sitting next to him or her.
3. The teacher will discuss the proper elements of a friendly letter based on the individual letters just written.
4. The teacher will then discuss the topic the class will be writing about, and together write a letter inviting a pre-selected Holocaust survivor to the class.

Closure: The students will revise the friendly letter they wrote to the person sitting next to them.

Evaluation: The students will prove comprehension of the friendly letter format by effectively revising the letters they wrote to the person sitting next to them.

Extension Activities: The students will write individual thank you notes to the visitor.

Activity #5: Select a Novel

Grade Level: Sixth

Goals:

- The students will develop deep understanding of the Holocaust through literature.
- The students will develop reading and writing skills.
- The students will be able to analyze and synthesize information.
- The students will increase their level of effective communication.
- The students will develop empathy and compassion.

Objectives:

- To develop an understanding of the time period through literature and class research.
- To analyze and synthesize information through discussion.

Grouping: The entire class

Materials Needed: Five novels for the students to choose from. They are *Number the Stars, Anne Frank: Diary of a Young Girl, Night, The Devil's Arithmetic, and Escape from Warsaw.*

Focus or Motivation: The novels

Procedure:

1. The teacher will introduce each novel to the class by reading a brief passage from each.
2. The students will choose a novel and begin reading.
3. The students will meet daily in literature circles and discuss the novel. Response journals will be kept as well.
4. The students will keep individual diaries from the perspective of any character in their novel. They may use art, poetry, music, passages from the novel, symbols, and class-guided research on the Holocaust to make their diary authentic.

Closure: The students will read portions of their diaries to the class.

Evaluation: Observation of the literature circles will take place. The teacher will know that children understand the time period through the information in their journals and diaries.

Extension Activities:

- The students will extend the novel and engage in reenactments in groups, based on various situations, (i.e., a Nazi rally, a scene from the novel, Kristallnacht, etc.).

- Upon completion of the diaries, they will be displayed in the Children's Museum.

Activity #10 Heil Hitler

Every child says "Heil Hitler!" from fifty to 150 times a day, immeasurably more often than the old neutral greeting. The formula is required by law; if you meet a friend on the way to school, you say it; study periods are opened and closed with "Heil Hitler!" "Heil Hitler!" says the postman, the streetcar conductor, the girl who sells you notebooks at the stationary store; and if your parents' first words when you come home to lunch are not "Heil Hitler!" they have been guilty of a punishable offence, and can be denounced. "Heil Hitler!" they shout, in the Jungvolk and Hitler Youth. "Heil Hitler!" cry the girls in the League of German Girls. Your evening prayers must close with "Heil Hitler!" if you take your devotions seriously.

Officially—when you say hello to your superiors in school or in a group—the words are accompanied by the act of throwing the right arm high; but an official greeting among equals requires only a comparatively lax lifting of the forearm, with the fingers closed and pointing forward. This Hitler greeting, this "German" greeting, repeated countless times from morning to bedtime, stamps the whole day.

Storm, M. & Parsons, W. (1982). *Facing history and ourselves: Holocaust and human behavior.* Watertown, MA: International Education.

Activity #23: Haiku

Grade Level: Sixth

Goals:

- The students will develop reading and writing skills.
- The students will be able to analyze and synthesize information.
- The students will increase their level of effective communication.

Objective: To have students learn the haiku form of poetry.

Grouping: The entire class

Materials:
Lined paper
Writing instruments
Various art supplies

Focus or Motivation: The students' recent trip to the museum

Procedure:

1. Examples of haiku will be shown to the students.
2. The elements of the poetry style will then be discussed, i.e., the syllable structure of 5-7-5.
3. The students will practice this style in groups and then share with the class; students who will critique one another's haiku based on proper use of elements.
4. The students will write their own haiku based on their recent trip to the U.S. Holocaust Memorial Museum in Washington, D.C.

Closure: Students will illustrate their haiku with a variety of art materials.

Evaluation: The students will prove comprehension of haiku by writing their own.

Extension Activities: The haiku and illustrations will be displayed in the Children's Museum.

Activity #27: Pastor Niemoller

Grade Level: Sixth

Goals:

- The students will be able to think critically.
- The students will develop a deep understanding of the importance of social responsibility.

Objective: To activate student's prior knowledge of action, and examine the consequences of non-action.

Grouping: The entire class

Materials:
Copies of the quote by Pastor Niemoller for the entire class
Journals
Writing instruments

Focus or Motivation: The Pastor Niemoller quote

Procedure:

1. The teacher will pass out copies of the quote to each student.
2. The teacher will read the quote aloud to the class.
3. The students will begin brainstorming and address ideas inherent in the quote, such as the consequences of nonaction.
4. The teacher will guide the students in defining the term "apathy."
5. The teacher will then ask the following questions: Has there ever been a time in your life where you did not speak up for something you believed in? If so, what were the consequences? The students will respond in their journals to these questions.

Closure: The class will break into small groups and share personal experiences with each other.

Evaluation: The journals will be read and responded to. The teacher will be looking for understanding of apathy and nonaction. Observation of group discussions will take place as well.

Extension Activities: The class will be made aware of other situations of nonaction, (i.e., the Kitty Genovese story).

"In Germany they first came for the communists and I didn't speak up because I wasn't a communist. Then they came for the Jews, and I didn't speak up because I wasn't a Jew. Then they came for the trade unionists, and I didn't speak up because I wasn't a trade unionist. Then they came for the Catholics, and I didn't speak up because I was a Protestant. Then they came for me—and by that time no one was left to speak up."

Pastor Martin Niemoller

Activity #28: Kitty Genovese

At 3:20 AM on March 13, 1964, Kitty Genovese parked her car in the lot adjacent to the railroad station and started to walk to her apartment, about 100 feet away. As she proceeded to the entrance she noticed a man at the far end of the parking lot. Kitty stopped and then nervously headed up the street toward Lefferts Boulevard, where there was a police call box. When she got to the street light, the man grabbed her. She screamed, and lights went on in the ten-story apartment house where she lived. Windows slid open and voices broke the early morning stillness. Kitty screamed: "Oh, my God, he stabbed me! Please help me! Please help me!" A man hollered from one of the upper windows: "Let that girl alone!" The assailant looked up at him, shrugged, and walked down the street toward a car.

Kitty struggled to her feet as the lights went out in the apartment house. The killer immediately returned and stabbed Kitty again as she screamed: "I'm dying! I'm dying!" Again, windows opened and lights came on. This time the assailant got into his car and drove away, while Kitty again struggled to her feet. But the killer returned a third time. By now Kitty had made her way to the rear entrance to the building. When the killer found her there, slumped on the floor at the foot of the stairs, he stabbed her a third time—the final, fatal blow.

Activity #33 Extra! Extra!

Grade Level: Sixth

Goals:

- The students will be able to analyze and synthesize information.

- The students will increase their level of effective communication.

- The students will develop reading and writing skills.

Objective: To have students synthesize all information received throughout the unit into a class newspaper.

Grouping: Individual

Materials:
Newsprint
Art supplies
Computers
Color laser printer
A variety of newspapers (i.e., *The New York Times, U.S.A. Today,* local newspapers, etc.)
Cameras and film

Focus or Motivation: The anticipation of having their work published.

Procedure:

1. Various types of newspapers will be available to the students. Different newspaper formats will be explored.

2. Learning centers in the classroom will be based on different sections of the newspapers we have become familiar with.

3. The newspaper will be a reflection of the Holocaust and the activities that took place in the classroom. The six learning centers will be Science (reporting on experiments that took place in our classroom and throughout the Holocaust); The Arts (political cartoons, illustrations, music of the time, etc.); International, National, and Local (writing of what was happening in these three areas); Book and Movie Reviews (of what we've read and seen about the Holocaust); Editorials (comments and reflections); and The War in Review (a time line and highlights such as Kristallnacht, etc.). To ensure that the paper has an equal balance, each student will rotate throughout the various centers. A list of topics will be provided at each center with limits for the number of articles needed. These limits can be negotiated, if necessary.

4. The students will pre-write, draft, revise, and publish work in their own classroom newspaper. They will also take photographs and illustrate the newspaper.

5. The teacher will move around the classroom and offer help, guidance, and suggestions when needed. The teacher also will check progress daily.

6. The students will bring all their work together into one large newspaper. They will do paste ups and layouts of their work to form the finished product.

Closure: The newspaper will be displayed and distributed in the classroom and throughout the school.

Evaluation: Developing writing skills will be assessed and the synthesis processes will be apparent throughout the activity.

Extension Activities:

• The newspaper will be displayed in the Children's Museum.

• A trip will be made to see an actual newspaper published.

Coverage Chart

Legend for activity columns:

1. INTRODUCTION
2. READ ALOUD
3. MAP SKILLS
4. FRIENDLY LETTER
5. SELECT A NOVEL
6. LITERATURE CIRCLES
7. RESPONSE JOURNALS
8. DIARY
9. "TRIUMPH OF WILL"
10. HEIL HITLER
11. "DANIEL'S STORY"
12. RESISTANCE
13. FOOD RATIONING

Category	Sub-area	1	2	3	4	5	6	7	8	9	10	11	12	13
SUBJECT AREA	SOCIAL STUDIES										✱			
	ARTS									✱	✱			
	GEOGRAPHY	✱		✱										
	HISTORY	✱	✱					✱	✱	✱	✱	✱	✱	✱
	MATH							✱						✱
	LANGUAGE		✱		✱	✱	✱	✱	✱	✱	✱	✱	✱	
GROUPING	INDIVIDUAL			✱	✱	✱		✱	✱	✱		✱	✱	
	GROUP						✱	✱						✱
	CLASS	✱	✱	✱	✱					✱	✱	✱	✱	✱
GARDNER'S CONCEPTS	KINESTHETIC													✱
	EXPERIENTIAL						✱	✱	✱					
	FOUNDATIONAL						✱	✱		✱	✱			
	QUANTITATIVE	✱		✱	✱					✱			✱	✱
	NARRATIONAL	✱	✱		✱	✱	✱	✱	✱	✱		✱	✱	
BLOOM'S TAXONOMY	EVALUATION													
	SYNTHESIS								✱					
	ANALYSIS					✱	✱	✱						
	APPLICATION			✱	✱						✱			✱
	COMPREHENSION									✱				
	KNOWLEDGE	✱	✱									✱	✱	

Coverage Chart

ACTIVITY	SUBJECT AREA						GROUPING			GARDNER'S CONCEPTS					BLOOM'S TAXONOMY					
	SOCI	ARTS	GEOG	HIST	MATH	LANG	INDIV	GROUP	CLASS	KINES	EXPER	FOUND	QUANT	NARR	EVAL	SYNTH	ANALY	APPLY	COMP	KNOWL
14. EXPERIMENT	★			★		★	★	★				★					★			
15. "THE WAVE"				★		★	★		★			★		★		★				
16. NO DIFFERENCE						★	★	★	★		★	★	★	★		★				
17. SIX-POINTED STAR				★		★	★	★	★			★		★		★				
18. NUMBER ON MY GRANDFATHER'S ARM				★		★			★			★	★	★		★		★		
19. FORMULATING QUESTIONS			★	★		★		★	★				★		★					
20. SURVIVOR		★		★		★	★		★				★	★				★		
21. THANK YOU NOTE						★	★						★					★		
22. MUSEUM	★	★	★	★		★	★	★	★	★	★	★	★	★						
23. HAIKU	★			★		★	★		★		★		★	★				★		
24. "SUSAN"	★			★		★	★		★					★				★		
25. CHILDREN'S QUILT		★		★	★		★	★	★	★	★		★			★				

Coverage Chart

ACTIVITY	SUBJECT AREA						GROUPING			GARDNER'S CONCEPTS					BLOOM'S TAXONOMY					
	SOCI	ARTS	GEOG	HIST	MATH	LANG	INDIV	GROUP	CLASS	KINES	EXPRES	FOUND	QUANT	NARR	EVAL	SYNTH	ANALY	APPLY	COMP	KNOWL
26. EXTEND NOVEL				★		★	★						★	★		★				
27. PASTOR NIEMOLLER				★		★	★	★	★			★		★		★				
28. KITTY GENOVESE				★		★	★	★	★			★		★	★					
29. BUSINESS LETTER						★			★				★					★		
30. LETTERS OF ACTION						★	★					★	★	★	★					
31. TALK SHOW	★	★		★		★	★	★	★	★	★	★		★	★					
32. WRITE A SONG		★		★	★	★		★		★	★			★		★				
33. EXTRA! EXTRA!	★	★	★	★	★		★	★	★		★	★	★	★	★					
34. REENACTMENTS		★		★				★		★						★				
35. TASTE EASTERN EUROPE	★	★		★	★		★	★	★	★	★	★	★					★		
36. CHILDREN'S MUSEUM		★	★	★		★	★	★	★		★			★	★					
37. HOL. REM. DAY	★	★	★	★	★	★	★	★	★		★	★		★	★					

Time Line

Week One

- Introduction: Historical Background
- Begin Read Aloud—ongoing
- Map Skills
- Mini Lesson on Friendly Letter Format
- Select a novel and begin reading—ongoing
- Literature Circles—ongoing
- Response Journals—ongoing
- Begin writing diary based on novel—ongoing
- Show parts of "Triumph of the Will"
- "Heil Hitler"
- Show "Daniel's Story"

Week Two

- Resistance
- Food Rationing
- Experiment—three days
- Show "The Wave"
- Shel Silverstein's "No Difference"
- Six-Pointed Star
- The Number of my Grandfather's Arm
- Formulating Questions
- Survivor Visit
- Thank You Note

Week Three

- Visit the U.S. Holocaust Memorial Museum in Washington, D.C.
- Mini Lesson on Haiku
- Show "Susan"
- Children's Quilt—ongoing
- Extend the Novel
- Pastor Niemoller Quote
- Kitty Genovese
- Mini Lesson on Business Letter Format
- Write a letter of action
- Talk Show

Week Four

- Write a Song
- Extra! Extra!—ongoing
- Reenactment
- A Taste of Eastern Europe
- Children's Museum
- Holocaust Remembrance Day

Students' Resources

Literature

Adler, D. A. *The number on my grandfather's arm*. New York: Union of American Hebrew Congregations, 1987.
> The Holocaust is explained to a young child by her grandfather.

Adler, D. A. *We remember the holocaust*. New York: Henry Holt, 1979.
> An illustrated book of the voices of survivors.

Asher, S. F. *Daughters of the law*. New York: Beufort Books, 1980.
> Deals with a young Jewish girl preparing for her bat mitzvah. Her mother is a survivor of the Holocaust and has difficulty discussing her past.

Atkinson, L. *In kindling flame: The story of Hannah Senesh, 1921-1944*. New York: Lothrop, Lee and Shepard Books, 1985.
> The story of Hannah Senesh, a Hungarian Jew who tried to rescue her people from the Nazis.

Fluek, T. *Memories of my life in a polish village, 1930-1949*. New York: Alfred A. Knopf, 1990.
> Tells the story of a young Jewish girl growing up on a Polish farm. Discusses the German occupation, ghettoization, hiding, and liberation.

Frank, A. *The diary of a young girl*. New York: Pocket Books, 1953.
> A Jewish girl's diary of hiding during the Holocaust. A classic.

Friedman, I. R. *Escape or die: True stories of young people who survived the holocaust*. Boston: Addison and Wesley, 1982.
> Personal stories of young people in many countries who survived the Holocaust. The author introduces with a short history of Jews in that country.

Hartman, E. *War without friends*. New York: Crown Publishing, 1982.
> The story of a teenage Dutch boy who begins having doubts about his father's Nazi sympathies.

Innocenti, R. *Rose Blanche:* Translated by Martha Coventry and Richard Graglia. Manako, MN: Creative Education, 1985.
> An artists view of the Holocaust as seen through the eyes of a child. The author says, "This book is meant to breed questions."

Isaacman, C. *Clara's story*. Philadelphia: Jewish Publication Society of America, 1984.
> Refugees from Romania, Clara's family is moving from one safe house to another to avoid deportation.

Lowry, L. *Number the stars.* New York: Dell Publishing, 1989.
A story about a girl in Denmark who helps save her best friend's life during the German occupation of Denmark.

Matas, C. *Daniel's story.* Kansas City, MO: Scholastic, Inc., 1993.
Based on the exhibit at the U. S. Holocaust Memorial Museum. An account of a boy named Daniel who portrays the experiences of children during the Holocaust.

Orgel, D. *The devil in Vienna.* New York: Puffin, 1988.
Set in Vienna, a Jewish girl discusses the difficulty of maintaining a close friendship with the daughter of a Nazi.

Richter, H. P. *Friedrich.* Translated from German by Edite Kroll. New York: Holt, Rinehart and Winston, 1970; Puffin, 1987.
An autobiography of a child who relates how the rise of the Nazi Party destroyed a friendship between the author and his Jewish friend Friedrich.

Samuels, G. *Mottele: A partisan odyssey.* New York: Harper and Row, 1976.
A fictionalized account of a boy who joins Uncle Misha's partisans, a Jewish resistance group, after his parents are killed by the Germans.

Sender, R. M. *The cage.* New York: Macmillan, 1986; Bantam Books, 1988.
A story about a girl's experiences from the Lodz ghetto to Aushwitz. Graphic, but not overwhelming.

Serraillier, I. *Escape from Warsaw.* Kansas City, MO: Scholastic, Inc., 1981.
Three polish children try to escape from their war-ravaged home during World War II.

Siegal, A. *Upon the head of a goat: A childhood in Hungary, 1939-1944.* New York: Farrar, Strauss and Giroux, 1981.

An account of the author's struggle in Hungary. Conveys the difficulty of maintaining hope and dignity in the face of hunger, death, and destruction.

Silverstein, S. *Where the sidewalk ends.* New York: Harper Collins Publishers, 1974.
A collection of poems and drawings on a wide range of topics including differences.

Spiegelman, A. *Maus.* New York: Pantheon Books, 1980.
A cartoon about the son of a survivor coming to terms with his father, history, and the Holocaust itself.

Spiegelman, A. *Maus II: And here my troubles began.* New York: Pantheon Books, 1986.
A sequel to Maus dealing with similar issues.

Staden, W. von. *Darkness over the valley.* New York: Penguin Books, 1982.
About a German girl who begins to see the evil in the Nazi movement. She and her mother decide to provide aid to prisoners of a Jewish labor camp near their home.

Suhl, Y. *Uncle Misha's partisan's,* 3rd ed. New York: Shapolsky Publishers, 1988.
A young Jewish boy joins a partisan group and is given an important assignment in the struggle against the Germans.

Treseder, T. W. *Hear o Israel: A Story of the Warsaw Ghetto.* New York: Atheneum, 1990.
A young Jewish boy describes life in the Warsaw ghetto and his eventual deportation to the Treblinka death camp.

Volavkova, H. (ed.). *I never saw another butterfly: Children's drawings and poems from the Terezin concentration camp, 1942-1944.* New York: Shocken Books, 1978.
Book of life in a concentration camp through the eyes of children.

Wiesel, E. *Night.* New York: Bantam, 1982.
A narrative account of Wiesel's own experiences in Auschwitz.

Yolen, J. *The devil's arithmetic.* New York: Viking Kestrel, 1988.
A young girl finds herself back in the time of the Holocaust.

Ziaben, J. B. *The fortuneteller in 5B.* New York: Henry Holt, 1991.
The story of an American Jewish girl and her friendship with a Holocaust survivor.

Research

Altshuler, D. A. *Hitler's war against the Jews: A young reader's version of "The war against the Jews, 1933-1945" by Lucy Dawidowicz.* New York: Behrman House, 1978.
A simplified and shortened version of Dawidowicz's history of the Holocaust. Includes photography and suggested topics for discussion.

Berwick, M. *The third reich.* New York: Putnam, 1971.
A simple illustrated history of the Holocaust. Includes a time line of events.

Chaikin, M. *A nightmare in history: The Holocaust 1933-1945.* New York: Clarion Books, 1971.
A history of anti-Semitism which sets the setting for the Holocaust. Examines concentration camps such as Auschwitz and ghettos such as the Warsaw ghetto.

Ramati, A. *And the violins stopped playing: A story of the gypsy Holocaust.* New York: Franklin Watts, 1986.
Ramati's struggles throughout the Holocaust. He is eventually captured and sent to Auschwitz.

Rogasky, B. *Smoke and ashes: The story of the Holocaust.* New York: Holiday House, 1988.
Includes a narrative and personal testimonies and poses questions such as: How did the Holocaust happen and why?

Rossell, S. *The Holocaust.* New York: Franklin Watts, 1981.
A history of the Holocaust with a good index and bibliography. Easy-to-read.

Rossell, S. *The Holocaust: The fire that raged.* New York: Franklin Watts, 1990.
A history of the Holocaust that is a good introduction for students.

Stadler, B. *The Holocaust: A history of courage and resistance.* New York: Behrman House, 1973.
A story of Jews and struggles in the camps, ghettos, etc. Great emphasis is placed on resistance.

Werstein, I. *The uprising of the Warsaw ghetto, November 1940-May 1943.* New York: Norton, 1968.
Discusses the terrible condition in the Warsaw ghetto which eventually led to its uprising.

Videos

"The Courage to Care." Culver City, CA: Zenger Video, 1986.
The film examines ordinary people who refused to succumb to Nazi tyranny and helped victims of the Holocaust.

"Daniel's Story." Washington, DC: United States Holocaust Memorial Museum.
This film tells the story of the Holocaust from a child's point of view. It is made especially for children ages 8-13 and therefore is not graphic.

"Dear Kitty." New York: Anne Frank Center
The life of Anne Frank is told with quotations from her diary, photos from the family album, and historic film footage. It also gives historical background on the Holocaust, anti-Semitism, racism, and fascism.

"Nazi War Crimes Trial." Sandy Hook, CT: Video Images, 1945.
Newsreels and documentary footage of Nazis brought to trial after the war.

"Susan." Kent, OH: KSU Productions, 1987.
A personal story of the youngest survivor of Dr. Mengele's experiments at Auschwitz.

"Triumph of Memory." Alexandria, VA: PBS Video, 1972.
Non-Jewish resistance fighters sent to concentration camps and their testimonies of the atrocities that took place.

"Triumph of the Will." Culver City, CA: Zenger Video, 1934.
This famous propaganda film is an effective tool for learning about Hitler's image of himself, his manipulation of the crowds, and his use of film propaganda.

"The Wave." Chicago: Films Incorporated.
The re-creation of how a high school teacher sets up an experiment of strict rules and behavior codes to show how peer pressure, conformity, and loyalty could work in a classroom the same way it had in Nazi Germany.

Teacher's Resources

Berenbaum, M. *The world must know: A history of the holocaust as told in the United States Holocaust Memorial Museum.* Boston: Little, Brown and Company, 1993.
> The story of the Holocaust as presented in the museum. It covers the Nazi's rise to power, the ghettos and concentration camps, and rescue, resistance, and the post-war period.

Cason, B. et al (Eds.), *Holocaust: The obligation to remember.* Washington, DC: The Washington Post, 1983.
> A collection of articles and speeches from the American Gathering of Jewish Holocaust Survivors in April of 1983.

Dawidowicz, L. *The war against the Jews 1933-1945.* New York: Bantam, 1986.
> Personalizes World War II as a direct attack on European Jewry, and solely to implement the "Final Solution."

Dawidowicz, L. *A Holocaust reader.* West Orange, NJ: Behrman House, 1976.
> Presents primary sources including letters, diaries, and reports from Jewish and German sources. A companion to the above mentioned title.

Epstein, H. *Children of the Holocaust.* New York: Viking Penguin, 1988.
> A story of survivors and children of survivors.

Gilbert, M. *The Holocaust: A history of the Jews in Europe during the Second World War.* New York: Henry Holt and Company, 1986.
> Historical research and personal narratives of survivors. Provides supplementary material for any aspect of the Holocaust.

Herstein, R. *The war that Hitler won: Goebbels and the Nazi media campaign.* New York: Paragon House, 1978.
> Illustration of the power of propaganda and the effective manipulation of mass media.

Kamenetsky, C. *Children's literature in Hitler's Germany: The cultural policy of national socialism.* Athens, OH: Ohio University Press, 1986.
> Tells the influence of the Nazi government on children's literature. Examines censorship, school reform, and control of libraries and publishers.

Kohl, H. *From Archetype to Zeitgeist: Powerful ideas for powerful thinking.* Boston: Little, Brown and Company, 1992.
> A book of words and concepts that help explain ideas.

Lifton, R. *The Nazi doctors: Medical killings and the psychology of genocide.* New York: Basic Books, 1988.
> German records and interviews of Nazi doctors, prison doctors, and survivors of the camps about the role of doctors and their rationalization of it.

Simon, R. *A. Selected bibliography of literature on the Holocaust for juvenile and young adult collections.* Rev. ed. New York: Association of Jewish Libraries, 1988.

Recipes

Latkes

Ingredients
6 medium-sized potatoes
1 small onion
2 small zucchini—optional
1 medium-large carrot—optional
1 egg, beaten
3 Tbs. flour
1/2 tsp. baking powder

Directions:

Grate potatoes and add grated onions. Add veggies if desired.

Press out potato juice.

Add the beaten egg, flour, and baking powder.

In heavy (or electric) skillet, fry by rounded teaspoons, flattening down. Use peanut or safflower oil and have it HOT.

Drain on absorbent paper.

Serve with applesauce, sour cream, maybe a pickle . . .?!

Applesauce

Ingredients
10 large apples
sugar to taste

Directions:

Peel and core the apples.

Dice the apples.

Put apples in a pan with just enough water to cover the bottom.

Bake at 350 degrees until soft, approximately 30-45 minutes.

Add sugar to taste.

Evaluation

Throughout the unit we will assess what the students have learned in many authentic ways. All students will keep a portfolio of their work from the beginning process until arriving at the finished product. The portfolio will be a source of pride and motivation for the students in that it will indicate progress. Other forms of assessment will take place as well. For example, the student journals will be read and responded to. The teacher will be looking for development of writing skills, maturation of thoughts, and understanding of the subject matter. The teacher will hold periodic interviews with the students to discuss their progress and reassess needs. Students' projects will be assessed in a similarly authentic manner. The students will have many opportunities for self and peer evaluation during interviews, in journals, and in group work. After the peer assessment, the teacher will evaluate each student's work.

The culminating project to be assessed in the newspaper. The teacher will set the following criteria:

- Does the newspaper demonstrate an understanding of the Holocaust?

- Is the information analyzed and synthesized in a coherent manner?

- Is the project empathic and tolerant of differences?

- Do the students effectively communicate their thoughts and ideas?

- Does the newspaper have a logical and sequential order?

- Do the students demonstrate critical thinking?

- Do the students demonstrate development of reading and writing skills throughout the unit?

- Is the newspaper aesthetically pleasing?

Some criteria address the group and will be assessed in that way, and other criteria will be assessed individually.

The teacher will know this unit has been successful through the use of student evaluations and the teacher's journal. The evaluation will give the teacher insight into what the students found enjoyable, purposeful, and useful. A daily record will be kept in the teacher's journal about what is occurring in the classroom. This includes, but is not limited to: evidence of student motivation and understanding; progress of the students; reactions to activities; and comments and reflections. The need for adjustments will be noted. The teacher will know the unit is successful by the reactions from the school and community to the newspaper, Children's Museum, and Holocaust Remembrance Day.

Psychology and the Media

by Mark Kenji Fulton
Teacher and Doctoral Candidate, Teachers College, Columbia University

Rationale

The Influence of Mass Media

In today's information-rich environment, where common experience derives as much from mass communication as from community and tradition, education stands at a crossroads. Every day we confront an overload of messages that we do not know how to process. We are overwhelmed with facts, ideas, images, sounds, statistics, and points-of-view. The danger is that much of this information is designed not to inform us, but to persuade us. However, while we are aware of media influence, our education does not prepare us to think critically about information.

Vulnerability to the media arises from two general weaknesses in education. First, we are unaware of the basic principles of persuasion. Without knowing the means by which others influence us, we cannot learn to pick up on the cues that signal hidden influence, faulty reasoning or misused information. Ignorance of the methods of persuasion increases the media's power over us.

Second, when we do think critically about the media, we tend to rely on convention. We develop "critical thinking heuristics," or rules-of-thumb for analyzing the media, but rarely go beyond these bits of conventional wisdom. On the other hand, these heuristics which help us analyze the media are essential, but they must be developed to match the sophistication of the persuasive techniques being used.

A Critical Thinking Curriculum for Psychology

This curriculum unit attempts to refine critical thinking with respect to information and the media. It is designed for a high school psychology course, focusing the study of influence and persuasion on an analysis of the media. The students begin by learning some of the psychological tendencies that make people vulnerable to persuasion. They will learn about information, how it is used to influence us, and how it is often misinterpreted. They will also learn about the most common techniques of advertising and propaganda. Finally, the students will learn more useful critical thinking heuristics to help them recognize and react to persuasion and influence in the media.

There are three important organizational elements in the curriculum plan which advocate its success in enhancing student learning. First, the unit takes advantage of familiarity to increase understanding. Research suggests that learning which draws from the students' prior knowledge is better understood and transferred (Glaser, 1984; Voss, 1987; Picus, 1983; Levin, 1979). The students already have a substantial base of experience with advertising and the media to keep the concepts and principles tangible. Furthermore, the students are more likely to develop a deeper understanding because they are applying principles to familiar problems.

The nature of the unit also promotes the retention of learning. Picus (1983) points out that students tend to lose trained thinking skills when they do not practice them with frequency. Personal experience suggests that students are truly fascinated with the effects of media. The high exposure and personal relevance of media influence should encourage the students to frequently apply their skills outside of school.

Finally, the unit promotes transfer of thinking skills to other contexts. Salomon and Perkins (1987) found that thinking skills are often transferred to other contexts when a student practices them to "near automaticity." Students should transfer critical thinking skills to a new context when they identify some cue that reminds them of persuasion in the media. We have tried to encourage this form of transfer by having the students actively identify cues to the presence of persuasion.

Critical Consumers of Mass Media

The primary purpose of teaching critical thinking is to enable individuals to make good decisions. The media is arguably the most relevant context for critical thinking because it has become the center of learning and experience. Whether we are driving past a billboard, reading a newspaper or relaxing in front of the television, we are exposed to the influence of the media. Teaching critical thinking skills and decision-making is incomplete unless students learn to turn a critical eye to this powerful modern environment.

Goals for Student Learning

Content Goals

The content goals in this unit revolve around the student's ability to grasp the psychological principles related to persuasion and influence. Furthermore, the students will be expected to actively use their skills of analysis to apply the principles and create their own examples of persuasion. The students will be able to:

- understand and explain the psychological needs and tendencies that make people vulnerable to media influence

- understand and explain the psychological principles behind persuasion

- identify and explain the specific techniques used in propaganda and persuasion

- understand and apply the concepts used in psychology and sociology to define and describe culture

- produce original projects which illustrate principles and techniques of persuasion using written, visual, audio, and/or video media

Process Goals

While the content goals aim at increasing the student's understanding of the psychological principles behind persuasion, the process goals involve using these concepts to think critically about the media. The students will learn to:

- examine media for persuasive messages

- identify and explain how information is used to persuade

- propose alternative interpretations of data or possible original contents for out-of-context information

- critically examine magazines, television, and movies for the covert messages that they convey about our society

- judge between sound and faulty argument

- develop methods for identifying interpersonal (verbal and nonverbal) and intrapersonal cues that signal the presence of influence and persuasion

Affective Goals

Teaching students to think critically about the media is incomplete by itself. The affective goals of this unit revolve around the students' ability to examine their own beliefs and reasoning. This completes the cycle of critical thinking by teaching the students critical self-examination. The students will:

- critically examine and re-evaluate the origins of their own beliefs about roles, norms, etc., in society
- begin the process of defining their opinions and standards about society based on their own values rather than the media's
- reject an argument when it is based on faulty reasoning in favor of an opinion which they hold
- reserve judgment on issues when they feel that there is not enough evidence to make a conclusion
- respect the right to hold an opinion which they don't hold when it is based on sound reasoning or another perspective

Organization

Organizing Structure

This curriculum is an organized analysis of persuasion and influence in the media. Through the course of twenty-five lessons (over a five-week period) the students study the psychological bases of influence and persuasion while refining their ability to both critically analyze and respond to the media. Their investigation of the media is divided into the three sub-units: information, exposure, and communication. While these topics represent the three basic means by which the media influences and persuades, they provide useful lenses through which the students can critically analyze the media.

The three sub-units comprise the core of the unit. The students begin with an analysis of how information is manipulated in the media. They investigate the various ways in which advertisers use information to make deceptive claims, draw false conclusions, and create an air of legitimacy. Next, the students will study the issue of exposure. They will consider how, through covert messages, the media defines both our culture and our perceived needs. Finally, the students study communication in the media. Here they will analyze persuasion and influence as it occurs in contexts such as argument, debate, and salesmanship.

In addition to the core there will be an introduction and conclusion. The introduction serves to orient the students with two general theories of persuasion and influence. It also provides a number of themes to which the students will return throughout the unit. The conclusion is a culminating activity that requires the students to synthesize their knowledge and integrate their skills.

Organizing Principles

The continuity of the unit is based on two elements. First, the psychological theories of persuasion and influence gain thematic continuity through the systematic analysis of the media. Second, in each of the three sub-units, the students go through three processes: they learn the relevant psychological principles and techniques; they will apply these ideas in an analysis of the media; and they determine ways to identify and guard against the various forms of media influence and persuasion. These processes provide continuity and coherence to the analysis itself.

The sequence of the unit is also created in two ways. First, within each sub-unit, the students build on prior knowledge in order to understand the particular dynamics of persuasion and influence in that area. Second, through the course of the unit the complexity of the learning experiences increases to require higher levels of thinking from the student. Students begin at the lower levels of Bloom's Taxonomy and gradually work their way to the highest levels, synthesis, and evaluation, in the culminating activity.

Content Outline

I. The Media and Society

A. Introduce to the Notions of Mass Media and Influence

B. What Makes Us Vulnerable to Persuasion? Packard's Eight Hidden Needs

C. How Does Media Persuasion Operate? Rank's "Downplay and Intensify" Model of Persuasion

II. Information and Influence—The Use and Misuse of Information

A. Principles

   1. The Misuse of Random and Ambiguous Data

   2. The Sleeper Effect

   3. Indirect Influence

B. Applications

   1. Emotional Evidence (the use of anecdotes and appeals)

   2. Rational Evidence (misread and out-of-context data)

C. Cues / Short Quiz #1

III. Exposure and Influence—The Media and Culture

A. Principles

   1. Weak Messages

   2. Repetition

B. Applications

   1. Covert Messages, Norms, and Socialization in the Media

   2. Status, Roles, and Stereotypes in the Media

C. Cues / Review

IV. Communication and Influence—Techniques of Persuasion

A. Principles

    1. Influence through Commitment

    2. Faulty Reasoning Designed to Persuade

B. Applications

    1. Foot-in-the-Door-Phenomenon and Low-Ball

    2. Faulty Reasoning and Other Devices Used in Propaganda

C. Cues / Short Quiz #2

V. Wrap-Up

A. Identifying Cues

    1. Verbal Cues (Repetition and Intonation)

    2. Non-Verbal Cues (Body Language)

    3. Internal Cues (Sensing Conformity Pressure)

B. Culminating Activity: Projects and Open House

Learning Experiences

Introduction to Media Influence (Week One)

Ad Count: (comprehension) Have the students count the number of times they encounter any kind of advertisement during the course of one day (this should include billboards on the way to school, radio or television ads, or any ads that they might encounter in school). The next day, the teacher should find the average number of ads seen by the students, multiply that number by 365, and start a discussion on the importance of studying media and media influence.

Scrapbook: (comprehension, application, and analysis) The students will create a scrapbook in which they keep examples of magazine advertisements or descriptions of television and radio advertisements which illustrate the principles and techniques studied in class. Each example is accompanied by a brief description of the idea it illustrates and an explanation of how it illustrates that idea. This activity will be ongoing throughout the unit.

Information and Influence (Week Two)

The Consumer Challenge: (comprehension, application, and analysis) Have the students discuss some of the outlandish claims and "evidence" used to sell products. Good examples include claims made by crazy glue or language tapes which claim to teach you while you sleep. Then call the company and ask it to substantiate its claims about the product. Either record the conversation or take notes. If the students seem up to it, you can have them study different products and call the companies. Report your findings to the class. Have the students compare and contrast the claims, evidence, and implied evidence in the ads and those given over the phone. Have them discuss how one detects unreasonable claims, implied evidence or misused data in other contexts. If there is a political election going on, this learning experience could be carried out with political ads.

Appeals to Reason vs. Emotion: (comprehension, application, analysis, and synthesis) Give each student an example of an emotional appeal and a rational appeal in ads or politics (the two appeals should be for different issues or products). Have the students compose their own appeals by rewriting the emotional appeal as a rational appeal, and vice versa. Have them include it in their scrapbooks with an analysis.

Exposure and Influence (Week Three)

Media and Culture: (comprehension, application, and analysis) Have the students break up into discussion groups. Give each group a topic and have them discuss the ways in which media defines our notions of people. Sample discussion topics: racial or gender representation, racial stereotypes, sex-roles, representations of religion, and symbols of status. Have the students share their observations with their classmates. Finally, have the students look for examples of their ideas and add them to their scrap books with an analysis.

Compare Magazines: (comprehension, application, analysis, and synthesis) Have the students compare two magazines that are targeted for audiences which are similar in some respect and different in another respect (for example, *Cosmopolitan* and *Family Circle*, or *Seventeen* and *Guitar Player*, or *Daily News* and *Wall Street Journal*). Have the students compare and contrast the ads. How are they similar? Have the students graph the number of times each of Packard's hidden needs are appealed to. You can have the students hypothesize which kinds of appeal will occur most in each magazine and then see if they are right. Have the students infer what assumptions are made about the populations.

Communication and Influence (Week Four)

Propaganda Film Analysis: (comprehension, application, and analysis) Have the students compare and contrast the propaganda techniques used in a Nazi propaganda film and a U.S. Cold War newsreel. Have the students compare and contrast the propaganda techniques used in each. Discuss the control of news during the Gulf War. Discuss the pros and cons of government control of the media during war and peace.

Presidential Debate: (comprehension, application, analysis, synthesis, and evaluation) Have the students watch the second presidential debate between George Bush, Bill Clinton, and Ross Perot. Have them identify and analyze faulty reasoning typical of propaganda. (Note: all three of the candidates provide examples.) Have the students suggest/predict alternative arguments or retorts. Stop the video and have the students evaluate the reasoning when they call it to question.

Wrap-Up (Week Five)

Nonverbal Persuasion: (comprehension, application, analysis, and synthesis) Show the students a series of television ads with the sound turned off. Have them identify principles of persuasion in body-language, facial expression, and camera maneuvers. Have the students add to their scrapbooks examples of nonverbal persuasion from magazine ads.

Verbal Persuasion: (comprehension, application, analysis, synthesis, and evaluation) To remind the students that there are positive uses for persuasion, have them listen to (not watch) Dr. Martin Luther King's Jr.'s "I have a dream" speech and/or John F. Kennedy's inaugural address. Have the students identify verbal cues of persuasion (like repetition or intonation). You can also bring in radio commercials and compare them to the speeches. Finally, have the students evaluate the persuasive elements in the speeches.

Culminating Experience: (comprehension, application, analysis, synthesis, and evaluation) As a culminating experience for the unit, let the students divide into groups of three or four. Have each group select four concepts, techniques or principles that they have learned in the unit. Each group will have to prepare three things:

First, each group must collect its members' scrapbook materials on the chosen concepts. Each group chooses its four favorite examples. These examples are entered into a template on a word processor. (The students might be given class time to do this.) The templates will be used to create a book on the techniques and principles of media persuasion.

Second, each group must design a political or commercial advertisement. This ad should illustrate the four principles of persuasion that the group has chosen. This ad can be produced in the medium of choice.

Finally, each group must prepare a presentation of its ideas for an open house. The open house can be for schoolmates and/or parents. (Since the students will need time to prepare, it should not take place until a couple of weeks after the completion of the unit). The teacher will correct the templates and compile a class book about the psychology of persuasion in the media.

Evaluation Plan

Evaluation of Student Learning

One of the basic conditions of authentic assessment is that evaluation should resemble real-world tasks. This curriculum is well-suited for authentic assessment because it is designed to increase the students' ability to critically analyze the media. Students readily acknowledge the material as both relevant and practical.

Students are provided ample opportunities to exhibit their learning through presentations and projects which draw on other kinds of talent and learning. Variety is seen as a critical element in addressing differences in both learning style and types of intelligence.

Written Quizzes: Two short-essay quizzes should be given during the unit, which require students to explain and apply concepts learned in class. The quizzes should aim at encouraging the students to review what they have learned. The final evaluation, however, should come in the form of the open-house presentations rather than as a test.

Scrapbooks: The scrapbooks are a means of both learning and evaluation. The student can use the examples to enrich their understanding and reinforce their memory. The teacher should grade the completeness of the scrapbook, the quality of examples, and the accuracy of the analyses.

Class Participation: Because the topics are so familiar to students, discussion can easily be an integral part of evaluation. The teacher must create an environment that recognizes student 'expertise' and invites input. Teachers can achieve this by referring back to examples provided by the *students* and by using student scrapbook examples to illustrate ideas in class. Students should be graded on their ability to add to discussion (spontaneously or when encouraged).

Culminating Experience: The final grade for the unit will be based on the students' display of understanding and aptitude in the open-house presentation. Individual grades will be based on the four scrapbook examples chosen by the students and their individual part of the presentation. The examples should be graded on the quality of choice and analysis. The presentations should be graded on thoroughness, clarity, and accuracy. Finally, group grades should be given for the advertisement designed by the students. The ads should be graded on their workmanship, accuracy, persuasiveness, and originality.

Teacher's Self-Evaluation

Critique of Lesson Plan: Pedagogical content knowledge refers to the knowledge that a teacher has, not simply about the subject, but how the subject is best taught. This is one of the fundamental characteristics of quality teaching. Therefore, the teacher should also keep a record of which elements of the lesson went well. Likewise, the teacher should record the success of various activities and change or replace them as she/he sees fit.

Classroom Environment: As part of a self-evaluation, the teacher should also consider the classroom environment. Did the students participate freely or did they need a lot of prompting? Did the activities promote learning or were they seen as a free-period? Did certain students dominate the discussion time? Were students and teacher comfortable enough to share experiences? Was there any room for humor in the lectures of discussion?

Evaluation of the Curriculum

Anonymous Questionnaire: The teacher should distribute an anonymous questionnaire at the end of the unit (or semester) to solicit opinions from the students regarding interest, how time was spent, information learned, and application of information outside of school.

Informal Evaluations: Teachers are also recommended to solicit information from students in other, informal contexts. When students seem disinterested in the lecture, discussion or activity, the teacher should invite student input. This also promotes a closer-knit environment in the classroom.

Evaluation of Final Projects—Advertisements

This evaluation chart should be used to evaluate the advertisements that the students design for their culminating activity.

	Superior Achievement (5-10)	Commendable Achievement (10-15)	Mediocre Achievement (15-29)	Minimal Achievement (20-25)
Application of Concepts	Demonstrates understanding through subtle application of the concepts.	Demonstrates understanding of both concepts and application.	Demonstrates only a vague understanding of the concepts.	Does not demonstrate understanding.
Effectiveness of Message	Presents a compelling problem and solution.	Presents a clear problem and solution.	Generally defines a problem and/or solution, but is not clear.	Vague, unclear message.
Originality	Creative. Innovative use of both techniques and/or medium.	Original. Uses traditional ideas in new ways.	Uses ideas from other ads, changing some features.	Not original. Taken from a pre-existing ad.
Overall Workmanship	Polished work. Exhibits artistry and style. Attractive display.	Demonstrates effort and attention to detail.	Incomplete. Less attention to detail, but well-designed.	Incomplete. Sloppy work with no attention to design.

Sample Lesson Plans

Lesson Plan #1—Introduction to Mass Media

Goals

The student will:

- understand and apply the concepts used in psychology and sociology to define and describe culture.

Objectives

The student will:

- define the terms "media," "persuasion," and "influence" as well as supply examples to illustrate the terms.

- consider and discuss the differences between positive, negative, and neutral forms of influence and persuasion in the media.

Materials

- Some examples of well-known slogans for products or public awareness campaigns (like "Just say no," "Friends don't let friends drive drunk," "Nike—Just do it," "Bugle Boy—a common thread," "You've come a long way, baby").

Outline of Lesson

- Before class, write the title of the lesson on the board along with the three definitions. Also write the slogans with the second half of each statement missing (e.g., "Nike-Just _____" or "Friends don't let friends _____").

- (10 minutes) Then tell the students that this is a quiz and that they will have a couple of minutes to finish the ten sentences. When they are finished, have the students volunteer the answers. Find out the average score in the class and discuss why so many students did so well (don't worry, they will all do well).

- (15 minutes) Define the three words and give a brief introduction to influence and persuasion in the media. Even lectures should be interactive, so have students supply parts of your points along the way.

- (15 minutes) Conclude by having the students consider what are good, bad, and neutral examples of persuasion and influence in the media.

Homework

- Have the students count all of the ads that they encounter in one day (see Learning Activities— "Ad Count").

Lesson Plan #2—Packard's Eight Hidden Needs

Goals
The student will:

- understand and explain the psychological needs and tendencies that make people vulnerable to media influence.

- examine media for persuasive messages.

Objectives
The student will:

- work with others to identify the Eight Hidden Needs which advertisements appeal to in people.

- consider how these needs, often intensified by the media, make people more vulnerable to media influence.

Materials

- Magazine advertisements which illustrate Packard's Eight Hidden needs. You should have ten to fifteen examples of each.

- Overhead projector and transparency with definitions for Packard's Eight Hidden Needs.

- Photocopies of the transparency for the students' notebooks.

- Reading assignment on Rank's "Downplay and Intensify" Model of Persuasion.

Outline of Lesson

- (15 minutes) Divide the class into eight groups, hand each group one packet of magazine ads (which illustrate one of Packard's Needs), and have the students infer a common theme among them. Have the students write out the common element on a piece of paper. Walk around the room and help students along if they are having difficulty, by modeling inductive thought processes. Coach them through induction if they still have problems.

- (25 minutes) Go over each group's conclusions and have them describe the common element that they found in the ads. Then put the transparency on the overhead and discuss Packard's Eight Hidden Needs with the students.

Homework

- Reading on Rank's Model of Persuasion.

Lesson Plan #3—Rank's "Downplay and Intensify" Model of Persuasion

Goals
The student will:

- understand and explain the psychological principles behind persuasion.

- identify and explain the specific techniques used in propaganda and persuasion.

- examine media for persuasive messages.

Objectives
The student will:

- apply Rank's notion of intensifying through repetition and association by comparing two political advertisements.

- apply Rank's notion of downplaying through omission, diversion, and confusion by comparing two political advertisements.

Materials

- A series of ads (on videotape) produced by two competing political candidates arguing issues back and forth.

- Television and VCR.

Outline of Lesson

- (15 minutes) Review Rank's three types of downplaying (omission, diversion, and confusion) and three types of intensifying (repetition, association, and composition). Make sure the students understood the examples from the reading. If not have the students who did understand supply further examples.

- (25 minutes) View the ads in the sequence that they appeared on television. Have the students look for which points were intensified and downplayed by each candidate. Have the students suggest which claims might be true (due to omission, confusion or diversion). Are any relatively insignificant points being overemphasized (repetition and association)?

Homework

- Have the students add examples of these techniques for commercial products in their scrapbook with analyses.

Lesson Plan #4—The Misuse of Information: The Absence of Evidence

Goals

The student will:

- identify and explain the specific techniques used in propaganda and persuasion.

- examine media for persuasive messages.

- identify and explain how information is used to persuade.

Objectives

The student will:

- identify deceptive claims in advertising which imply, but do not provide, valid evidence.

- recognize and understand the significance of disclaimers and qualifiers in the media.

- relate these claims to Rank's Model.

Materials

- Copy of *The National Inquirer*.

- Some examples of spurious claims made by commercial products like subliminal message learning tapes and outrageous weight-loss programs.

- Overhead projector and a transparency of the ad(s).

Outline of Lesson

- Before class, write the definitions of "disclaimer" and "to qualify" on the board.

- (5 minutes) Ask someone in the class to explain what a disclaimer is. Ask for someone to explain the verb "to qualify" (as in, "to reduce the strength or limit the meaning of a statement with exceptions").

- (20 minutes) Show the students the cover of *The National Inquirer* and start a discussion about evidence and claims in the media. Read through one of the articles in class and get the students to identify any statements in which the authors qualify their outrageous claims. Relate to Rank's Model.

- (15 minutes) Show the students the deceptive advertisement. Have them critique the claims that it makes. Explain to the students about the existence of laws against false advertising. Have them hypothesize how the advertisers were able to make their claim without breaking the law. The students should record their hypotheses. Tell the class that you will call the company and have them substantiate their claims. This could also be done by some very motivated students, but go over the questions that they should ask with them (see Lesson Plan #6 for an explanation of the follow-up activity).

Homework

- Have the students find examples and add them to their scrapbooks with analyses.

Lesson Plan #5—The Misuse of Information: Misinterpreted Evidence

Goals

The student will:

- understand and explain the psychological principles behind persuasion.

- identify and explain the specific techniques used in propaganda and persuasion.

- examine media for persuasive messages.

- identify and explain how information is used to persuade.

Objectives

The student will:

- explain ways in which random, inconclusive, and ambiguous information can be manipulated in advertising and politics to persuade.

- understand "the sleeper effect" in psychology and how it affects our judgment of inconclusive evidence.

Materials

- Photocopied reading on incomplete, random, and inconclusive evidence.

Outline of Lesson

- (20 minutes) Define ambiguous, random, and inconclusive data. Explain how they can be manipulated for persuasive ends in situations like the diet programs and psychic phone services.

- (10 minutes) Discuss how Packard's needs allow people to accept misused information even when their better judgment would counsel them otherwise.

- (10 minutes) Ask the students "have you ever asked someone 'how do you know that' and had them reply 'I read it somewhere'?" This could be the truth, a lie, or "the sleeper effect." Discuss how this effect leaves us vulnerable to the misuse of information.

Homework

- Reading on incomplete, random, and inconclusive evidence.

Lesson Plan #6—The Consumer's Challenge

Goals
The student will:

- examine media for persuasive messages.

- identify and explain how information is used to persuade.

- propose alternative interpretations of data or possible original contexts for out-of-context information.

Objectives
The student will:

- compare and contrast claims and actual evidence for a product.

- analyze how advertisers get around false advertising laws by using deceptive claims.

- generate a list of cues that might help them identify deceptive claims.

Materials

- A recording of or notes from the interview with the advertisers of the product discussed in Lesson Plan #4.

- Overhead projector and transparency of the deceptive claim from Lesson Plan #4.

Outline of Lesson

- (5 minutes) Share your notes or recording with the students.

- (20 minutes) Have the students compare and contrast the claims and evidence used in the two contexts. Have them explain how the advertisers skirted false advertising laws.

- (15 minutes) Have the students divide into groups of three. Then have use this situation as well as *The National Inquirer* article from Lesson #4 to generate a list of cues for deceptive claims. In other words, have them list out the different ways in which one might detect deceptive claims in the media. Have them share some conclusions at the end of class.

Homework

- Have the students enter their list of cues into their scrap books.

- Remind the students to study for the quiz at the beginning of next week. The quiz will include: Packard's Eight Needs, Rank's "Downplay and Intensify" Model of Persuasion, the Sleeper Effect, and Out-of-Context Device. The students will also be responsible for explaining disclaimers; qualifiers; how random, ambiguous, and inconclusive evidence can be used; and the different aims of emotional and rational persuasion. (Some of these topics will be covered in the next two lessons.)

Glossary

body language—nonverbal communication of ideas through gestures, posture, and facial expressions.

conformity pressure—an implicit or explicit demand that an individual act like the group.

covert messages—value messages or assumptions about our society that are implicitly stated in media.

downplay—part of Rank's theory that suggests that persuaders de-emphasize both their own faults and the assets of their opponents. This can be achieved through omission, diversion or confusion.

foot-in-the-door phenomenon—the technique of persuasion by which a person persuades someone to accept a large, costly request by first getting them to accept a series of smaller, insignificant requests. This technique operates on the principle that people are driven by the need to be consistent.

influence—to affect the thoughts, beliefs or actions of another person.

intensify—part of Rank's theory that suggests that persuaders emphasize both their own asset and the faults of their opponents. This can be achieved through repetition, association, and composition.

low-ball technique—the technique of persuasion by which a person persuades someone to accept a request by first asking for a small request and then raising the request. This technique operates on the principle that people feel uncomfortable when they back out of commitment.

mass media—a medium of communication (like television, radio, magazines) that is designed to reach a large number of people.

norm—a belief or value which is held by a group which may not be accepted by individual members of a group.

Packard's Eight Hidden Needs—a theory put forward by Vance Packard which suggests that advertisers generally attempt to persuade by appealing to one or more of eight psychological needs that people have. These needs are: the need for reassurance of worth, ego gratification, emotional security, creative outlets, love objects, a sense of power, roots, and immortality.

persuasion—the active attempt to change the thoughts, beliefs or actions of another person.

propaganda—ideas, facts or allegations that spread deliberately to further one's cause or damage an opposing cause.

role—the behaviors that we learn which meet the expectations or satisfy the needs of others. Each person plays many roles in society.

sleeper effect—the tendency for certainty about information to increase over time. This is usually attributed to the fact that we remember the information, while we forget the source that we got it from.

socialization—the process by which an individual consciously or unconsciously adopts the values and beliefs of the group.

status—the position, rank or prestige held by a person in a group. It can also refer to the position of groups of people in a society.

stereotype—a group-shared image of another group of people. They can be positive or negative.

weak message—a small seemingly insignificant bit of false information that people accept without questioning.

Bibliography

Glaser, R. (1984). Education and thinking: The role of knowledge. *American Psychologist, 21*(1-2), 99–120.

Levin, T. (1979). Instruction which enables students to develop higher mental processes. *Evaluation in Education: An International Review Series, 3*(3), 174–220.

Picus, L. (1983). *Teaching problem-solving: A research synthesis.* Portland, OR: Northwest Regional Educational Laboratory.

Salomon, G. & Perkins, D. (1987). Transfer of cognitive skill from programming: When and how? *Journal of Education Computing Research, 3*(2), 149–169.

Voss, J. F. (1987). Learning and transfer in subject-matter learning: A problem-solving model. *International Journal of Educational Research, 11*, 607–622.

Resource and Materials

Books

Berger, A. A. (1982). *Media analysis techniques.* Beverly Hills: Sage Publications.

Brembeck, W. & Howell, W. (1976). *Persuasion: A means of social influence.* Englewood Cliffs, NJ: Prentice Hall.

Burton G. & Dimbleby, R. (1990). *Teaching communication.* London: Routledge and Kegan Paul.

Crespi, I. (1989). *Public opinion, polls, and democracy.* Boulder, CO: Westview Press.

Gilovich, T. (1991) *How we know what isn't so: The fallibility of reason in everyday life.* New York: The Free Press.

Heinz, A. C. (1970). *Persuasion.* Chicago: Loyola University Press.

Larson, C. (1986). *Persuasion: Reception and responsibility.* Belmont, CA: Wadsworth Publishing Company.

Parkins, A. & Aronson, E. (1991). *Age of propaganda: The everyday use and abuse of persuasion.* New York: W. H. Freeman Company.

West, C. (1981). *The social and psychological distortion of information.* Chicago: Nelson Hall.

Zimbardo, P. & Leippe, M. (1991). *The psychology of attitude change and social influence.* Philadelphia: Temple University Press.

Video Resources

Road to the White House (57 minutes)—VHS. Purdue University Public Affairs Video Archives, 1988.
Summary: Shows several commercials from the 1988 presidential campaign, with analysis from a specialization political advertising.

Sexism, Stereotype, and Hidden Values (29 minutes)—VHS. Nancy Reeves / Films, Inc., 1987.
Summary: Sexism and other forms of stereotyping are identified. Suggestions for how to recognize and avoid hidden presumptions and values.

Media and Society: News Military and the Media (90 minutes)—VHS. Columbia University and WNET, 1985.
Summary: Note: only part of the video is relevant—the role of the media in the Gulf War. Issues of censorship and propaganda discussed.

The Uses of the Media (26 minutes)—VHS. Films for the Humanities, Inc., 1989.
Summary: Examines the impact of television on the way we see ourselves as a society. Explores the hidden messages that television communicates and discusses how these messages influence viewers.

Media Probes: Political Spots (30 minutes)—VHS. Time Life Video, 1982.
Summary: Introduction to the techniques used by political advertisers. Samples from around the country, representing all political parties and various levels of government.

Media Probes: Language (30 minutes)—VHS. Time Life Video, 1982
Summary: Demonstrates how language is a powerful medium that has an impact in every corner of society.

Magazine, Radio, and TV Advertisements

Of course, the success of this unit depends on the ability of the teacher to relate the material to the media. Therefore, the teacher must collect up-to-date examples of advertising and propaganda from the media. Consult magazines, radio, and television. Also, collect a "library" of magazines for the students to use. Many students will not have access to a variety of magazines.

Appendix D—Chart of Learning Experiences

Learning Experiences

	comprehension	application	analysis	synthesis	evaluation
Ad Count	X	X			
Scrapbook	X	X	X		
Political Ad Comparison	X	X	X		
Consumer Challenge	X	X	X		
Ad Rewrite	X	X	X	X	
Magazine Comparison	X	X	X		
Covert Messages	X	X	X	X	
T.V. Debate Analysis	X	X	X		
Propaganda Film Analysis	X	X	X		
Body Language on T.V.	X	X	X	X	
Persuasive Speeches	X	X	X	X	X
Open House Projects	X	X	X	X	X

POWER:
Untitled and Unbridled

by Catherine Franklin Talon
Teacher and Doctoral Candidate, Teachers College, Columbia University
and Judith King-Calneck
National Public Radio and Doctoral Canadiate, Teachers College Columbia University

> *"(Life is a) game, my ass. Some game. If you get on the side where all the hot-shots are, then it's a game, all right—I'll admit that. But if you get on the other side, where there aren't any hot-shots, then what's a game about it? Nothing."*

> Holden Caufield in J. D. Salinger's
> *The Catcher in the Rye* (1951:8)

Overview

J. D. Salinger in his novel, *The Catcher in the Rye,* captured the bitter mood of adolescence in the above passage. To Holden Caufield, the main hero (anti-hero) in this story, life was a struggle of power. This story strikes the soul of countless generations of adolescents. They see themselves in Holden. They, too, question the meaning of power. The honesty and security of childhood fades the more one looks into the ambiguous and hypocritical world of the future.

How should I live? What is the right action to take? How do I know it to be right? These are some of the questions that people continually ask themselves throughout their lives. Kohlberg (in Howard, 1991, (p. 43) suggests that humans are essentially philosophers. Adolescents, according to Kohlberg and Gilligan (1972) are the quintessential philosophers and the age is marked by the (re)discovery and (re)definition of self.

Are young adolescents ready to experience and intellectualize power? Is it too explosive an issue for them? Bruner (in Egan, 1992, pp. 50-51) states that "the foundations of any subject may be taught to anybody at any age in some form." The key is to involve the individual's mind to construct, compose, and reassess the learning experience. Classroom strategies used to explore power in this curriculum are sensitive to the diversity of the human mind. As there are different ways of thinking, there are different ways of learning. The lessons prepared in this curriculum address the iconic (visual-spatial), enactive (kinesthetic action), and symbolic (deductive logic) regions of the mind (Bruner et al., 1967)

Rationale

What is this Curriculum?

The aim of this curriculum is to create a safe learning environment in which students can explore historical and contemporary aspects and applications of power. It takes into account issues such as race, gender, and class and how are they linked to power. The curriculum probes three levels: the identity of the individual, the role of the individual in society, and the role of social institutions.

At a time in life when many physical, social, and emotional changes are happening, this curriculum enables the young adolescent to analyze his/her own questions of identity. This hands-on approach asks pertinent questions about the student's struggle for peer, familial, and societal power. It provides a process for the adolescent to explore a variety of possible issues.

Within a context of civic power and responsibility, constitutional democracy is critically analyzed. The curriculum serves as an open and safe forum for looking at the social, political, and legal obstacles that individuals have had to overcome in our society to establish their rights. An analysis of the subsequent consequences of their actions is addressed. In the same context, students will consider how society's institutions and organizationss reflect different aspects of power. Furthermore, a study on how these institutions help and/or hinder individuals and groups in society is conducted.

Who is this Curriculum for?

This curriculum is designed especially for early adolescents. It responds specifically to the needs and concerns of adolescents by including the following elements:

1. a diversity of opportunities by incorporating concrete and abstract learning activities that make use of sensory modes and rhythms;

2. time for personal reflection, self-exploration, and self-definition to help students respond to their changing identities (physical and social), and relations with peers and adults;

3. opportunity to take risks, show initiative, develop, and respect their own creativity;

4. physical activity (from Dorman in Lipsitz, 1984; p.10).

Why is Curriculum Important?

It Serves the Needs of the Student. The adolescent can identify with this curriculum. The theme it addresses reflects the same issues that a young person faces on a daily basis: identity, belonging, justice. As the study of power progresses, the student will have the opportunity to explore interpersonal dynamics, citizen rights, and civic responsibilities. In this stage of development the adolescent is forming an identity, the development of a positive self-image, is crucial (Edwards, 1982; Martin, 1972). Unlike the alienated Holden in *The Catcher in the Rye,* the student in this curriculum can acquire confidence to handle power effectively.

It Serves the Needs of the Community. Ensuring and empowering the democratic spirit in community situations is the primary aim of this curriculum. Throughout the curriculum, the community is alternately defined as students' immediate surroundings (local community), the national community, and the global community. A viable democracy depends on an informed, demanding, and interested populace. Banks' (1991, p. 140) multicultural literacy approach captures the essence of this:

> The major goals of a curriculum ...should be to help students to know, to care, and to act in ways that will develop and foster a democratic and just society where all groups experience cultural democracy and empowerment...students also must develop commitment to personal, social, and civic action...

Through an intense study of power, students will embark on a cognitive and affective journey. Through this exploration, the student will develop a keener understanding of the relationships between his/her own immediate community to larger communities. Ideally, the participant will identify concerns of the neighborhood and explore possible solutions that could address the obstacles faced by the people.

It Serves the Needs of the Society. With grim frequency, school violence and teenager crime are key items in the media today. No longer isolated to only urban settings, school violence threatens to become a national trend. To determine the effectiveness of civic education on student behavior, the U. S. Department of Justice in 1979 initiated a four-year study. Startling results were attained:

> The evaluators found that students who are exposed to properly implemented law-related education programs are less likely than others of the same age to engage in theft, to use violence against other students, and to be involved in gang fights, to avoid payments for goods and services, to cheat on tests, to be truant, . . .
>
> Teachers in the study overwhelmingly reported that the curricular programs had favorable effects on the development of a number of general student skills and attitudes. These included participating competently in classroom activities, understanding a variety of views, and working cooperatively with students of different backgrounds. (Letwin, 1991, pp. 210-11).

Similar studies have been done around the nation (Valett, 1991, pp. 243-58). The results tend to concur with the above report. This points to the relevance and timeliness of civic education.

What is Unique About this Curriculum?

There are two areas that distinguish this curriculum from others: its educational orientation and its differentiation for the gifted and talented adolescent. The philosophical tone of this curriculum is influenced by social reconstructionism and pragmatism as well as feminist applications of critical education theory (Eisneer, 1985; Weiler, 1988 which is discussed later in this paper). In the social reconstructionist model, people are perceived as viable change agents. It is also assumed that cognitive processes can be nutured, that teaching/learning objectives should partially stem from students' cognitive levels/orientations, and assessments should consider students' individual cognitive growth. Within the classroom, the vision of battering the human condition is advocated. The pragmatic approach is also appropriate for this student population as it focuses on the new *ways* to think rather than new *things* to think. It recognizes the fluid state of knowledge which is in a constant movement of dynamic development.

Social reconstructionism and pragmatism complement each other. One is involved in providing the individual with the process to strive for self-realization, and the other links the individual to the group. Both philosophies focus on the hands-on exploration of defining issues and solving problems. Neither is taken to the extreme. The curriculum uses these two perspectives to allow the individual and the group to experience democracy.

Along with its educational orientation, this curriculum has another unique aspect. It is differentiated for the gifted and talented. The underlying assumption in this curriculum is that all students have strengths and weaknesses: All students are gifted in one way or another. It is the responsibility of the curriculum and the teacher(s) to tap into and respond to the giftedness of each student.

In order to stimulate the youth's creativity and provide opportunities for gifted expression through different learning modalities, the curriculum is differentiated at various points and in different ways. Using a multiple talent approach (Taylor as discussed in Tannenbaum, 1983; Gardner, 1983, divides talents into linguistic, musical, logical/mathematical, personal, spatial, and bodily-kinesthetic), six broad areas of talent are addressed: academics, creativity, planning, communicating, forecasting, and decision-making. It allows one to achieve success in an area that makes sense to the student. At the same time, this approach challenges the student to develop and explore areas where his/her natural talent is not utilized.

This curriculum is sensitive to the specific talents and needs of students. At the same time, it is flexible to the learning modalities of the students. Throughout the lessons, a variety of activities are used that legitimize the various ways we learn. Using Bob Samples' (1992) learning modalities, five areas are addressed: symbolic abstract, visual-spatial, kinesthetic, auditory, and synergic. Integrated within the scope and sequence of this curriculum, all major ways of learning are supported.

How was this Curriculum Created?

This curriculum was written by a team of people with unique talents: Catherine Franklin Talon, Judith King-Calnek, and Sylvia Dimino. Each member of this team brings certain dimensions to the curriculum (see "Biographies" for detail on the authors' backgrounds). As a collaborative effort, we acknowledge the experience that each of us has had with particular student populations: Hispanic-Americans, Asian-Americans, African-Americans, European-Americans, adults, and children, within the United States and internationally. In addition, we have expertise in a variety of educational settings: public, private, and community-based organizations. Professionally, our roles include classroom teacher, administrator, and consultant.

The process of writing this curriculum has been a learning experience for us all. Catherine Franklin Talon took the initiative of pulling together the group (which originally consisted of Talin, Dimino, and King-Calnek). We decided upon the theme of power by coming at it from different angles. This is reflected in our individual units. The first few meetings consisted of a mixture of focus on the task at hand. Getting to know one another a was major goal as it was the first time we had worked together. Establishing a group rhythm or dynamic was an unspoken task on which we constantly worked.

In our first meeting Talon, Dimino, and King-Calnek discussed our individual interests, exchanged copies of our rationales, and began brainstorming ways of approaching the theme of power. We also discussed the needs of the student population. We thought of exploring power in terms of gender, class, race, age, and economics. At this stage, the group ran out of creative fuel. We became re-energized when we decided not to think of power an adults, but to think of it as an adolescent. Immediately we generated a long list of issues and topics that can relate to power. They include:

> music, dance, friends, health and human development (changing bodies, sex), alcohol, drugs, peers, adults, fun and games, family, sports and athletics, television, movies and videos, in and out groups, gangs and cliques, parties, boyfriends and girlfriends, the environment, school, authority.

From the above list, activities were considered that could serve as building blocks to units related to the theme of power. One of our challenges has been to keep the curriculum and the units interdisciplinary and resist the tendency to fall back into the traditional divisions by discipline. Also we have each struggled to incorporate the idea of having the units reflect multiple perspectives not only by being multicultural, but by drawing on different learning modalities. Our group meetings focused on the body of the curriculum rather than the individual units. We also shared our units with each other as we developed them.

Perhaps our biggest challenge was trying to get all of our voices heard equally in the curriculum. It was a struggle to harmonize our voices because, although we have some similarities, we also have many differences.

Catherine Franklin Talon was the lead writer for the first draft of the overview. She also assisted in the design of the "Rationale," "General Context," "Goals and Purposes," and "Evaluation and

Assessment." Talon edited and collaborated on the other parts of the curriculum body. She is solely responsible for her unit "Power in The Political Process."

Judith King-Calnek was the principle coordinator for the working drafts and final copy of this curriculum. She did considerable work on the writing of the rationale and on the curriculum philosophy. In addition, King-Calnek was the lead editor on all other parts of the curriculum body. She synthesized the ideas from group meetings to reflect one voice. Her organizational skill helped the curriculum progress smoothly through its various stages of development. In addition, she is solely responsible for the unit "Rapping for Power."

Sylvia Dimino contributed to the "Theoretical Foundations" section with some ideas about giftedness. Dimino is responsible for her unit on math and power. Scheduling constraints often made it difficult to find a common time to meet. We all felt that we needed more time to develop the curriculum, our individual units, and solidify our group dynamic.

Concurrent Classroom Study

Catherine Franklin Talon provided insight into the curriculum from her work at Bank Street's School for Children. At the same time she was writing her unit, she was implementing the curriculum in her eighth-grade social studies class. As the lessons are student-centered, its overall effectiveness is determined by how well the students drive the curriculum. Talon had considerable apprehension about allowing the students to "run" this curriculum.

At one point the class senate devised a process to elect a president. Talon shared her concern with the curriculum design team when she asked, "How does one ensure that the best senatory is elected to the position?" We all felt that this was the crux of the "Power" curriculum: As teacher, Talon had to put trust in not only the democratic system, but in her students' newfound power as well. The following week, Talon reported her delight with the students' ability to handle power effectively and constructively.

Philosophy

Biographies and Personal Philosophies

> Schools must breathe life . . . hope . . . and the confidence to effect needed societal change. Knowledge and awareness of the right to use one's own power to effect life is critical. Curiosity should drive the learner to further expand his/her knowledge and experience base. Within this spirit of inquiry, a healthy tension can assert itself. The demands of both the affective and cognitive domains can be met. Education must develop and challenge the whole being. Its aim must ultimately be centered on reflective thought and reflective action.
>
> —Catherine Franklin Talon

Catherine Franklin Talon has taught in a variety of locations around the world. In Fukuoa, Japan, she taught English to housewives, corporate executives, and students. In Bogota, Columbia, she worked in an international school. Talon was the core teacher for a bilingual second grade, as well as the enrichment coordinator for an after-school elementary project. In New York City, she was the coordinator and teacher of social studies for the middle grades in a private, single-sex school. Currently Talon is at Bank Street's School for Children, where she is the head teacher for an eighth-grade class. Using the disciplines of social studies and literature, she teaches a yearlong curriculum on ancient Greece and American democracy.

> I often wonder about the places that race, gender, and class intersect in one's life. How are these places shaped by one's educational experiences? Different from educators such as Tannenbaum (1979), I believe that we must stop looking at education equality and gifted education as mutually exclusive. In my experience as an African-American woman, I believe that education should be truly democratic. Our challenge is to make sure that both educational equality and gifted education happen simultaneously. Then, and only then, can students better understand the nature of power and learn to use their own power in positive and constructive ways.
>
> —Judith King-Calnek

Over the past twelve years, Judith King-Calnek has worked in education in a variety of positions. Most recently she participated in a project that aimed at transforming the workplace of a major manufacturing corporation in Stamford, Connecticut. In that consultancy, King-Calnek conducted needs analyses, designed and piloted employee assessments and courses in technical and team skills, and diversity training. She has conducted numerous consultancies in the Washington, DC, area involving needs assessment, course design and delivery in private and government organizations, and workshops in intercultural training for international students, business people, and Americans. While in Washington, Judith King-Calnek provided project support for U. S. A. I. D.-funded projects in nonformal education and training. She wrote reports on lessons learned, trends in the field, and project findings. King-Calnek works in English, Spanish, and Portuguese, and has traveled extensively throughout the Americas and Caribbean. She taught English language to elementary students and adults in Brazil while she was there conducting research on a Watson fellowship.

Theoretical Foundations

Giroux and Freire (in Weiler, 1988, p. xi) describe school as "a matrix of institutional, personal, and social forces caught up in deeply contradictory tensions that are neither exclusively dominating nor liberating." The authors of this paper were very much influenced by the writings of Freire (1985; in Weiler, 1988) and Weiler (1988) which look at the dynamics within school through the lens of production and reproduction theories and feminist pedagogy (evolved from critical education theory). In general, the approach considers the role of school (curriculum, instruction, teachers, administrators and students) in reproducing the existing social structure (reproduction theory). At the same time, it gives equal consideration to the ways people validate their own experience and effect society on the bases of cultural, sexual, racial, and/or class characteristics (production theory).

It is important to consider both production and reproduction theory in schooling and realize that, as Giroux and Freire (in Weiler, 1988, p. x) note, the two are not "dichotomous social practices. . . [but] are mutually informing relations" that get played out in different areas of our daily lives. They reflect and echo the various forms of power that shape our thoughts, behaviors, relations, and the way we construct knowledge. Therefore, it is only fitting that this be the theoretical foundation upon which a curricular study of power is built.

This curriculum does not accept the concept of a universal form of oppression (Giroux in Freire, 1985, p. xii), rather there are certain "modes of domination" and "diverse forms of collective [and individual] struggle and resistance" that vary depending on the context. This curriculum looks at power in positive, negative, and neutral ways, and as a "combination of historical and contemporary ideological and material practices" (Giroux in Freire, 1985, p. xii). One aspect of power and oppression that is unique to both Freire (Giroux in Freire, 1985, p. xix) and Weiler's approach is that they both call for the need to scrutinize the way people internalize certain tenets of power. Both Freire and Weiler discuss how people participate in their own subjugation. This is explored throughout the curriculum.

Gifted adolescents have many of the same needs as other teenagers. However, they often are more sensitive to their needs and challenges. Often, the emotional and social issues that face the gifted adolescent are a result of their isolation from their peers, their frustration with the curriculum that does not challenge them, and boredom in traditional schools that do not address civic and ethical issues. Gifted adolescents in traditional education programs often feel like round pegs in square holes.

An interdisciplinary approach to the curriculum and differentiation for the gifted go hand in hand. They create a vehicle by which gifted students can view problems from unique perspectives and are able to engage in divergent and convergent thinking. Interdisciplinary teaching/learning provides a natural setting so the student can make connections among many subjects and themes. This curricular approach also facilitates "non-gifted" students' appreciation of new perspectives. That is, it allows for better, more complete learning. Furthermore, it brings out the giftedness of each student. Through the interdisciplinary curriculum, students are stimulated to use cognitive styles not usually invoked in the traditional curriculum. As a result, learning becomes richer, and students see the whole rather than mere fragments of themes. In studying a theme like power, this is especially important as it facilitates the adolescent's ability to think and act in relation to real-life issues.

Key Concepts*

There are many meanings of power that can be applied to scientific entities in world matter, like energy, light, radioactive molecules, scientific abstracts, mathematical ideas, and human beings. The power in human relations can be considered as an individual's power to do something, the capacity of an actor to attain some goal (Russell, 1938), or as interpersonal power, when individuals are interdependent. This curriculum looks at power in the macro sense, or collective power, and the micro sense, individual power.

There are a myriad of shapes, forms, and configurations of power that are touched on throughout the units in this curriculum. Some of them include authority, influence, manipulation, coercion, force, compliance and noncompliance, hegemony and counterhegemony, control, accommodation, choice, persuasion, legitimacy, rights (who defines and assigns rights to whom, when, where, and how), preferences, oppression, subjugation, and freedom. These concepts are explored in great detail in the units, particularly the power relationships in various forms of social, political, and economic realities.

It is essential to notice that power relationships are transcendental. Power as energy flows between the physical world and the world of living organisms. Each living organism is a source of power, because it is able to go on living and it can also empower other living organisms. Human society is something more than a group of interdependent living organisms. People with their intellectual, emotional, physical, spiritual, political, and other forms of power can (as individuals and groups) consciously change the allocation of all kinds of energies and resources. In this context we place the statement that "power works both on and through people" (Freir, 1985).

---

*The background for this section comes from an article contributed by Ryszard Stowowy, the design team's reactions to the article, and conversations with Stowowy.

General Context

Students

This interdisciplinary curriculum is geared for young adolescents in an urban school setting. It can also be easily adapted to suburban and rural environments as well. Typically, the student pool comes from a broad spectrum. Diversity of socioeconomic backgrounds, ethnic and racial heritage, family structure, and learning style indicate the multiplicity of characteristics within the student population.

Institutional Settings

As the creators of this curriculum work in different settings, it was designed for use in a variety of environments. It was created for use in a progressive educational institution. This could be either a formal school or an alternative setting such as a community center. The environment, however, must be one that perceives education as a way to strengthen both the individual and the community. Faculty and student alike are encouraged to develop a sense of societal responsibility. Learning to solve problems together is considered an important task. Furthermore, the learner is seen as a whole entity—made up of social, emotional, and intellectual facets. In this setting, both the teacher and the student are learners and together they create the experience (Lusted as discussed in Weiler, 1988, p. 1).

Activities are experiential and adolescent centered in design. Making coherent and continuing connections between the student's daily life, the community, and the curriculum are particularly important. Within this progressive climate, a rigorous intellectual standard is supported and reflected in the individual units.

Goals and Purposes

Power is at the core of various forms of social, political, and economic realities. Some people have it, some people don't. By reflecting and acting upon one's image of a more equitable world, students begin the journey towards building a better society.

Geared for the young adolescent, this curriculum seeks to develop the individual's knowledge of self and critical consciousness of the world. At a time in life when many physical and emotional changes are happening, this curriculum is designed to help the student deal with his/her own identification with power.

Specifically, "Power" has three ultimate goals for the learner:

1. to participate consciously in the transformation of a "better" society. Different concepts of a "better" society will be defined by students.

2. to consider multiple perspectives for viewing society. These perspectives are informed by gender, class, race, religion, etc.; and

3. to increase the level of consciousness where the student will be aware that "power works both on and through people" (Freire, 1985).

Guiding Questions

A circular of learning and teaching is followed in this curriculum. Like the infinity sign, the study of power is never ending. Certain guiding questions are asked throughout the study of this topic:

1. **How is power identified? (a) How does one keep it? (b) How does one share it?** This question breaks down the mystique power. Its purpose is to begin to look at power in nontraditional as well as traditional ways. Distinguishing the elements related to power and how those elements related to one another is a key part of identifying power. What forces promote power? What are the elements within power that can be seen, felt, heard, touched, etc.? These are some of the issues that frame this guiding question.

2. **What are some forms of power?** This deceptively straightforward question challenges the student to analyze forms of power. It then proceeds to analyze the value of various forms of power. In a given situation, is one form of power more effective than another? In addition, the student validates her/his responses to this provocative question through experience, research, and discussion.

3. **How is power manifested in daily life?** Power can be a subtle, invisible force, or a blatant, tangible entity. By becoming more sensitive to the ways power is manifested, it allows the individual to be critically conscious of power. By being able to intellectualize and emotionalize power, sharing positive and negative experiences with it, the participant in this curriculum will

become more aware of this force. This, in turn, gives her/him an educated edge when found in a "powerless" or "powerful" role.

Specifically, this question addresses the verbal and nonverbal issues related to power. Words and weapons are two ways that power is expressed. It is a travesty that adolescents and adults resort to guns to resolve issues of power. They need to develop their awareness of other more peaceful alternatives to the expression of power. This need is not an adult agenda to teach the younger generation. Rather, it is a civilized, humane response generated by society to get back in touch with the power within us all.

Framework

Each of the four units within this curriculum is based on the three-dimensional model depicted on the next page. The three dimensions addressed are curricular modalities (skills areas), students learning modalities, and guiding questions. Within the classroom setting, a variety of instructional modes are used, including individual, small group (cooperative and competitive), and whole class. The specific lesson and student/teacher preference will determine the type of setting that is used. The curriculum is composed of various projects that are experiential and hands-on. In addition, projects vary in depth and length. Some are short-term, others extend throughout the semester. Lastly, lessons are differentiated for the specific talents and gifts of the individual student. Units are differentiated in numerous ways in order to draw out the range of giftedness that is assumed to be present in the student population.

The curriculum is equally concerned with process and content. Students use and further develop certain skills that are a part of the first dimension of the framework. The skills are academic, creativity, planning, communicating, forecasting, and decision-making. Student learning modalities make up the second dimension. Using Samples' (1992) model, five modalities are reflected in the curriculum: symbolic abstract, visual-spatial, kinesthetic, auditory, and synergetic. The third dimension examines the three guiding questions of this curriculum: How is power identified? What are forms of power? How is power reflected in daily life? Each question generates a myriad of follow-up questions that are determined by the particular unit.

The authors of this curriculum consider it important to utilize all cognitive approaches of Bloom's taxonomy (knowledge, comprehension, application, analysis, synthesis, and evaluation). By involving different learning modalities and processing experiences, all cognitive approaches will be touched on. We interpret Bloom's Taxonomy through the lens of critical education theory and not view the taxonomy as circular (see diagram next page) and that all cognitive levels must be present to complete the learning cycle and build true knowledge.

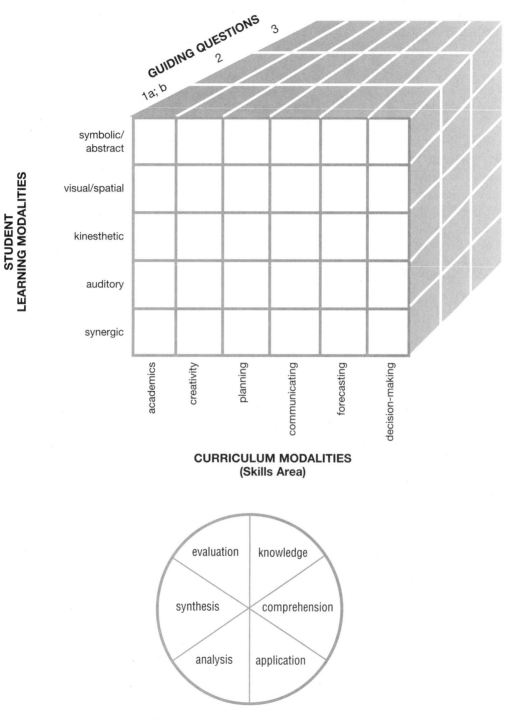

GUIDING QUESTIONS

1a; b   2   3

STUDENT
LEARNING MODALITIES

symbolic/
abstract

visual/spatial

kinesthetic

auditory

synergic

academics

creativity

planning

communicating

forecasting

decision-making

CURRICULUM MODALITIES
(Skills Area)

evaluation | knowledge

synthesis | comprehension

analysis | application

A WHOLISTIC APPROACH TO BLOOM'S TAXONOMY

Scope and Sequence

Implementation

This curriculum was developed with the expectation that teachers will adapt it to meet the specific needs of their students. The lessons follow a circular sequence. The teacher(s) should feel free to use the units in the order which is more relevant to his/her classroom. To optimize its impact, however, it is recommended that all units be utilized. In addition to the guiding questions, several driving questions are probed throughout the curriculum. Why explore power? What does power have to do with me? How does the experience of the democratic process feel? Am I effective in the democratic process? Does the democratic process actually empower its participants? How do I make myself or others powerful/powerless? Is only the majority voice heard in this process?

Implementation is also flexible and can take place in a series of all-day intensive workshop settings or in daily lesson segments throughout the semester. In its optimum state, this curriculum is envisioned to be truly interdisciplinary and transcend the traditional academic departments.

Description of Units

Below is a brief description of each unit. Each unit uses the framework to track which modalities and skills are addressed in relation to the guiding questions.

Power and The Political Process (Catherine Franklin Talon). This interdisciplinary unit examines the human capacity for power through an intensive study of the U. S. Congress. The key part of this unit is its hands-on approach. The students become senators. They hold various roles of power: majority leader, minority leader, whips, etc. In addition, they serve on committees and consider various bills that have been researched and proposed by the class. Giving students the "power" of the senate enables them to experience and reflect upon one institution's structure of the political process.

Rapping for Power (Judith King-Calnek). This is a unique blend of historic and contemporary aspects of power. It looks at the intersection of individual power through the spoken (sung or chanted) word and political power of the larger societal structure. Through a creativity study of the use of the oral tradition in West Africa, the Caribbean, and contemporary urban United States, students explore, analyze, and interpret constructions and interactions of power. The cross-cultural approach provides an opportunity to make connections from a broad spectrum of experiences, thus stimulating students to think critically and use all cognitive approaches.

Evaluation and Assessment

Ongoing assessment is an integral component of this curriculum. It is determined by examining the students' growth over time in relation to the stated objectives. While each unit carries an individual evaluation, the teacher(s) views each unit as an infinite entity. Students responses are viewed in the long-term, not in the short-term. Teacher(s) will consider the students' responses to different modes of instruction. The teacher(s) will also consider the learning modalities that the students employ. The objectives probe the overall guiding questions. Each lesson addresses a part of the guiding question(s). The effectiveness of the lesson is determined by how well the students met the stated objectives.

In terms of an evaluation component for determining curriculum effectiveness, teacher and student feedback is continually solicited. At the end of each lesson, participants are given the opportunity to provide feedback on the lesson. This is done by asking: (1) what worked well?; (2) what are student suggestions for improvement?; (3) what are teacher suggestions for improvement? Depending on time constraints, feedback is attained using informal techniques such as discussions and written responses. A continuous state of evaluation, adaptation, and reassessment is central to this curriculum. Formal evaluations are included in individual units.

Power in the Political Process

Context

"Power in the Political Process" is a unit from a larger interdisciplinary curriculum entitled "Power: Untitled and Unbridled." As is expressed in the collaborative document (written by C. Franklin Talon, J. King-Calnek, S. Dimino, and R. Stawowy), the curriculum, as a whole, probes two levels: the identity of the individual and the role of the individual in society. At a time in life when many physical, social, and emotional changes are happening, this program enables the young adolescent to analyze in an active way his/her own questions of identity and power. This hands-on approach asks pertinent questions about the participant's struggle for peer, familial, and societal power; it provides a safe and informed process for the adolescent to explore a variety of issues.

Curriculum Approach

"Power in the Political Process" is an accordion-like curriculum. Depending upon the time element within the semester, it can be done in two weeks or in two months. To extend this curriculum, suggestions are given at the end of each lesson. To optimize the impact of this program, it is suggested that each lesson be extended to meet the needs, talents, and interests of the participants.

In the last two lessons "Republican or Democrat" and "The Power of the Committee" it is highly recommended that extensions be taken. The lessons are so rich and profound. It would be a shame not to extend this learning experience. By the time one reaches the final lessons of the curriculum, it will be evident that the program has a life of its own. One will notice the student conversations outside of class will focus on the curriculum! It becomes a student-driven curriculum by the end of the semester.

The approach is engaging and student centered. Using hands-on activities, each of the six sample lessons, combined with the suggested extensions, could make up a full semester-long course. Theoretical contexts are provided for each learning experience; an explanation is given at the start of each lesson.

Synopsis

"Power in the Political Process" examines the human capacity for power through an intensive study of the U.S. Congress. The key part of this unit is its hands-on approach. The students become senators. They hold various roles of power: president pro tempore, majority leader, minority leader, whips, etc. In addition, they serve on committees and consider various bills that have been researched and proposed by the class "Senate." Giving students the "power" of the Senate, enables them to experience and actively reflect upon the political process.

Goals and Purposes

Power is at the core of various forms of political realities. The principle aim of this unit is to empower the student to reflect and act upon his/her image of a more equitable world. The following are the goals stated in the collaborative rationale "Power: Untitled and Unbridled." These goals are closely linked to the specific thrust of "Power in the Political Process."

1. to participate consciously in the transformation of a "better" society. Different concepts of a "better" society will be explored and defined by the student.

2. to consider multiple perspectives for improving society.

3. to heighten the level of consciousness where he/she will be aware that "power works both on and through people."

Key Concepts

Six lessons were designated that reflect the specific concepts that form the basis of "Power in the Political Process." Although each lesson deals with the three concepts stated below, some activities address one concept more than the others.

1. creation and identification of forms of power

2. role of perception within power structures

3. informed participation in a representative democracy

Guiding Questions

Three questions are contiually asked in this unit: (1) How is power identified?;(2) What are some forms of power?;(f 3) How is power manifested in daily life? These questions are dynamically probed within the curriculum. As a circular form of learning and teaching is advocated, these guiding questions are asked, answered, and re-asked in a variety of ways. The collaborative document "Power: Untitled and Unbridled" has a detailed discussion concerning each of these questions.

Differentiation for the Gifted and Talented

Howard Gardner's theory of multiple intelligences is used throughout this unit. Not only does his framework fit the range of broad talents, it is also sensitive to a culturally diverse student population. As different cultures value and develop specific areas of intelligence, Gardner's theory enables the teacher to develop an "intellectual profile" of the individual. This identifies the unique strengths and weaknesses of the student. Gardner outlines six areas of intelligence: linguistic, musical, logical-mathematical, spatial, bodily kinesthetic, and personal.

Each lesson is followed with differentiation for the gifted. This approach allows the gifted student to be motivated and recognized. At the same time, his/her project when shared and presented will further broaden the horizon and the motivation for the "regular" student.

Plan of Action

Having implemented this curriculum in her own classroom, this writer speaks from experience in suggesting that one be flexible with its time frame. Lessons range the full gamut. Some are geared for one lesson, others for several months. Detailed explanation is provided in the actual lesson plans. The following outlines the time scope of the curriculum:

1. **Creating the Classroom Environment**
   This lesson sets the tone for the whole curriculum. It is a classroom management technique which is used daily throughout the study of Power. The students take over some of the administrative procedures within the classroom. Using the roles and responsibilities of the Presidential Cabinet as a foundation, students are given power and responsibility.

2. **Power: Implications for Democracy**

   This is one lesson activity. It speaks to drama and impact. By sparking the student's attention and energy from the beginning, it sends a signal that full and total participation is expected in this program.

3. **Knowledge as Power: Explore the Issues**
   This lesson is a precursor to "Power in the Political Process." The student could begin this current events project, a full semester before this curriculum is in place. The purpose is to allow the student to follow a current events issue over an extended amount of time (two months, six weeks? . . .) This information will then be used when the student becomes a "Senator" and uses the collected data for a bill proposal.

4. **Using the Power of Action**
   Seven to eight periods are required for this lesson. As research needs to be done, students need to secure time in the library. Teacher and peer feedback is also required at this stage. The following breaks down the lesson components:

   State selection and research ....3 lessons
   Discussion "How do Ideas for Bills Begin" ....1 lesson
   Bill writing...2 lessons

5. **Republican of Democrat: The Power of Perception**
   This lesson is the heart of "Power in the Political Process." This is where the student finds his/her political identity. As can be seen below, six periods are required for this lesson.

   Survey—Define terms: Republican/Democrat ...homework
   Class discussion ....1 lesson
   Party caucus...1 lesson
   Bill presentation to the party ....1 lesson
   Extension:
   Election of party leader and whip ....1 lesson
   Election of president pro tempore ....2 lessons

6. **The Power of Committee**

   This is the final thrust of "Power in the Political Press." Here the student works in committee to help solidify a bill. He/she then moves it through the senatorial process. Approximately, fourteen periods are needed for this lesson.

   Class discussion ....1 lesson
   Committee selection ....1 lesson
   Committee work...5 lessons
   President pro tempore selection ....1 lesson

   Extension:
   Committee hearings ....3 lessons
   Senate debate ....2 lessons
   Senate roll call...1 lesson

Not including the current events segment as explained in Lesson 2, this curriculum is a twenty-five to thirty period piece. Each period is approximately forty-four minutes. As explained earlier, the curriculum could expand or contract accordingly—deepening if all the suggested extension activities are used. In addition, each lesson is differentiated for the gifted and talented. This would allow further time to be added to the curriculum.

Scope and Sequence

On page 445 is a scope and sequence chart. Using Bloom's Taxonomy as a guide, this chart uses six regions of knowledge: comprehension, application, analysis, synthesis, evaluation, and creation. Knowledge is seen in its broad context—it encompasses various forms of intellectual energy. In this curriculum, the various forms of knowledge is seen in a circular context, rather than a sequential one. Within each lesson, several areas of knowledge are tapped.

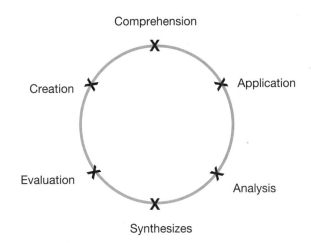

An "X" notes that the primary lesson addresses a given frame of knowledge. "E" refers to the extended lesson that focuses on a given area—when it is not addressed by "X." When applicable, "D" refers to the gifted and talented differentiation.

Evaluation

A. Participant Assessment. As explained in the rationale of the interdisciplinary curriculum "Power: Untitled and Unbridled", ongoing assessment is an integral component to this curriculum. It is determined by examining the student's growth over time in relation to the stated objectives for each lesson. Thus, the effectiveness of the lesson is determined by how well the student met the stated objective. Did the student demonstrate the skills necessary to complete the lesson? Did the student demonstrate control over the knowledge base presented in the lesson? Has the student shown the capacity and motivation that she/he isready to move on to new material? How has the student expressed inquiry?

There are several formal assessments within this curriculum: (1) the bill that is proposed by the individual "Senator", (2) the behavior and attitude of the committee members during: committee work and committe hearings, (3) the written statement of testimony by the witness called to the hearing, (4) the lobbying efforts of the party whips, etc. (5) the bill that is proposed by each committee. Each lesson has several components within it that allow the evaluator to assess student achievement. These formal and informal assessments are part of the whole learning process within the lesson.

B. Curriculum Assessment. In terms of an evaluation component for determining curriculum effectiveness, teacher and student feedback is continually solicited. At the end of each lesson, participants are given the opportunity to provide feedback on the lesson. This is done by asking: (1) What worked well? (2) Student suggestions for improvement. (3) Teacher suggestions for improvement. Depending on time constraints, feedback is attained using informal techniques (discussions, written responses). A continuous state of evaluation, adaption, and re-assessment is central to the curriculum.

SCOPE AND SEQUENCE

Lessons	Comprehension	Applicaton	Analyze	Synthesize	Evaluate	Create
1. Creating the Classroom Environment	X	X	X	E	E	D
2. Power: Implications for Democracy	X	X	X	X	E	D
3. Knowledge as Power: Explore the Issues	X	X	X	X	X	X
4. Using the Power of Action	X	X	X	X	X	X
5. Republican or Democrat: The Power of Perception	X	X	X	E	E	E
6. The Power of Committee	X	X	X	X	X	X

Sample Lesson #1:

Creating the Classroom Environment

General Context:

In Joseph Adelson's "The Political Imagination," he notes that young adolescents tend to identify with authoritarian rule. (1) Students within this age bracket gravitate to concrete, absolute concepts. This lesson is a beginning step to challenge students to experience the powers within representative democracy. The goal is to create a daily situation where the student will participate in a form of representative democracy. Through this experience of being president, the individual will evaluate the various perspectives that members of the executive department give to the president.

Guiding Questions: What are some forms of power?

Objective:

The objective of this starting lesson is to immediately empower students to take over some of the administrative procedures of the classroom. This will also expose them to key positions within the president's cabinet. Given the responsibility and power, students will do their job to the best of their ability. To enable students exposure to a variety of responsibilities, these jobs will change each week.

Materials: poster board, markers

Procedures:

- In a prominent location in the classroom, have students create a working poster entitled: The President's Cabinet. Explain the official job description of each post. In the appendix to this unit, an explanation is given of the various responsibilities of each of the cabinet posts.
- Lead the class into a discussion of how these official jobs can relate to classroom jobs.
- Explain each classroom job. Explain that in our morning and afternoon meetings (fifteen minutes at the start and end of the day), the president is in charge. He/she will follow (or create) an agenda for the meeting. The president is expected to control the meeting.
- Lead a discussion on cabinet power. In times of a nation crisis (or international crisis—economic, political, social, natural disaster) who would the president want to see on a priority basis? Why is it important for the president to seek the counsel of several cabinet members?
- Simulate an international crisis. Have the members of the cabinet give appropriate counsel to the president.
- When the class meets for meeting time, give the president a clipboard with an agenda to follow. He/she will call out certain names of the cabinet. When a position is called, that person has to do his/her job.

Resources:

Any American Civics book is helpful. The appendix includes material from:

Hartley, W. H. & Vincent, W. S. (1987). *American Civics. Constitution Edition.* Chicago: Harcourt Brace Jovanovich.

New York Times—a copy should be available in the classroom (This will enable the members of the Cabinet to update their news information)

Note:

The president's cabinet is an integral part of this writer's eighth-grade classroom. It is used daily through out the semester-long study of "Power in the Political Process." Although the roles change weekly, the format is consistent throughout the term. On Mondays, the students eagerly await their new cabinet assignments.

On Mondays, the first day of job assignments, coach the key players in the new roles. The president may need help in keeping control of the class. Make sure the following "officers" know where to locate their specific information in the *New York Times:*

Vice President—National News
Secretary of State—International News
Secretary of Commerce—Weather and Business

It is expected that from Tuesday onward, the vice president and secretary of state would not have to refer to the paper for news. As they have to inform the public, and make policy decisions, they need to get informed summaries at home. (Sources of good information: McNeil Lehrer Report, substantive reading of the paper)

Attorney General—Open Forum

This is a fascinating role. This person calls upon his/her peers to investigate any gripes or issues that need to be aired. Sometimes, the open forum turns into a venting session . . . a chance for the student to let off steam. Other times, it is an opportunity for the attorney general to inform his/her peers about upcoming events. Whatever the case, the teacher's role is as a listener and observer. Remember the power is in the hands of the cabinet.

Future Adaptations:

This worked: _____

_____

_____

Student suggestions for improvement: _____

_____

_____

Teacher suggestions: _____

_____

_____

Extensions:

- Have each student write a business letter to his/her assigned cabinet. Find out who is the person in charge of that position. In the letter, request further information about the responsibilities of this cabinet post. (For cabinet addresses, see Appendix p. 31)

- Draw a political cartoon that satires a political issue that involves a cabinet desicion and/or personality.

- Have students memorize excepts from some of the key documents in our history. (Excerpts from these documents are included in the Appendix on p. 33.)

  — The Declaration of Independence

  — The Constitution of the United States

  — Nathan Hale's Speech

  — The New Colossus by Emma Lazarus

  — "I Have A Dream by Dr. Martin Luther King

- Have students explore Article 2 (Section 1 and 2) of The Constitution of the United States. This explains the executive department and the specific powers of the president.

Differentiation for the Gifted and Talented

Howard Gardner's theory of multiple intelligences is used throughout this unit. Not only does his framework fit the range of broad intelligences, it also it sensitive to a culturally diverse student population. As different cultures value and develop specific areas of intelligence. Gardner's theory enables the teacher to develop an "intellectual profile" of the individual. This would identify the specific strengths and weaknesses of the student. Gardner outlines six intelligences: linguistic, musical, logical-mathematical, spatial, bodily kinesthetic, and personal.

- *Linguistic:* Have students locate and summarize news articles that center on cabinet positions. This summary could be broadcast on video or tape.

- *Musical:* Have students who are musically gifted to create a song (rap, rock, new age . . .) that has as its focal point a symbol of the U.S.. Through this song, the listener will understand the meaning of this symbol. Possible symbols: liberty bell, donkey and elephant, great seal, eagle, Uncle Sam.

- *Logical—Mathematical:* Stage a debate between two cabinet members. Whose job is more important? Use the federal budget and deficit. Using your reasoning and logic, explain why, as cabinet member, your reasons for recommending cuts.

- *Spatial:* Design and create a statue commemorating an outstanding cabinet member. Past or present. This statue could be made of paper-mache or clay.

- *Bodily Kinesthetic:* Mime the role and responsibility of a given cabinet member. Create a dance on the theme of power.

- *Personal:* Write a letter to a member of a cabinet. Find out what key decisions they are facing. Include your opinions on the issues related to these decisions. What would you decision be? Include evidence, viewpoint, connection to other issues, relevance, etc.

Sample Lesson #2:

"Power: Implications for Democracy"

General Context:

As the individual progresses from early to middle adolescence, there is a cognitive development in the ability to abstract. (3) The adolescent moves from concrete reasoning to a more sophisticated level of abstraction. This lesson provides a fun, hands-on strategy for looking at power. The goal is to create and evaluate the various ways that power can be expressed.

Guiding Question: How is power identified?

Objective:

By active participation in this activity (listening-response) and in the debriefing afterward, students will demonstrate an awareness of the complex components of power. In their discussion, students will address the topic of democracy as a form of power.

Materials: none

Procedures:

- Ask the class: Who has the most power in this room? Why? How is this person showing power?

- Can anyone think of another way to show power? How? (Let that person demonstrate his/her power). "FREEZE" (Freeze that person showing power.) Ask the class: How is that person showing power? Who now is the most powerful person in the class? Why? Can anyone think of another way to show power? How? (Let that person show you.) FREEZE. (Freeze that person also, you should now have two "frozen" volunteers.) Who is the most powerful? Why? Continue to invite more volunteers to demonstrate their power. Freeze them once they have demonstrated their power. Invite a brief discussion after each freeze.

- Discuss: What is power? How did it feel to have power? What were some ways that people showed power?

(Taken and adapted from a Global Kids presentation on 4/11/92 at the Americas Society)

Future Adaptions:

This worked: _____

_____

_____

Student suggestions for improvement: _____

_____

_____

Teacher suggestions: _____

_____

_____

Extensions:

- Explore power-play situations in our lives. Pay particular attention to the non-verbal component of power. Here are a few examples to get started:

  — State trooper pulling over a speeding car. Symbols of power: flashing lights, siren, loud-speaker, sunglasses worn by the police—can't see their eyes.

  — Take a field trip to the principal's office. Does this room communicate power? How? Is it as powerful a room as the classroom? Why? Why not?

Differentiation for the Gifted and Talented

- *Linguistic:* Have students research and present recent power issues in current events (i.e., David Koresch—Waco, Texas or the World Trade bombing). How were they able to set up their own power structure? What was their agenda? How does their agenda relate to the dominant culture of this society? Create a trial situation. Defend your client—defend the position of the government.

- *Musical:* Have students look at the lyrics of popular songs. Explore one that deals with the issue of power. How do the lyrics and the melody work together to express power. How does rhythm come into play?

  In a group (or alone) create an instrumental song. Its purpose is to express forms of power.

- *Logical—Mathematical:* Working in a group, design a pattern of sound (beat, volume) that expresses power. How should this sound begin? Communicate? Conclude? Why? Perform this sound. Explain the nuances behind it.

- *Spatial:* How does a map show power? Survey the various maps that have been designed throughout the centuries. Explore the various projections that a cartographer might use (Oblique Azimuthal, Mercator, conical). How does a map tell a story of power? The Cooper Hewitt Museum (212-860-8698) recently had an exhibit on the power of maps. This would be a good resource for this project. Create a map that uses no projection!

- *Bodily Kinesthetic:* In a group, choreograph a dance on the theme of power.

- *Personal:* If the school has access, watch C-SPAN on cable. Note the rhetoric used by the politicians. How do they communicate knowledge? power? What non-verbal skills are also being used. Research the skills used by leaders of our day. If resources are available, make a film using clips from broadcasts by these leaders (politicians, spokespeople, Richard Gere's Tibetian plea at the Oscar's).

Sample Lesson Plan #3:

Knowledge as Power: Explore the Issues

General Context:

Middle school curriculum should reflect the educational issues pertinent to young adolescents. James Beane identified a number of issues that concern adolescents. Some of them include: environmental problems, distribution of wealth, advancing pace of technology, conflict among peoples.(4) This lesson, empowers the student to track a relevant issue in the media over an extended period of time. This enables the student to become a "specialist" in his/her chosen topic. This information will then be used when the student as "Senator" writes a bill on a key issue. (See lesson "Using the Power of Action" p. 18).

Guiding Question: How is power manifested in daily life?

Objective:

The student will follow a current events issue over a two-month period. This work could be done in school or at home. At the end of this time period, the student will present an in-depth analysis of a current events issue.

Materials: newspapers
construction paper
scissors, scotch tape
lined paper

Procedures:

- Discuss with the class issues that they are facing as adolescents. Broaden this discussion with topics that concern them about the world.

- Give students a few days to think of a topic that they would like to individually cover for two months. The selected topic must be "hot" and controversial. As it will be covered for the next two months, the student needs to be able to find weekly articles on this issue.

- Once topic has been chosen, have them decorate the cover to their news scrapbook.

- In written or oral form, have them explain to the class why they are interested in this topic. Include this information in their scrapbook.

- Have students do research on this topic. Explore the geographical, historical, and cultural connections to their selected issue.

- Each week, have students hand in a news article and a written summary of their topic. Students will paste the article and a news summary on a piece of construction paper.

- At the end of two months have each student use his/her news scrapbook as a resource. He/she will present to the class an in-depth analysis of the selected issue. Each presentation must include: multiple perspectives of the issue, historical background, global connections, possible "solutions" to identified obstacles. The presentation may be done in a variety of ways: written report, video broadcast, radio broadcast, skit.

Future Adaptions:

This worked:_____

_____

Student suggestions for improvement: _____

_____

Teacher suggestions:_____

_____

Extensions:

- Create a classroom newspaper devoted to adolescent concerns. Have a news team organize this project. Included on the staff might be the following positions: international correspondent, economic specialist, family and home lift-expert, Op Ed writers.

- Have students bring in a variety of newspapers showing various voices from the community (i.e., African-American, Irish, Jewish, Liberal, Conservative, Wall Street). By having the students explore the articles in these papers, they will understand the "bias" or world view that this newspaper promotes. This enables the student to realize that newspapers do not necessarily report straight fact. The fact is reported within a given context.

Differentiation for the Gifted and Talented

- *Linguistic:* Have students research and present poetry written on the chosen current events topic. Poetry is in many forms (i.e., lyrics from songs, or published poems). Have students write poetry (or a song) on this current events issue. Various poetic styles could be explored: haiku, free verse, ballad, sonnet, limerick, rhyming.

- *Musical:* Have the student find a relevant quote from a person involved in his/her current events issue. Compose a song from that quote. Perform it live or on tape.

- *Logical—Mathematical:* Have the student conduct a school survey on the controversial issues related to the selected topic. Analyze this data. Was there a correspndence in the answers given by sex, age, ethnic background, education experience?

- *Spatial:* Visualize your current events topic! Create a visual display comparing the various perspectives to the given issue.

- *Body Kinesthetic:* Create a fashion statement (i.e., jewelry, button, hat, T-shirt) that articulates your topic. What world view is this statement promoting?

- *Personal:* Write an editorial to key community newspapers about this issue. Work on getting this article published. The public needs to hear and understand your view on this controversial issue. A good resource for this are books that list a directory of publishers (i.e., *1993 Writer's Guide to Getting Published*).

Sample Lesson #4:

Using the Power of Action

General Context:

John Dewey coined the expression "the eclipse of the public." This is when people feel powerless and do nothing. This phenomena runs counter to Dewey's belief of democracy; diverse people should come together to articulate their given concerns, to take action, and to make changes.(5) In this lesson, students have been elected by their constituents to act upon state, national, and international concerns. In addition, they are put into political parties. Their bill writing may also take into account the idealogy of the party. The goal of this lesson is for the senator to research the key concerns of his/her state. From this lesson, a bill will be proposed.

Guiding Question: What are some forms of power?

Objective:

The specific objective of this lesson is for the student to use his/her current events research (see lesson "Knowledge as Power: Explore the Issues" p. 15), and state research to prepare a bill for the Senate.

Materials: 1993 Almanac
Congressional Staff Directory
World Book Encyclopedia
The Almanac of American Politics 1993

Procedures:

- Have each student select a state. Explain that they have been elected by the voters of this state to represent their concerns. Give each student a senator and state research worksheet. Using the above materials, have the students complete this worksheet.

- Go around the room and have students share their state findings and ideas for bills.

- Explain that at the state level, the proposed bills tend to reflect national concerns that are shared by a number of states. Remind them about their current events projects and encourage them to think of ways to connect their state issue with a national concern.

- Lead discussion on "How Do Ideas for Bills Begin?" From student responses generate the following possibilities:
  — The Voters: favor a particular bill.
  — Individual Members of Congress: may introduce a bill.
  — Large Groups of Americans: lobby for a specific bill.

— Congressional Investigating Committees: may recommend a bill.

— The President: may urge certain laws in his/her speeches to Congress and the public.

- Have each student write a draft of a bill. (In the Appendix on p. 37 there is a copy of an official bill form.) In informal response groups, have students share their bills. This is an opportunity for them to get feedback on it. Is it clear? Well thought out? What evidence supports the rationale for having this bill? (In the Student Work Section on p. 42 there is a copy of a student bill.)

Differentiation for the Gifted and Talented

- *Linguistic:* Have the student give an extended oral argument expressing the merits of the bill that he/she designed.

- *Musical:* Have student survey patriotic songs through the years. What are common themes that come up in these songs. Compare them to songs from another country. How do the themes and imagery compare?

- *Logical—Mathematical:* Have the student hypothesize on the ramifications of the bills proposed in the class "Senate." Take one bill and explore its consequences on the economy, environment, quality of life.

- *Spatial:* To promote the passage of a specific bill, create an advertising poster for it. The poster should include the primary purpose of the bill.

- *Bodily Kinesthetic:* Have students explore co-sponsored bills. Put two to three ideas from similar bills into one main bill.

- *Personal:* Write a letter to your state's senators. Request copies of bills they are working on in committee. In your letter, explain the bill that you are drafting. Ask them for feedback on it. *Note:* In the Reference section of this document (pp. 53-68), there is a lot of statistical data that could be used as a basis for drafting a bill.

Sample Lesson #5:

Republican or Democrat: The Power of Perception

General Context:

As the young adolescent approaches the formal-operational stage, he/she should be given opportunities to discover the power of perception. Kohlberg and Gilligan in "The Adolescent as a Philisopher" believed that at this age ambivalence is discovered and conflicts of feeling often result. In this lesson, the student is given a role to play—either Republican or Democrat. Through party caucuses and discussions, a group idealogy is established. The goal of this lesson is to provide a context for the student to understand party lines and loyalties. What truly defines a Republican or a Democratic?

Guiding Questions: How is power identified?

Objective:

By canvassing the opinions of three adults on the question—What is a Republican? What is a Democratic?—the student will begin to discover that perception plays a key role in how power is identified. Through discussion, the student will explore the varied definitions shared by the class of their adult survey.

Materials: 2 large pieces of newsprint
heavy markers
poster board

Procedures:

- Have students for homework ask three adults their definitions of a Republican and a Democrat.

- Share this information in class. On one piece of newsprint write: What is a Republican? On the other—What is a Democrat? Write the responses to these questions. Discuss. Is there an absolute concept that defines each party? What determines the perception of the party?

- Determine the actual number of democrats and republicans in the Senate. Using this data as a guide, determine the ratio of democrats and republicans that should exist in the class senate. The class senate should minimize as close to possible the real senate—in terms of the party numbers.

- At this stage each student has already selected a state and had done research on it. Some states are solid Republican—others are all Democrat. Some states are a mix of the two. Go around the class, and give each "Senator" his/her party name.

- Have a party caucus. Have each party define their own idealogy. Write it down on poster board. It could be similar to the ones discussed earlier.
- Have each senator present his/her bill to the party. Does it fit with the party idealogy. Solicit help from other senators on improving it.
- Have each group fill out one Party Status on Bills report.

FutureAdaptations:

This worked: _____

_____

Student suggestions for improvement: _____

_____

Teacher suggestions: _____

_____

Recommended Extensions:

- Have each party determine the following roles: Party leaders and party whip. Have students research the importance and responsibilities of these roles.

- Once party lines have been delineated, an election should take place on who should lead the Senate. The president pro tempore is the official name of the Senate leader. He/she is typically chosen from the majority party. Elections however, could include nominations from the minority party as well. Have each party nominate a leader. For the minority party, discuss strategies that could split the majority party (i.e. have the minority party elect two people: one from the majority and one from the minority).

- Have the nominees give speeches (see sample of nominee speech in Student Work Section p. 45).

- Encourage the whips to pressure party members to stay within the party and not to vote outside of it. Have the party leaders call party caucuses to solidify the voting decision.

- Have the election.

Differentiation for the Gifted and Talented

Note: It is recommended that the extension to the above lesson be followed. This would allow the following projects for the gifted and talented to be implemented.

- *Linguistic:* Have the student give an extended speech within his/her party on the merits of a given nominee for president pro tempore.

- *Musical:* Have student design a campaign song for his/her choice of president pro tempore.

- *Logical—Mathematical:* Have this student work closely with the party leader and whip to determine the minimum amount of votes that are needed to elect the president pro tempore. Explore party cross overs. How do cross overs effect the results of the election? Does it effect party morale? What are the chances of it happening?

- *Spatial:* To promote the election of a given candidate, have this student in charge of campaign posters. Why is your candidate the best one to lead the Senate.

- *Bodily Kinesthetic:* Have this student work closely with the party whip and leader. What body languages are being exhibited in party caucuses? Will all party members toe the line and vote according to the party recommendation? Does body language tell you differently? Will anyone vote outside the party?

- *Personal:* This student is critical. Have him/her work closely with the party and the party leaders. Have him/her work with party members that are not as involved in the group dynamics. Make these people feel and believe that they belong to this party.

Sample Lesson #6:

The Power of the Committee

General Context:

One of the characteristics of children between the ages of eight to fifteen is their "willingness to investigate exhaustively the details of a given topic." (7). This unique trait is acknowledged and valued in this lesson. The goal is to channel the student's energies and "obsessions" into the political arena. By working with other members of his/her committee, the student will become invested in the viability of a selected bill.

Guiding Question: What are some forms of power?

Objective:

This lesson moves the student from party loyalties into committee work. The purpose is to have the committee members work together to select one of their bills for consideration. The underlying objective is to have the committee identify the qualities of a good bill and to work on making it a solid piece of legislation.

Materials: copies of all the students generated bills
(From lesson "Using the Power of Action" p. 18)

Procedures:

• Looking at all the bills generated by class, group similar bills together. In the appendix on p. 39, is a list of the standing committees of the Senate. Put each bill in a group. Have no more than four to five committees to a class.

• Explain to the class that the majority of the work in Congress is done in committees. Before the Congress can consider a bill, the selected committee investigates the bill and holds hearings on it to gather evidence on it. Depending upon the outcome of this process, the committee will than recommend (or discourage) this bill to the Senate.

• Put each bill into committee. Explain that each committee should select a person to chair the meetings.

• At this stage it is helpful to design a class list showing where everyone is on committee. It is also helpful to show leadership positions.

• Within committee, have each member discuss his/her bill. At this stage, senators might want to jointly create a bill that would encompass like concerns.

- Have the committee select a bill (or a joint bill) for consideration.

- Give the committee several sessions to work on this bill—to hammer out the details on it and to do research that would support it.

- When committees have selected, researched and revised one bill, have them each present it to the president pro tempore. The president pro tempore (along with the majority/minority leaders and whips) and review the committees' bills. See The Student Work Section pp. 47 for examples of committee bills.

- The president pro tempore will select one bill for consideration. Have him/her explain the selection process. Was it a choice based on politics? person concerns? Belief that it was the best bill? Best for the american people?

- Debrief. What was the process like within your committee? What leadership roles were taken? Was power shared? Why? Why not? Did the process help your bill in the long run? Now that you know the process, what would you have done differently with your bill?

Future Adaptations:

This worked: _____

_____

Student suggestions for improvement: _____

_____

Teacher suggestions:_____

_____

Recommended Extensions:

- Explain the process of having a hearing to gather evidence on a bill. Evidence may be in favor or against the purposes stated in the bill. Generate a list of witnesses that will be effected by this bill. Assign members of the class to role play these witnesses. Each witness must do research on the bill and present a witness statement to the hearing.

- A day before the hearing make copies of the witness statements. Give them to the committee sitting together at a table. In front of them having a smaller table with a glass of water on it. This table will seat the witness.

- Have the witness read his/her statement to the committee. Committee members should address each other as Senator so and so. They should refer to the witness as Mr. (Ms., Dr.,

Mrs., Rev.). After the committee has finished listening and questioning the witness, have the other senators ask him/her questions.

- One must remind the class that this is not time for debate. The process is simply to gather information from the witness.

- After the hearing, the committee then deliberates to determine the status of the bill. Do they want to recommend it for debate in the Senate? Do they want to amend it? Do they want to drop it?

Differentiation for the Gifted and Talented

Note: It is recommended that the extension to the above lesson be followed. This would allow the following projects for the gifted and talented to be implemented.

When called as a witness, the gifted and talented individual should feel able to use his/her special gifts within the testimony. Coaching by the teacher is recommended.

Footnotes

[1] Joseph Adelson. "The Political Imagination of the Young Adolescent," in Jerome Kagan and Robert Coles. 12 to 16 Early Adolescence. (New York: W. W. Norton. 1972). p. 115-120.

[2] Howard Gardner. Frames of Mind: The Theory of Multiple Intelligences. (New York: Basic Books. 1983).

[3] Adelson. Ibid. p. 108-110.

[4] James Beane. "Intersections of Personal and Social Concerns." in Paul S. George, et al. The Middle School—and Beyond. (Virginia: Association for Supervision and Curriculum Development, 1992). pp. 89-93.

[5] John Dewey quoted in Maxine Greene. "Perspective and Diversity: Toward a Common Ground." in Frank Pignatelli and Susanna W. Pflaum, eds. Celebrating Diverse Voices. (California: Corwin Press, 1992). p. 16-19.

[6] Lawrence Kholberg and Carol Gilligan. "The Adolescent as a Philosopher." in Jerome Kagan and Robert Coles. 12 to 16 Early Adolescence. (New York: W. W. Norton. 1972).

[7] Kieran Egan. Imagination in Teaching and Learning: the Middle School Years. (Chicago: University of Chicago Press, 1992) p. 89.

Bibliography

Adelson, J. (1972). The political imagination of the young adolescent. In J. Kagen & R. Coles, *12 to 16 Early Adolescence.* New York: W. W. Norton.

Banks, J. A. (1991, Spring). Multicultural literacy and curriculum reform. *Educational Horizons,* 135-140.

Beane, J. (1992). Intersections of personal and social concerns. In Paul S. George et al. *The middle school—and beyond.* Virginia: Association for Supervision and Curriculum Development.

Bruner, J. S. et al. (1967). *Studies in cognitive growth.* New York: Wiley.

Dewey, J. (1992). Quoted in Maxine Greene, Perspective and diversity: Toward a common ground. In F. Pignatelli & S. W. Pflaum (Eds.), *Celebrating diverse voices.* California: Corwin Press.

Edwards, C. P. (1982). Moral development in comparative perspective. In D. A. Wagner & H. W. Stevenson, (Eds.), *Cultural perspectives on child development.* San Francisco: W. H. Freeman.

Egan, K. (1992). *Imagination in teaching and learning: The middle school years.* Chicago: University of Chicago Press.

Eisner, E. (1985). *The educational imagination,* (2nd ed.). New York: Macmillan.

Freire, P. (1983). *The politics of education.* New York: Bergin and Garvey Publishers.

Gardner, H. (1983). *Frames of mind: The theory of multiple intelligences.* New York: Basic Books.

Howard, R. (1991). Lawrence Kohlberg's Influence on moral education in elementary schools. In J. S. Benninga, (Ed.), *Moral character and civic education in the elementary school* (p. 44-45). New York: Teachers College, Columbia University.

Kohlberg, R. & Gilligan, C. (1972). The Adolescent as a philosopher: The discovery of the self in a post-conventional world. In J. Kagan & R. Coles, (Eds.), *Twelve to sixteen, early adolescence* (p. 144-179). New York: W. W. Norton and Company.

Letwin, A. Z. (1991). Promoting civic understanding and civic skills through conceptually based curricula. In J. S. Bennings, (Ed.), *Moral, character, and civic education in the elementary school.* New York: Teachers College, Columbia University.

Lipsitz, J. (1984). *Successful schools for young adolescents.* New Brunswick, NJ: Transaction Books.

Martin, E. C. (1972). Reflections on the early adolescence in school. In J. Kagan & R. Coles, (Eds.), *Twelve to sixteen, early adolescence* (p. 180-106). New York: W. W. Norton and Company.

Salinger, J. D. (1951). *The catcher in the rye.* Boston: Little, Brown and Company.

Samples, R. (1991, Samples). Using learning modalities to celebrate intelligence. *Educational Leadership,* 62–66.

Tannenbaum, A. J. (1979). Pre-sputnik to post-watergate concern about the gifted. In 78th Yearbook of the National Society for the Study of Education, *The gifted and talented: Their education and development.* Chicago: University of Chicago Press.

Valett, R. E. (1991). Teaching peace and conflict resolution. In J. S. Bennings, (Ed.), *Moral character, and civic education in the elementary school.* New York: Teachers College, Columbia University.

Weiler, K. (1988). *Women teaching for change, gender, class and power.* New York: Bergin and Garvey Publishers.

Weather

by Michelle Mnnion
Teacher and Master Degree Candidate, State University of New York,
College at New Paltz

Overview

It is important to note that I am a special educator and work with children who function at a pre-k to late kindergarten levels. Much of the writing activities have to be completed by myself or my aide.

Because of their capabilities, most lessons are between fifteen to twenty-five minutes. A lot of visual, hands-on projects are necessary to keep their attention and to stay within the means of their capabilities.

Evaluation for my children is quite different from a secondary class or even a "regular" elementary class. No assigned recorded grade will be given in any of the lessons. Each lesson does explain what I will be looking for according to the level at which they are capable of working.

Michelle Mannion
June 1994

Rationale

A unit on weather is part of the early childhood science curriculum in my special education classroom. Observing weather, learning about the weather types and how the weather changes, feelings created by the weather, and dressing appropriately for the weather are all facets of the unit on weather. The activities in this particular unit are only a part of the unit that is presented as whole during the week we study the letter "W."

It is important to note that, throughout the entire year, we have graphed the daily weather, interpreted the graph, and have also made daily predictions on the future weather. This particular activity builds and fosters graph interpretation, counting, concepts of more and less, and beginning addition and subtraction. It is a fun learning activity and our morning circle time would not be complete without it.

Lesson Plans

Lesson 1

Organizing Idea: Weather changes
Taxonomy Level: Knowledge and application
Writing Domain: Practical/informative

Objectives:

Thinking Skills:

Students will:
- observe the daily weather (knowledge)
- record the daily weather (knowledge)
- illustrate the daily weather (application)

Writing Skills:

Students will: write a description of the daily weather using the sentence frame—Today is "Monday." It is "cloudy." The frame remains consistent throughout the week; the day of the week and the weather will obviously change daily.

Lesson Overview:

This activity will take place in the morning along with the other morning activities, such as calendar and attendance. A weather journal will be the completed project, with each child having a record of the daily weather. Through this activity children will hopefully realize that the weather does indeed change on a day-to-day basis. The illustrations (a sun for a sunny day, clouds for a cloudy day) along with the printed word will provide the proof that weather changes daily.

Evaluation:

No specific grade would be assigned for this project. Each child will be evaluated individually according to their individual capabilities. Participation, completion of project, correct observation of weather, and appropriate drawings of weather type are all elements that all children can have evaluated by the teacher.

Writers will be evaluated on proper letter formation, spacing and size, and left-to-right orientation. Use of punctuation and capitalization will also be evaluated. Spelling is not an area of evaluation since we will use invented spelling.

Nonwriters will be evaluated on tracing skills, eye/hand coordination, and, depending on the child, willingness to print by themselves.

Lesson 2

Organizing Idea: Weather dictates the type of clothing we wear
Taxonomy Level: Knowledge and application

Objectives:

Thinking Skills:

Students will:
- apply their previous knowledge to the situation at hand with a hat and the weather it represents (knowledge and application)
- name the type of hat worn by teacher (knowledge)
- describe the type of weather it would be if this hat would be worn (comprehension)
- type of hat worn, i.e., a ski hat for a snowy day (knowledge)

Lesson Overview:

An assortment of hats such as a rain hat, a stocking hat, a straw hat, a baseball hat, and sun visor will be placed in a large shopping bag. A hat is placed on top of my head. Students are asked to describe what the weather might be if a person chose to wear this hat. Retrieve another hat from the bag and place it on a child's head. Ask student to describe the type(s) of weather this hat might be worn in. Continue in this manner until all hats are being worn.

Evaluation:

Evaluation would be in the area of participation and appropriate responses to the type of hat and the weather type described.

Lesson 3:

Organizing Idea: Weather dictates the type of clothing we wear

Taxonomy Level: Knowledge, comprehension, and application

Writing Domain: Sensory/descriptive and practical/informative

Objectives:

Thinking Skills:

Students will: • recall, name, and explain a weather type and appropriate dress for that weather (knowledge and comprehension)
  • illustrate an appropriate picture to coincide with descriptive written words (application)

Writing Skills:

Students will: fill in appropriate responses using the sentence frame—In _____ weather, we wear _____. The frame remains the same on all pages of the book each child will create.

Lesson Overview:

Each major weather type will be written about and illustrated. Each page will be put into book format. Each individual child will create a "Dressing for the Weather" book. Because the sentence frame is repetitive, non-readers will be able to read the book by using the sentence frame and picture clues.

Evaluation:

Each child can be evaluated on participation, appropriate responses, and appropriate illustrations. Writers can be evaluated on letter size and spacing, letter formation, left to right orientation, punctuation, and capitalization.

Non writers can be evaluated on tracing skills, eye/hand coordination, and, depending on the child, a willingness to try to print by themselves.

Lesson 4

Organizing Idea: Different weather types make us feel different feelings
Taxonomy Level: Knowledge, comprehension, analysis, and evaluation

Objectives:

Thinking Skills:

Students will:
- recall a specific weather type (knowledge)
- describe, discuss, and explain weather and the ideas and feelings represented by that weather, and the ideas and feelings represented by that weather (comprehension)
- differentiate between the weather types and the different types of feelings a specific weather type makes us feel (analysis)
- construct a word web from their discussion of feelings and ideas—teacher-made (synthesis)
- compare the different feelings and ideas represented by the different weather types (evaluation)

Lesson Overview:
In a group format, a discussion about weather type will take place. Questions such as "What do you think of when you hear the word rain?" and "How do you feel when it rains?" will serve as the motivating questions to begin discussion in the group. Their responses will be put on chart paper in concept idea webbing format. Major weather types will be discussed in this manner.

Evaluation:
All children will be evaluated on participation and appropriate response to questions asked.

Lesson 5

Organizing Idea: Different weather types make us feel different feelings
Taxonomy Level: Knowledge and synthesis
Writing Domain: Sensory/descriptive

Objectives:

Thinking Skills:

Students will:
- recall and name the ideas and feelings represented by the certain weather types webbed in Lesson 4 (knowledge)
- create an original poem with ideas and feelings about a weather type (synthesis)

Writing Skills:

Students will create and write a descriptive poem.
(Nonwriters will dictate their poems to an adult and the adult will transcribe their ideas onto paper. The nonwriter will then trace the written poem.)

Lesson Overview:

Having read poems throughout the year on a daily basis, students will be familiar with poems, their format, and their purpose. Published poems about weather will be shared, read, and explored prior to this experience also.

Using the ideas and feelings generated in Lesson 4 in the webbing experience, students will pick a weather type and write a brief four-line poem. The format of the poem will be structured in that it is repetitive and simple.

An example would be:
Rain is wet
Rain makes puddles.
Rain is umbrellas and raincoats.
Rain means we stay inside!!!

Evaluation:

Each child will be evaluated on participation, appropriate descriptors for the weather type chosen, and creativity and originality.

Writers will be evaluated on letter size, formation, spacing, capitalization, punctuation, and left to right orientation.

Spelling is not evaluated since we use invented spelling.

Nonwriters will be evaluated on tracing skills, eye/hand coordination, and, depending on the child, willingness to print by themselves.

Lesson 6

Organizing Idea: People have weather preferences
Taxonomy Level: Analysis and evaluation

Objectives:

Thinking Skills:
Students will:
- analyze, compare, and contrast weather types (analysis)
- evaluate and choose a favorite weather type (evaluation)
- explain why they made a particular choice (comprehension)
- assess, measure, and compare which weather type has the most votes—the least votes (evaluation)
- judge and predict why we had these particular outcomes in our choosing a favorite weather type (evaluation)

Lesson Overview:
Children will select a favorite weather type. Using a bar graph format that the children are familiar with, the children will place their favorite weather vote in the appropriate column on the graph. Children must then explain why they made that particular choice. Once all votes are in we will compare and contrast the voting choices. Which type has the most and which has the fewest, and why do we think we had this type of outcome, are all questions that will be asked.

Evaluation:
All children will be evaluated on participation, their justification and reasoning behind their choice, and their assessment of the graph and its results.

Name Index

Subject Index